Microsoft® Publisher 2002

PUBLISHER

Microsoft® Publisher 2002

SHELLEY GASKIN

PUBLISHER

PEARSON

Prentice
Hall

Upper Saddle River, New Jersey, 07458

Library of Congress Cataloging-in-Publication Data

Gaskin, Shelley.
   Microsoft Publisher 2002 / Shelley Gaskin.
       p. cm.
   Includes index.
   ISBN 0-13-101467-6
   1. Microsoft Publisher.   2. Desktop publishing.
3. Websites—Design.   I. Title.
   Z253.532.M53 G37 2003
   686.2′25445369—dc21   2002156324

Publisher and Vice President: Natalie E. Anderson
Executive Acquisitions Editor: Jodi McPherson
Senior Project Managers, Editorial: Eileen Clark and Thomas Park
Assistant Editor: Melissa Edwards
Senior Media Project Manager: Cathleen Profitko
Editorial Assistant: Jodi Bolognese
Development Editor: Christy Parrish
Senior Marketing Manager: Emily Knight
Marketing Assistant: Danielle Torio
Manager, Production: Gail Steier de Acevedo
Project Manager, Production: Audri Anna Bazlen
Associate Director, Manufacturing: Vincent Scelta
Manufacturing Buyer: Natacha St. Hill Moore
Design Manager: Maria Lange
Art Director: Pat Smythe
Cover Design: Marjorie Dressler
Cover Illustration: Marjorie Dressler
Full-Service Composition: Impressions Book and Journal Services, Inc.
Cover Printer: Coral Graphics
Printer/Binder: Quebecor World Color-Dubuque

Credits and acknowledgments borrowed from other sources and reproduced, with permission, in this textbook appear on the appropriate page within the text.

Microsoft, Windows, Windows NT, MSN, The Microsoft Network, PowerPoint, Outlook, FrontPage, Hotmail, the MSN logo, and/or other Microsoft products referenced herein are either trademarks or registered trademarks of Microsoft Corporation in the United States and/or other countries. Screen shots and icons reprinted with permission from the Microsoft Corporation. This book is not sponsored or endorsed by or affiliated with Microsoft Corporation.

Pearson Education is independent from Microsoft Corporation, and is not affiliated with Microsoft in any manner.

10 9 8 7 6 5 4 3 2 1
ISBN 0-13-101467-6

Contents at a Glance

Table of Contents

Dedication

This book is dedicated to my students, who inspire me every day, and to my husband, Fred Gaskin, who works tirelessly to create new opportunities for both students and faculty who teach students.

Acknowledgments

Many talented individuals worked to produce this book, and I thank them for their continuous support. My Executive Acquisitions Editor, **Jodi McPherson**, gave me much latitude to experiment with new things. **Thomas Park**, Project Manager, and **Christy Parrish**, Developmental Editor, patiently worked with me through each stage of writing and production. **Emily Knight** and the Prentice Hall marketing team worked with me throughout this process to make sure both instructors and students are informed about the benefits of using this text. My new home state of **Arizona** provided a beautiful backdrop for the book.

Thanks to all!
Shelley Gaskin, Author

About the Author

Shelley Gaskin is a professor of Business and Computer Technology at Pasadena City College in Pasadena, California. She holds a master's degree in Business Education from Northern Illinois University and a doctorate in Adult and Community Education from Ball State University. Dr. Gaskin has 15 years of experience in the computer industry with several Fortune 500 companies and has developed and written training materials for custom systems applications in both the public and private sector. She is also the author of books on Microsoft Outlook and word processing.

Introduction

Publisher 2002 is anchored in the practical and professional needs of all types of students. The goal of the text is to provide you with the skill to produce attractive publications and simple Web sites for yourself and for the organizations for which you work. This goal is accomplished by using an approach that is based on clearly-defined publications that you produce. The instructional objectives, which focus on the features of the software, are clustered around these actual publications.

There are no lengthy passages of text. Rather, important information about how the software operates is introduced in the context of performing an action. All of the publications within the text are based upon publications developed for one organization—the City of Desert Park.

Key Features

❏ **Step-by-Step Publications.** Activities within the Lessons include numbered step-by-step instructions that show you how to use the software in a clear, concise, and direct manner. Unlike other textbooks that begin steps with an action verb, this text uses Microsoft procedural syntax that places you at the point of the action and then describes the action to take. This prevents you from doing the right thing in the wrong place. Additionally, important information about how the software operates is introduced within the steps—at the time when they are in context with the actions you are performing. Accompanying data files eliminate unnecessary typing.

❏ **Using Publisher Help.** At the end of each Lesson, there is an exercise to practice using Publisher's extensive Help feature. Because no one can memorize all the features of a rich program like Publisher, efficient use of the Help system will facilitate your long-term skill in using Publisher. If you elect to take the MOUS certification test in Microsoft Publisher, you are permitted to use the Help feature during the test.

❏ **End-of-Lesson Publications.** The end-of-lesson publications emphasize hands-on skill development. You will find two levels of reinforcement—Skill Assessments and Performance Assessments. Each end-of-lesson publication is independent of other publications, so you can complete them in any order. Accompanying data files eliminate unnecessary typing.

Skill Assessments Skill Assessments reinforce publication skills. Each skill reinforced is the same, or nearly the same, as a skill presented in the Lesson. Each exercise includes a brief narrative introduction, followed by detailed instructions in a step-by-step format.

Performance Assessments Performance Assessments expand on the skills presented in the Lesson. Each exercise provides a brief narrative introduction, followed by instructions in a numbered-step format that are not as detailed as those in the Skill Assessments section.

❏ Two other sections precede the end-of-project exercises—**Summary** and **Concepts Assessments**. The Summary provides a brief recap of tasks learned in the project. The Concepts Assessments section includes Short Answer and Matching questions designed to check your comprehension of overall concepts and familiarity with terms.

❏ **Notes.** Publication projects include two types of notes: "Does your screen differ?…" and "To extend your knowledge…" The first type displays between hands-on steps. These short troubleshooting notes help you anticipate or solve common problems quickly and effectively. Many activities in the projects end with "To extend your knowledge…" notes that provide extra tips, shortcuts, and alternative ways to complete a process, as well as special hints. You may safely ignore these for the moment to focus on the main task at hand, or you may pause to learn the additional information.

❐ **Illustrations.** Multiple illustrations reinforce learning in each publication project. Each publication is introduced with a visual summary that graphically illustrates the concepts and features included in the publication you will produce. Each time a new button is introduced, its icon displays in the margin. Screen shots display after key steps for you to check against the results on your screen. These figures, with ample callouts, make it easy to check your progress.

How to Use This Book

This text contains six Lessons, and each Lesson presents two or three new publications to complete while practicing the features of the software. At the end of each Lesson, additional new publications for you to complete are presented, so that you can practice what you have learned. The following elements are designed to maximize your learning experience:

❐ **Objectives.** Starting with an objective gives you a short-term, attainable goal. Using Lesson objectives that closely match the titles of the step-by-step tutorials breaks down the possibly overwhelming prospect of learning several new features of an Office XP application into small, attainable tasks. Look over the objectives on the opening page of the Lesson before you begin, and review them after completing the Lesson to identify the main goals for each Lesson.

❐ **Key Terms.** Key terms introduced in each Lesson are listed, in alphabetical order, immediately after the objectives on the opening page of the Lesson. Each key term is defined during its first use within the text, and is shown in bold italic within that explanation. Definitions of key terms are also included in the Glossary.

❐ **Publication Design Tips.** Each Lesson begins with Publication Design Tips that provide information about preparing professional publications. Here you will find information about the layout, design, and production of your publications.

❐ **Publication Identification and Illustration.** Each publication within the Lesson is identified with the Lesson number and a letter. Thus, publication 3B is the second publication in the third Lesson. Each publication begins with an illustration of what the completed publication will look like when it is printed.

 ❐ **Does your screen differ?... .** These short troubleshooting notes help you anticipate or solve common problems quickly and effectively. You may not encounter the difference described, but if you do, you will be able to move ahead without interruption.

❐ **To Extend Your Knowledge... .** These notes provide extra tips, shortcuts, alternative ways to complete a process, and special hints about using the software.

Typeface Conventions Used in This Book

Publisher 2002 uses the following conventions to make it easier for you to understand the material:

❐ Key terms appear in ***italic and bold*** the first time they are defined in a project.

❐ Monospace type appears frequently and looks `like this`. It is used to indicate text that you are instructed to key in.

❐ *Italic text* indicates the name of a file to be used in a lesson or exercise.

Accessing Student Data Files

The data files that students need to work through the publications can be downloaded from the book's companion Web site at *www.prenhall.com/gaskin*. Data files are provided for each Lesson. The filenames correspond to the filenames called for in this book. The first character indicates the Lesson number and the second character indicates the publication letter within the Lesson.

For the Instructor

Instructor Resources

Instructor's Resource CD-ROM

The **Instructor's Resource CD-ROM** that is available with *Microsoft Publisher 2002* contains:

- ❏ Instructor's Manual in Word and PDF.
- ❏ Solutions to all questions and exercises from the book and Web site
- ❏ Publications for demonstration for each Lesson
- ❏ Data and Solution files
- ❏ A Windows-based test manager and the associated test bank in Word format

Tools for Online Learning

www.prenhall.com/gaskin

This text is accompanied by a companion Web site at *www.prenhall.com/gaskin*. This Web site is designed to bring you and your students a richer, more interactive Web experience. The site will also include the data files for students to download and a **For instructor** site that will contain the solution files for instructors.

Getting Started With Publisher 2002

Objectives

In this lesson, you learn how to:

- ✔ Start Publisher and Identify Components of the Publisher Window
- ✔ Create a Publication
- ✔ Save and Close a Publication and Open an Existing Publication
- ✔ Insert a Footer on Every Page of a Publication
- ✔ Preview and Print a Publication
- ✔ Create a Personal Information Set
- ✔ Insert a Logo in a Publication
- ✔ Delete and Move an Object
- ✔ Format Text in a Letterhead
- ✔ Use Publisher's Help System

Key terms in this Lesson include

- ❑ desktop publishing
- ❑ flyers
- ❑ footers
- ❑ frames
- ❑ grayed out
- ❑ handles
- ❑ headers
- ❑ help
- ❑ keyboard shortcut
- ❑ logo
- ❑ Master page
- ❑ menus
- ❑ object
- ❑ Office Assistant
- ❑ personal information set
- ❑ placeholder text
- ❑ Quick Publications
- ❑ ScreenTip
- ❑ selecting
- ❑ sizing handles
- ❑ submenu
- ❑ task pane
- ❑ templates
- ❑ wizard
- ❑ word wrap
- ❑ zoom

Publication Design Tips—What Is Microsoft Publisher, and How Does It Differ From Microsoft Word?

Microsoft Publisher 2002 is a ***desktop publishing*** program with which you can mix text and graphics on a page to create publications of professional quality. There are other desktop publishing programs on the market, but they are designed to be used by professional typesetters and can take much more time to learn. Publisher, on the other hand, was created for office professionals and individuals who want to create professional publications, but do not have access to the services of professional graphic designers and typesetters—and who do not have the time to learn complex desktop publishing programs!

Microsoft Publisher 2002 helps you create publications such as ***flyers*** (one-page messages with minimal text and graphics ideal for quick communications), brochures, advertisements, business forms, colorful reports, newsletters, and Web sites. These types of publications can also be created using Microsoft Word. Because both programs are capable of creating some of the same types of publications, when would you choose Publisher instead of Word?

There are three reasons why Publisher is a better tool than Word for creating most publications. Publisher gives you much more flexibility in designing the page than Word does. Whereas Word focuses on the page as a whole, Publisher lets you design the layout of the page by positioning different ***frames*** on the page. Frames are boxes into which you place text or images. Once they are placed on the page, frames can be resized, formatted, and rearranged by moving them on the page.

Also, Publisher has a much wider variety of ***templates*** from which you can choose. A template is a model publication upon which you can build your own new publication. Publisher provides hundreds of templates that already have a professional design and color scheme in place. The graphic design has been done for you! Additionally, Publisher assists you in using each of its pre-designed templates with a ***wizard***. A wizard is a tool that takes you step-by-step through a process. A publication wizard guides you through the process of building a publication based on a pre-designed template.

The final reason that you would use Publisher instead of Word is if you plan to use a commercial printer for your publication. Commercial printers are interested in color processing and other sophisticated techniques for producing color publications. Word cannot prepare your file in the precise way that a commercial printer needs to transform your electronic file into a beautifully printed color publication.

Publication 1A

New Park

In Activities 1.1–1.9 you will create a Quick Publication announcing a new park for the City of Desert Park, Arizona. Your completed publication will look similar to the one shown in Figure 1.1. Using your own first and last name, you will save your publication as *Firstname Lastname-1A New Park*.

New Park

The City of Desert Park is pleased to announce that the City Council has approved the plan for a new park to be built on the City's north side. Go to the City's Web site for more information.

Student Name-1A New Park

Figure 1.1

Objective 1: Start Publisher and Identify Components of the Publisher Window

In the following Activities, you will start Publisher and become familiar with the Publisher window.

Activity 1.1   Starting Publisher and Exploring the Publisher Window

1 On the left side of the Windows taskbar, click the **Start** button.

The Start menu displays.

2 On the computer you are using, locate the Publisher program and then click **Publisher** to open the program.

Organizations and individuals store computer programs in a variety of ways. The Publisher program might be located under All Programs, or Microsoft Office, or some other arrangement. Refer to Figure 1.2 as an example.

Figure 1.2

Publisher opens, and the opening screen displays (see Figure 1.3). Depending upon your screen's resolution, you may see fewer or more model publications on the screen. The default Publisher working environment consists of a menu bar, toolbars on the top and left side of the window, and a main window divided into two sections—the *task pane* on the left, and the Publication Gallery on the right. The task pane is a window within a Microsoft Office application that provides commonly used commands. Its location and small size allow you to use these commands while still working on your files.

Activity 1.1   Starting Publisher and Exploring the Publisher Window

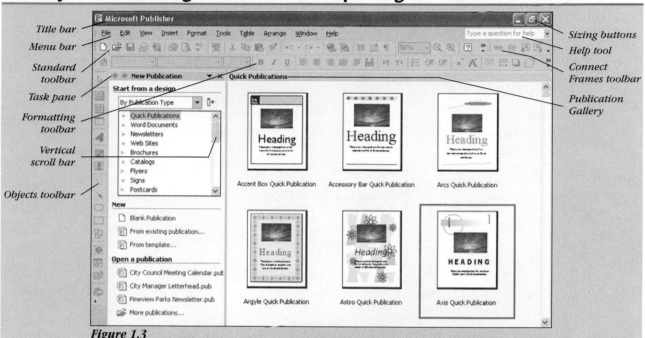

Title bar
Menu bar
Standard toolbar
Task pane
Formatting toolbar
Vertical scroll bar
Objects toolbar

Sizing buttons
Help tool
Connect Frames toolbar
Publication Gallery

Figure 1.3

Does your screen differ?

Upon starting Publisher, if you do not see the New Publication task pane on the left, or if you do not see the Publication Gallery on the right, it is possible that the settings have been changed on the computer you are using. From the Tools menu, click the Options command to display the Options dialog box. Click the General tab, and if necessary, select (click to place a check mark in) the Use New Publication task pane at startup check box. Then, click the User Assistance tab, and if necessary, select the Use Quick Publication Wizard For Blank Publications check box.

❸ Using Figure 1.3 and Table 1.1 as a guide, take a few moments to study the elements of the Microsoft Publisher screen.

Table 1.1 lists and describes the default screen elements.

(Continues)

Activity 1.1   Starting Publisher and Exploring the Publisher Window (continued)

TABLE 1.1   ELEMENTS OF THE MICROSOFT PUBLISHER SCREEN

Element	Description
Title bar	Shows the name of the program and file that is currently in use. If you have not saved the publication, Publisher displays a document number, such as *Publication1*.
Sizing buttons	Enables you to minimize, maximize, restore, and close the Publisher window.
Help tool	Enables you to type a question whenever you need help using a feature.
Menu bar	Contains a series of menus that contain related Publisher commands.
Standard toolbar	Contains a row of buttons that provide a one-click method to perform the most common commands in Publisher.
Formatting toolbar	Contains a row of buttons that provide a one-click method to perform the most common formatting commands in Publisher.
Connect Frames toolbar	Contains buttons for specific Publisher commands that provide a method to connect frames.
Objects toolbar	Contains the Publisher tools with which you can draw shapes, insert text boxes, and draw picture frames.
Task pane	Displays task-specific commands and options that you can access without displaying the menus.
Publication Gallery	Displays thumbnails (small images) of the pre-designed publications available in the category that is currently selected in the New Publication Task pane.
Vertical scroll bars	Move up and down to display more choices.

To Extend Your Knowledge...

Displaying the Standard and Formatting Toolbars on Separate Rows

If your Standard and Formatting toolbars do not display as two separate rows, go to the menu bar and click View, and then click Toolbars. On the Toolbars submenu, click Customize. In the Customize dialog box, click the Options tab, and then click to place a check mark in the Show Standard and Formatting Toolbars on Two Rows check box.

Activity 1.2   Using the Menu Bar

 On the menu bar, click **File**.

The menu displays in either the full format (see Figure 1.4) or in a short format (see a menu in short format in Figure 1.5.). Publisher's commands are organized in ***menus***—lists of commands within a category. A short menu will display fully after a few seconds, or alternatively you can click the small double arrows at the bottom to display the full menu. The File menu, when displayed in full, lists the last four to nine Publications used on your computer. Whether your full menu displays instantly or is delayed by a few seconds depends upon how your software was set up by your system administrator. Likewise, the number of previous document names displayed depends upon how the software is set up.

Activity 1.2   Using the Menu Bar

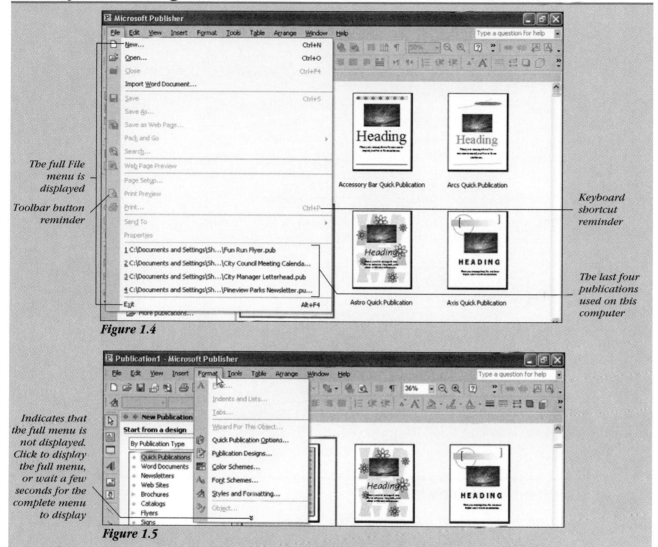

The full File menu is displayed

Toolbar button reminder

Keyboard shortcut reminder

The last four publications used on this computer

Figure 1.4

Indicates that the full menu is not displayed. Click to display the full menu, or wait a few seconds for the complete menu to display

Figure 1.5

2 If necessary, click the double arrows to expand the File menu (see Figure 1.5).

On the left side of some command names, you see an image of the button that represents this command on a toolbar. This is just a reminder that the toolbar button can also be used to start this command. Likewise, to the right of some commands, there is a reminder that there is also a *keyboard shortcut* (holding down a combination of keys) to start this command.

3 Look at the full menu on your screen.

On the right side of the menu commands, you will see symbols or characters. These characters are standard across all Microsoft products. The following is a list of these characters and a description of what will happen when that command is chosen:

(Continues)

Activity 1.2   Using the Menu Bar (continued)

Characteristic	Description	Example
... (ellipsis)	Indicates that a dialog box requesting more information will display	Print...
▶ (triangle)	Indicates that a submenu—another menu of choices—will display	Send to ▶
No symbol	Indicates that the command will perform immediately	Exit
✔ (check mark)	Indicates that an option is turned on or active	✔ Standard
Gray option name	Indicates that the option is currently unavailable (grayed out)	Properties

4 On the menu bar, click **File** again to close the menu.

If you decide not to select a command from a displayed menu, close the menu either by clicking its name, or clicking somewhere outside of the menu.

? Does your screen differ?

If you do not see the short version of the File menu as shown in Figure 1.5, your system has been set so that full menus always display. Many individuals prefer the full menu display. To set a system to always display the full menu, click to display the Tools menu, click Customize, and then click the Options tab. Select (place a check mark in) the Always show full menus check box. Click Reset my usage data and then click Yes.

To Extend Your Knowledge...

Selecting Menus from the Keyboard

You can use the keyboard to display a menu from the menu bar. Notice that one letter of each menu name is underlined. For example, F is underlined in File. To open a menu, press and hold down Alt and the underlined letter. Thus, pressing Alt + F displays the File menu.

Activity 1.3   Using Toolbars

1 On the Standard toolbar, move the mouse pointer over the Open button on the Standard toolbar.

When you position the mouse pointer over a button, Publisher displays the button's name in a box called a ***ScreenTip***. You should see the ScreenTip "Open."

2 On the menu bar, click **View** to display the View menu and then click **Toolbars**.

A list of available toolbars and the Customize command displays (see Figure 1.6). The check marks indicate the active toolbars.

Activity 1.3   Using Toolbars

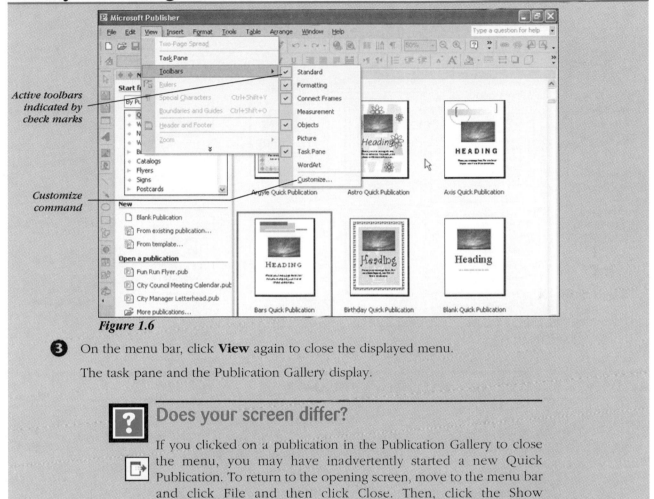

Active toolbars indicated by check marks

Customize command

Figure 1.6

3 On the menu bar, click **View** again to close the displayed menu.

The task pane and the Publication Gallery display.

Does your screen differ?

If you clicked on a publication in the Publication Gallery to close the menu, you may have inadvertently started a new Quick Publication. To return to the opening screen, move to the menu bar and click File and then click Close. Then, click the Show Publication Gallery button located at the top of the task pane, just to the right of the By Publication Type arrow.

Objective 2: Create a Publication

The New Publication task pane is the fastest way to start new publications or to display existing publications. The New Publication task pane on the left presents you with three methods to display a publication (see Figure 1.7).

The first method is to start a new publication from a design—either one of the hundreds of pre-formatted templates available within Publisher, or from a blank publication containing basic margins and page layouts. Each of the pre-formatted template designs has a name and is presented in alphabetical order.

The second method is to start a new publication from either a Blank Publication, an existing publication, or a template that you may have created in the past.

The third method to display a publication is to open an existing publication. Publisher conveniently lists the names of the last several publications on which you worked. You can access other existing publications by clicking More publications at the bottom of the task pane to display the Open Publication dialog box, from which you can locate any stored publication file.

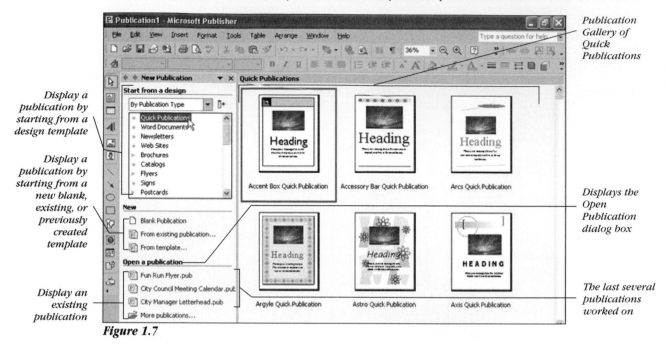

Display a publication by starting from a design template

Display a publication by starting from a new blank, existing, or previously created template

Display an existing publication

Publication Gallery of Quick Publications

Displays the Open Publication dialog box

The last several publications worked on

Figure 1.7

Activity 1.4   Opening a Quick Publication

❶ In the New Publication task pane, under Start from a design, click **Quick Publications**. Then, use the scroll arrow to view the many pre-formatted templates available in the Quick Publications Gallery.

The available Quick Publication templates display in the Publication Gallery (see Figure 1.8). Each **Quick Publication** is a one-page, pre-formatted design that consists of three frames—one each for a picture, a heading, and a message—plus some color and graphic design elements.

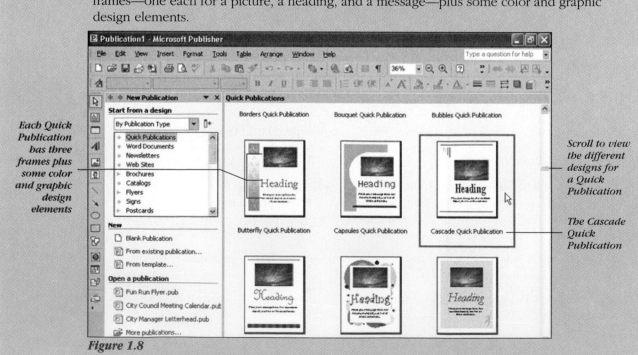

Each Quick Publication has three frames plus some color and graphic design elements

Scroll to view the different designs for a Quick Publication

The Cascade Quick Publication

Figure 1.8

Activity 1.4   Opening a Quick Publication

2 Scroll to locate and then click the **Cascade Quick Publication**.

If you see a message regarding your name and address, click OK, and then in the displayed dialog box click Cancel. The Quick Publication Wizard builds your selection using the default layout for the Cascade Quick Publication (see Figure 1.9). Notice that a new task pane is opened—the Quick Publication Options task pane—with options for changing the Design, Color Scheme, and Font Scheme of the current publication. You will learn more about these options.

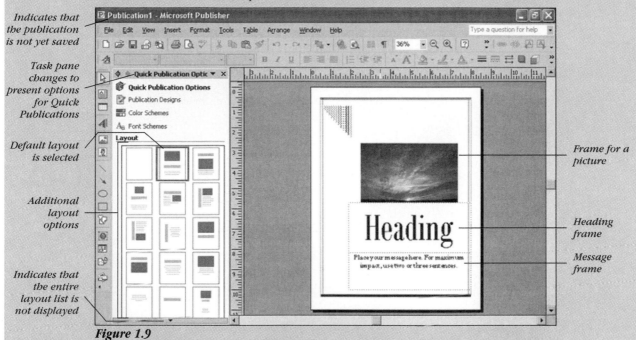

Indicates that the publication is not yet saved

Task pane changes to present options for Quick Publications

Default layout is selected

Additional layout options

Indicates that the entire layout list is not displayed

Frame for a picture

Heading frame

Message frame

Figure 1.9

? Does your screen differ?

If previous users of your computer have not utilized the "personal information set" feature in Publisher, you may see the message, "The wizard will fill in your name, address, and other information for you, so you don't have to enter it each time. Click OK to tell the wizard about yourself."

Click the OK button, and then, on the Personal Information dialog box, move to the lower right corner, and click Cancel. In subsequent Activities in this lesson, you will learn about this feature.

3 In the Quick Publication Options task pane under Layout, in the fourth row, point to the second layout. When the ScreenTip "No picture" displays, click once to choose this layout.

As you just saw in the Layout section of the task pane, each pre-formatted design template offers further options for arranging the frames on the page. In the layout that you just selected, there is no picture. The Heading and Message frames contain ***placeholder text***, which is text that you will replace with your own text.

4 In the publication pane, move the mouse pointer anywhere over the word "Heading" and click once.

(Continues)

Activity 1.4   Opening a Quick Publication (continued)

The placeholder text "Heading" is highlighted in black, indicating that it is selected. *Selecting* refers to using the mouse to highlight text or images so that they can be edited, formatted, copied, moved, or deleted.

5 Type `New Park`

6 In the frame that contains the placeholder text that begins "Place your message here," click once to select the text and then type the following text, letting the text wrap as you type (in other words, do not press `←Enter` to end any lines) and inserting just one period at the end of a sentence. `The City of Desert Park is pleased to announce that the City Council has approved the plan for a new park to be built on the City's north side. Go to the City's Web site for more information.`

As you type, there is no need to press `←Enter` to end lines because Publisher will automatically use *word wrap* to wrap the text to the next line. Word wrap is the action that takes place when the insertion point reaches the right margin of a frame, and is automatically moved down and to the left margin of the next line.

Although you may have learned that two spaces should follow punctuation at the end of a sentence, the accepted practice now is to place only one space after the end of sentence punctuation. This is especially true of desktop publishing programs such as Publisher—two spaces might result in a noticeable gap between sentences.

7 Compare your screen to Figure 1.10.

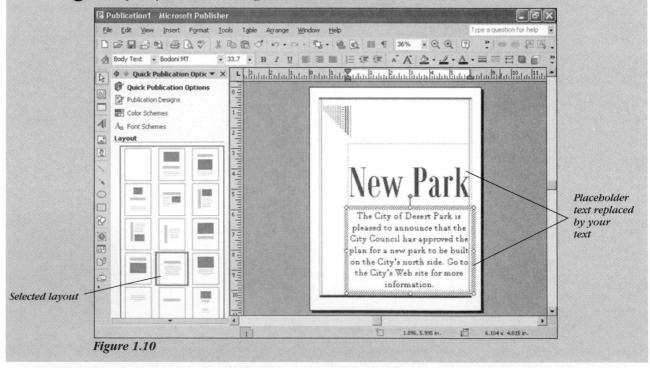

Selected layout

Placeholder text replaced by your text

Figure 1.10

To Extend Your Knowledge...

Correct Typing Mistakes

If you make a mistake as you type, you have two options for making corrections. Press `←Backspace` to delete text to the *left* of the insertion point, or press `Del` to delete text to the *right* of the insertion point. After deleting incorrect letters, type the correct letters.

Objective 3: Save and Close a Publication and Open an Existing Publication

In the same way that you use file folders to organize your paper documents, Windows uses a hierarchy of electronic folders to keep your electronic files (publications) organized. Using Windows' hierarchy of folders, you can group your files in a logical manner.

As you create, edit, and save publications, you may wish to create a logical group of electronic file folders in which to store them. For example, you could create a folder for each lesson of this book so that all your activities and assignments for each lesson are kept together. Check with your instructor or lab coordinator to see where you will be storing your documents (for example, on your own disk or on a network drive), and whether there is any suggested file folder arrangement.

Activity 1.5 Creating a New Folder and Saving a Publication Using Save As

1 On the menu bar, click **File** to display the File menu, and then click **Save As**.

The Save As dialog box displays (see Figure 1.11).

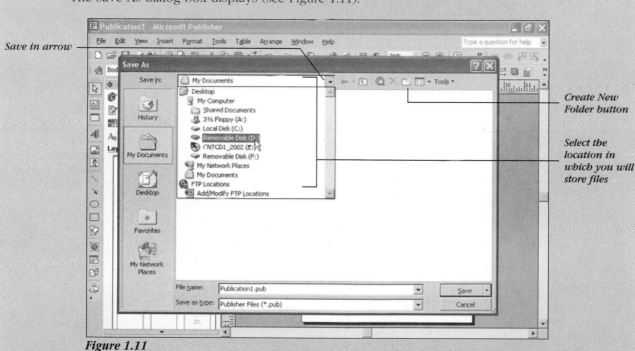

Figure 1.11

2 Click the **Save in arrow** (the downward-pointing arrow at the right edge of the Save in box) to view a list of the drives available to you.

3 Click to select the drive on which you will be storing your folders and documents; for example, Removable Disk (D:).

4 Click the **Create New Folder** button.

The New Folder dialog box appears as seen in Figure 1.12.

5 In the New Folder dialog box, click in the Name box, type Lesson 1 to create a folder on your disk, and then click **OK**.

(Continues)

Activity 1.5   Creating a New Folder and Saving a Publication Using Save As (continued)

Publisher creates the Lesson 1 folder, and makes it the active folder in the Save As dialog box.

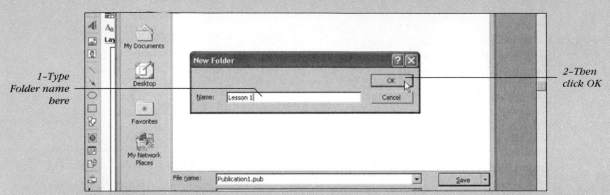

1-Type Folder name here

2-Then click OK

Figure 1.12

6 In the File name box, type `Firstname Lastname-1A New Park`

7 Click the **Save** button in the lower right corner of the dialog box, or press ↵Enter.

The new file name appears in both the title bar and the taskbar, and the document has been saved in the Lesson 1 folder.

Activity 1.6   Closing a Publication and Exiting Publisher

1 On the menu bar, click **File**, and then click **Close** (see Figure 1.13).

Your publication is closed. The Publisher program remains open with the New Publication task pane on the left, and a blank publication on the right.

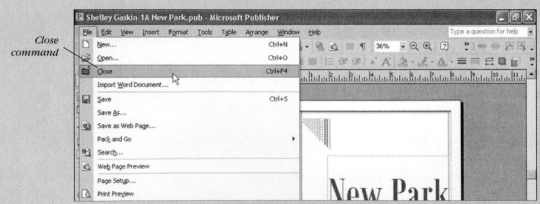

Close command

Figure 1.13

2 In the upper right corner of the task pane, click the **Shows Publication Gallery** button to re-display the Publication Gallery on the right.

Click this button (see Figure 1.14) to re-display or hide the Publication Gallery.

Activity 1.6   Closing a Publication and Exiting Publisher

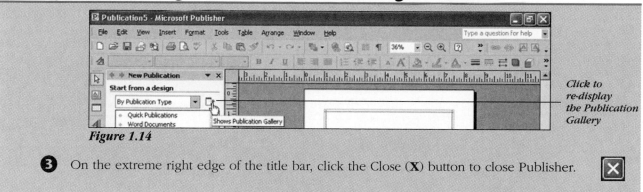

Figure 1.14

❸   On the extreme right edge of the title bar, click the Close (**X**) button to close Publisher.

Activity 1.7   Re-Starting Publisher and Opening an Existing Publication

❶   Using the **Start** button, start the Publisher program as you learned to do in Objective 1 of this lesson.

The Publisher program opens, and your most recently used files display at the bottom of the task pane.

❷   Open your 1A New Park publication by pointing to it on the task pane and then clicking once (see Figure 1.15).

Alternatively, you could click the Open button on the Standard toolbar (or click File and then Open from the menu bar) and locate your files by navigating the Windows folder hierarchy.

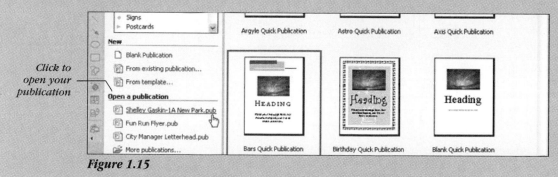

Figure 1.15

Objective 4: Insert a Footer on Every Page of a Publication

Because you might be working in a classroom or lab environment, you will put your name at the bottom of all the pages in your publications. Publisher provides a method by which you can place text or graphics on every page of a publication. This feature is the ***Master page***. The Master page is a special page that acts as a background for your publications. Items placed on the Master page will display on any or all pages in the publication.

It is common to have ***headers*** or ***footers*** on every page of a publication. Headers and footers are text, page numbers, graphics, and formatting that print at the top (header) or bottom (footer) of every page.

Activity 1.8   Creating a Footer on the Master Page

❶ On the menu bar, click **View**, and then click **Header and Footer**.

A background page that looks like a blank page displays in the work area. The status bar in the lower left corner of the publication pane shows the page number as R, indicating that the Master Page view is displayed.

❷ On the small Header and Footer toolbar, click the **Show Header/Footer** button once to display the Footer frame.

The Footer frame is displayed and selected (see Figure 1.16).

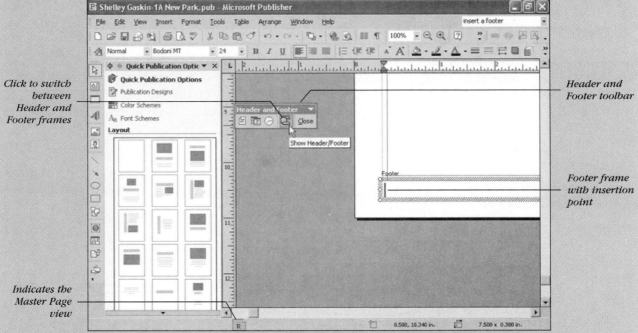

Figure 1.16

❸ On the Formatting toolbar, click the **Font Size arrow** (see Figure 1.17) and then click **10**. If necessary, click in the Footer frame; then, using your own first and last name, type `Firstname Lastname-1A New Park`

❹ Compare your footer frame to Figure 1.18.

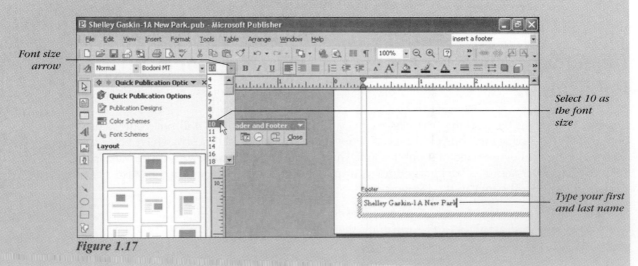

Figure 1.17

Activity 1.8   Creating a Footer on the Master Page

5 On the small Header and Footer toolbar, click **Close**.

The Master Page view is closed, and your publication, with its footer, displays (see Figure 1.18). Notice that the page number in the status bar indicates 1.

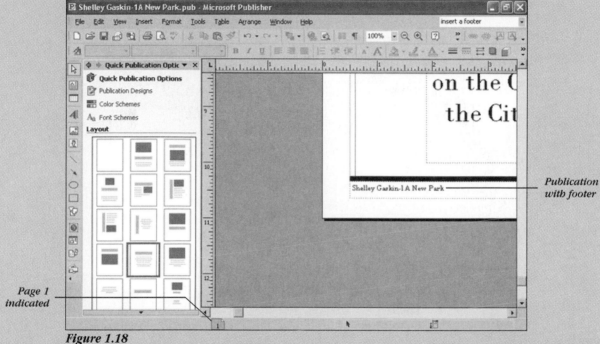

Page 1 indicated

Publication with footer

Figure 1.18

6 On the Standard toolbar, click the **Save** button.

Clicking the Save button will save the changes you have made to your publication since the last save operation. Recall that a toolbar button is simply a one-click method for performing a command that could otherwise be performed from the menu bar (clicking the File menu and then the Save command).

Objective 5: Preview and Print a Publication

Before you print a publication, it is always a good idea to use Publisher's Print Preview command to see what your publication will look like on the printed page. You can make a quick visual check to be sure that the formatting, placement, and layout are correct before actually printing the document on paper.

The simplest way to print a document is to click the Print button on either the Standard toolbar or the Print Preview window's toolbar. This will print one complete copy of the document on the default printer. If you wish to print anything other than one complete copy—such as multiple copies; some, but not all pages; or to select a different printer—you must use the Print command from the File menu.

Activity 1.9   Previewing and Printing a Publication

❶ On the Standard toolbar, click the **Print Preview** button.

Figure 1.19 shows the Print Preview button. Your publication displays as it will look on the printed page (see Figure 1.20). Notice the graphic elements that were added by Publisher, and which you did not have to create yourself! This is the main advantage of using Microsoft Publisher, as opposed to Microsoft Word, for creating publications.

Print Preview button

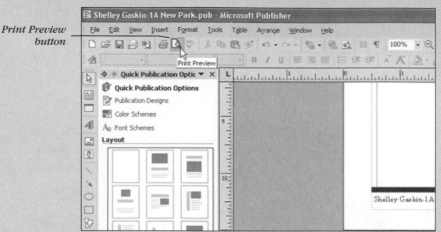

Figure 1.19

Graphic elements and design added by Publisher

Close Preview button

Your name and publication name here

Figure 1.20

❷ On the toolbar of the Print Preview screen, click the **Close Preview** button to return to the publication window.

❸ On the menu bar, click **File**, and then click **Print**.

The Print dialog box displays (see Figure 1.21).

Activity 1.9   Previewing and Printing a Publication

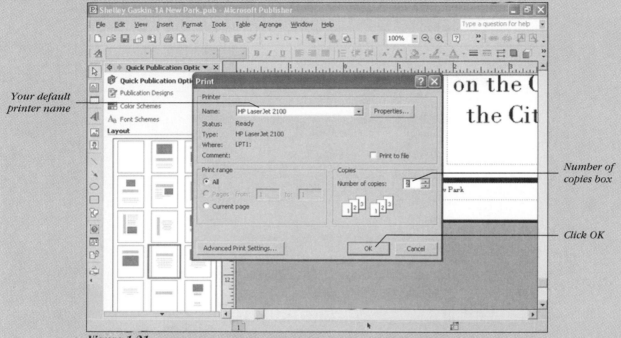

Your default printer name

Number of copies box

Click OK

Figure 1.21

4   Under Copies, locate the Number of copies box.

5   In the Number of copies box, change the number of copies to **2** either by deleting 1 and typing **2,** or clicking once on the upward-pointing arrow in the spin box (see Figure 1.21).

6   Click **OK**.

Collect your two printouts from the printer. Note that if you are printing on an ink jet printer, you may have to move the footer frame up slightly. Publication 1A New Park is complete!

7   On the menu bar, click **File**, and then click **Close** to close the publication. Save any changes if prompted to do so.

Publication 1B

City Letterhead

In Activities 1.10–1.13 you will create a letterhead for the City of Desert Park. Your completed publication will look similar to the one shown in Figure 1.22. You will save your publication as *Firstname Lastname-1B City Letterhead.*

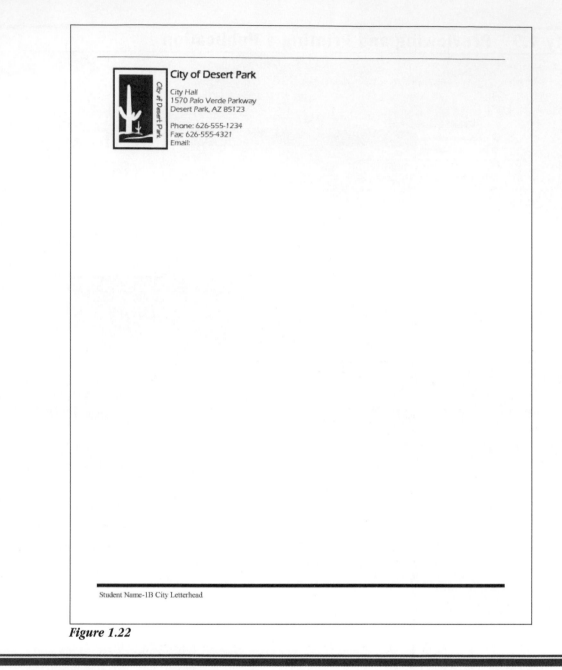

City of Desert Park

City Hall
1570 Palo Verde Parkway
Desert Park, AZ 85123

Phone: 626-555-1234
Fax: 626-555-4321
Email:

Student Name-1B City Letterhead

Figure 1.22

Objective 6: Create a Personal Information Set

In many of the pre-designed publications in Microsoft Publisher, commonly used business information such as the name, address, phone numbers, and logo of an organization is automatically inserted. For example, if you create a letterhead or a business card, Publisher takes your business information from a feature called the ***Personal Information Set***. This feature saves you time, because once you insert the information, you do not have to re-type your business information each time it is needed in a publication.

The Personal Information Set is stored on the computer's hard drive—not on your disk. While the feature is quite useful for individuals or organizations, if you are working in a classroom or lab, the Personal Information Set will be subject to change. Depending upon who has used the computer at which you are seated, you may be prompted to create a Personal Information Set, or another user may have already filled in some of the personal information. Whichever is the case, you can always change the personal information.

Activity 1.10   Creating the Personal Information Set

1 If necessary, start Publisher, and make sure that the task pane and the Publication Gallery are displayed.

If the task pane is not visible, go to the menu bar and click View and then click Task Pane. If the Publication Gallery is not displayed, click the Shows Publication Gallery button in the upper right corner of the task pane.

2 In the New Publication task pane under Start from a design, be sure that By Publication Type is displayed. If it is not, click the Start from a design arrow and then click By Publication Type. Scroll down, and click **Letterheads** (see Figure 1.23). In the Publication Gallery, scroll down, point to the small image of the **Cascade Letterhead,** and click. (If a message displays regarding your name and address, click OK and then click Cancel in the displayed dialog box.)

The Cascade letterhead displays, and the Letterhead Options task pane displays on the left. The Cascade letterhead design contains frames for the organization name, address information, and telephone number. Additionally, the graphic elements are contained within frames.

? Does your screen differ?

Depending on previous use of the computer you are using, you might see actual address information included in the letterhead instead of placeholder text. This is because Publisher will automatically insert information from the Personal Information Set, which a previous user could have entered. If that is what you see, simply ignore it. You can always replace the information in a Personal Information Set with your own data.

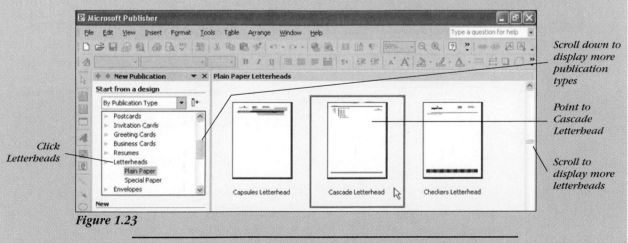

Figure 1.23

(Continues)

Activity 1.10   Creating the Personal Information Set (continued)

3 On the menu bar, click **Edit**, and then click **Personal Information** (see Figure 1.24).

The Personal Information dialog box displays (see Figure 1.25).

Notice that in addition to the Primary Business set, three additional personal information sets are available.

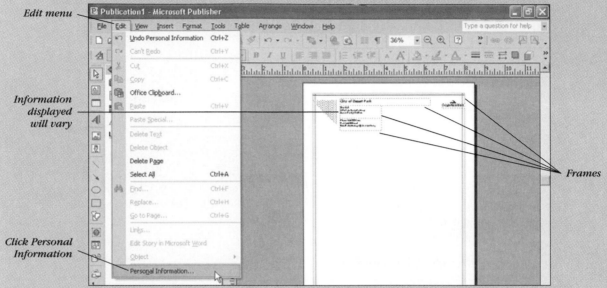

Edit menu

Information displayed will vary

Click Personal Information

Frames

Figure 1.24

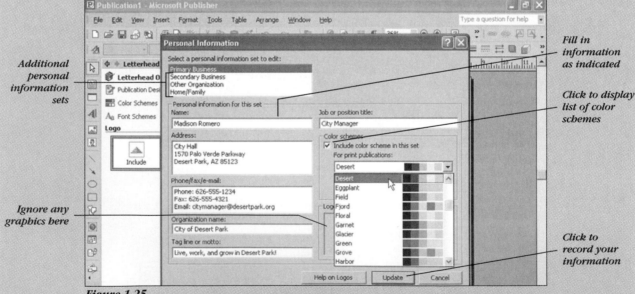

Additional personal information sets

Ignore any graphics here

Fill in information as indicated

Click to display list of color schemes

Click to record your information

Figure 1.25

4 Under Select a Personal Information Set to Edit, be sure that **Primary Business** is selected; then, using Figure 1.25 as your guide, fill in the Personal Information as shown in the following table. Use the (Tab⇆) key or mouse to move from field to field.

Recall that depending on previous use of the computer at which you are seated, some or all of the information may already be in the dialog box. Ignore any graphics under Logo.

Activity 1.10   Creating the Personal Information Set

Name:	Madison Romero
Address:	City Hall
	1570 Palo Verde Parkway
	Desert Park, AZ 85123
Phone/fax/e-mail:	Phone: 626-555-1234
	Fax: 626-555-4321
	Email: citymanager@desertpark.org
Organization name:	City of Desert Park
Tag line or motto:	Live, work, and grow in Desert Park!
Job position or title:	City Manager
Color schemes:	Desert (If necessary, select the Include color scheme in this set option.)

If there is information already entered in the Personal Information Set, simply type over it. Ignore any graphics under Logo.

5 In the lower portion of the dialog box, click the **Update** button to record your information.

The Cascade letterhead with the new personal information displays.

6 In the task pane's upper right corner, click the Close button to close the task pane. On the Standard toolbar, click the **Zoom arrow** and then zoom to **75%** (see Figure 1.26).

To *zoom* means to make the page view larger or smaller. Throughout this text, a zoom size will be suggested, but you may change the zoom size to whatever is comfortable for you.

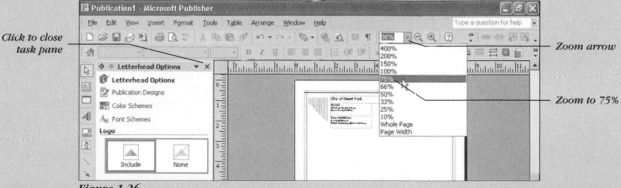

Click to close task pane   *Zoom arrow*

Zoom to 75%

Figure 1.26

7 Use the vertical and horizontal scrollbars to position the top portion of the letterhead in the center of your screen, as shown in Figure 1.27.

Depending upon how the computer at which you are seated has been used, either a default or some other logo displays in the upper right corner of the letterhead (see Figure 1.27).

(Continues)

Activity 1.10   Creating the Personal Information Set (continued)

Information you inserted in the personal information set displays in the frames

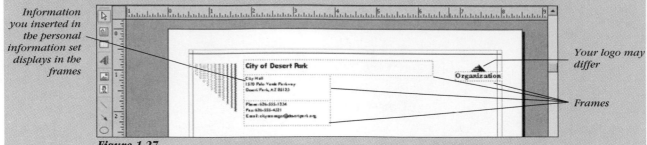

Your logo may differ

Frames

Figure 1.27

8 On the menu bar, click **File** to display the File menu, and then click **Save As**.

The Save As dialog box displays.

9 Click the **Save in arrow** and then navigate to the drive and folder in which you are storing your publications.

For example, in the last publication, you may have created a file folder for Lesson 1 on your disk.

10 In the File name box, delete any existing text; then, using your own first and last name, type `Firstname Lastname-1B City Letterhead`

11 Click the **Save** button in the lower right corner of the dialog box, or press `↵Enter`.

Objective 7: Insert a Logo in a Publication

Most organizations use a ***logo***—a letter, symbol, or sign used as an identifying statement—on all publications. You can probably think of a logo used by your school or employer. In the next Activity, you will insert a logo in the City letterhead.

Activity 1.11   Inserting a Logo in a Publication

1 Display your publication *1B City Letterhead* so that you can see the top of the page. If necessary, close the task pane, and zoom to 75% (see Figure 1.27).

2 In the upper right corner of the letterhead, click on the logo (see Figure 1.28).

Note that a different logo than the one pictured in Figure 1.28 may be displayed, depending on previous use of the computer at which you are working. ***Handles*** (also called ***sizing handles***), which are small circles or squares at the corners and sides of a frame, text box, or other object, display around the logo. Sometimes handles display in dark gray with an x in the center, which indicates that the logo was created by combining several different graphic elements. The handles are used to change the size of the object, and also indicate that an object is selected. Additionally, a Wizard icon displays (see Figure 1.28).

Activity 1.11   Inserting a Logo in a Publication

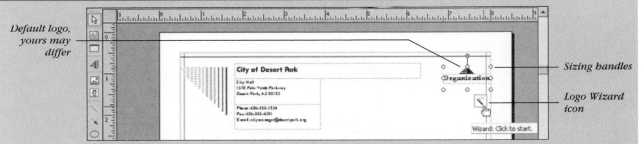

Default logo, yours may differ

Sizing handles

Logo Wizard icon

Figure 1.28

❸ Point to the **Wizard icon** (see Figure 1.28) and then click.

The Logo Designs task pane opens on the left.

❹ In the Logo Designs task pane, point to **Logo Options**, and click.

The Logo Options task pane displays.

❺ In the Logo Options task pane, under New or existing, click **Inserted picture**.

The Choose picture button becomes active, as shown in Figure 1.29.

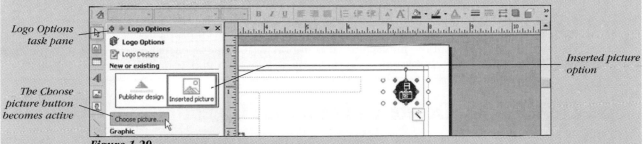

Logo Options task pane

The Choose picture button becomes active

Inserted picture option

Figure 1.29

❻ Click the **Choose picture** button.

The Insert Picture dialog box displays.

❼ Click the **Look in arrow**, and then navigate to the folder containing the student files that accompany this textbook.

❽ Click the file **1B_DesertParkLogo,** and then, in the lower right corner of the dialog box, click the **Insert** button.

The City of Desert Park logo is inserted in the letterhead. If you see sizing handles that are dark gray with an X, this simply indicates that the logo was built from more than one graphic element.

❾ Close the task pane, and scroll as necessary to view the entire width of the top portion of the letterhead. If the Picture toolbar displays, click its Close (**X**) button.

❿ On the Standard toolbar, click the **Save** button to save the changes to your publication. If you see the message asking if you want to save the logo, click **Yes**. See Figure 1.30.

Clicking Yes will store, on the computer's hard drive, the logo as a permanent part of the Primary Business Personal Information Set. In this instance, permanent simply means that you do not have to find where the logo is stored each time you need it. It has become part of the Personal Information Set. A permanent logo can be replaced with another permanent logo at any time.

(Continues)

Activity 1.11   Inserting a Logo in a Publication (continued)

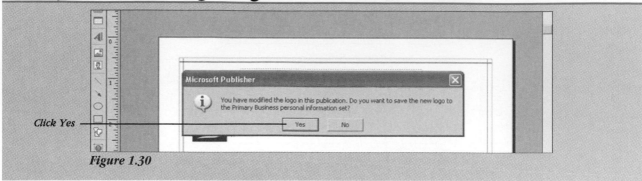

Click Yes

Figure 1.30

To Extend Your Knowledge...

Attaching a Logo to the Personal Information Set

You can attach a specific logo to a personal information set. The result is that whenever a publication includes a logo, the stored logo is automatically inserted. After a logo is attached to a personal information set, it cannot be deleted; however, it can be replaced with another logo. And of course, in any specific publication, the logo can simply be deleted and another one inserted without changing the permanent logo. After a logo has been attached to a personal information set, however, you cannot return to a state of no logo attached. Certainly this is not a problem because the logo can be changed or deleted from the publication. It is important to remember that after a logo is attached, it will display on the Personal Information dialog box unless the Publisher software is re-installed.

Objective 8: Delete and Move an Object

In Publisher, an ***object*** is any element that can be selected, such as a graphic or frame. Selecting the object results in the object's being surrounded by handles that enable you to move or resize the object.

Activity 1.12   Deleting, Resizing, and Moving an Object

1 Position your mouse pointer over either the dark gray lower left sizing handle as shown in Figure 1.31, or the lower left white handle slightly outside of the picture.

The Resize pointer activates.

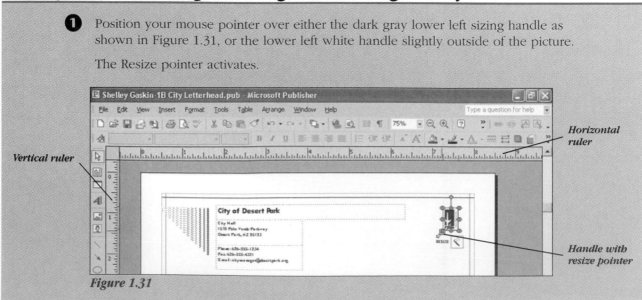

Vertical ruler

Horizontal ruler

Handle with resize pointer

Figure 1.31

Activity 1.12   Deleting, Resizing, and Moving an Object

2   Look at the screen to locate the vertical ↕ and horizontal ⇔ rulers.

Does your screen differ?

If your rulers are not visible, move to the menu bar, click View and then click Rulers. If you see white handles surrounding the area outside of the logo, you can use these to resize the object.

3   Hold down the left mouse button, and then drag the resize handle down and to the left until the logo is about 1 inch wide and 1.5 inches tall. Release the left mouse button.

You can use the rulers as a guide, or use your eye to judge the measurement; it does not need to be exact at this point. See Figure 1.32. If you do not like your results, click the Undo button on the Standard toolbar, and begin again.

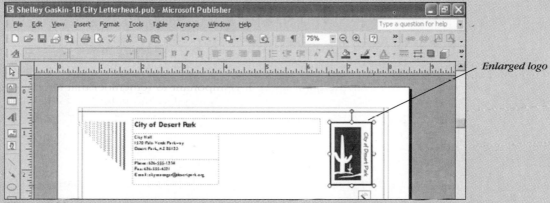

Enlarged logo

Figure 1.32

4   On the upper left corner of your letterhead, locate the graphic element object that is composed of a series of colored lines of varying lengths. Move the mouse pointer over the graphic element object until you see the **Move** pointer, and then click to select the graphic element. See Figure 1.33.

Notice that a new button (two overlapping squares) displays. For now, you can ignore this button, which you will learn about in a subsequent Lesson.

Handles indicate the object is selected

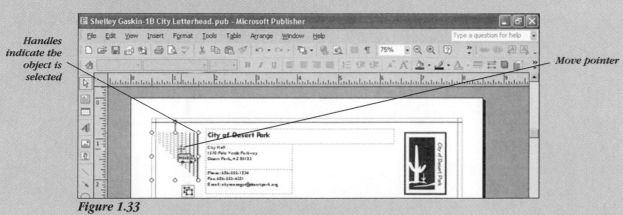

Move pointer

Figure 1.33

(Continues)

Activity 1.12   Deleting, Resizing, and Moving an Object (continued)

5 On your keyboard, press the ⌈Del⌋ key.

The graphic element is deleted.

6 Position the mouse pointer over the Logo Picture until the Move pointer is displayed. Hold down the left mouse button, and drag the logo to the left side of the letterhead as shown in Figure 1.34, and then release the left mouse button.

Notice that a shape of dotted lines moves with the mouse so that you get a visual picture of how the object is moving. If you do not like your results, click the Undo button on the Standard toolbar, and begin again. Resize as necessary.

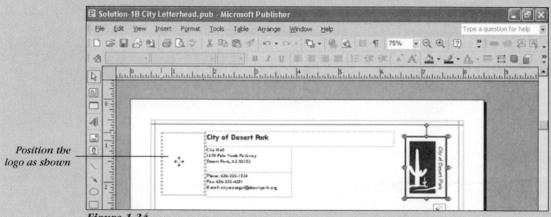

*Position the
logo as shown*

Figure 1.34

7 Click anywhere outside of the logo picture to cancel the selection of the object. If necessary, select the logo again, and make any necessary size or position changes. Then, on the Standard toolbar, click the **Save** button to save the changes you have made to your publication. If asked to save the modified logo, click No.

Objective 9: Format Text in a Letterhead

The default text in the Cascade design that you are using to build your letterhead does not coordinate with the font of the text in the inserted logo. You can easily format the text in a publication using the same kinds of methods that you would use in Word or another word processing program.

Activity 1.13   Formatting Text in a Letterhead

1 With your mouse, point to the left of the C in the text City of Desert Park at the top of the letterhead until you see the I-beam pointer with the ScreenTip "Text." Then drag to select the text in the first frame (see Figure 1.35).

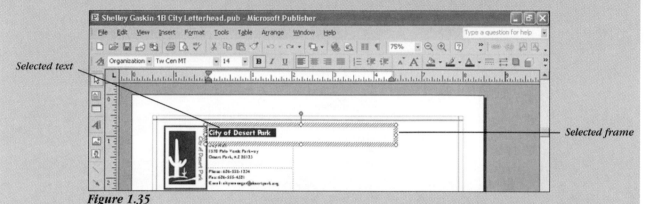

Figure 1.35

2 On the Formatting toolbar, click the **Font arrow**, scroll as necessary and then click **Eras Medium ITC** (see Figure 1.36).

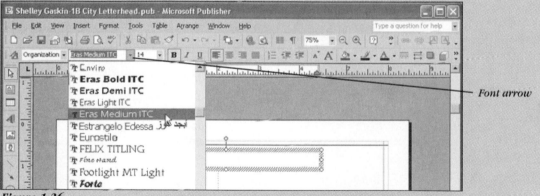

Figure 1.36

3 Click in the three-line address frame, hold down the Ctrl key, and press A to select all of the text in the frame. Change the font to **Eras Medium ITC**.

After you have selected a font, that font name will appear at the top of the list as a recently used font, making it quicker to select the font again.

4 With the address block text still selected (highlighted in black), move to the Formatting toolbar, click the **Font Size arrow**, and click **10** (see Figure 1.37).

(Continues)

Activity 1.13   Formatting Text in a Letterhead (continued)

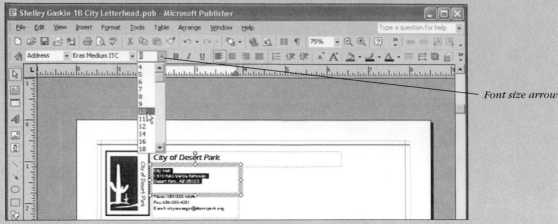

Font size arrow

Figure 1.37

5 Using the technique above, select the three lines in the Phone/Fax/E-mail frame, and change the Font to **Eras Medium ITC**. Then click outside to cancel the selection of any elements that were selected.

Remember that you can always use the Undo key if you are not satisfied with your results.

6 On the menu bar, click **View** and then click **Header and Footer**.

A blank page displays in the work area. At the lower left, in the status bar just above the task bar, notice an R displays. This indicates that the Master page is displayed.

7 On the small Header and Footer toolbar, click the **Show Header/Footer** button until the Footer frame is displayed.

The footer frame displays. (Recall that you can point to a button until its ScreenTip displays to be sure of clicking the correct button.)

8 On the Formatting toolbar, click the **Font Size arrow**, and then click **10**. If necessary, click in the Footer frame to position the insertion point, and then, using your own first and last name, type `Firstname Lastname-1B City Letterhead`

9 On the Header and Footer toolbar, click **Close**.

The Master page is closed, and your publication, with its footer, displays. Notice that in the status bar, the page number 1 displays in a small box. This is how you can determine that the Master page is closed, and that the publication is once again displayed.

10 On the Standard toolbar, click the **Print Preview** button.

Your letterhead displays in print preview, similar to Figure 1.38.

Activity 1.13   Formatting Text in a Letterhead

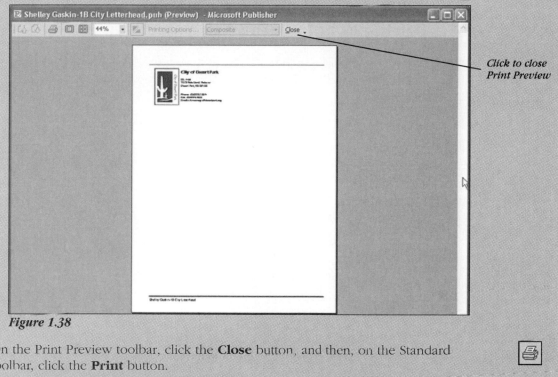

Figure 1.38

⓫ On the Print Preview toolbar, click the **Close** button, and then, on the Standard toolbar, click the **Print** button.

One copy of your publication prints. Recall that clicking the Print button prints one complete copy of the displayed document on the default printer. If you desire some other printing arrangement, such as more copies or specific pages (in a longer document), you must initiate printing from the Print dialog box.

⓬ On the menu bar, click **File**, and then click **Close**. Click **Yes** to save the changes you have made to your publication. Publication 1B is complete!

Objective 10: Use Publisher's Help System

As you work with Publisher, you can get answers to questions about how to perform tasks by using the Help feature. The **_Help_** feature provides information about Publisher features, and step-by-step instructions for performing tasks.

The fastest way to use Help is to type a question in the Ask a Question text box, located at the right edge of the menu bar as shown in Figure 1.39.

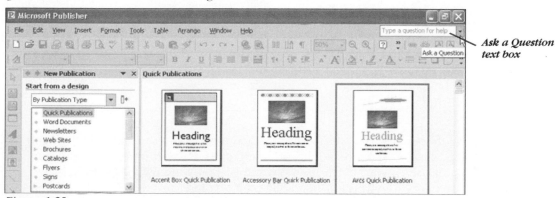

Figure 1.39

In the following Activity, you will find out how to change the color of text in a publication.

Activity 1.14 Getting Help from the Ask a Question Box

① If necessary, start Publisher and then display the New Publication task pane and the Publication Gallery. In the Ask a Question text box, type `How do I change the color of text?`

Recall that to display the task pane and Publication Gallery, move to the menu bar, click View, and click Task Pane. In the displayed task pane, click the Show Publication Gallery button.

② Press ↵Enter.

A list of Help topics displays (see Figure 1.40).

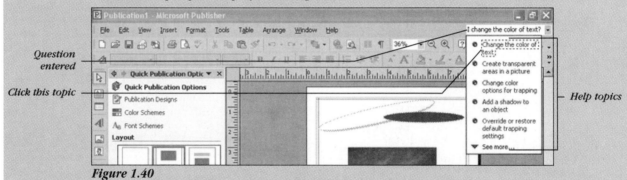

Figure 1.40

③ On the list of Help topics, click **Change the color of text**.

The Microsoft Publisher Help window opens. See Figure 1.41.

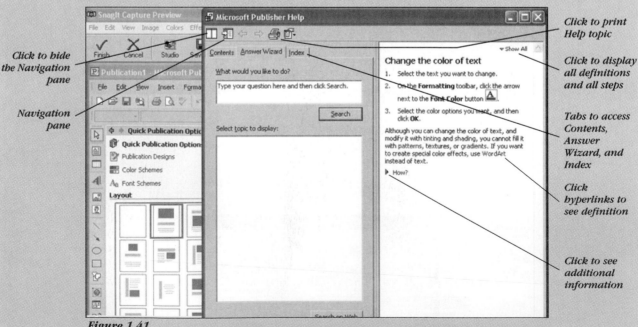

Figure 1.41

The left side of the window has tabs to access different ways to use Help, and the right side contains information about the topic you selected. Although the Help window may be covering all or part of your publication, the publication window will be in full view when you close the Help window. Underlined blue text indicates a hyperlink that will take you to additional information.

Activity 1.14   Getting Help from the Ask a Question Box

 Does your screen differ?

 If you don't see the Navigation pane, click the Show button on the Help toolbar.

4 Click the blue word **tinting** on the right pane.

A definition displays in green letters.

5 Click **How?** at the bottom of the right pane.

When you click a hyperlink preceded by a triangle, Publisher displays additional information, such as specific steps. Click the hyperlink again to hide the information.

6 Click the **Close** button—the **X** in the top right corner of the Help window—to close the Help window.

 ## To Extend Your Knowledge...

Help Index

The Index feature lets you type a topic and search through the alphabetical index of topics. The first step is to enter keywords (particular words that would be found in the Help topics) and then click the Search button. Alternatively, you can scroll through the list of keywords in the index to find the listing that you want.

Double-click the topic listed in the Or choose keywords list box. You see a list of topics in the Choose a topic list box. Click a topic to read more about it.

Office Assistant

You might see the ***Office Assistant***, an animated character that provides general and specific help in response to your questions. You can display or hide the Office Assistant by choosing your preferences from the Help menu.

Help on the Web

If you cannot find the information you need within Publisher, you can access resources available on the World Wide Web. Assuming you have Internet access, you can choose Help, Office on the Web to view information on Microsoft's Web site for Publisher.

Summary

Microsoft Publisher 2002 is an easy-to-use desktop publishing program designed for individuals who do not have access to a professional graphic design department. Unlike Microsoft Word, Publisher focuses on the arrangement of frames on the page, rather than words on the page. For a variety of reasons, Publisher is usually a better choice than Word when there is a mixture of text and graphics on a page.

Publisher contains hundreds of pre-designed templates upon which you can base your publications. The Publisher environment uses various task panes to assist in completing your tasks.

The Personal Information Set feature enables you to enter commonly used business information, such as an organization's address and phone numbers, into a form that can be accessed by Publisher any time such information is needed in a publication.

The Master page feature within Publisher enables you to create text or graphics that will display on every page—a header or footer, for example. This saves you time because you do not have to enter such elements on every page of your publication.

Using Publisher Help

The Publisher Help system contains an entire Help Manual. In this exercise, you will view the hierarchy of the online Help Manual.

1. If necessary, start Publisher, and display the New Publication task pane and the Publication Gallery.

2. On the menu bar, click Help and then click Microsoft Publisher Help.
    The Office Assistant character displays.

3. In the Office Assistant's text box, type How can I get help?

4. Click Search and then on the displayed list, click About getting help while you work.
    The Help pane displays.

5. On the left side, click the Contents tab. If necessary, drag the Office Assistant character to the side.
    The list of books displays.

6. Click the + to the left of any book.
    The + becomes a –, and various topics display. You can click on any topic preceded by a blue question mark and then view the information associated with the topic (see Figure 1.42). Take a few minutes to explore several topics and several books. Clicking the – collapses (hides the subordinate levels of) the topic.

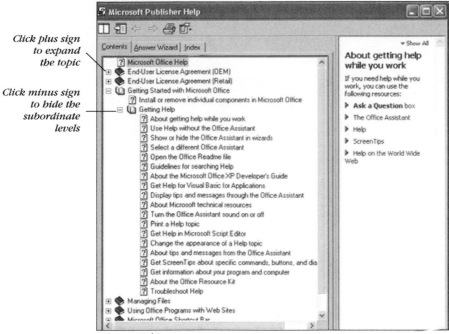

Click plus sign to expand the topic

Click minus sign to hide the subordinate levels

Figure 1.42

7. Click the Close button—the **X** in the top right corner of the Help window—to exit the Help system.

Concepts Assessment

Short Answer

Write the correct answer in the space provided.

1. Microsoft Publisher 2002 is a good tool for office professionals and individuals who do not have access to the services of _____.

2. One reason that Publisher is a better tool than Word to create publications is because Publisher gives you more _____ in designing the page than Word does.

3. Another reason that Publisher is often a better choice than Word is because Publisher has hundreds of templates that already have in place _____.

4. You should use Publisher if you plan to have a _____ produce your publication.

5. Clicking the Print button on the Standard toolbar will print _____.

6. The Personal Information Set is stored on the computer's _____.

7. After a logo is attached to a Personal Information Set, it cannot be deleted in such a way that the software returns to having no logo, but the logo can be _____ by another logo.

8. Selecting an object results in the object's being surrounded by _____.

9. The fastest way to use Publisher's Help system is to type a question in the _____.

10. If you cannot find the Help information you need within Publisher, you can access more Help on the _____.

Matching

Match each term in the second column with its correct definition in the first column. Write the letter of the term on the blank line to the left of the correct definition.

_____ **1.** A program that allows you to mix text and graphics on a page to create publications of professional quality.

_____ **2.** Lists of commands within a category.

_____ **3.** Commonly used business information such as the name, address, phone numbers, and logo of an organization.

_____ **4.** Any element, such as a graphic or a frame, that can be selected.

_____ **5.** A small box that displays the name of a button on a toolbar or some other part of a Windows screen when you pause the mouse pointer over it.

_____ **6.** Highlighting text or clicking on objects for the purpose of editing, formatting, copying, or moving.

_____ **7.** Default text in a frame that you replace with your own text.

_____ **8.** A special page that acts as a background for your publication. Items placed here will display on any or all pages in the publication.

_____ **9.** A letter, symbol, or sign used as an identifying element for an organization.

_____ **10.** Model publications upon which you can build your own new publication.

_____ **11.** Small black circles or squares on the edges of a frame, text box, or other object used to change the size of the object.

_____ **12.** The action that takes place when the insertion point reaches the right margin and automatically moves down and to the left margin of the next line.

_____ **13.** Text, page numbers, graphics, and formatting that print at the bottom of every page, or on specific pages.

_____ **14.** Boxes into which you place text or images, and which can be moved, resized, and formatted.

_____ **15.** A system that provides information about Publisher features and step-by-step instructions for performing tasks.

A. Desktop publishing program

B. Footers

C. Frames

D. Help

E. Logo

F. Master page

G. Menus

H. Object

I. Personal Information Set

J. Placeholder text

K. ScreenTip

L. Selecting

M. Sizing handles

N. Templates

O. Word wrap

Skill Assessments

Publication 1C

Arizona Skies

In the following Skill Assessment, you will create a publication announcing a trip for City employees to the Flandrau Science Center and Planetarium. Your completed publication will look like the one shown in Figure 1.43. You will save your publication as *Firstname Lastname-1C Arizona Skies*.

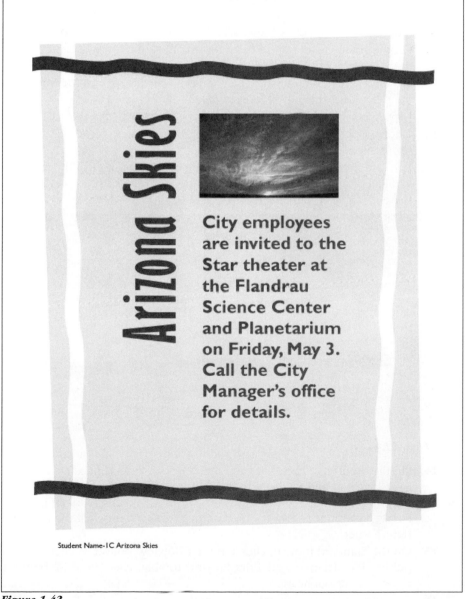

Figure 1.43

1. Start Publisher, and display the New Publication task pane and the Quick Publications Publication Gallery.

2. In the Quick Publications gallery, scroll down to the bottom and then click to select the Wavy Frame Quick Publication.

3. In the Quick Publication Options task pane under Layout, in the second row, click the third layout (Sidebar heading, picture at the top).

4. In the task pane, click Color Schemes. If necessary, under Apply a color scheme, click the Desert color scheme. Close the task pane to allow more space in which to work. On the Formatting toolbar, click the Zoom arrow and then click 50%.

5. In the Heading frame, click the Heading placeholder text to select it. Type `Arizona Skies`

6. In the Message frame, click the placeholder text to select it. Type the following, allowing the text to wrap automatically and the font size to adjust automatically. `City employees are invited to the Star Theater at the Flandrau Science Center and Planetarium on Friday, May 3. Call the City Manager's office for details.`

7. In the message frame, select all of the text that you just typed by either dragging with the mouse or holding down `Ctrl` and pressing `A`. On the Formatting toolbar, click the Font Size arrow and then click 24.

8. On the menu bar, click View, and then click Header and Footer.

9. On the small Header and Footer toolbar, click the Show Header/Footer button as necessary to display the Footer frame.

10. On the Formatting toolbar, click the Font Size arrow, and then click 10. Leave the Font as the default for this publication template—Gill Sans MT.

11. Using your own first and last name, type `Firstname Lastname-1C Arizona Skies`

12. On the Header and Footer toolbar, click Close to close the Master page and return to your publication.

13. Because the large vanilla-colored frame is blocking part of the footer, click to select the vanilla-colored frame. With the resize pointer (see Figure 1.44), drag it upward so that the footer with your name is in view.

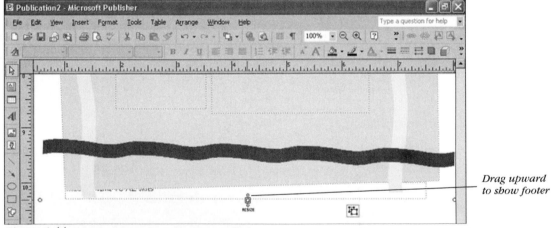

Drag upward
to show footer

Figure 1.44

14. On the menu bar, click File, and then click Save As. In the Save As dialog box, click the Save in arrow and navigate to the location in which you are storing your files for this Lesson. In the File name box, using your first and last name, type the following: `Firstname Lastname-1C Arizona Skies`. Then click the Save button in the lower right corner.

15. On the Standard toolbar, click the Print Preview button to check the overall look of your publication. Then, on the Print Preview toolbar, click the Print button to print one complete copy of your publication.

16. Close the Print Preview window. On the menu bar, click File, and then click Close. If necessary, click Yes to save any additional changes. Publication 1C is complete!

Publication 1D

Fine Arts and Parks

In the following Skill Assessment, you will create a personal information set for the City's Fine Arts and Parks Department, create an informational flyer for the department, and attach a logo to the personal information set. Your completed publication will look like the one shown in Figure 1.45. You will save your publication as *Firstname Lastname-1D Fine Arts and Parks*.

CITY OF DESERT PARK

Grand Opening
North Park

North Park will open on May 1. Everyone is welcome to attend the opening ceremony, which will be held at sundown at the park entrance located at 27 Mariposa Drive.

DISCOVER THE ARTS AND PARKS IN DESERT PARK!

CITY OF DESERT PARK

Fine Arts and Parks Department
One Cholla Plaza
Desert Park, AZ 85123

Phone: 626-555-9876
Fax: 626-555-6789
Email: fineartsandparks@desertpark.org

Student Name-1D Fine Arts and Parks

Figure 1.45

1. If necessary, start Publisher and display the New Publication task pane and the Publication Gallery.
2. In the New Publication task pane, under Start from a design, be sure that By Publication Type is displayed. Scroll down and next to Flyers, click the gray arrow to display the list of

flyers available. Click Informational. In the Publication Gallery of Informational Flyers, click to open the Edge Informational Flyer.

3. In the task pane, click Color Schemes, and, if necessary, click Desert. In the upper right corner of the task pane, click the X button to close the task pane. On the Standard toolbar, click the Zoom arrow, click 75%, and use the scroll bars as necessary to position the top portion of the publication in the middle of your screen. Information from the Primary Business personal information set stored on your computer will be automatically inserted.

4. On the menu bar, click Edit and then click Personal Information to display the Personal Information dialog box. Under Select a personal information set to edit, click Secondary Business. Using the information in the table below, complete the personal information set. Recall that the Tab↹ key is useful for moving from field to field. (Note that if another student has completed this exercise on this computer, the information may already be entered.)

Name:	Ray Hamilton
Address:	Fine Arts and Parks Department
	One Cholla Plaza
	Desert Park, AZ 85123
Phone/fax/e-mail:	Phone: 626-555-9876
	Fax: 626-555-6789
	Email: fineartsandparks@desertpark.org
Organization name:	City of Desert Park
Tag line or motto:	Discover the arts and parks in Desert Park!
Job position or title:	Director
Color schemes:	Mountain (If necessary, select the Include color scheme in this set option.)

5. At the lower right corner of the Personal Information dialog box, click the Update button. The informational flyer displays with the Secondary Business personal information set information filled in.

6. In the upper left corner of the flyer, position the mouse pointer over the current logo picture until you see the Move pointer and the ScreenTip Logo Picture. Click to select the logo.

7. To attach a new picture as the logo for the Fine Arts and Parks Department (the Secondary Business Personal Information Set), click the Wizard button below the selected logo. The Logo Designs task pane displays on the left.

8. In the Logo Designs task pane, click Logo Options, and then under New or existing, click Inserted picture. Click the Choose picture button. Navigate to your student files and click 1D_SunClip. Then, in the lower right corner of the dialog box, click the Insert button.

9. Close the task pane. With the newly inserted logo selected, use the lower right sizing handle and the Move pointer as necessary to resize and position the logo similar to Figure 1.45.

10. Click to select all of the text in the Product/Service Information frame, and type the following:
Grand Opening
North Park

11. In the frame with the placeholder text that begins "Place text here," click to select all of the placeholder text and type the following text, using just one space at the end of a sentence:
North Park will open on May 1. Everyone is welcome to attend the opening ceremony, which will be held at sundown at the park entrance located at 27 Mariposa Drive.

12. Hold down the Ctrl key and then press A to select all of the text you just typed, or alternatively, drag to select all of the text. On the Formatting toolbar, click the Font Size arrow and then click 22.

13. Click in the frame directly below the sunset picture, and use Ctrl + A to select the text. Change the font to Perpetua (from the default Perpetua Titling MT) and the font size to 20.

14. In the address frame at the left, select all of the text, and change the font to Eras Medium ITC and the font size to 10.

15. In the Phone/Fax/E-mail frame, select all of the text, and change the font to Eras Medium ITC.

16. On the menu bar, click View, and then click Header and Footer.

17. On the small Header and Footer toolbar, click the Show Header/Footer button as necessary to display the Footer frame.

18. Using your first and last name and the default font and font size (Times New Roman 10), type `Firstname Lastname-1D Fine Arts and Parks`

19. On the Header and Footer toolbar, click Close to close the Master page and return to your publication.

20. On the menu bar, click File, and then click Save As. Click the Save in arrow and navigate to the folder in which you are storing your Publications for this Lesson. Using your first and last name, in the file name box type `Firstname Lastname-1D Fine Arts and Parks`

21. Click the Save button. When prompted to save the new logo in the Secondary Business personal information set, click No.

22. Print and close your publication, saving any additional modifications if necessary. Publication 1D is complete!

Performance Assessments

Publication 1E

Surplus Auction

In the following Performance Assessment, you will create a publication announcing a Surplus Auction being held by the City of Desert Park. Your completed publication will look similar to the one shown in Figure 1.46. You will save your publication as *Firstname Lastname-1E Surplus Auction*.

Looking for a forklift? You can have one if you are the highest bidder at the City's Surplus Auction. All bidders need to register and must show photo identification to receive a bidder's card. Purchases must be removed from the auction yard within 10 working days after the auction.

Date: July 27

Surplus Auction

Time: 8 am—noon

- Forklifts
- Tow trucks
- Motorcycles
- Desks and chairs
- Scrap wire

Public Works yard behind City Hall

City of Desert Park

City Hall
1570 Palo Verde Parkway
Desert Park, AZ 85123

Phone: 626-555-1234
Fax: 626-555-4321
Email:
citymanager@desertpark.org

Student Name-1E Surplus Auction

Figure 1.46

1. Start Publisher, and display the New Publication task pane and the Publication Gallery. In the task pane under By Publication Type, click Flyers so that the types of flyers display, and then click Sale. In the Publication Gallery, click Book Sale Flyer.

2. In the task pane, click Color Schemes, and if necessary, click Desert. Close the task pane. On the menu bar, click Edit and then click Personal Information. If necessary, click Primary Business. Check to ensure that the Primary Business information is filled in for the City Manager, as described in Publication 1B, and update it if necessary. Click the Update button to close the dialog box.

3. Zoom the publication to 75%. Click in the frame beginning "Tell your readers," and replace the text with the following (remember, just one space at the end of a sentence): Looking for a forklift? You can have one if you are the highest bidder at the City's Surplus Auction. All bidders need to register and must show photo identification to receive a bidder's card. Purchases must be removed from the auction yard within 10 working days after the auction.

4. At the left, click on any of the zeroes after Date: to select them. Type July 27

5. Replace the text "Book Sale" with Surplus Auction
6. Click any of the zeroes after Time: and type 8 am-noon
7. Click in the frame with the items beginning "List" to select the entire bulleted list. When you press ⏎Enter at the end of each list item, a new bullet will display. Type the following list:
Forklifts
Tow trucks
Motorcycles
Desks and chairs
Scrap wire
8. Select the list you just typed, change the font to Franklin Gothic Book, and change the font size to 14.
9. Click in the frame that begins "Describe your location" to select the text. Change the font to Franklin Gothic Book and the font size to 20; then replace the highlighted text with Public Works yard behind City Hall
10. Click the logo in the lower left corner. If the logo is not the City logo shown in Figure 1.46, click the default logo and use the Wizard button to insert the logo picture file 1E_DesertParkLogo—similar to the steps in Publication 1D.
11. Move and resize the logo picture as necessary to look similar to Figure 1.46.
12. Using the Header and Footer feature, create a footer on the Master page, using the default font and font size (Times New Roman, 10 point), as follows: Firstname Lastname-1E Surplus Auction
13. Using the Save As command, save the publication in your storage location as *Firstname Lastname-1E Surplus Auction*. Click No if asked to save the modified (enlarged) logo as part of the information set.
14. Use Print Preview to view the overall look of your publication. Then print the publication, close the Print Preview, and close the publication. Publication 1E is complete!

Publication 1F

Fund Raiser

In the following Performance Assessment, you will create a personal information set for the City's Public Information Officer, and create an informational flyer for the Public Information Office. Your completed publication will look similar to the one shown in Figure 1.47. You will save your publication as *Firstname Lastname-1F Fund Raiser*.

Figure 1.47

1. Start Publisher, and display the New Publication task pane. Under By Publication Type, click Flyers, and in the Flyers subset, click Fund-raiser. In the Fund-raiser Flyers gallery, click the Car Wash Fund-raiser Flyer.

2. In the task pane, click Color Schemes, and if necessary, click Desert. Close the task pane and zoom to 75%. Display the Personal Information dialog box, and click Other Organization. Insert the information from the following table and then click Update:

Name:	Gloria French
Address:	Office of Public Information
	One Cholla Plaza
	Desert Park, AZ 85123
Phone/fax/e-mail:	Phone: 626-555-5000
	Fax: 626-555-5001
	Email: pio@desertpark.org
Organization name:	City of Desert Park
Tag line or motto:	Information for citizens of Desert Park
Job position or title:	Public Information Officer
Color schemes:	Navy (If necessary, select the Include color scheme in this set option.)

3. Change the date to May 3, and change the time to 8 a.m.–5 p.m.

4. In the frame beginning "Place text here," replace the placeholder text with the following: To pay for their trip to visit Desert Park's international sister cities, our 15 high school students who are members of the Ambassador Exchange program will hold a car wash. The students will depart in July and live with a host family in their designated sister cities for one week. Stop by for a car wash and help these students meet their goal!

5. In the lower right corner, replace the text beginning "Describe Your Location" with the following and then change the font size to 16: Parking lot of Hammond's Hardware store!

6. Click the logo picture, if any, at the bottom of the flyer, and delete it.

7. Using the Header and Footer feature, create a footer on the Master page, using the default font and font size (Times New Roman, 10 point), as follows. Firstname Lastname-1F Fund Raiser

8. Save the publication in your storage location as follows: Firstname Lastname-1F Fund Raiser

9. Print and close the publication, saving any changes if necessary. Publication 1F is complete!

On the Internet

The Web site for a major U.S. city can be found using the following pattern for its Web page name: www.ci.cityname.two-letter state abbreviation.us. For example, to locate the Web site for Chicago, type www.ci.chicago.il.us. (Do not type a period at the end.) If the city has two words, use a hyphen instead of a space. For example, type www.ci.las-vegas.nv.us for Las Vegas, Nevada.

If you have Internet access, try finding the Web site for your favorite city, and discover what's going on there.

Working With Text in a Publication

Objectives

In this lesson, you learn how to:

✔ Open an Existing Publication and Save It With a New Name
✔ Navigate and Select Text
✔ Align and Format Text
✔ Format a Text Box
✔ Format Bullets and Line Spacing
✔ Identify the Parts of a Newsletter
✔ Insert Word Files and Text in Text Boxes
✔ View Connected and Layered Frames
✔ Flow Text in a Publication
✔ Use Spelling, Hyphenation, AutoCorrect, and Editing Tools

Key terms in this Lesson include

❑ AutoCorrect
❑ Autoflow
❑ Booklet
❑ Brochure
❑ Callouts
❑ Continued notice
❑ Copyfitting
❑ Entry blank
❑ Fill color
❑ Fill effects
❑ Formatting
❑ Gradient fill
❑ Hyphenation
❑ Hyphenation zone
❑ Import

❑ Justify
❑ Layered
❑ Line spacing
❑ Newsletter
❑ Overflow
❑ Points
❑ Program
❑ Pt.
❑ Scratch area
❑ Selecting
❑ Story
❑ Text boxes
❑ Text frames
❑ White space
❑ Word count

Publication Design Tips—Types of Publications

Businesses and organizations use many types of publications in their day-to-day operations. Publisher has pre-planned templates for many of these publications. For example, in Lesson 1 you created a flyer, which is a one-page message with minimal text and graphics ideal for quick communications. In a flyer, you can use large print and bold colors because the goal is speed and eye-catching design.

A *brochure* is a small pamphlet that describes an event, product, program, or service. Whereas a flyer tends to be informal and useful only for a short period of time, people often keep a brochure to remind them of a product or service. A brochure is usually folded into two, three, or four folds. It can include an *entry blank* (a printed form to be filled out), an order form, and space for a mailing label. A brochure is not the place for extensive information. Rather, it is designed to introduce the reader to the information and encourage them to obtain more information by submitting the entry blank, consulting the organization's Web site, phoning, or e-mailing the organization.

A *newsletter*, usually produced as a periodical on a monthly or quarterly basis, is used to distribute news and information to a specific group. For example, newsletters are often written for and distributed to employees of an organization. A newsletter can also be produced to communicate with customers or shareholders of a business. College alumni associations frequently produce newsletters for past graduates informing them of activities at the college.

A *catalog* is a printed list of items arranged systematically. For example, your college catalog likely includes a list of degrees, programs, and courses. A catalog in a business organization is usually a list of products or services for sale. Microsoft Publisher 2002 is an ideal tool for producing a catalog because it can not only accommodate a large number of pages in a publication, but also combinations of text, columns, and graphics on individual pages.

Business stationery such as letterhead, envelopes, and business cards personalized with your organization's name, address, and logo can be produced using Publisher. *Business forms* such as invoices, shipping documents, purchase orders, expense reports, and customer information forms, all of which are used to document transactions within a business, are another type of publication easily produced with Publisher. Ordering custom forms with your organization's logo and address from a professional printing company can be costly. With Publisher, you can create custom forms from your desktop printer!

Postcards—cards on which a message is written and mailed without an envelope—are another type of publication easily produced with Microsoft Publisher 2002. Many postcard templates are provided and include designs for both the front and the back of the postcard.

Mass mailings, also called *bulk mailings*, occur when you send a copy of the same publication to a large number of addresses—for example, sending a newsletter to each of 100 employees, or sending a postcard to each of 500 customers. These are also easily done with Microsoft Publisher.

A *program* is a printed outline describing the events, people, and features of a play, dinner, agenda, performance, or public event. The finished size of a program is often 5 1/2 inches by 8 1/2 inches, which is letter-size paper, folded in half to create a small booklet of four separate pages.

A *booklet* is a publication that describes products, services, or other information in detail. A booklet's finished size is usually either 5 1/2 inches by 8 1/2 inches (like a folded program) or the size of regular paper—8 1/2 inches by 11 inches.

Finally, you can use Publisher to create a *Web site*. A Web site is one or more Web pages stored together on the World Wide Web. For large and complex Web sites, you would select a more sophisticated tool such as Microsoft FrontPage 2002, but to create a simple Web site for an individual or small organization, Microsoft Publisher is an ideal tool.

Publication 2A

Volunteer Awards

In Activities 2.1–2.8, you will format text in a program for the City of Desert Park's annual Volunteer Awards. The publication is based on one of Publisher's pre-defined templates. The four pages (two printed sheets of letter-size paper) of your completed publication will look similar to Figure 2.1. You will save your publication as *Firstname Lastname-2A Volunteer Awards*.

Reading Volunteers Needed

Last year approximately 4,000 Desert Park children signed up for this award-winning program. By reading 20 minutes, 50 pages, or one book, participants advance on a colorful game board, earning prizes along the way. Children who are too young to read play by having someone read to them. This is a free program co-sponsored by the Desert Park News and the Desert Park Jackrabbits, our wonderful minor league baseball team.

VOLUNTEER HOURS ADD UP!

Cholla Valley Senior Center	4,956 Hours Given This Year
Desert South Senior Center	12,845 Hours Given This Year
Canyon Community Center	16,268 Hours Given This Year
Kid's Corner Park Center	9,489 Hours Given This Year

City Hall
1570 Palo Verde Parkway
Desert Park, AZ 85123
Phone: 626-555-1234
Fax: 626-555-4321
Email: citymanager@desertpark.org

Volunteer Awards

The City of Desert Park is pleased to present the

annual Volunteer Awards to the outstanding

individuals who give freely of their time and talents

to make Desert Park a better community for all

residents.

Saturday, June 20 at 8:00 p.m.
In the Plaza at City Hall
Music Provided by
Desert Park Community College String Quartet

Student Name-2A Volunteer Awards

Figure 2.1A

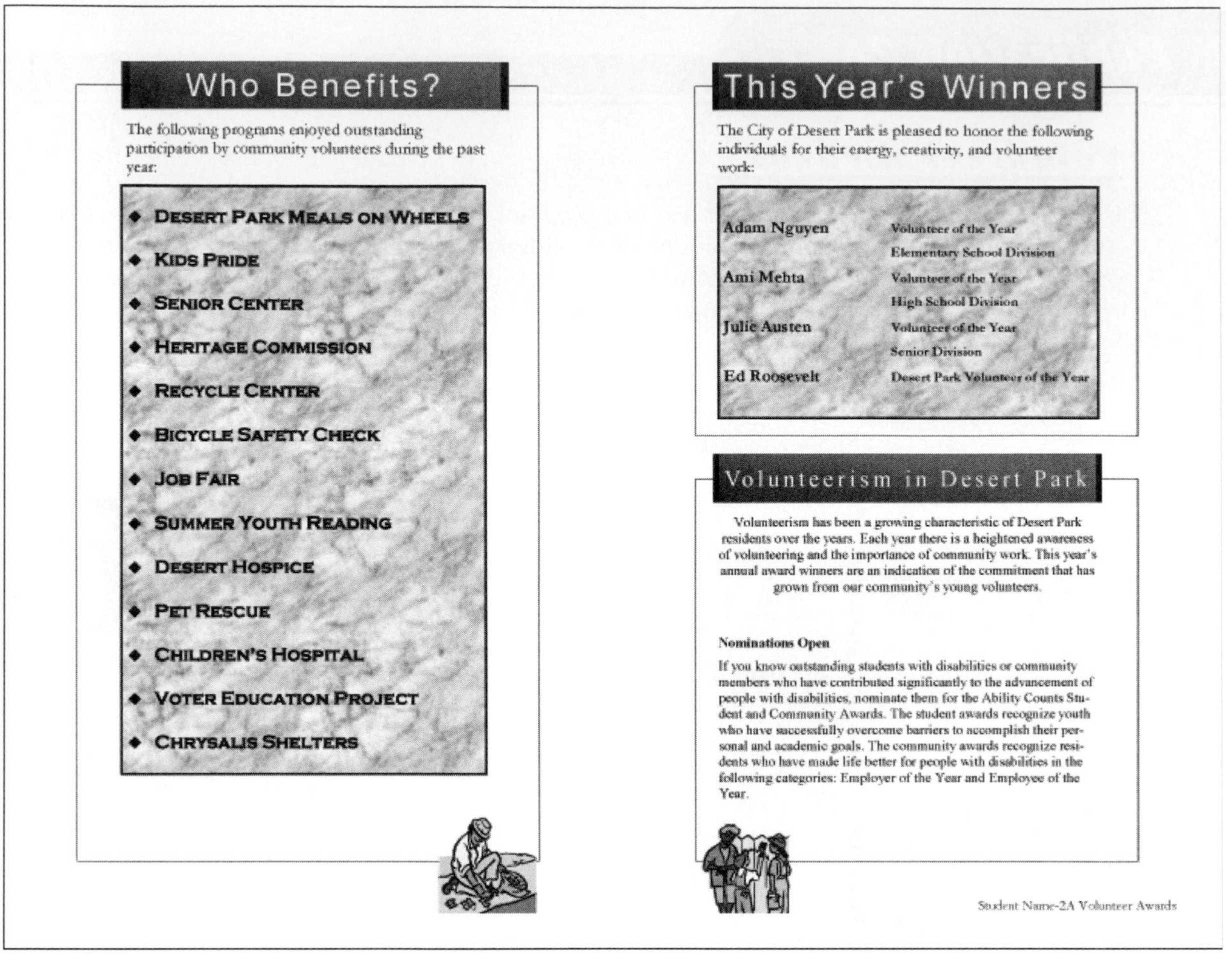

Who Benefits?

The following programs enjoyed outstanding participation by community volunteers during the past year:

- ◆ **DESERT PARK MEALS ON WHEELS**
- ◆ **KIDS PRIDE**
- ◆ **SENIOR CENTER**
- ◆ **HERITAGE COMMISSION**
- ◆ **RECYCLE CENTER**
- ◆ **BICYCLE SAFETY CHECK**
- ◆ **JOB FAIR**
- ◆ **SUMMER YOUTH READING**
- ◆ **DESERT HOSPICE**
- ◆ **PET RESCUE**
- ◆ **CHILDREN'S HOSPITAL**
- ◆ **VOTER EDUCATION PROJECT**
- ◆ **CHRYSALIS SHELTERS**

This Year's Winners

The City of Desert Park is pleased to honor the following individuals for their energy, creativity, and volunteer work:

Adam Nguyen	Volunteer of the Year
	Elementary School Division
Ami Mehta	Volunteer of the Year
	High School Division
Julie Austen	Volunteer of the Year
	Senior Division
Ed Roosevelt	Desert Park Volunteer of the Year

Volunteerism in Desert Park

Volunteerism has been a growing characteristic of Desert Park residents over the years. Each year there is a heightened awareness of volunteering and the importance of community work. This year's annual award winners are an indication of the commitment that has grown from our community's young volunteers.

Nominations Open

If you know outstanding students with disabilities or community members who have contributed significantly to the advancement of people with disabilities, nominate them for the Ability Counts Student and Community Awards. The student awards recognize youth who have successfully overcome barriers to accomplish their personal and academic goals. The community awards recognize residents who have made life better for people with disabilities in the following categories: Employer of the Year and Employee of the Year.

Student Name~2A Volunteer Awards

Figure 2.1B

Objective 1: Open an Existing Publication and Save It With a New Name

Activity 2.1   Opening an Existing Publication and Saving It With a New Name

1 **Start** Publisher, and on the Standard toolbar, click the **Open** button. In the Open Publication dialog box, navigate to your student files, and open the file *2A_VolunteerAwards*.

Publication 2A Volunteer Awards displays.

Does your screen differ?

If Publisher displays a message indicating that the printer cannot be initialized, simply click OK to change to the default printer for the computer you are using.

2 On the menu bar, click **View**, and then click **Header and Footer**.

Publisher switches to the Master Page view.

3 On the Header and Footer toolbar, click the **Show Header/Footer** button to switch to the Footer frame. Then scroll to the extreme right of the page and click in the Footer frame. See Figure 2.2. Type Firstname Lastname-2A Volunteer Awards

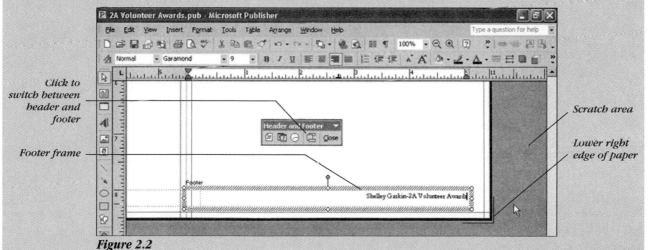

Figure 2.2

4 On the Header and Footer toolbar, click **Close** to close the Master page and return to your publication.

The Master page view is closed, and page 1 of your publication displays.

5 On the menu bar, click **File**, and then click **Save As**.

The Save As dialog box displays.

6 Navigate to the folder in which you are storing your files for Lesson 2, creating a new folder if you want. Then, in the File name box, type Firstname Lastname-2A Volunteer Awards

(Continues)

Activity 2.1   Opening an Existing Publication and Saving It With a New Name (continued)

7 In the lower right corner of the Save As dialog box, click the **Save** button.

The publication redisplays with the new name in the Title Bar.

8 So that you have a draft of the program to look at, click the **Print** button.

This printout is not to be submitted to your instructor. Rather, use it as a printed reference as you work through the remainder of this publication. Two sheets will print.

9 Place the two sheets with their blank sides together, and fold in half to form a booklet. Be sure that the booklet pages are folded so that the picture of the ribbon is on the front page, the Desert Park logo is on the back page, and the sheet that forms the two inside pages is right side up.

The size and format of the booklet is probably similar to those you have seen for a play or a religious service. Depending on your printing capabilities, the final document could be printed on one sheet front and back, or on two sheets as you have just done. Also, you might or might not have access to a color printer in your classroom or lab. If you are printing on a black and white printer, recall that colors will print as shades of gray.

Objective 2: Navigate and Select Text

Editing is the process of making changes to text or objects in a publication. *Formatting* is the process of determining the overall appearance of the text within the publication and of the publication itself. *Selecting* text refers to highlighting areas of text so that the text can be edited, formatted, copied, or moved. Publisher recognizes a selected area of text as one unit, to which you can make changes. After text or any other object such as a text frame is selected, you can cancel the selection by clicking anywhere in the *scratch area*—the gray area of your screen (see Figure 2.2).

Selecting and editing text in Microsoft Publisher works in much the same manner as selecting and editing text in Microsoft Word. As in Word, Publisher operates in *insert mode*, which means that when you place your insertion point within existing text and begin to type, the existing text moves to the right to make space for the new text.

Activity 2.2   Navigating and Selecting Text Using the Mouse and Keyboard

 1 On the Standard toolbar, locate the **Zoom Out** button and click it three times.

Page 1 of the displayed publication zooms to 50%. The Zoom In and Zoom Out buttons on the Standard toolbar are convenient to use when you want to zoom in and out in increments by clicking, as opposed to clicking the Zoom arrow to display the Zoom list.

2 Click the **Zoom In** button three times to Zoom to 100%, and then scroll to position the top of page 1 in the middle of your screen as shown in Figure 2.3.

Activity 2.2   Navigating and Selecting Text Using the Mouse and Keyboard

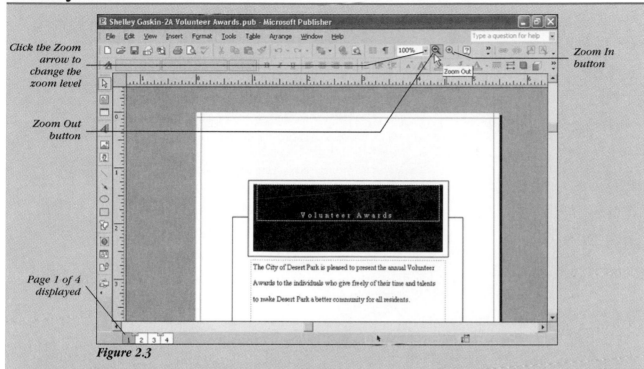

Click the Zoom arrow to change the zoom level

Zoom Out button

Page 1 of 4 displayed

Zoom In button

Figure 2.3

③ In the status bar at the lower left of your screen, note that four pages are indicated in this publication (see Figure 2.3).

Even though this publication prints on two standard sheets of paper, the publication is composed of four separate pages for the purpose of arranging the frames of text and graphics.

④ On page 1 of the publication, click anywhere in the text beginning "The City of" and notice that your insertion point is positioned within the text, and the text frame is selected.

Because this text has been inserted and it is not placeholder text, none of the text is selected.

⑤ You can use various key combinations to **navigate** (move the insertion point) within a block of text. Take a moment to examine the following table, and experiment with moving the insertion point within this block of text.

(Continues)

Activity 2.2   Navigating and Selecting Text Using the Mouse and Keyboard (continued)

TABLE 2.1

Keys	Action
Arrow Keys	Moves the insertion point one character at a time (left or right) or one line at a time (up or down).
Ctrl + →	Moves the insertion point one word to the right at a time.
Ctrl + ←	Moves the insertion point one word to the left at a time.
Ctrl + ↑	Moves the insertion point to the beginning of the previous paragraph.
Ctrl + ↓	Moves the insertion point to the beginning of the next paragraph.
Ctrl + Home	Moves the insertion point to the beginning of the text in the frame.
Ctrl + End	Moves the insertion point to the end of the text in the frame.
End	Moves the insertion point to the end of the line.
Home	Moves the insertion point to the beginning of the line.

6 Click to position the insertion point in front of the "C" in the word "City." Then, press and hold down both the ✦Shift key and the Ctrl key, and press the → key.

The word City is selected.

7 Take a moment to examine the following table, and experiment with selecting text in this paragraph.

TABLE 2.2

To Select:	Do This:
A portion of text	Click to position the insertion point at the beginning of the text you want to select, hold down the ✦Shift key, and then click at the end of the text you want to select. Alternatively, hold down the left mouse button and drag from the beginning to the end of the text you want to select.
A word	Double-click the word.
A paragraph	Triple-click anywhere in the paragraph.
One character at a time	Hold down the ✦Shift key and press the → or ← key.
A string of words	Hold down ✦Shift and Ctrl and then press the → or ← key.
Consecutive lines	Hold down the ✦Shift key and press the ↑ or the ↓ key.
Consecutive paragraphs	Hold down the ✦Shift and Ctrl keys and press the ↑ or the ↓ key.
A story	Click to position the insertion point in any text frame, display the Edit menu, and then click Select All. Alternatively, hold down Ctrl and press A.

Objective 3: Align and Format Text

Alignment refers to the placement of text relative to the left and right boundaries of the text frame or column in which it is contained. Text frames in pre-designed templates have various default settings for alignment.

Align Left aligns text at the left boundary leaving the right margin uneven. *Center* alignment aligns text so that it is centered between the left and right boundary. *Align Right* aligns text at the right boundary leaving the left margin uneven. The *Justify* alignment option adds additional space between words so that both the left and right margins are even. Justify is often used when formatting newspaper-style columns (see Figure 2.4).

A *font* is a set of characters with the same design and shape. There are two basic types of fonts—serif and sans serif. *Serif fonts* contain extensions or lines on the ends of the characters, and are good choices for large amounts of text because they are easy to read. Examples of serif fonts include Times New Roman, Garamond, and Century Schoolbook. *Sans serif fonts* do not have lines on the ends of characters. Sans serif fonts are good choices for headings and titles. Examples of sans serif fonts include Arial, Impact, and Comic Sans MS (see Figure 2.4).

Fonts are measured in *points*, with one point equal to 1/72 of an inch. A higher point size indicates a larger font size. For large amounts of text, font sizes between 10 point and 13 point are good choices. Headings and titles are often formatted using a larger font size, such as 14 points or more. The word "point" is usually seen abbreviated as *pt.* (see Figure 2.4).

Font styles refer to the ways in which you can add emphasis to text by applying bold, italic, and underline styles. Using the Font Color button, you can also change the color of a font (see Figure 2.4).

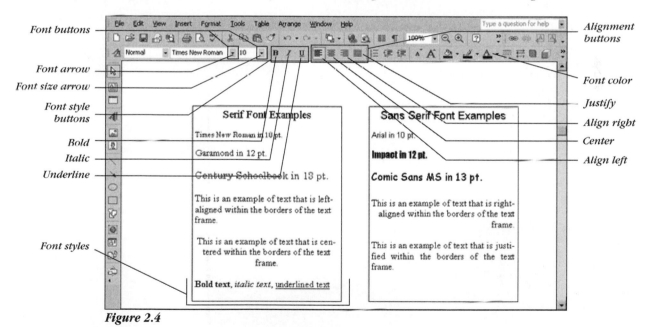

Figure 2.4

Activity 2.3   Formatting Paragraphs and Text

1 On page 1 of your publication, click anywhere in the paragraph beginning "The City of" and notice that on the Formatting toolbar, the Align Left button is **pushed** (highlighted and bordered) as shown in Figure 2.5.

Left Align button "pushed"

Figure 2.5

2 Hold down Ctrl, and press A to select all of the text in the frame, and then, on the Formatting toolbar, click the **Center** button.

The text is centered between the left and right edges of the frame.

3 With the text still selected, move to the Formatting toolbar, click the **Font arrow**, scroll as necessary, and then click **Garamond**.

4 With the text still selected, move to the Formatting toolbar, click the **Font Size arrow**, and then click **12**.

5 Find the word "individuals," click in front of the "i" and, with a space after it, type outstanding

Notice how insert mode moved the existing text to the right to make space for your new typing.

6 Scroll to the top of page 1, select the text "Volunteer Awards" and change the font to **Arial,** the font size to **20**, and then on the Formatting toolbar, click the **Bold** button to apply the Bold style. Click after the "s" in "Awards." Compare your screen to Figure 2.6.

Notice that the text in this frame was already center aligned.

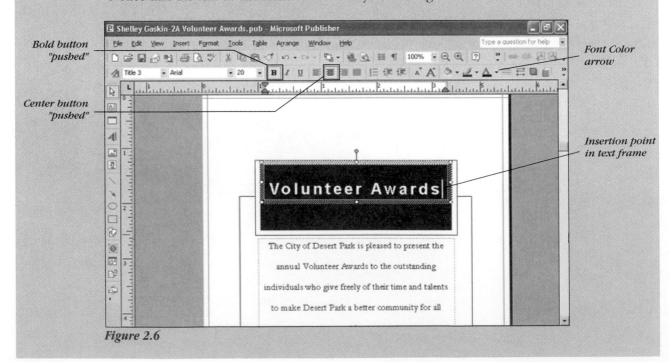

Bold button "pushed"

Center button "pushed"

Font Color arrow

Insertion point in text frame

Figure 2.6

Activity 2.3 Formatting Paragraphs and Text

7 Scroll to the bottom of page 1, click to position the insertion point after the "l" in "Hall" and then press ↵Enter. Type on two lines:

Music provided by

Desert Park Community College String Quartet

8 Select all of the text in this text frame by holding down Ctrl and pressing A, and then change the font to **Footlight MT Light** and the font size to **10**.

9 With the text in this frame still selected, move to the Formatting toolbar and click the **Font Color arrow** (small arrow to the right of the Font Color button). See Figure 2.4.

10 On the displayed palette, click **More Colors** and then, if necessary, click the **Standard tab** on the Colors dialog box.

11 On the displayed honeycomb, in the last row, point to the fifth color and click once to select the color (see Figure 2.7).

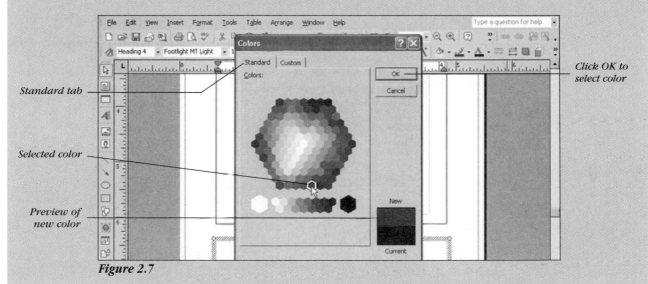

Standard tab

Selected color

Preview of new color

Click OK to select color

Figure 2.7

12 In the upper right corner of the dialog box, click **OK**, and then click in the gray scratch area of your screen to cancel the selection and view your changes.

13 On the Standard toolbar, click the **Save** button to save the changes you have made to your publication.

When you insert text in a text box, you can experiment with various font sizes until the text fills the entire frame. A faster way to do this is to have Publisher determine the font size that will automatically make the text fill the frame.

Activity 2.4   Using Best Fit to Adjust Text Size in a Text Box

1 Using the page navigation buttons in the status bar, click **4** to display page 4 of your publication.

2 At the top of the page, select the text "Reading Volunteers Needed" and then change the font to **Arial**. Leave the text selected.

3 With the mouse pointer hovering over the selected text, right-click to display a shortcut menu, point to **Change Text**, point to **AutoFit Text**, and then click **Best Fit** (see Figure 2.8).

Publisher automatically determines the best font size for the text to fill the frame. This process is known as *copyfitting*.

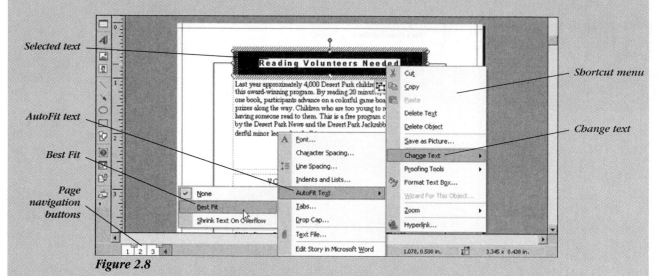

Selected text

AutoFit text

Best Fit

Page navigation buttons

Shortcut menu

Change text

Figure 2.8

4 Click in the next frame and then use Ctrl + A to select all of the text beginning "Last year."

5 Change the font to **Garamond**, and then use **Best Fit** to have Publisher determine the best font size for the text to fill the frame.

6 Click in the scratch area of your screen to cancel the selection. Compare your screen to Figure 2.9.

7 On the Standard toolbar, click the **Save** button to save the changes you have made to your publication.

Activity 2.4   Using Best Fit to Adjust Text Size in a Text Box

Best Fit used to determine font size

Indicates page 4 of the publication

Reading Volunteers Needed

Last year approximately 4,000 Desert Park children signed up for this award-winning program. By reading 20 minutes, 50 pages, or one book, participants advance on a colorful game board, earning prizes along the way. Children who are too young to read play by having someone read to them. This is a free program co-sponsored by the Desert Park News and the Desert Park Jackrabbits, our wonderful minor league baseball team.

VOLUNTEER HOURS ADD UP!

Cholla Valley Senior Center	4,956 Hours Given This Year
Desert South Senior Center	12,845 Hours Given This Year
Canyon Community Center	16,268 Hours Given This Year
Kid's Corner Park Center	9,489 Hours Given This Year

Figure 2.9

Activity 2.5   Applying Font Effects

1 In the next text frame, select the text "VOLUNTEER HOURS ADD UP!". Move to the menu bar, click **Format**, and then click **Font**.

The Font dialog box displays. Font effects, such as Shadow, Embossing, All caps, and Small caps, provide additional options for font formatting (see Figure 2.10).

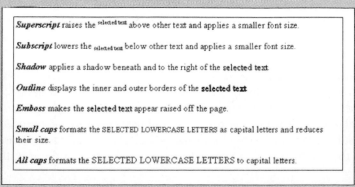

Superscript raises the selected text above other text and applies a smaller font size.

Subscript lowers the selected text below other text and applies a smaller font size.

Shadow applies a shadow beneath and to the right of the **selected text**

Outline displays the inner and outer borders of the **selected text**

Emboss makes the **selected text** appear raised off the page.

Small caps formats the SELECTED LOWERCASE LETTERS as capital letters and reduces their size.

All caps formats the SELECTED LOWERCASE LETTERS to capital letters.

Figure 2.10

2 In the displayed Font dialog box, under General, click the **Font arrow**, and then scroll as necessary to click **Arial**.

3 Click the **Font style arrow** and click **Bold**, and then click the **Size arrow** and click **12**.

Recall that toolbar buttons are simply a one-click method to perform a task that would otherwise be performed from the menu bar and a dialog box. The Formatting toolbar

(Continues)

Activity 2.5   Applying Font Effects (continued)

contains buttons for changing the Font, Font style, and Font size. However, this is a good example of a time when it would be better to use the dialog box because additional font formatting can be applied that is not available on the toolbar. It is also useful because a combination of various font formats can be applied at one time.

4 Under General, click the **Underline arrow**, and then click **Single**.

5 Under Effects, click to place a check mark next to **Small caps**.

Notice that as you add formatting and effects, your choices are reflected under Sample.

6 Click **OK**, and then click in the scratch area to cancel the selection. Compare your screen to Figure 2.11.

Font formatting applied —
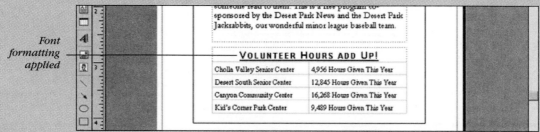

Figure 2.11

7 On the Standard toolbar, click the **Save** button to save the changes you have made to your publication.

To extend your knowledge...

Applying Alignment, Fonts, and Font Styles

You want people to read your publications—that is why you create them. To make your publications more readable, here are some guidelines regarding alignment, fonts, and font styles that have been established by professional graphic designers.

Use no more than two alignment formats in one publication. For example, use center alignment for headings, and left alignment for text. Or use right alignment for headings, and justified alignment for text. Justified alignment is best for text in long publications such as books, articles, and reports. Right-aligned text is not often used in publications and, when used, should be reserved for headings and subheadings. Text within a frame can also be aligned vertically ⇕—between the top and bottom of the frame. You can vertically align text relative to the top, the bottom, or the middle of the frame.

Avoid using more than two or three different fonts in a publication. A good standard to apply is to choose a serif font for body text, and a sans serif font for headings. Serif fonts, with their tiny line extensions at the bottom of characters, tend to move the reader's eye along. That is why serif fonts are a good choice for body text. Good combinations are Times New Roman and Arial or Bookman and Lucida.

Other good serif fonts for text include Bookman Old Style, Century Schoolbook, Garamond, Georgia, Goudy Old Style, and Times New Roman. Good fonts for headings and subheadings include Arial, Arial Black, Bauhaus, Bernard MT Condensed, Elephant, Eras, Franklin Gothic, Lucida,

Rockwell, and Verdana. Courier, which looks like an old-fashioned typewriter font, is not acceptable for any publication.

Do not over use font styles and effects. Within the text of your publications, never use any font style (bold, italic, underline) or effect (all caps, shadow, and so on) for more than a few words, because it is difficult to read. This is especially true of all uppercase text, which is extremely difficult to read and should be reserved for headings only. Use italic and bold to add emphasis to words, or for the title of a book or article. Do not underline text (another carryover from the old-fashioned typewriter), although underlining headings is acceptable.

Objective 4: Format a Text Box

Not only can you format text within a text box, but you can also format the text box itself. A text box is a type of object, and similar to all objects it has two basic parts—the inside area and the border around the inside area. A simple line border can be added around a text box. Or, you can apply a custom border or one of the Publisher-designed BorderArt elements. Additionally, you can apply fill colors and fill effects, such as patterns or textures, to the inside area of a text box. *Fill color* is the inside color of an object.

Activity 2.6   Applying a Border and Fill Color to a Text Box

1 On page 4 of your publication, scroll to the bottom of the page and select all of the text in the text box under the City's logo.

2 Change the font to **Eras Medium ITC**, and then apply **Bold**.

3 With the mouse pointer anywhere over the selected frame, right-click to display the shortcut menu and then click **Format Text Box**. (Alternatively, you can move to the menu bar, click Format, and then click Text Box.)

The Format Text Box dialog box displays.

4 If necessary, click the **Colors and Lines tab**. Notice that this dialog box tab is divided into the two basic parts of the text box—Fill (inside area) and Line (outside border).

5 Under Line, click the **BorderArt** button (see Figure 2.12).

6 In the BorderArt dialog box, scroll down and click the **Southwest** border.

(Continues)

Activity 2.6   Applying a Border and Fill Color to a Text Box (continued)

The selected border displays under Preview (see Figure 2.12).

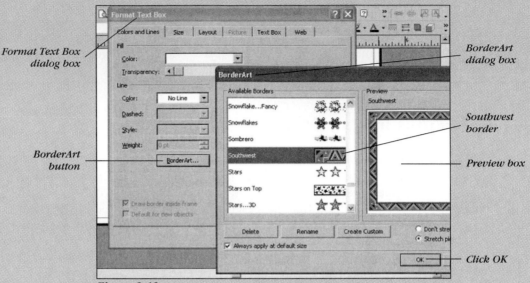

Figure 2.12

❼ In the lower right corner of the BorderArt dialog box, click **OK**, and then in the upper portion of the Format Text Box dialog box under Fill, click the **Color arrow**. Click the third color block (a light gold color) in the color scheme.

The light gold color is inserted into the Preview box.

❽ In the lower right corner of the Format Text Box dialog box, click **OK** and then click in the gray scratch area to cancel the selection and view your changes.

The textbox is bordered with the Southwest border and the fill color is light gold.

❾ On the Standard toolbar, click the **Save** button to save the changes you have made to your publication.

Applying a fill color to the inside of a frame, as you did in the previous Activity, allows you to apply a single color. There are many other fill options, called ***fill effects***, which you can apply to the inside of an object. Fill effects are textures, patterns, color fades, and pictures that can be applied to the inside of an object. A ***gradient fill*** is a color combination in which one color fades into another.

Activity 2.7   Applying a Gradient Fill to a Text Box

❶ Using the page navigation buttons on the left side of the status bar, click page **2**.

Notice that both pages 2 and 3 are highlighted on the page navigation buttons, and that both pages 2 and 3 display. This is called the ***Two-Page Spread***.

❷ On the Formatting toolbar, click the **Zoom arrow**, and then click **Page Width**.

When the Two-Page Spread is active, the Page Width zoom option will display two pages. In the case of an event program, which is what this publication is, the two pages represent one sheet of paper. At any time you can turn off the Two-Page Spread by dis-

Activity 2.7   Applying a Gradient Fill to a Text Box

playing the View menu and clicking to remove the check mark next to Two-Page Spread. For this publication, leave the Two-Page Spread displayed.

③ Zoom back to **100%**, scroll to position the top of page 2 in the middle of your screen, and then click in the text box with the text "Who Benefits?"

The text frame is selected.

④ In the status bar at the bottom right of your screen, notice that when a frame is selected, Publisher indicates the Object Position and Object Size in the status bar, and the frame's size on the horizontal rule (see Figure 2.13).

For example, this frame is 3.362 inches wide and 0.432 inches tall. The object is positioned 1.149 inches from the left edge of the paper and 0.500 inches from the top edge of the paper. You won't often need information this precise, but it's nice to know it's available.

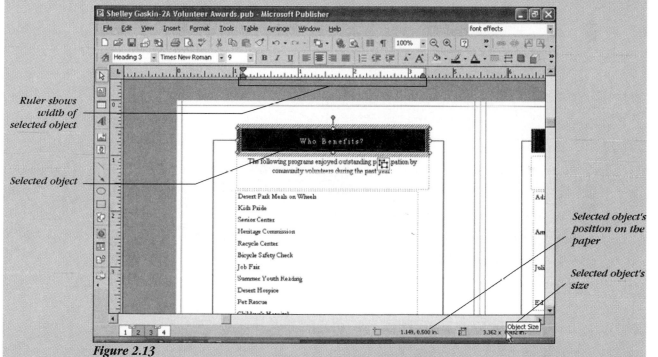

Ruler shows width of selected object

Selected object

Selected object's position on the paper

Selected object's size

Figure 2.13

⑤ On the menu bar, click **Format** and then click **Text Box**.

The Format Text Box dialog box displays. Alternatively, you can reach this dialog box by right clicking over the selected frame and then selecting Format Text Box from the shortcut menu.

⑥ If necessary, click the **Colors and Lines tab**, and then under Fill, click the **Color arrow** and click **Fill Effects**.

The Fill Effects dialog box displays.

⑦ If necessary, click the **Gradient tab**. Under Colors, click the **One color** option and then click the **Color 1 arrow**.

(Continues)

Activity 2.7   Applying a Gradient Fill to a Text Box (continued)

8 Click the **7th color** (rust) in the row, and then under Shading styles, click the **Diagonal down** option. Under Variants, click the **first variant in the first row** (the default). See Figure 2.14.

The Sample box displays your selections. If you do not have a color printer in your classroom or lab, gradient fills will print as shades of gray. Regardless of your printer arrangement, you will be able to view and experiment with colors on your screen.

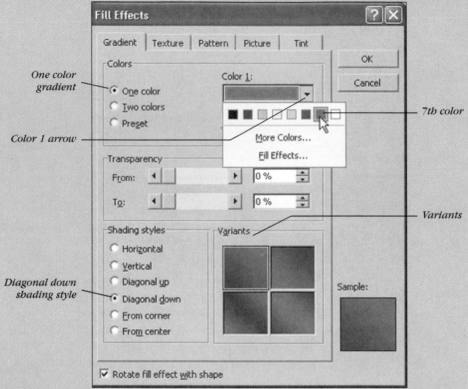

Figure 2.14

9 In the upper right corner of the Fill Effects dialog box, click **OK**, and then click **OK** again at the bottom of the Format Text Box dialog box.

10 Select the text in the frame and change the font to **Arial** and the font size to **Best Fit** (hover over the selected text, right-click, Change Text, AutoFit, Best Fit).

11 Scroll over to view page 3, select the text box with the text "This Year's Winners" and apply the same gradient fill as you did in the previous steps. Then apply the same font and **Best Fit**.

12 Scroll down and apply the same gradient fill and font formatting to the text frame containing the text "Volunteerism in Desert Park."

13 Scroll over and up to view the top of page 2, select all of the text beginning "The following," and change the font to **Garamond**. Use **Best Fit** to select the font size, and apply **Align Left** to the text.

14 At the top of page 3, select all of the text beginning "The City of," and change the font to **Garamond**. Use **Best Fit** to select the font size and apply **Align Left** to the text.

15 On the Standard toolbar, click the **Save** button to save your changes.

Objective 5: Format Bullets and Line Spacing

Instead of numbers or letters, you can use bullets to introduce items in a list. You can modify bullets by changing the bullet character, color, and size.

The amount of space between lines of text in a paragraph is called **_line spacing_**. In addition to setting line spacing for lines of text within a paragraph, space can be added before and after entire paragraphs. The Spacing Before and Spacing After options do not add additional space between each line in the paragraph; rather, these commands add space to the line immediately before or immediately after the paragraph. Line spacing in Publisher is accomplished through the Line Spacing dialog box, which is displayed from the Format menu.

Activity 2.8 Formatting Bullets and Line Spacing

1 On page 2 of your publication, click anywhere in the text frame that begins "Desert Park Meals on Wheels."

2 With the mouse pointer positioned anywhere over the selected frame, right-click to display the shortcut menu, and click **Format Text Box**.

The Format Text Box dialog box displays.

3 If necessary, click the **Colors and Lines tab**. Under Fill, click the **Color arrow**, click **Fill Effects**, and then click the **Texture tab**.

4 On the texture tab, in the second row, click the second texture.

"White marble" displays at the bottom of the dialog box, and the marble texture displays under Sample.

5 In the upper right corner of the Fill Effects dialog box click **OK**.

6 In the Format Text Box dialog box, under Line, click the **Color arrow**, and then click the first color block—**Black** (see Figure 2.15).

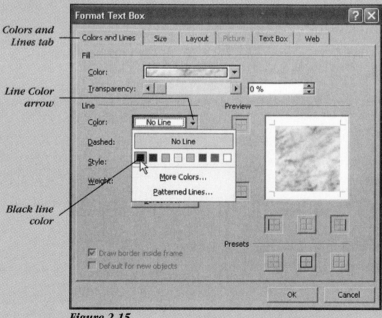

Figure 2.15

(Continues)

Activity 2.8   Formatting Bullets and Line Spacing (continued)

7 Under Line, click the **Style arrow**, and then click the **1 1/2 pt** line style.

The Preview area displays the marble texture and the line border.

8 Click **OK** to close the Format Text Box dialog box.

The texture and border are applied to the frame.

9 Use Ctrl + A to select all of the text in the frame.

10 Change the font to **Copperplate Gothic Bold** and the font size to **12**.

11 With the text in the frame still selected, move to the menu bar, click **Format**, and then click **Indents and Lists**.

The Indents and Lists dialog box displays.

12 Under Indent settings, click the **Bulleted list** option button.

13 Under Bullet type, click the **New Bullet** button.

The New Bullet dialog box displays.

14 In the New Bullet dialog box, under Font, click the **Font arrow**, scroll down the displayed list, and click **Wingdings** (see Figure 2.16).

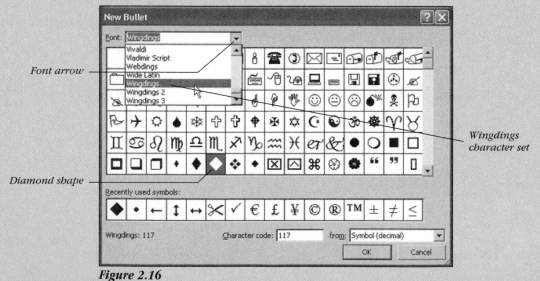

Font arrow

Diamond shape

Wingdings character set

Figure 2.16

15 In the sixth row, click the sixth character—the **large diamond shape**.

16 At the bottom of the New Bullet dialog box, click **OK**, and then click **OK** again in the Indents and Lists dialog box.

17 With the bulleted text still selected, move to the menu bar, click **Format**, and then click **Line Spacing**.

The Line Spacing dialog box displays.

18 To the right of the Between lines box, click the up arrow in the spin box until **1.75** is displayed (see Figure 2.17).

Activity 2.8   Formatting Bullets and Line Spacing

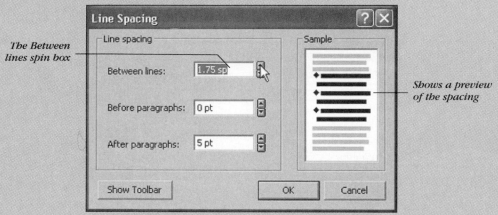

The Between lines spin box

Shows a preview of the spacing

Figure 2.17

19 Click **OK** to close the Line Spacing dialog box.

20 On the Standard toolbar, click the **Zoom Out** button twice to zoom down to 66%, and notice that the bulleted list is not quite centered vertically ↕ in the frame—there is a little more space at the bottom of the frame than at the top.

21 Right-click over the selected frame to display the shortcut menu, click **Format Text Box**, and then click the **Text Box tab**.

22 Click the **Vertical alignment arrow**, and then click **Middle** (see Figure 2.18). Click **OK** to close the dialog box and apply the formatting, and then click in the scratch area to cancel the selection and view your changes.

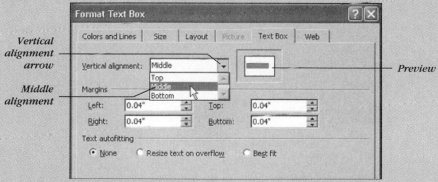

Vertical alignment arrow

Middle alignment

Preview

Figure 2.18

23 On page 3, select the frame containing the names of the award winners and then apply the **White marble** texture and a **1 1/2 pt** black border. Vertically center the text in the frame.

24 On the Standard toolbar, click the **Print Preview** button.

25 To display both sheets (4 pages) in the preview window, move to the toolbar, click the **Multiple Pages** button, and then hold down the left mouse button and drag to select two sheets (see Figure 2.19).

The two sheets display as shown in Figure 2.20.

(Continues)

Activity 2.8   Formatting Bullets and Line Spacing (continued)

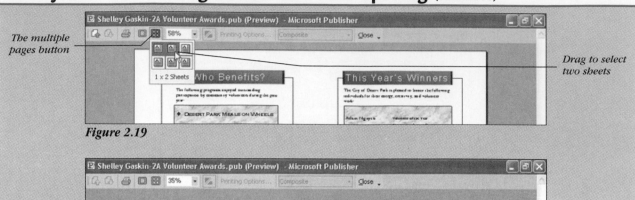

The multiple pages button

Drag to select two sheets

Figure 2.19

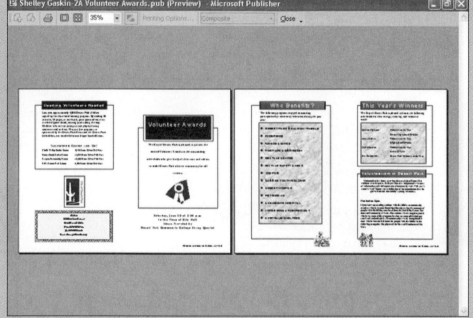

Figure 2.20

26 On the Print Preview toolbar, click the **Print** button, and then click the **Close** button to close Print Preview. Publication 2A Volunteer Awards is complete!

27 On the menu bar, click **File**, and then click **Close**. Click **Yes** to save any changes.

Publication 2B

Summer Newsletter

In Activities 2.9–2.18, you will insert and arrange text in the Summer Edition of the Fine Arts and Parks Newsletter, which is sent to all households in the City of Desert Park. The four pages of your completed publication will look like Figure 2.21. You will save your publication as *Firstname Lastname-2B Summer Newsletter*.

The Strawberry Hedgehog

Fine Arts and Parks News for Residents of Desert Park

Finalists In Trail Design Competition

Residents of Desert Park are invited to preview what future enhancements to the Agave Trail may look like. Three architectural teams have been selected to design comprehensive improvement plans for the trail. Their prospective designs will be on display for public viewing and comment in the lobby of City Hall during the week of July 12.

The finalist teams' display will include artist renderings and maps showing proposed improvements such as interpretive signs, waterway enhancements, bicycle and pedestrian bridges, ramadas, lighting, transit shelters and other architectural and artistic features.

Final judging of the Trail Design Competition, which will be open

to the public, will take place at noon on Saturday, July 17, at the Desert Park Botanical Garden located on the northwest corner of Agave Parkway and Ironwood Boulevard.

The winning team will be selected based on its ability to address the functional needs of the project, while providing complementary solutions to the area's unique environment and rich cultural traditions.

The Agave Trail is a 10-mile loop linking many of the area's significant historic, natural, cultural and recreational attractions. The Agave Trail was begun in 1975 as a short, one-mile hiking

Agave Trail will be enhanced and expanded.

path. When complete, the Agave Trail will serve as an inviting destination for cyclists, pedestrians and hikers to enjoy the landscape of Desert Park. The competition is coordinated by the Fine Arts and Parks Department, led by Director Ray Hamilton.

Volume 5, Issue 2

Summer

Special points of interest:

- *Agave Trail to be Enhanced*
- *Increased Fire Danger!*
- *Bicycling Important Here*
- *Cool Off at the Beach*
- *Public Artists Needed*
- *Youth Resource Guide Available*
- *Keep Your Child Healthy*
- *Youth Golf Will Benefit*

Inside this issue:

Seasonal Fire Danger!

An unusually dry winter and spring, rising temperatures, and low humidity have combined to create extreme fire danger in Desert Park's mountain preserves and desert parks.

To reduce the risk of brush fires, a fire ban has been declared. This

is the third straight year such a ban has been enacted.

The ban stipulates: no open or wood fires of any kind in any part of the preserves or parks; charcoal briquettes may be used only in established, department-installed grills in designated

cooking areas; propane or gas grills may be used only in established picnic areas; motorists may not throw smoking materials from cars.

The fire restrictions are needed to

(Continued on page 2)

Figure 2.21A

Bicycling in Desert Park

The "Golden Age" of bicycling occurred during the development of Desert Park many years ago. Early photographs show street scenes with bicycles, horses, trolleys, and pedestrians. In fact, our first streets were arranged for these users. But Desert Park was ahead of its time, because this development pattern is actually an essential element of a livable community.

Desert Park is a city in which people can get around without cars, and the City hopes to make this a place where it is easier to ride a bicycle than to drive a car. Ideally, bicyclists

should be able to circulate along city streets freely and safely. At the bicyclist's destination there should be safe, free, and accessible parking.

The City is working on a plan that identifies a network of bikeways that will connect bicycle riders to their destinations. The enhancements to the Agave Trail are an important part of this plan. The plan includes a list of other projects and pro-

grams, similar to the Agave Trail program, to be added to the Transportation Improvement Plan.

Desert Park has a long history of encouraging bicycling.

Fire Danger, continued

(Continued from page 1)

protect against devastating wildfire during these times of extreme fire danger and severe drought. The complete text of the fire restrictions for the city limits is posted on the City's Web site.

Residents living on preserve boundaries can obtain a free informational brochure with tips on identifying vegetation they can legally remove from preserve boundary areas by calling 626-555-2222.

> *Don't play with fire! Visit the City's Web site to learn now to protect your property from wild fires.*

City Beaches Are Open

Looking to cool off? The City's two beaches—at Blue Rock Lake and at Lake Roadrunner—are open now. And staying cool will be a bargain again this summer. Regular admission is just 50 cents for youths and seniors and $1 for adults. Coupon books and season

Cool off at the City's beaches.

passes are available by calling 626-555-SWIM.

The Desert Park Fine Arts and Parks Department will offer a variety of special summer programs and classes, which will include learn-to-swim and water safety instruction. Call the number above for more information and

reservations.

Daily hours begin May 1, with the beaches open from 10 a.m. - 8 p.m. through the end of August. After August 31, beaches revert to weekend operations through October 15. Lifeguards are on duty during all open hours.

Figure 2.21B

Volume 5, Issue 2

Page 3

Call for Artists

The Desert Park Fine Arts Commission is accepting applications from individual artists and artistic teams to design several public art projects for the City Hall Plaza mall. The goal of the public art projects is to provide an aesthetic link among intersections, bikeways, pedestrian bridges, and trails. Additionally, enhancements and artistic improvements to gateways to residential areas will be considered. The Commission hopes to add additional gardens, sculptures, walking paths, and pedestrian bridges to the area.

A team can include artists, architects, and landscape architects. A selection committee will choose finalists to develop a preliminary proposal. Selected finalists must present their conceptual approach at a City Council meeting, and will receive a $1,000 honorarium for the proposals. Local artists and architects are encouraged to apply.

Students from the departments of Art and of Landscape Architecture at Desert Park University will assist the Fine Arts Commission in organizing submissions for judging. Dr. Betty Frank, the university's president, said, "We are proud to be a part of this artistic endeavor."

The deadline to apply is 5 p.m. Friday, August 1. Each team member should include a resume and a portfolio of relevant work. For more information or detailed submission requirements, call the City Manager's office at 626-555-1234.

Join the public art project.

Youth Guide Available

Desert Park Community College is pleased to announce this year's Desert Park Summer Youth Resource Guide. It is full of information about summertime programs for children, youths and families. It is published by the Desert Park Human Services Division.

Activity categories include Creative Arts, Camping, Services for Kids with Special Needs, Support Services for Families, Desert Wilderness Appreciation, Rocks and Flowers, and Fun Stuff to Learn in Desert Park.

Listings in the guide feature more than 75 programs and organizations, including such public providers as the City of Desert Park and the Desert Park Community College.

There's something for everyone in the guide. You can pick up a free guide in the City Hall lobby or get one mailed to you by calling the City Manager's office at 626-555-1234.

Come to City Hall and pick up your free guide, or call 626-555-1234

Child Health Fair Coming

The 5th annual Desert Park Children's Health Fair, entitled Take Time to Feel Fine! will be held on Saturday, August 15 from 10 a.m. – 5 p.m. at Meadow Park Center.

The Fair will focus on the health and safety of the whole child, from dental care to the importance of play time. Over 40 children's activity booths will be sponsored by local child care centers and medical professionals, as well as organizations such as the Tooth Mobile, the Desert Park Police Department, and the county Health Department.

Nursing students will have free disk copies of a spreadsheet that can track your child's immunizations and health checkups.

The Fair will also feature three inflatable fun jumpers, a gymnastics demonstration, free tooth brushes, coloring books, and bicycle helmets.

The Fair is part of the Desert Park Month of the Child celebration, which strives to raise awareness of the needs of children. The Fair is an annual tradition that gives families time to learn and play together without spending money.

Figure 2.21C

Fine Arts and Parks News
for Residents of Desert Park

City Hall
1570 Palo Verde Parkway
Desert Park, AZ 85123

Phone: 626-555-1234
Fax: 626-555-4321
Email: citymanager@desertpark.org

Mailing Address Line 1
Mailing Address Line 2
Mailing Address Line 3
Mailing Address Line 4
Mailing Address Line 5

Live, work, and grow in Desert Park!

Visit us on the Web:
www.desertpark.org

Golf for a Cause

The Desert Park Fine Arts and Parks Department is hosting a golf clinic and nighttime golf benefit at the North Park Golf Course on Friday, August 21 to benefit the city's Youth Golf Program.

A PGA Tour Professional, recognized as one of the most accomplished golfers to play the game, will be at the North Park Golf Course to offer a free Golf Clinic. The clinic will run from 9 a.m. – 10:30 a.m. It's open to the public and there is no charge for admission. Come on out and learn some valuable tips from a pro!

Play golf to benefit Youth Golf Program.

Want to see how a pro applies those clinic techniques to an actual round of golf? As a follow-up to the clinic, our pro will join tournament guests in an exhibition round beginning at 12 noon. Plan to follow this foursome to see how they perform.

The nighttime event begins at 8 p.m. Pre-registration is required. The cost is $25 per person. Registration includes greens fees, glow balls, prizes, soft drinks, and pull carts. The tournament is a four-person scramble with a shotgun start at 8:15 p.m.

The tournament, which is played on the nine-hole course, is limited to the first 12 teams (48 players). The Youth Golf Program provides free golf lessons to youth at six of Desert Park's municipal golf courses. Funding makes it possible to provide year-round instruction, golf clubs, balls and other equipment for use during the classes. For more information, call 626-555-1131.

"The Golf Benefit is a fun and informal way to support hundreds of young people in Desert Park and the surrounding county," said Fred Stein, president of the Youth Golf Program Foundation. "The golf clinic is a great opportunity for children to learn about the game and be exposed to business leaders who can have an influence on their lives."

Figure 2.21D

Objective 6: Identify the Parts of a Newsletter

Recall that a newsletter is a periodical used to communicate news and information to a specific group. A newsletter usually has at least two pages, but might have four, six, or more pages. Additionally, every newsletter contains specific parts.

Activity 2.9   Identifying the Parts of a Newsletter

1 **Start** Publisher. From your student files, open the publication *2B_SummerNewsletter*.

This publication is based upon one of the templates provided by Publisher.

2 On the menu bar, click **View**, and then click **Header and Footer**. On the displayed Header and Footer toolbar, click the **Show Header/Footer** button to navigate to the footer frame.

The Master page view displays, and the publication zooms to 100%.

3 In the footer frame, type Firstname Lastname-2B Summer Newsletter

4 On the Header and Footer toolbar click **Close** to close the Master Page view and return to the publication.

5 On the Standard toolbar, click the **Zoom Out** button once to zoom to 75%. Scroll to position the top portion of page 1 in the middle of your screen.

6 On the menu bar click **File**, click **Save As**, and then navigate to the location where you are storing your files for this lesson. In the File name box type Firstname Lastname-2B Summer Newsletter

7 Click the **Save** button, and then on the Standard toolbar, click the **Print** button to print a copy of the newsletter for your reference as you work through the publication. Four pages will print.

8 Look in the lower left portion of the screen, and notice that the Page Navigation buttons in the status bar indicate that there are four pages in this publication. Then, take a few moments to examine the placeholder text on each of the four pages of your printout. The placeholder text offers good tips about how to arrange a newsletter and the number of words that can fit in the various text boxes.

9 Take a moment to examine Figure 2.22, which shows the first and last page of the newsletter, and Table 2.3 to learn the parts of a newsletter. You can also use the printout you just produced as a reference.

(Continues)

Activity 2.9   Identifying the Parts of a Newsletter (continued)

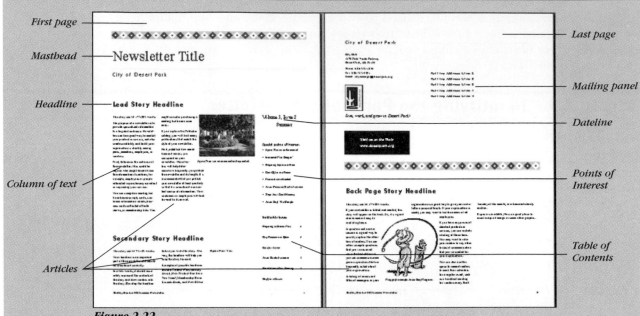

Figure 2.22

TABLE 2.3   PARTS OF A NEWSLETTER

Newsletter Part	Description
Masthead	The top of the first page. This frame contains the title of the newsletter, and is often in a different font than the rest of the newsletter.
Dateline	Lines of text that indicate the date and/or the volume or issue number of the newsletter. The dateline informs the reader how long the newsletter has been published, and can be used to distinguish one issue of the newsletter from another.
Points of Interest	A list of key points from the various articles, intended to entice readers to read the entire article.
Table of Contents	The titles of the articles in the newsletter.
Headline	The title of an article written in a way that informs the reader of the article content.
Column	An arrangement of short lines of text in a newsletter, such as a newspaper. Shorter lines of text are easier to read than long lines.
Pull quotes (also called **callouts**)	Interesting quotations taken from the text of the story to draw the reader into the story—usually in a larger font size than the story, and in bold or italic.
Mailing panel	Space provided on the back of the newsletter for the recipient's name and address (or a preprinted label containing the recipient's name and address), and which includes the organization's name, address, logo, and phone number.
Articles	The informative stories contained in the newsletter.

Objective 7: Insert Word Files and Text in Text Boxes

Recall that all text and images in a publication are contained in frames—boxes into which you place text or images. Recall also that ***text frames***, also called ***text boxes***, are containers into which you can type or ***import*** text. To import text means to bring into your publication text from another electronic file. Publisher includes tools that enable you to do this.

It is easy and convenient to type text directly into a text frame. It is also easy to import text created in Microsoft Word format, Rich Text Format (RTF), or other suitable formats. Importing text is often necessary when several people are working on various stories for the publication. Additionally, Microsoft Word provides more extensive editing features; therefore, it might be easier to format your text in Word and then import it into your publication.

Activity 2.10   Inserting Word Files and Text in Text Boxes

1 On page 1 of the newsletter, click anywhere in the text "Newsletter Title" to select the placeholder text, and type The Strawberry Hedgehog

2 Click in the text box under the newsletter title, and either drag or use Ctrl + A to select the text "City of Desert Park." Replace the text with Fine Arts and Parks News for Residents of Desert Park

Notice that because this was inserted text and not placeholder text, it was not automatically selected when you clicked in the frame.

3 Click anywhere in the text "Lead Story Headline" to select the placeholder text in the text frame, and then type Finalists In Trail Design Competition

4 In the text box below the Lead Story Headline that you just typed, click anywhere to select all of the placeholder text, and scroll the publication so that you can see all of the selected text.

Notice that text is selected in two text boxes, but only the first text box is selected. This is because both frames are connected by Publisher, so clicking the placeholder text in one selects the placeholder text in all.

5 On the menu bar, click **Insert** (see Figure 2.23), and then click **Text File**.

The Insert Text dialog box displays.

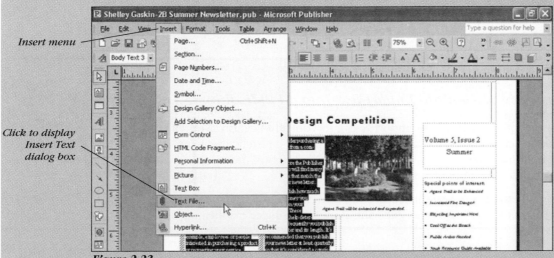

Figure 2.23

(Continues)

Activity 2.10   Inserting Word Files and Text in Text Boxes (continued)

6 Navigate to the student files that accompany this textbook, click *2B_AgaveTrailText*, and then in the lower right corner of the dialog box, click **OK**.

The text from the Word file is inserted into three frames of the newsletter. Because the three frames are connected by Publisher, when the first frame filled, the text flowed over to the second and third frames.

7 If necessary, click to position the insertion point at the end of the text in the last frame. Press Spacebar once, and then type The competition is coordinated by the Fine Arts and Parks Department, led by Director Ray Hamilton.

8 Compare your screen to Figure 2.24. On the Standard toolbar, click **Save** to save the changes you have made to your publication.

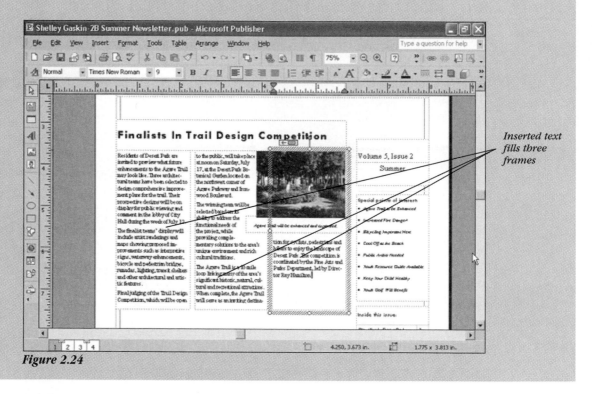

Inserted text fills three frames

Figure 2.24

To extend your knowledge...

Alternative Methods to Import Text Into a Publication

There are other methods to import text into your Publication. You can position the mouse pointer over a selected text frame, right-click to display a shortcut menu, point to Change Text, and then click Text File. This will open the Insert Text dialog box, from which you can navigate to a file and insert it into your publication.

Another method is to use the Copy and Paste commands in a manner similar to other Office XP programs to copy text from other files and paste them into a publication.

Objective 8: View Connected and Layered Frames

In Publisher, a chain of connected text boxes is called a **story**. For example, the article that was imported into your newsletter in the previous Activity is considered a story because it spans a series of connected text boxes (text frames).

Connected frames are indicated by the Go to Next button and the Go to Previous button. You can both create and break a connection between frames by using the buttons on the Connect Frames toolbar. When you use a pre-designed template, such as the one for this newsletter, you will notice that some frames are already connected to accommodate a story.

Frames in Publisher can also be **layered**; that is, one frame can overlap another. Various tools are provided to manipulate the order of the layered frames.

Activity 2.11   Viewing Connected and Layered Frames

❶ Click anywhere in the first frame of the lead story, which begins "Residents of," and then locate the Go to Next Frame button at the bottom of the frame. See Figure 2.25.

Figure 2.25

❷ Click the **Go to Next Frame** button once.

The second frame of the story is selected. Notice that at the top of the frame there is a Go to Previous Frame button and at the bottom of the frame there is a Go to Next Frame button. Thus, within a story—a chain of connected frames—you can navigate from frame to frame either forward or backward by clicking one of the buttons.

❸ At the bottom of the second frame of the story, click the **Go to Next Frame** button.

The third and final frame of the story is selected. Notice that there is no Go to Next Frame button at the bottom of the frame. That is how you know that this is the final frame in the story and that no further frames are in the chain.

❹ With the third frame selected, look at the third frame's upper border and notice that it extends over the picture of the trail.

This indicates that the text frame and the picture frame are layered. When the text frame is on the bottom, the text wraps around the picture as it does in this instance (see Figure 2.26).

(Continues)

Activity 2.11   Viewing Connected and Layered Frames (continued)

Text frame border extends over picture indicating layering of frames—text frame is on the bottom

Go to Previous Frame button

There is no Go to Next Frame button because this is the last frame in the story

Finalists In Trail Design Competition

Go to Previous Frame

Volume 5, Issue 2

Summer

Figure 2.26

5 Position the mouse pointer over the picture of the trail, and click once.

Sizing handles surround the picture and its caption, which have been grouped together as one large object. Recall that if text wraps around the picture, as it does here, then the text frame is on the bottom. (In subsequent Lessons, you will learn more about grouping and ungrouping objects.)

6 With the picture and its caption selected, move to the menu bar, click **Arrange**, point to **Order**, and then click **Send to Back**.

The picture frame is moved to the bottom layer, and the text no longer wraps around the picture; rather the text covers most of the picture (see Figure 2.27).

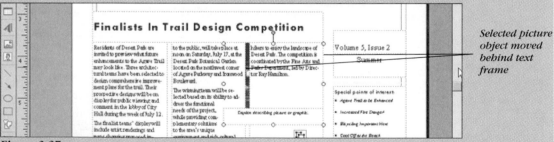

Finalists In Trail Design Competition

Volume 5, Issue 2

Summer

Selected picture object moved behind text frame

Figure 2.27

7 With the picture frame still selected, move to the menu bar, click **Arrange**, point to **Order**, and then click **Bring to Front**.

The picture frame is once again layered on top of the text frame, and the text wraps around the picture.

8 Zoom the publication to **100%**, and scroll so that you can view the bottom of the middle column of this story.

Some words within the story, for example "Agave" and "ramada," might not be recognized by your computer's spelling dictionary, and thus might be flagged with a wavy red line. These red lines will not print. (You will learn about Spelling in Activity 2.16.)

9 In the middle column, in the next to last line, click to position the insertion point in front of the word "When" and then type the following text with a space at the end of the sentence `The Agave Trail was begun in 1975 as a short, one-mile hiking path.`

Activity 2.11   Viewing Connected and Layered Frames

10   Notice that as you typed, the existing text moved to the right, and the text flowed into the connected frame. See Figure 2.28. On the Standard toolbar, click **Save** to save the changes you have made to your publication.

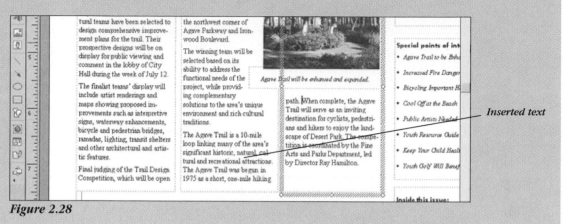

Figure 2.28

Recall that a chain of connected text boxes is called a story. In a publication using a pre-designed template such as 2B Summer Newsletter, Publisher has already connected text boxes to form stories on the pages. If you are working with a pre-designed template, it is a good idea to familiarize yourself with the basic story layouts, which you can then adopt or change to suit your needs.

Activity 2.12   Viewing Frames in a Story

1   On the Standard toolbar, click the **Zoom Out** button four times to zoom the publication to 33%.

2   On page 1, click in the first text box under "Secondary Story Headline."

The placeholder text in the three text boxes in the story chain is selected, and a Go to Next Frame button displays beneath the first frame (see Figure 2.29).

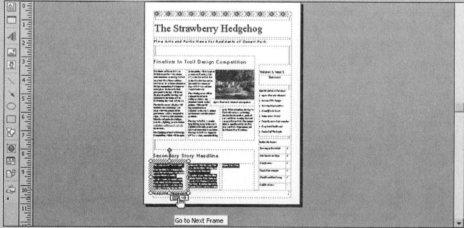

Figure 2.29

(Continues)

Activity 2.12   Viewing Frames in a Story (continued)

❸ On the Page Navigation buttons in the status bar, click **2** to display page 2, and then click in the first story frame on page 2.

The placeholder text in the three frames that comprise the story is selected. Notice also that because a newsletter is usually printed on large paper that folds in the middle, such as a newspaper, the Two-Page Spread displays.

❹ Continue to select some frames in the newsletter pages so that you gain an understanding of how a pre-designed template presents you with frames already connected as stories.

❺ Navigate back to page **1**, zoom to **75%**, and position the lower portion of page 1 in the middle of your screen.

❻ On the Standard toolbar, click **Save**.

To extend your knowledge...

Printing on Large Paper Sizes

Tabloid paper is 11 inches wide and 17 inches high. It can be folded in half—to 8 1/2 inches by 11 inches—to create a four-page newsletter in the same manner as you folded your 8 1/2 inch by 11 inch paper in half to produce four pages of a program. Tabloid-size paper is commonly used for newsletters, but it will not fit in most desktop printers. However, commercial printers and quick copy shops can print tabloid-size paper. If you take your four printed newsletter sheets to them, they will be able to copy the four sheets onto the front and back of one large tabloid sheet to produce your newsletter. You can then fold the sheet in half to form your newsletter.

Objective 9: Flow Text in a Publication

When you type or import more text than the selected text box (or group of connected text boxes) can hold, Publisher displays a message. The message offers two choices—to flow text automatically, or to connect text boxes yourself.

If you elect to flow the text automatically, called ***Autoflow***, Publisher will look for the next available text box in the publication (or offer to create a new text box if none is available), and then "flow" the extra text into it. It will then connect the new text box to the chain of boxes that comprise your story. Although the feature is called *Auto*flow, Publisher actually waits for your permission before it flows the extra text into any text box.

If you elect instead to connect text boxes yourself, the lower right corner of the final text box in the story will display the Text in Overflow indicator, which is a small box containing the letter "A" followed by an ellipsis (3 dots). ***Overflow*** is an area where extra text is held until you decide how you to want deal with it. You can do so in several ways:

> ❯ Select all of the text and then change to a smaller font size. Because text cannot be shrunk to extremely tiny sizes, this will work only if there is a small amount of text in the overflow area. Additionally, good design suggests that you should not use varying font sizes for text within the same publication.

> ❯ Use the sizing handles to make one or more of the text boxes bigger. This will work only to the extent that you have space on the page in which to enlarge the text box.

> ❯ Locate or create another text box, manually connect it to the story chain, and then flow the overflow text into it. You can insert a new text box and even new pages if necessary, but the overall design and plan of your publication must be considered.

> ❯ Consider deleting some of the text to shorten the article so that it will fit.

In the following Activities, you will work with text flow.

Activity 2.13 Using Autoflow

❶ On page 1 of the newsletter, click in the "Secondary Story Headline" to select the placeholder text. Type Seasonal Fire Danger!

❷ Under the Secondary Story Headline that you just typed, click in the first text frame to select the placeholder text.

❸ With the mouse pointer over the selected text, right-click to display the shortcut menu, point to **Change Text**, and then click **Text File**.

This is another method to display the Insert Text dialog box.

❹ Navigate to the student files that accompany this textbook, click the Word document *2B_FireDangerText*, and then click **OK**.

Because the text is too large to fit into the selected frames, a message displays (see Figure 2.30). If you elect to flow the text automatically by clicking Yes, Publisher will look for the next empty text box and wait for your permission to flow the extra text into it. The boxes will be automatically connected.

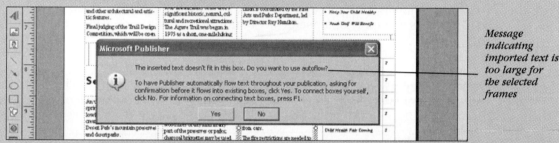

Message indicating imported text is too large for the selected frames

Figure 2.30

If you elect to connect text boxes yourself by clicking No, the lower right corner of the text box will display the Text in Overflow indicator. You will then have to decide how to handle the text stored in the overflow area.

❺ Click **Yes** to have Publisher flow the text automatically in the publication.

Publisher locates the next empty text frame, which is on page 2 of the newsletter. Publisher asks if you want to Autoflow into this box (see Figure 2.31). If you click Yes, Publisher will flow the remaining text into this text box. If you click No, Publisher will move to the first frame in the *next* empty story chain of text boxes. It might be helpful here to refer to the printout you made so that you can see how Publisher is determining what story frames are empty and available.

Suggested text box is selected and Publisher awaits your decision

Figure 2.31

(Continues)

Activity 2.13   Using Autoflow (continued)

6 Click **No** to skip this story chain and move to the next one available.

Because you have rejected the first available chain of connected frames, Publisher will move to the first frame of the next available chain of connected frames.

7 Click **Yes**.

The remaining Fire Danger text flows into the text box of the middle story chain on page 2.

8 Scroll so that you can see the newly added frame in the story chain, and then on the Standard toolbar, click **Save** to save the changes you have made to your publication.

Sometimes your story will not fill up all of the frame space available. Although a publication needs some empty space, called **white space**, to make it readable, large blocks of unused space do not look professional. Nor does it look professional to enlarge the font size of a story. To the extent possible, maintain consistent font sizes across all stories in your publication. A better way to fill unused space is to add more information to the story, insert an additional element, or enlarge an existing element—such as a graphic or a pull quote. In the next Activity, you will enlarge a pull quote to fill in unused space.

Activity 2.14   Deleting and Enlarging Text Boxes

1 On page 2 of the publication, click to select the frame into which the remainder of the Fire Danger story was placed, and notice at the bottom of the frame there is a Go to Next Frame button (see Figure 2.32).

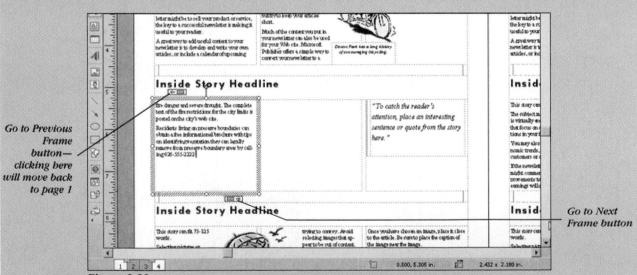

Go to Previous Frame button— clicking here will move back to page 1

Go to Next Frame button

Figure 2.32

2 Click the **Go to Next Frame** button to select the empty frame to the right, and press the Del key to delete this empty frame.

3 Select, again, the frame into which the remainder of the Fire Danger story was placed, and then click the **Go to Next Frame** button.

The text box containing the pull quote, which is part of this story chain, is selected.

Activity 2.14 Deleting and Enlarging Text Boxes

4 Click anywhere in the text beginning "To catch" and then position the mouse pointer over the lower left resize handle until the Resize pointer displays (see Figure 2.33).

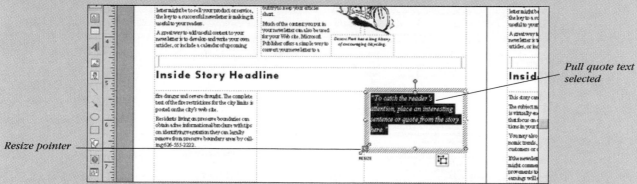

Figure 2.33

5 Keeping your eye on the horizontal and vertical rulers, hold down the left mouse button and drag down and to the left—until the ruler lines that move as you drag are at **3 1/2 inches on the horizontal ruler** and **7 1/2 inches on the vertical ruler** (see Figure 2.34), and then release the left mouse button.

If you do not like your results, click the Undo button on the Standard toolbar and begin again.

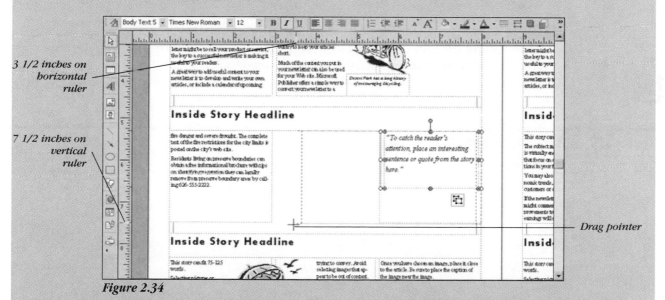

Figure 2.34

6 Click to select the placeholder text for the pull quote and type Don't play with fire! Visit the City's Web site to learn how to protect your property from wild fires.

7 Select the text you just typed, change the font size to **24**, and apply **Bold**.

8 Click the placeholder text for the headline above these frames and type Fire Danger, continued

Compare your screen to Figure 2.35.

(Continues)

Activity 2.14   Deleting and Enlarging Text Boxes (continued)

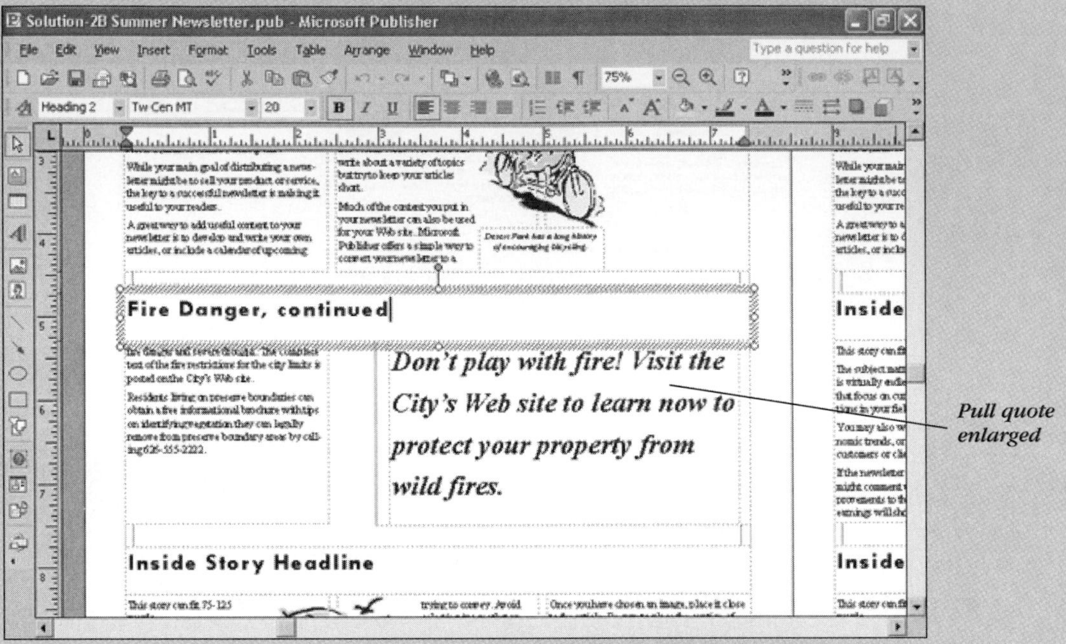

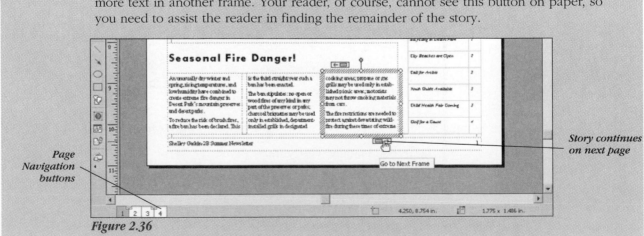

Figure 2.35

9   On the Standard toolbar, click **Save** to save your changes.

If you connect text boxes on separate pages as you have just done in the previous Activity, you can help your reader find connected text boxes by adding a ***continued notice***. You are probably familiar with this type of notice from newspaper and magazine articles. It tells the reader on what page the story is continued, and on the *continued to* page, there is an indication of what page the story was continued *from*. Publisher provides a simple method to do this.

Activity 2.15   Adding a Continued Notice

1   Use the Page Navigation buttons to navigate to page 1, scroll so that you can see the story at the bottom of page 1, and then click in the last text frame on the page (see Figure 2.36).

The frame is selected, and a Go to Next Frame button displays indicating that there is more text in another frame. Your reader, of course, cannot see this button on paper, so you need to assist the reader in finding the remainder of the story.

Figure 2.36

Activity 2.15   Adding a Continued Notice

2 Position the mouse pointer over the selected text box, right-click to display a shortcut menu, and then click **Format Text Box**.

The Format Text Box dialog box displays.

3 Click the **Text Box tab**, and then in the lower left portion of the dialog box, move to the *second* check box and click the **Include "Continued on page..."** check box (see Figure 2.37).

Click check box

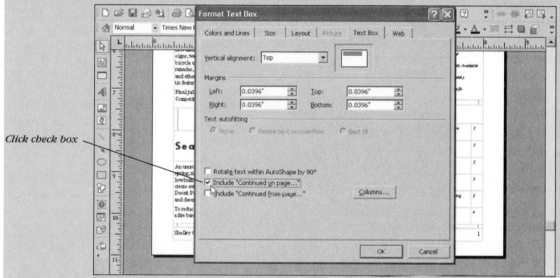

Figure 2.37

4 In the lower right corner of the Format Text Box dialog box, click **OK**.

A small notice is inserted at the bottom of the frame.

5 Click the **Go to Next Frame** button to move to the text box on page 2 that contains the continuation of the story.

6 Move the mouse pointer over the selected frame, right-click to display the shortcut menu, and then click **Format Text Box**.

The Format Text Box dialog box displays.

7 Click the **Text Box tab**, and in the *third* check box, click to place a check mark in the **Include "Continued from page..."** check box. Click **OK**.

A small notice is inserted at the top of the frame (see Figure 2.38).

Continued from notice

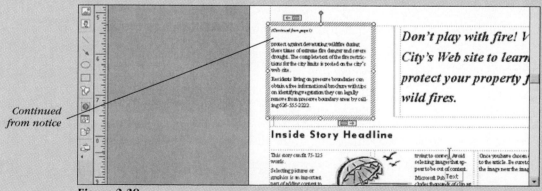

Figure 2.38

8 On the Standard toolbar, click **Save** to save your changes.

Objective 10: Use Spelling, Hyphenation, AutoCorrect, and Editing Tools

Unless the default settings have been changed, Publisher checks spelling as you type. Spelling errors are flagged with wavy red lines. If you right-click on a flagged word, a list of suggested spellings displays. From that menu, you can choose to replace the word, ignore that one instance or all instances, or add the word to your dictionary so it is not flagged in the future. You can also check an entire publication for misspellings by clicking Spelling on the Tools menu. Then from the dialog box, you can select Check all stories to check the spelling in every text box in the current publication. Because the majority of the text in a publication is usually imported from other sources, it is probably best to check the spelling of the entire publication when it is complete.

Hyphenation is the process of breaking—between syllables—long words that occur at the end of a line of printed text for the purpose of making the right margin look more even. Publisher automatically hyphenates unless you elect to turn the feature off. Because Publisher uses text boxes that are usually much narrower than a sheet of paper, hyphenation occurs more frequently than it would in longer lines of text. However, more than three consecutive lines of text ending with a hyphen make reading difficult. If possible, adjust the text to avoid such an occurrence. Also, check for words that Publisher might have hyphenated awkwardly and adjust accordingly.

AutoCorrect corrects common typing, spelling, and grammatical errors as you type. For example, if you type "teh," AutoCorrect replaces it with "the." If you type "aboutt," AutoCorrect replaces it with "about." AutoCorrect contains corrections for many common typing errors. Not only are a number of misspellings and corrections already built into this feature, but you can also add words that you frequently misspell or mistype.

Activity 2.16   Using Spelling and Hyphenation

① Scroll to position the top of page 2 in the middle of your screen. Click in the first story frame, and notice from the selected placeholder text that the three frames surrounding the bicycle picture are connected.

② With the placeholder text selected, move the mouse pointer over the selection, right-click to display the shortcut menu, point to **Change Text**, and then click **Text File**.

③ Navigate to the student files that accompany this textbook, click *2B_BicycleText*, and then click **OK**.

Notice that some of the words are flagged with red wavy lines indicating that they are misspelled.

④ Zoom to **100%** and scroll so that you can see the entire story clearly.

⑤ Position the mouse pointer over the first misspelled word, right-click to display a shortcut menu, and then click the correct word—**photographs**.

⑥ Repeat the process for the other two misspelled words, selecting **trolleys** and **accessible**. If necessary, right-click on "Agave," and add it to your dictionary if you are permitted to do so. If not, click Ignore All. (Computers in college labs and classrooms usually restrict individuals from adding to the dictionary.)

⑦ Click the headline text box for this story and type Bicycling in Desert Park

Activity 2.16   Using Spelling and Hyphenation

8 Zoom back to **75%**. Scroll to the bottom of page 2 so that you can view the three frames around the beach umbrella picture, click to select the placeholder text, and then from your student files insert the file *2B_BeachText*.

Notice that at the bottom of the middle frame and the top of the last frame the word "reservations" is awkwardly hyphenated because it must move up to a new column.

9 On the menu bar, click **Tools**, point to **Language**, and then click **Hyphenation**.

The Hyphenation dialog box displays. Notice that the ***Hyphenation zone*** is set to .25″ (1/4 inch). This is the amount of space at the end of a line within which automatic hyphenation will be activated. The smaller the value the more even the right margin. A very small value can result in too many hyphens; however for most publications this is an appropriate hyphenation zone.

10 Click to *remove* the check mark from the Automatically hyphenate this story check box, and then click **OK**.

In this instance, turning the hyphenation feature off gives the desired result; that is, the word "reservations" is no longer awkwardly hyphenated, and the remainder of the story is still attractively arranged. The ability to turn off automatic hyphenation for a single *story*—and not the entire publication—is a very convenient feature.

11 Make the headline for this story City Beaches Are Open

12 Scroll to position the top of page 3 in the middle of screen. Above the picture of the artist, replace the headline with Call for Artists

13 Click the first text box to select the placeholder text for the three frames in the story. Insert the file *2B_ArtistsText*.

14 Click the second text box in the story, and notice how the text frame extends over the picture frame, then click the third text box in the story and notice again how the text frame extends over the picture frame.

Recall that if a text frame extends over a picture frame, it indicates that the frames are layered. When the text frame is on the *bottom*, the text wraps around the picture as it does in this instance.

15 On the Standard toolbar, click **Save** to save the changes to your publication.

Activity 2.17   Using AutoCorrect and Editing Tools

1 Scroll down to the middle story on page 3. It has no picture or graphic, but it does have a pull quote as part of the story.

2 Click in the first frame to select the placeholder text, move to the menu bar, click **Tools**, and then click **AutoCorrect Options**.

The AutoCorrect dialog box displays.

3 In the Replace text box, type dp

4 In the With text box, type Desert Park (see Figure 2.39).

(Continues)

Activity 2.17   Using AutoCorrect and Editing Tools (continued)

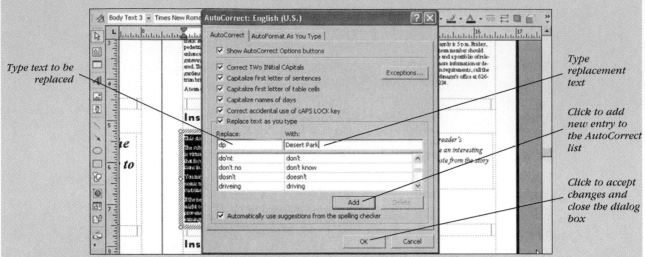

Type text to be replaced

Type replacement text

Click to add new entry to the AutoCorrect list

Click to accept changes and close the dialog box

Figure 2.39

Does your screen differ?

AutoCorrect entries are stored on the hard drive of the computer. If another student recently completed this exercise on the computer at which you are seated, the With box might already display "Desert Park" and you will not have to type it. If so, just click the Close button. It is also possible that another student has used the letters "dp" to refer to something else. If this is the case, delete the With text, and type "Desert Park" as indicated.

5 Click **Add** (see Figure 2.39) and then click **OK**.

The result of this action will enable you to speed your typing. Every time you type "dp" and then press the [Spacebar], Publisher will insert the text "Desert Park."

6 With the placeholder text selected, type the following text, including the typing errors. As you type, try to watch how AutoCorrect fills in "Desert Park" and corrects the words "about" and "the" after you press [Spacebar].

dp Community College is pleased to announce this year's dp Summer Youth Resource Guide. It is full of information aboutt summertime programs for children, youths, and families. It is published by teh dp Human Services Division.

7 After typing the text in the previous step, press [↵Enter] once. On the Standard toolbar, click the **Save** button to save your changes.

8 On the Windows taskbar, click the **Start** button, and then locate and open **Microsoft Word**. Within Word, navigate to the student files that accompany this textbook and open the document *2B_YouthGuideText*.

9 Use [Ctrl] + [A] to select all of the text, and on the Standard toolbar of Word, click the **Copy** button (see Figure 2.40).

Activity 2.17   Using AutoCorrect and Editing Tools

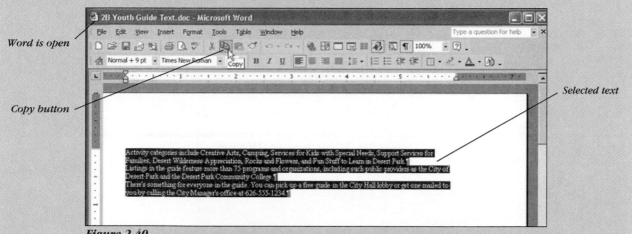

Figure 2.40

10 Close the document, and close Word.

11 In Publisher, with the text box still selected, move to the Standard toolbar and click the **Paste** button.

The text is pasted into the story (see Figure 2.41).

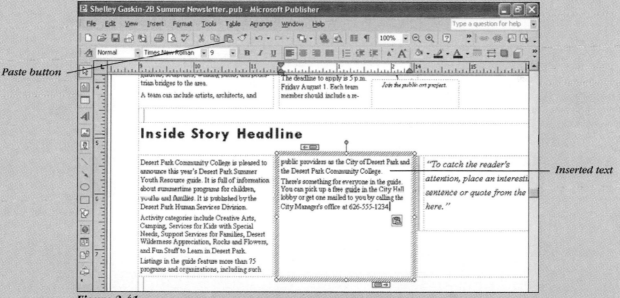

Figure 2.41

12 Click to select the placeholder text in the pull quote and type Come to City Hall and pick up your free guide, or call 626-555-1234.

13 Select the pull quote text, and change the font size to **16**, and then change the headline for the story to: Youth Guide Available

14 On the Standard toolbar, click the **Save** button to save your changes.

You can edit text directly in Publisher, or you can edit text in Microsoft Word. Text that you import into your publication and text that you type directly into your publication can be edited with Microsoft Word. Because of Word's advanced editing features and ease of use, you will likely want to edit in Word if extensive editing is needed.

Word Count, a feature in Microsoft Word 2002 that automatically counts the words in a document, is useful when inserting text from Word into a publication. Word Count can give you an idea of how well the inserted Word document will fit into the story chain with which you are working.

Activity 2.18   Editing a Story in Microsoft Word

1 Scroll to the bottom of page 3 and insert the text file *2B_HealthFairText* in the story frames surrounding the picture of the child, and then change the story headline to
Child Health Fair Coming

2 Click anywhere in the Child Health Fair story.

3 On the menu bar, click **Edit**, and then click **Edit Story in Microsoft Word** (see Figure 2.42).

The text of the Child Health Fair story displays.

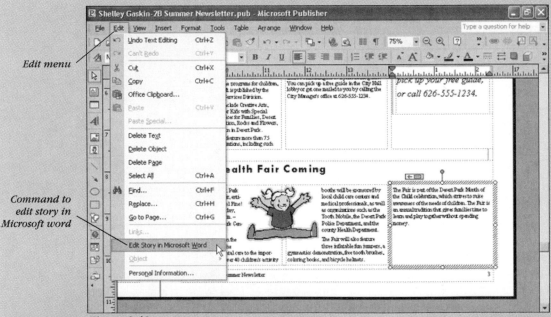

Figure 2.42

4 Click to position the insertion point in front of the 7th line of text, which begins "The Fair will also feature" and then, followed by one press of the ⏎Enter key, type:

Nursing students will have free disk copies of a spreadsheet that can track your child's immunizations and health checkups.

5 On the menu bar, click **File**, and then click **Close & Return** (see Figure 2.43).

Your publication displays with the inserted text.

Activity 2.18   Editing a Story in Microsoft Word

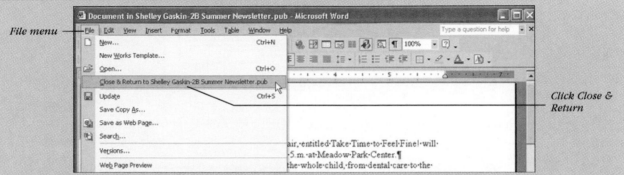

File menu ————

Click Close & Return

Figure 2.43

6 Use the Page Navigation buttons to navigate to page 4, scroll to the bottom to see the Back Page Story Headline, and then replace the headline with Golf for a Cause

7 Select the story's placeholder text, and insert the text file *2B_GolfText*.

Because the text in the file is too large for the available frames in the story, Publisher displays a message (see Figure 2.44).

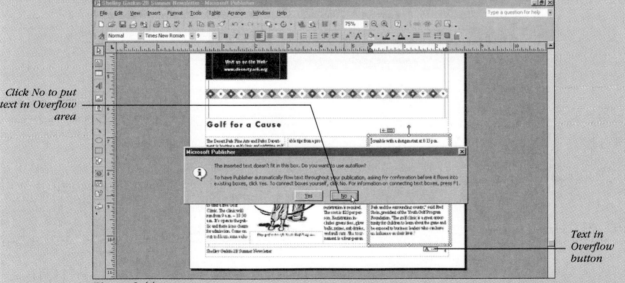

Click No to put text in Overflow area

Text in Overflow button

Figure 2.44

8 Rather than flowing the extra text into other frames, click **No** to place the remainder of the text into the overflow area.

Now you need to decide what to do with the extra text that is being held in the overflow area. Recall that sometimes decisions about the length of articles must be made. Because you are at the end of the newsletter, you have no other frames with which to work. Unless you create a new page, or otherwise rearrange the articles in the newsletter, you will have to adjust the length of this article.

9 At the bottom of the third frame, point to the Text in Overflow button to see its ScreenTip (see Figure 2.45).

You cannot view the overflow area, nor can you know how much text is held there. In this instance, however, you have the Word file from which the text was imported.

(Continues)

Activity 2.18   Editing a Story in Microsoft Word (continued)

Figure 2.45

⑩ With the third frame of the story still selected, move to the menu bar, click **Edit**, and then click **Edit Story in Microsoft Word**.

⑪ The text of the Word document that was inserted displays. Select the last paragraph of text and press the ⒹⒺⓁ key to delete this text and shorten the article (see Figure 2.46).

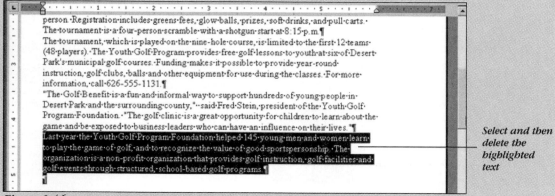

Figure 2.46

⑫ On the menu bar, click **File**, and then click **Close & Return**.

Your publication displays. Notice that the Text in Overflow indicator no longer displays, indicating that no text remains in the overflow area.

⑬ On the Standard toolbar, click the **Print Preview** button, and use the **Multiple Pages** button to display all 4 pages—either 1 × 4 Sheets or 2 × 2 Sheets (see Figure 2.47).

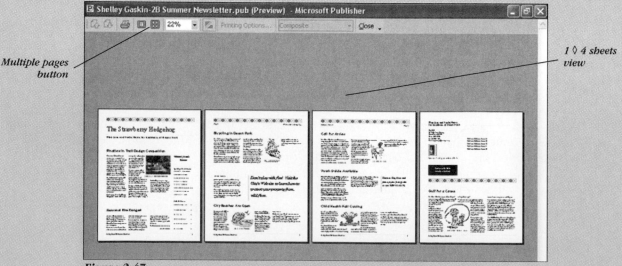

Figure 2.47

⑭ **Close** the Print Preview screen. On the Standard toolbar, click **Save** to save your changes. **Print** one copy of your publication. 2B Summer Newsletter is complete! Close the publication.

Summary

Among the many types of publications for which Microsoft Publisher 2002 is a good tool are flyers, brochures, newsletters, catalogs, business stationery, business forms, postcards, programs, booklets, and small Web sites. In this Lesson you worked with a program and a newsletter.

In this Lesson you learned about working with text within a publication—how to get text into a publication and how to format text within a publication. There are a variety of methods by which you can insert text into a publication. You can type directly into a text box, import a text file from a word processing program, such as Microsoft Word 2002, or copy and paste text from Word or another Office XP application.

After text is in a text box, formatting the text is similar to formatting text in Microsoft Word. You can change font and font size, apply font styles and font colors, align text in various ways within the text box boundaries, and apply font effects, such as underline and small caps. The container for text—a text box—can also be formatted with fill color, fill effects, and borders.

Because Publisher depends entirely on frames—containers for text and graphics—it is important to view and understand the way text flows among text boxes. For text that is too large for one text box, Publisher has a system of connecting text boxes to form a story.

Finally, Publisher provides a variety of ways in which you can edit text in a frame. You can edit directly in the text box, or work with the text in Microsoft Word. Proofreading and hyphenation tools found in Word, such as hyphenation, spell checker, and AutoCorrect, are also available in Publisher.

Using Publisher Help

Because of the nature of the short lines of text within a text box, Publisher uses more frequent hyphenation than a normal word processing document. In a normal Word document, hyphenation can often be avoided altogether. But with short lines of text, such as those found in columns or text frames, hyphenation occurs frequently. In this exercise, you will use Help to view additional tips for dealing with hyphenation in Publisher.

1. If necessary, start Publisher and display the New Publication task pane and the Quick Publications Publication Gallery.

2. At the right edge of the menu bar, click in the Ask a Question box and type How can I change the frequency of hyphens in a publication?

3. Press ⏎Enter and then on the displayed list, click **Hyphenate text manually**.
   The Help pane displays.

4. At the top of the Help pane, click **Show All**.
   The information for manual hyphenation displays.

5. If you want to keep a copy of this information, click the **Print** button. It will print on one page, but your name will not print on the document.

6. Click the **Close** button, the **X** in the top right corner of the Help window, to close the Help window.

Concepts Assessment

Short Answer

Write the correct answer in the space provided.

1. Selecting and editing text in Microsoft Publisher works in much the same manner as selecting and editing text in _____.

2. As in Microsoft Word, when you place your insertion point within existing text and begin to type, the existing text moves to the right to make space, which is known as _____ mode.

3. Toolbar buttons are simply one-click methods to perform commands that would otherwise be performed from the menu bar and a _____.

4. In terms of font designs, it is a good idea not to use more than _____ in a publication.

5. Serif fonts are a good choice for _____.

6. Because they are more difficult to read, _____ fonts are best used for headings only.

7. The font called _____, which looks like an old-fashioned typewriter, is not acceptable for any publication.

8. Text formatted in all _____ letters is difficult to read and should be used only for headings.

9. Although it will not fit in most desktop printers, a paper size known as _____ is often used for newsletters, and is usually available at copy shops and commercial printers.

10. The Spacing Before and Spacing After commands are used to add space above and below _____.

Matching

Match each term in the second column with its correct definition in the first column. Write the letter of the term on the blank line to the left of the correct definition.

_____ **1.** A small pamphlet that describes an event, product, program, or service.

_____ **2.** Textures, patterns, color fades, and pictures that can be applied to the inside of a frame.

_____ **3.** A set of characters with the same design and shape.

_____ **4.** Alignment of text that adds additional space between words so that both the left and right margins are even.

_____ **5.** A periodical used to distribute news and information to a special group.

_____ **6.** Interesting quotes taken from the text of the story to draw the reader into the story, usually in a larger font size than the story and in bold or italic.

_____ **7.** Fonts with no lines on the ends of characters, and which are more suitable for headings and titles.

_____ **8.** The process of sizing text to fit in a text box.

_____ **9.** A chain of connected text boxes.

_____ **10.** A color combination in which one color fades into another.

_____ **11.** An area where extra text is held until you decide how you want to distribute it.

_____ **12.** The unit of measurement of fonts, with one equal to 1/72 of an inch.

_____ **13.** A process to distribute text that is too large to fit into the selected frames and in which additional frames are automatically located by Publisher.

_____ **14.** Fonts with lines or extensions on the ends of the characters and that are a good choice for large amounts of text because they are easy to read.

_____ **15.** A feature that corrects common typing, spelling, and grammatical errors as you type.

A. AutoCorrect

B. Autoflow

C. Brochure

D. Copyfitting

E. Fill effects

F. Font

G. Gradient fill

H. Justify

I. Newsletter

J. Overflow

K. Points

L. Pull quotes

M. Sans serif fonts

N. Serif fonts

O. Story

Skill Assessments

Publication 2C

Spring Calendar

In the following Skill Assessment, you will create a Calendar of Events for the Desert Park Fine Arts and Parks Department for the months of May and June. Your completed publication will look similar to the one shown in Figure 2.48. You will save your publication as *Firstname Lastname-2C SpringCalendar*.

May

Sun	Mon	Tue	Wed	Thu	Fri	Sat
						1
2	3	4	5	6	7	8
9	10	11	12	13	14	15
16	17	18	19	20	21	22
23	24	25	26	27	28	29
30	31					

Schedule of Events

- May 3, 6pm-Migratory Bird Festival: Celebrate birds, birdhouse and feeder making at the City Garden Center
- May 5, 7pm-Dance Recital: Ballet, tap and jazz performances by Movement Dance, Cholla Recreation Center
- May 7, 10am-Golden Age Club President's Breakfast Meeting at the Desert Café on Main Street
- May 14, noon-Sports Day: Basketball, dodge ball, soccer, relays and more, North Branch Park Center
- May 15, 6pm-Pot Luck Dinner with talent exhibitions by participants, Town Hall Dining Room
- May 22, 6pm-Annual Sleep Over, games, story telling, movies, swimming, snacks, and breakfast, North Branch Park Center
- May 23, 10am-Nature Walk, Desert Park Botanical Garden
- May 24, 5:30pm-Parent Appreciation Ceremony, participants will entertain parents and present certificates, Desert Park Elementary School auditorium
- May 26, 6pm-Spring Arts Program, dance, choral and poetry recitals, refreshments, Susan Anthony Recreation Center
- May 30, 10am-Nature Center Day, naturalists will be on hand to answer nature questions, Desert Park Botanical Garden

Discover the arts and parks in Desert Park!

City of Desert Park

Fine Arts and Parks Department
One Cholla Plaza
Desert Park, AZ 85123

Phone: 626-555-9876
Fax: 626-555-6789
Email: fineartsandparks@desertpark.org

Student Name-2C Spring Calendar

Figure 2.48A

June

Sun	Mon	Tue	Wed	Thu	Fri	Sat
		1	2	3	4	5
6	7	8	9	10	11	12
13	14	15	16	17	18	19
20	21	22	23	24	25	26
27	28	29	30			

Schedule of Events

- June 1, 9am-Senior Walk: Guided walk for seniors along the Agave Trail
- June 5, 6pm-Evening Canoe Floats on Roadrunner Lake, meet at the dock
- June 6, 8am-Market Day: Annual plant and craft sale, tours and more, Desert Park Arboretum
- June 10, 3pm-Roller Skating Show: North Branch Park Center
- June 12, 1pm-Community Clean-Up at North Park—volunteers will cut grass and plant flowers
- June 15, noon-Fifth Annual Flower Mart on the City Mall—flower sales, arts, crafts, hat contest
- June 17, 10am-Draw From Our Collections: Professional and amateur artists invited, bring your own drawing materials, Desert Park Nature Center
- June 21, 9pm-Stars in Your Skies—Search the Arizona night sky for stars, planets, and constellations with Professor Florence Morrison from Desert Park University, at the Mt. Estrella Center
- June 22, 1pm-Awards Program, boys and girls in the after-school program will receive awards for sports and academic achievements, Desert Park Middle School Auditorium

Discover the arts and parks in Desert Park!

City of Desert Park

Fine Arts and Parks Department
One Cholla Plaza
Desert Park, AZ 85123

Phone: 626-555-9876
Fax: 626-555-6789
Email: fineartsandparks@desertpark.org

Student Name-2C Spring Calendar

Figure 2.48B

1. Start Publisher, navigate to your student files, and open the publication *2C_SpringCalendar*.

2. On the menu bar, click View, and then click Header and Footer. On the displayed Header and Footer toolbar, click the Show Header/Footer button to navigate to the Footer frame, and then type `Firstname Lastname-2C Spring Calendar`

3. On the menu bar, click File, click Save As, navigate to the location in which you are storing your files for this Lesson, and in the File name box type `Firstname Lastname-2C Spring Calendar`

4. Close the Header and Footer toolbar, which will close the Master page and return you to the publication. The publication zooms to 100%.

5. Scroll so that you can view the upper right portion (Schedule of Events) of the calendar for May.

6. Click anywhere in the text frame containing the word "Date" to select the placeholder text. Move the mouse pointer over the selected text, right-click to display the shortcut menu, point to Change Text, and then click Text File.

7. In the displayed Insert Text dialog box, navigate to the student files that accompany this textbook, click *2C_MayCalendarText*, and then click OK.

8. Use Ctrl + A to select the inserted text. Change the font to Garamond.

9. With the inserted text still selected, move to the menu bar, click Format, click Indents and Lists, and in the Indents and Lists dialog box under Indent settings, click the Bulleted list option button.

10. Under Bullet type, click the New Bullet button. In the New Bullet dialog box, click the Font arrow and navigate to the Wingdings character set. In the sixth row, click the 12th character—a small flower—and then click OK. Click OK again to close the Indents and Lists dialog box. The flower character becomes the bullet for the bulleted list.

11. With the inserted text selected, move to the menu bar, click Format, and then click Line Spacing to display the Line Spacing dialog box. In the After paragraphs spin box, click the up arrow until 3 pt displays. Click OK.

12. With the inserted text selected and the mouse pointer positioned anywhere over the selected text, right-click to display the shortcut menu, point to Change Text, point to AutoFit Text, and then click Best Fit. Publisher adjusts the font size to fill the text box. Click in the gray scratch area of your screen to cancel the selection and view your changes.

13. Notice that there is a little more space at the bottom of the text box than at the top. To center the text vertically within the text box, click anywhere in the text box to select it, right-click to display the shortcut menu, click Format Text Box, and then click the Text Box tab. Click the Vertical alignment arrow, click Middle, and then click OK to close the dialog box. If necessary, zoom to 75% so that you can view the entire text box on your screen. Notice that the text is vertically centered within the text box.

14. If necessary, click anywhere within the text box to select it. On the menu bar, click Format, and then click Text Box. If necessary, click the Color and Lines tab. Under Fill, click the Color arrow, and then click Fill Effects. If necessary, click the Gradient tab. Under Colors, click the Two colors option button.

15. Click the Color 1 arrow and then click the third color in the row (robin's egg blue). Click the Color 2 arrow, and then click the fifth color in the row (gray). Under Transparency, use either the slider or the up arrow in the spin box to set the Transparency From to 38% and the Transparency To to 16%. Under Shading styles, click the From corner option button. Under Variants, click the first variant in the first row—the default. Click OK once to return to the Format Text Box dialog box.

16. In the Format Text dialog box, under Line, click the Color arrow, and then click the 6th color in the row (Navy). Click the Style arrow, and then click 3 pt. Click OK to close the Format Text Box dialog box. Click in the gray scratch area to cancel the selection and view your changes.

17. Click inside the small text box above the list of events. On the Formatting toolbar, click the Center button to center the text horizontally. Then, use the Text Box tab of the Format Text

dialog box to center the text vertically. Place a 3 pt border around this text box, using the same line color as the step above.

18. On the menu bar, click the Save button to save your changes. Navigate to page 2. In the text box containing the word "Date" insert the text file *2C_JuneCalendarText*. Then repeat steps 8–17 above. When you are finished, go to step 19. Note that the flower bullet will be displayed under Bullet type, and you will not have to retrieve it from the Wingding character set.

19. On the menu bar, click the Save button to save your changes. On the Standard toolbar, click the Print Preview button, and use the Multiple Pages button to view both pages, either side by side or one above the other. Then, on the Print Preview toolbar, click the Print button to print one complete copy of your publication.

20. Close the Print Preview. On the menu bar click File, and then click Close. If necessary, click Yes to save any additional changes. Publication 2C is complete!

Publication 2D

City News Brief

In the following Skill Assessment, you will edit a newsletter for the City Manager of Desert Park. Your completed publication will look like the one shown in Figure 2.49. You will save your publication as *Firstname Lastname-2D City News Brief*.

Volume 2, Issue 3

Fall Issue

CITY OF DESERT PARK

City News Brief

Siren Noise A Concern

The Desert Park Emergency Medical Services (EMS) team recognizes that siren noise is of concern to residents, especially those in the higher density areas of the city. Noise pollution is a growing concern among urban residents.

EMS strives to balance the concerns about noise with the need for quick response to life-threatening situations. The City has taken some steps to help reduce the frequency and level of siren noise.

Special light sensors have been installed at certain intersections, which detect the approach of an ambulance and control the traffic lights accordingly.

This not only cuts down on noise, but also permits a much safer flow of traffic.

In the main dispatch office, software is being installed that will prioritize ambulance calls and allow ambulances on some less serious calls to proceed to the scene without sirens. This will reduce a significant number of sirens.

Upgraded, high-output strobe lights are being installed on all ambulances to improve the visibility of the ambulance and reduce the need to use the siren. In addition, newer ambulances have sirens located under the front bumper that directs noise down toward

the street so it can be heard by vehicles, but is less noticeable away from the street.

EMS will continue to research and evaluate new methods for reducing noise while maintaining the ability to respond quickly to the needs of residents. For more information, call the Desert Park EMS team at 626-555-HELP.

New Museum Location

Thanks to a bond issue passed by the residents of Desert Park in 1998, the Desert Park Museum of Art has relocated to a new facility at 20th Street and Via Colinas. A gala dedication ceremony will be held on November 12, at

8:00 p.m. The ceremony is open to the public.

The new space was designed to allow a permanent exhibit area as well as changing exhibits area, museum store, collection storage, and children's

museum. "I know that residents and visitors to the city will be impressed by the new museum," said Elizabeth Viejo, museum curator. "The space was specially designed with our collection in mind and
(Continued on page 2)

Special points of interest:

- *New museum location enhances visitor experience*
- *Desert Park teens will benefit from new program*
- *Your non-profit organization can get computer help!*
- *West side will be focus of new development*

Figure 2.49A

Non-Profits Get IT Assistance

The Desert Park Community Information Technology Resource Center matches computer-skilled volunteers with area non-profit organizations needing technology assistance. Organizations that use the services of the Center include art associations, environmental groups, health centers, legal assistance centers, and social service agencies.

The Resource Center was developed after the results of a collaborative survey of the Department of Information Technology, the Human Services Department, and County Community Services Division were released. The survey looked at information technology access and

needs within the non-profit community, and was designed to guide the City, the County, and other funding organizations in offering technology assistance to non-profits.

Respondents in the survey were asked to identify what sort of training or assistance would help them use technology more effectively. Almost every agency that responded to the survey cited the need for basic training for staff in software and hardware, and the need for increased technology support and troubleshooting.

All the agencies in the survey said that technology was essential to their operation, and yet they are not finding the funding to maintain their infrastructure and update their equipment and skills. Many organizations noted that the volunteers they use for their technology support
(Continued on page 3)

Museum, continued

(Continued from page 1)

it shows it off to the fullest."

This investment will ensure that the residents of Desert Park will have a beautiful museum to enjoy for many years to come. At the next meeting of the City Council, the various organizations that worked to get the bond measure passed will be recognized. They

include the Heritage Commission, Friends of Fine Arts and Parks, Desert Park Citizens United, and many other individual citizens.

For exhibit information and museum hours, call 626-555-4ART or visit the Web site at www.desertparkmuseum.org.

"The space was specially designed with our collection in mind."
Elizabeth Viejo, Curator

Anyone Can Use the Law Library!

Public Law Library was established in 1965 to provide citizens of the City and the surrounding county access to legal reference materials on city, state, federal and international statutes, case law and supporting materials. The Law Library is open to residents, judges, attorneys, students—anyone who needs access to the materials for legal, personal or academic research.

The Law Library is governed by a six-member board of trustees consisting of representatives from the County Superior Court and the County Bar Association. Law Library operations are financed through a portion of the filing fees paid by parties involved in civil cases in the County Court, not by general tax funds. The County provides the library housing and maintenance.

Figure 2.49B

New Youth Program

The City of Desert Park's Office of Youth Initiatives was established to assist every young person in the city to become a productive citizen and valuable contributor to society. Through programs and partnerships, we strive to provide education, community resources, and career development assistance to young people in our community. Working closely with the City's public schools we help assure that every student has the skills needed to allow full participation in the community.

The office has just launched a program called "Reach Out Youth!" The program will offer detailed and up-to-date information on recreational events,

leadership development opportunities, corporate partners, and career development and job placement. The program will link youth to other programs of interest such as those offered by local parks, libraries, science centers, and sports teams. The program will maintain a list of local companies who are actively recruiting young people for part-time and summer jobs.

For information, call 626-555-TEEN.

Look Up A Law

Did you ever wonder about the City ordinances and other items that get passed at a City Council meeting? The City Clerk's Office maintains the records of the City Council. You can obtain copies of ordinances, resolutions, and related items for free or at a nominal cost.

Ordinances: Copies of legislation are available for $1 per printed page. However, for ordinances proposed since May of 1988, you may view and print from the City's Web site. These copies are for your information only. Official copies are available in the City Clerk's Office. The online ordinances are updated weekly.

Charter and Code: Copies of the annotated City Charter may be purchased for $25 from the City Clerk's Office. For a complete copy, there is a charge of $250. Call the City Clerk's office for information about a subscription. An informational copy of the Charter and Code of Ordinances is available on the City's Web site.

Non-Profits, continued

(Continued from page 2)

are essential. There is a gap in technology planning and training for non-profit organizations.

The volunteers assist the staffs with all types of Information Technology projects including planning and installation of network capability, planning future IT needs, selection of

hardware and software, database design, building Web sites, and training staff and clients.

If you are an IT professional or have solid computing skills and would like to share your expertise with Desert Park non-profit organizations, please fill out an interest form at the Center's Web site at www.dpitvolunteer.com. Volunteers are currently needed in the

areas of Web site design and development, accounting spreadsheets, Microsoft Office training, and networking.

Figure 2.49C

CITY OF DESERT PARK

City Hall
15.70 Palo Verde Parkway
Desert Park, AZ 85123

Phone: 626-555-1234
Fax: 626-555-4321
Email: citymanager@desertpark.org

Live, work, and grow in Desert Park!

We're on the Web
www.cityofdesertpark.org

Mailing Address Line 1
Mailing Address Line 2
Mailing Address Line 3
Mailing Address Line 4
Mailing Address Line 5

City of Desert Park

West Side Development Plans Announced

The mayor has announced a new plan that will begin to implement the recommendations of a Task Force appointed to study the redevelopment of the west side of downtown Desert Park.

Under the plan, the mayor will issue a Request for Proposals (RFP) through the Department of City Planning that will look for a private development partner. The selected partner will work with the City to develop a financing plan for the project.

The Department of Engineering and Construction has already begun to draft a major infrastructure investment project on Central Avenue, with particular focus on the intersecting streets of Mesa Drive and Town Lake Avenue. This plan was presented at last month's City Council meeting.

The mayor stated that he has spent the

past weeks carefully reviewing the plan and is pleased with the new blueprint for investment in the west side. The mayor further stated that invigorating the west side retail corridor remains

one of our most critical challenges.

"I am confident that we can come together as a community to develop fiscal recommendations that will allow

Desert Park to grow and prosper well into the future" said the mayor. "I look forward to working with the Task Force and our development partners."

The West Side Redevelopment Authority will expand the façade grant program, and will create new loan programs to allow existing buildings and tenants to make improvements to their businesses. The grant program will also attract new businesses to the corridor, and provide for some financial assistance to start-up companies.

Of note is the new Convention Center, which is the latest in a series of cultural, recreational and commercial assets that have been added to the west side in the last few years.

Figure 2.49D

1. Start Publisher, navigate to your student files, and open the publication *2D_CityNewsBrief*. View the Footer frame and type `Firstname Lastname-2D City News Brief`

2. Close the Header and Footer toolbar, which will close the Master page and return you to the publication. The publication zooms to 100%. On the Standard toolbar, click the Print button to print a copy of the newsletter for your reference as you work through the publication. Four pages will print.

3. On the menu bar, click File, click Save As, navigate to the location in which you are storing your files for this Lesson, and in the File name box type `Firstname Lastname-2D City News Brief`

   In the Save As dialog box, click the Save button.

4. On the Standard toolbar, click the Zoom Out button once to zoom to 75%, and then scroll to position page 1 in the middle of your screen. On the left side of page 1, click the Newsletter Title placeholder text. On the Formatting toolbar click the Center button, and then type `City News Brief`

5. Scroll to position the top of page 1 on your screen. Click to select the Lead Story Headline placeholder text and type `Siren Noise A Concern`

6. Click anywhere in the first text box beneath the Lead Story Headline that you just typed. The placeholder text is selected. Click the Go to Next Frame button to select the second frame, and then click its Go to Next Frame button to select the third text box. Notice that because there is no Go to Next Frame button at the bottom of the third frame, this is the final text box in the story chain. Click again in the first text box.

7. With the placeholder text selected, move to the menu bar, click Insert, and then click Text File. Navigate to the student files that accompany this textbook, click *2D_SirenNoiseText*, and click OK to insert the text into the publication. The template upon which this newsletter was based uses a font size of 9.5. Use (Ctrl) + (A) to select all the text in the story, and change the font size to 10. Click in the scratch area to cancel the selection and view your changes and then click Save to save your changes.

8. In the middle of page 1, click the Secondary Story Headline, and type `New Museum Location`

9. Click to select the placeholder text in the three text boxes beneath the headline you just typed. With the mouse pointer positioned anywhere over the selected text, right-click to display the shortcut menu, point to Change Text and then click Text File. Insert the text file *2D_MuseumText*.

10. The inserted text is larger than the story chain. To have Publisher assist you in finding another location for the remaining text, click Yes to use autoflow. Publisher selects the next available empty story chain, which is at the top of page 2. Click No to reject this suggestion and to have Publisher seek the next available story chain. Click Yes to select the story chain in the middle of page 2.

11. Navigate to page 1. Click in the first text box of the Museum story, and then use (Ctrl) + (A) to select all the text in the story. The continuation of the story on page 2 will also be selected, because Publisher has automatically connected the frames. On the Formatting toolbar, click the Font Size arrow and change the font size to 10. Because the continued text on page 2 is connected to the story chain, it is also changed to font size 10.

12. On page 1, click anywhere in the third frame of the Museum story. Right-click to display the shortcut menu, click Format Text Box, and then click the Text Box tab. At the bottom of the dialog box, click the Include "Continued on page" check box, and then click OK.

13. On page 2, scroll to the left as necessary and then click in the first frame of the Museum continuation. (Because the Two-Page Spread is active, you might have to scroll to the left to view the Museum frames.) On the menu bar, click Format, and then click Text Box. Click the Text Box tab, and at the bottom, click the *third* check box Include "Continued from page." Click OK to close the dialog box.

14. To the right, click to select the text box containing the pull quote. Position the mouse pointer over the edge of the selected pull quote until you see the Move pointer, and then

move the pull quote into the third text box. Use your eye to center it vertically and horizontally in the frame. The text of the story now ends in the second continuation frame. Click to select the placeholder text in the headline above the story continuation and type `Museum, continued`

15. If the Web site name at the end of the story is flagged with a wavy red line, right-click on it and then click Ignore All. The red lines will not print, but sometimes it is distracting to see them. Click to select the placeholder text in the pull quote and type, including the quotation marks:
`"The space was specially designed with our collection in mind."`
`Elizabeth Viejo, Curator`

16. Click the Save button to save your changes. At the top of page 2, click the headline above the computer picture, and type `Non-Profits Get IT Assistance`

17. In the story chain below the heading you just typed, insert the text file *2D_ITResourceCenterText*. Click Yes to use autoflow to flow the text, and then click No three times until you can click Yes to flow into the story chain at the bottom of page 3, which contains a picture of a computer connector plug.

18. Click in any of the story's frames, and then select all the text in the story. Change the font size to 10. If necessary, remove the red wavy line from the end of the story by right-clicking and then clicking Ignore All. Replace the headline above the story continuation with `Non-Profits, continued`

19. On page 2 and page 3, use the Text Box tab of the Format Text Box dialog box to insert appropriate "Continued on page" and "Continued from page" notices for the Non-Profits story. Look at the first frame of this story on page 2 and notice that in both the first and second paragraphs, three consecutive lines are hyphenated. To remove hyphenation from this story, click anywhere in the story, move to the menu bar, click Tools, click Language, click Hyphenation, and then click to remove the check mark from the Automatically hyphenate this story check box. Click OK and then click Save to save your changes.

20. Scroll to the bottom story chain on page 2. Select the placeholder text, and insert the file *2D_LawLibraryText*. Change the font size to 10. Change the headline to `Anyone Can Use the Law Library!`

21. Scroll to the top of page 3. Select the placeholder text surrounding the picture of the teenagers working, and insert the file *2D_YouthText*. Change the font size to 10. Change the headline to `New Youth Program`

22. Click Save. On page 3, scroll to view the middle story chain. Insert the text file *2D_CityClerkText*. Click No, which instead of using autoflow, will place the extra text in the overflow area. Recall that you cannot view the text in overflow, but the "A" at the bottom of the last frame indicates that some text is being held in the overflow area. Rather than deleting any of the text, click on the frame edge of the pull quote to select it. If necessary, click again so that the sizing handles surround the frame. Press the Del key on your keyboard. Change the font size of the story to 10. Without the pull quote text frame, there is adequate space to accommodate the text. At the bottom of the first column, click in front of the word "Ordinances" and press ↵Enter once. Adding a blank line here arranges the two columns in a more logical manner. These are the kinds of adjustments you can make as you edit your newsletter. Change the story's headline to `Look Up A Law`

23. Click Save. Navigate to page 4. For the Back Page Story, insert the text file *2D_WestSideText* and change the font size of the story to 10. Change the headline to `West Side Development Plans Announced`

24. There is some additional text that needs to be added to the story, and notice that there is space available to do so. Click anywhere in the story, move to the menu bar, and click Edit, and then click Edit Story in Microsoft Word. In the 12th line, click in front of the line beginning "The West Side Redevelopment Authority" and then type the following making sure that you end your typing by pressing ↵Enter.
`"I am confident that we can come together as a community to develop fiscal recommendations that will allow Desert Park to grow and`

prosper well into the future" said the mayor. "I look forward to working with the Task Force and our development partners."

On the menu bar, click File, and then click Close and Return.

25. In the last column of the Back Page Story, three lines in a row contain hyphenation. Also, there is still space in the column to expand the text slightly. On the menu bar, click Tools, click Language, click Hyphenation, and then remove the check mark to turn off automatic hyphenation.

26. Save your changes. Navigate to page 1, scroll to the bottom of the page, and select the first occurrence of the text "Inside Story." You might want to zoom up to make it easier to see. Fill in the information as follows, and change the page numbers as necessary. You can use `Tab⇆` to move from field to field.

Non-Profits Get IT Assistance (page 2)

Anyone Can Use the Law Library (page 2)

New Youth Program (page 3)

Look Up A Law (page 3)

West Side Development Plans Announced (page 4)

27. To the right, click anywhere in the bulleted text. All of the bulleted text is selected. Type the following, and notice that each time you press `⏎Enter`, a new bulleted line is added.

New museum location enhances visitor experience

Desert Park teens will benefit from new program

Your non-profit organization can get computer help!

West side will be focus of new development

28. On the menu bar, click the Save button to save your changes. On the Standard toolbar, click the Print Preview button, and use the Multiple Pages button (use a 2×2 view) to view the four pages. Then, on the Print Preview toolbar, click the Print button to print one complete copy of your publication.

29. Close the Print Preview. On the menu bar click File, and then click Close. If necessary, click Yes to save any additional changes. Publication 2D is complete!

Publication 2E

Concert Program

In the following Performance Assessment, you will edit a program for an outdoor concert at the Desert Park Botanical Garden. Your completed publication will look like the one shown in Figure 2.50. You will save your publication as *Firstname Lastname-2E Concert Program*.

Special Thanks

Programming	Fred Molinaro, Professor of Music
Programming	Carmen Lear, Professor of Music
Staging	Bernice Gilels, Professor of Fine Arts
Staging	Colin James, Symphony Hall Director

Sponsors

♪ *Desert Park Community College Board of Trustees*

♪ *Desert Park Symphony Orchestra Board of Directors*

♪ *Desert Park University Board of Regents*

♪ *Music Store of Desert Park*

♪ *Desert Park Gas and Electric*

♪ *Health Partners of the Desert*

♪ *Friends of the Botanical Garden*

Outdoor Concert Series

Fall Concert in the Botanical Garden

Date: September 31
Time: 7 p.m.

Student Name-2E Concert Program

Figure 2.50A

Tonight's Program

Under the direction of
Dr. Fred Molinaro, Professor of Music

◆

Program Part One

Sonatina for Guitar, Jorge Morel composer

Piano Sonata in A Op 1/2, John Field composer

15 Minute Intermission

Program Part Two

Suite Italienne, Igor Stravinsky composer

String Quartet No. 2 in G Op 18 No. 2, Ludwig Van Beethoven composer

15 Minute Intermission

Program Part Three

Piano Trio No. 45 in E-Flat, Franz Joseph Haydn composer

Brandenburg Concerto No. 3 in G, Johann Sebastian Bach composer

The Performers

Part One *Peter Tallis, Guitar*

Part One *Vivian Emerson, Piano*

Part Two *Hoa Pham, Violin and Chun Xie, Piano*

Part Two *Mario Rios, Dee Ford, Sung Lee, Ed Amit*

Part Three *Rose Horn, Dave Bronson, Austin Stroup*

Part Three *Desert Park University Orchestra*

About the Series

Classical music is alive and well in Desert Park! Since 1986, the Desert Park Botanical Garden Outdoor Concert Series has presented over 600 high-quality events to audiences from Desert Park and from around the nation. With steady growth, the series has become a major public-private coalition of organizations.

The series started with an idea of a group of music faculty members at Desert Park University and Desert Park Community College. During its history, the series has never compromised its level of world-class excellence, bringing to its audiences a mix of well-known and up-and-coming performers.

Please feel free to bring your picnic supper to enjoy in the Garden before the performance begins. Many of our attendees love to bring their bright table linens and vases of fresh flowers to accompany their picnics. (Due to fire danger, please no candles.)

Student Name-2E Concert Program

Figure 2.50B

1. Start Publisher. From your student files, open Publication *2E_ConcertProgram*. In the same manner as you have done in previous publications, insert a footer with your first and last name and the file name. Save the file using your first and last name and the file name. Print a copy of the program for your reference as you work through the program. Fold the two pages into a program booklet, and be sure that "Program Title" displays on the front cover.

2. Zoom the publication to 75%. On page 1, select the text "City of Desert Park" and replace it with `Outdoor Concert Series`

3. In this frame, change the font to Eras Medium ITC, and use Best Fit to adjust the font size. In the Format Text Box dialog box, use the Line commands to place a 3 pt border line around the frame using the 7th color block displayed from the Line color arrow—a brown rust color. Use the Fill commands to apply a solid fill color to the text box as follows: After clicking the Fill color arrow, click More Colors, and then click the Standard tab to display the color honeycomb. Locate the center white hexagon in the honeycomb and then click the hexagon one row down and to the left—a vanilla color.

4. In the text box containing "Program Title," replace the text with `Fall Concert in the Botanical Garden`

5. Change the font to Eras Medium ITC, and then apply the same border and fill as the text box above. Change the date to `September 31` and change the time to `7 p.m.` Change all the date and time text to the Eras Medium ITC font and apply Bold.

6. Save your changes. Navigate to page 2, and notice that the Two-Page Spread is active. At the top of page 2, select the text box containing "Tonight's Program" and change the font to Eras Medium ITC and use Best Fit to change the font size to fill the frame.

7. Select the text box containing "Program Part One" and change the font to Eras Medium ITC. Apply the Stationery texture as a fill effect. Repeat this formatting for the "Part Two" and "Part Three" text boxes. Under each Program Part, select the text for the two musical pieces and change the font to Bodini MT, and the font size to 10. Change each occurrence of "15 Minute Intermission" to Bodini MT.

8. Save your changes. At the lower portion of page 2, select "The Performers" text, change the font to Eras Medium ITC, and use Best Fit to adjust the font size. Change the text of the performer's names and instruments to Bodini MT. (Hint: You can drag down to select the entire group and format them all at once.)

9. Save your changes. Navigate to page 3. Select the text "Heading" and type About the Series

10. Change the font of the heading to Eras Medium ITC and use Best Fit to adjust the font size. Click on the musical note graphic and delete it. Click in the text box containing the Latin placeholder text, and insert the file *2E_ConcertText*. Remove automatic hyphenation from this text box. To this text box, apply the Music Notes BorderArt border. Change the font of the inserted text to Eras Medium ITC and use Best Fit to adjust the font size to fill the frame. At the end of the 9th line of text, click in front of "The" and press ↵Enter once to create a new paragraph. Center the text in the frame vertically.

11. Save your changes. Navigate to page 4. Select "Special Thanks" and change the font to Eras Medium ITC, then use Best Fit to adjust the font size. Select the names of the individuals in the list below and change the font to Bodini MT. (Hint: You can drag down and select the entire group.)

12. At the bottom of page 4, change "Sponsors" to Eras Medium ITC and use Best Fit to adjust the font size. Drag to select the list of sponsors, and apply a musical note bullet (you can find a music note in the Webdings character set, 9th row, last column) to each of the names. Change the font size of the sponsors to 12 and apply Bodini MT font.

13. Save your changes. Use Print Preview to view the overall look of your publication. Then print the publication, close the Print Preview, and close the publication. Publication 2E is complete!

Publication 2F

Mayor News

In the following Performance Assessment, you will edit a newsletter published by the Mayor's Office in Desert Park. Your completed publication will look similar to the one shown in Figure 2.51. You will save your publication as *Firstname Lastname-2F Mayor News*.

Figure 2.51A

CITY OF DESERT PARK

Mayor's Office News

Volume 5, Issue 1   **Spring**

Special points of interest:

- Public comment encouraged at Council Workshop
- Have a party in your neighborhood!
- Drink the water
- Watch City Council meetings on TV
- City internships available for college students

Inside this issue:

City Council Workshop Planned

Citizens are invited to attend a City Council workshop on September 10 to discuss the City's Strategic Five-Year Plan. The workshop will take place at 2 p.m. in the City Council Chambers at City Hall.

The workshop is an opportunity for the Council to receive an update on the "City of Neighborhoods" plan and to hear public comment. Citizens are encouraged to attend. Additional discussion will be held on the draft of a citizen committee document for this project. No formal action will be taken at the workshop.

The Strategic Five-Year Plan is the first step in updating the City's General Plan. A "City of Neighborhoods" strategy addresses our City's quality of life in light of our increasing population. The proposal builds upon our existing neighborhoods by creating a network of vibrant neighborhood centers, served by a world-class transit system, and linked by bike paths.

Guided by a 30-person citizen's committee, the City of Neighborhoods strategy is the product of an intensive three-year public involvement effort that has engaged citizens and City officials in a dialogue about our city's future each step of the way. Five phases of public outreach have included over 200 meetings and hundreds of residents in the decision making process.

New City Council Committees Announced

The Office of the City Clerk has announced that the City Council committees have been restructured. The restructuring follows several months of meetings with citizens and City employees to determine how best the Council can be organized to serve Desert Park residents.

The new committee names are listed below. Visit the city's Web site to view the committee heads, members, and agendas.

- Aviation
- Finance and Audit
- Legislative, Rules and Ethics
- Neighborhood Development
- Operations
- Planning, Zoning and Economic Development
- Housing and Development

Student Name-2F Mayor News

Figure 2.51A

Figure 2.51B

Block Clubs Prepare for Annual Party Night

Friday, September 28 is designated as the Annual Party Night for all neighborhood Block Clubs in Desert Park. Block Clubs are groups of neighbors who get out and get acquainted, who watch out for each other, and keep an eye on the neighborhood. Any neighborhood club that would like to close a street in their neighborhood for the purpose of a neighborhood party can call the Desert Park Police Department for assistance. An officer will be assigned to your party and will assist with traffic flow, barricade setup, and perhaps even grilling a few hot dogs! The officer will also provide any necessary city permits—one call does it all.

(Continued on page 3)

Storm Water Pollution Prevention Program

The City strives to protect the water quality of the lakes, rivers, and creeks.

Residents can visit the City's Web site to view the Urban Runoff Management Plan. The Plan details the City's action to protect and improve water quality of the lakes, rivers, and creeks in the region, and achieve compliance with the State Municipal Storm Water Permit. The Urban Runoff Management Plan has been posted to allow public access and understanding of the overall efforts of the City Manager's office to improve water quality in the City of Desert Park. Implementing the plan is one of the six objectives of the City's Storm Water Pollution Prevention Program to help improve water quality. The City Council approved the plan last January, and is effective through February of 2006. At the City's Web site, click on "City Services," and choose "Storm Water Pollution Prevention."

Water Quality Analysis

Regulations from the State Public Health Services Drinking Water Program and the Environmental Protection Agency (EPA) require all community water systems to deliver an annual Consumer Confidence Report (water quality report) to customers. The City of Desert Park Water Bureau began sending this information to all postal customers in 1996, before these regulations went into effect in 1999.

The most interesting information for most consumers is this: our drinking water supply continues to meet all state and federal regulations, without exception. This report includes other information of interest to many consumers: water quality test results; definitions; information on our sources of water supply; how to reduce exposure to lead in drinking water; and special notice for immuno-compromised persons. Copies of the report may also be ordered in Braille by calling the City Manager's office at 626-555-1234.

Student Name-2F Mayor News

Figure 2.51B

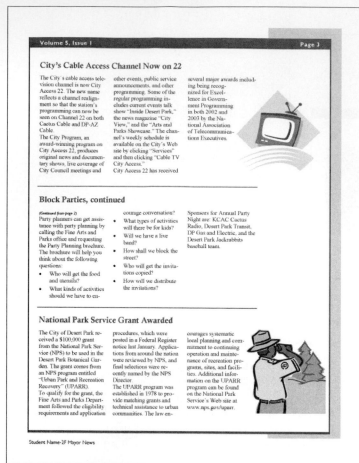

Figure 2.51C

Figure 2.51D

1. Start Publisher. From your student files, open the publication *2F_MayorNews*. In the same manner as you have done in previous publications, insert a footer with your first and last name and the file name. Save the file using your first and last name and the file name. Print a copy of the newsletter for your reference as you work through the newsletter. Four pages will print.

2. Zoom the publication to 75%. On page 1, type the newsletter title as Mayor's Office News

3. For the Lead Story Headline, type City Council Workshop Planned

4. In the story's frames, replace the placeholder text with the file *2F_CityCouncilText*. Select the text in the story, and change the font size to 10.

5. At the bottom of page 1, type the headline New City Council Committees Announced

6. Replace the story's placeholder text with file *2F_CommitteeText*. Change the font size to 10. Drag to select all the text after the word "agendas." To the selected text, apply bullets, using a small round bullet—normally found as one offered in the dialog box. With the bulleted text selected, apply line spacing of 2 pt before paragraphs.

7. Click the Save button on the Standard toolbar to save your changes. Navigate to and scroll as necessary to view the top of page 2. Type the headline Block Clubs Prepare for Annual Party Night

8. In the story frames, insert the file *2F_BlockClubsText*. Click Yes to use autoflow, click No three times to reject Publisher's suggested locations, and then click Yes to flow the remainder of the story to the middle story chain on page 3. Select all of the text in the story chain, and change the font size to 10.

9. Insert appropriate Continued on and Continued from notices. In the continuation of the story on page 3, change the headline to Block Parties, continued and then select the text that comprises the questions you should think about. Format the questions with a simple bullet of your choice. To the bulleted list, add spacing before paragraphs of 2 pt. At the bottom of the next-to-last frame, click in front of the word "Sponsors" and press ⏎Enter once to move the entire paragraph to the last frame. To the right, delete the pull quote text and its frame.

10. Save your changes. Navigate to the middle of page 2. In the story chain next to the fish picture, insert the file *2F_StormWaterText*, and change the font size to 10. Change the headline to Storm Water Pollution Prevention Program

11. Insert the following text into the pull quote: The City strives to protect the water quality of the lakes, rivers, and creeks.

12. In the story chain at the bottom of page 2, insert the text file *2F_WaterQuality Text*. Change the font size to 10. Insert the headline Water Quality Analysis

13. Save your changes. Navigate to the top of page 3, and in the story chain containing the TV set graphic, insert the text file *2F_CableAccessText*. Insert the headline City's Cable Access Channel Now on 22 and then change the font size in the story to 10.

14. Navigate to the bottom of page 3, and in the story chain, insert the file *2F_NPSGrantText*. The text fits into the frames. Change the font size to 10, and then click in the third frame. The "A" at the bottom of the frame indicates that changing the font size to 10 has forced some of the text into the overflow area. Edit the story in Microsoft Word, and delete the second paragraph (lines 4-5), which begins "UPARR grants can be used." Return to the publication. Insert the headline National Park Service Grant Awarded

15. Save your changes. Navigate to page 4. As the Back Page Story headline, type City Internship Program Seeking Applicants
In the story chain, insert the file *2F_InternshipText*. The text fits the story chain. Select all of the text and change the font size to 10. Click in the last frame. Changing the font size to 10 has caused some of the text to go into the overflow area. Use Ctrl + A to select all of the text in the story. In the Font Size box, click to select "10," type 9.5 and then press ⏎Enter. This will shrink the text slightly to make it fit into the story chain. Although good design technique suggests that all text within the newsletter should be the same size, sometimes a

design decision like this must be made. Additionally, because this story is on a page by itself, it is unlikely that the reader will notice this slight reduction in the font size. Of course, you could also delete some of the text, or reduce the size of the picture. Right-click on the two misspelled words in the story, and select the correct spelling.

16. Navigate to page 1. Fill in the "Special points of interest" section as follows:

```
Public comment encouraged at Council Workshop
Have a party in your neighborhood!
Drink the water
Watch City Council meetings on TV
City internships available for college students
```

17. Fill in the "Inside this issue" section as follows, using `Tab⇆` to move from field to field.

```
Block Clubs Prepare for Annual Party Night (page 2)
Storm Water Pollution Prevention Program (page 2)
Water Quality Analysis (page 2)
City's Cable Access Channel Now 22 (page 3)
National Park Service Grant Awarded (page 3)
City Internship Program Seeking Applicants (page 4)
```

18. Save your changes. View the newsletter in Print Preview, and then print one complete copy. Close the publication. Publication 2F is complete!

On the Internet

You can get a lot of additional information about using Microsoft Publisher 2002 by visiting the product's official Web site at www.microsoft.com/office/publisher.

Here you will find an Assistance Center with "Tips and Tricks for Publisher 2002." The site also has examples of publications and updates to the software. Plan to visit the site often if your organization uses Publisher frequently. You won't want to miss the important new information here!

Working With Graphics in a Publication

Objectives

In this lesson, you learn how to:

- ✔ Use Rulers, Guides, and Toolbars to Create Lines and Circles
- ✔ Create Ruler Guides
- ✔ Insert and Format AutoShapes
- ✔ Group, Ungroup, and Flip Objects
- ✔ Add Text to a Shape
- ✔ Rotate and Nudge an Object
- ✔ Create and Format WordArt
- ✔ Use a Wizard to Create a Brochure
- ✔ Insert and Format Pictures in a Publication
- ✔ Combine Text with Graphics
- ✔ Recolor Graphics

Key terms in this Lesson include

- ❑ adjustment handle
- ❑ aspect ratio
- ❑ AutoShapes
- ❑ bitmaps
- ❑ brochure
- ❑ caption
- ❑ clip art
- ❑ cropping handles
- ❑ cropping pointer
- ❑ crosshair pointer
- ❑ dingbats
- ❑ docked
- ❑ drop cap
- ❑ grayed out
- ❑ grouping
- ❑ gutters
- ❑ jpeg
- ❑ layout guides
- ❑ nudge
- ❑ object
- ❑ pixels
- ❑ raster objects
- ❑ rotation handle
- ❑ ruler guide
- ❑ text juxtaposition
- ❑ vector objects
- ❑ wrapping

Publication Design Tips—Graphics in a Publication

Desktop publishing is concerned with the layout of text and graphics on a page. Although approximately 80 percent of your publication's message is delivered in words (text), it is the **graphics** that catch the reader's attention. A graphic is anything on the page that is not text. Graphics include a wide variety of visual elements—for example, photographs, drawings, illustrations, maps, diagrams, and charts. Graphics also encompass other types of visual elements on the page, such as lines, boxes, shapes, frames, borders, and **dingbats**. A dingbat is a small typographical symbol or ornament used to embellish a printed page, often at the start and end of chapters in a book.

When placing graphics on a page, consider basic design principles so that the graphics work toward your main objective—getting people to read your publications. Appropriate use of design principles, such as **text juxtaposition** (the relationship of graphics to the surrounding text) and **layout** (the size, number, and placement of graphics on a page), is key to the success of your publication. One of the primary advantages to using Publisher's pre-designed templates for your publications is that professionals have thoughtfully created the designs.

There are a number of ways to find graphics for your publications. Publisher provides tools with which you can create graphic elements, such as lines, circles, boxes, and shapes. You can insert graphic elements provided to you from Microsoft, either from the installed software or from Microsoft's Web site called **Design Gallery Live**. You can acquire, for free or for a fee, visual elements from other organizations. Finally, you can create your own images with a digital camera or with graphic editing software, such as Microsoft Visio, Microsoft MapPoint, Adobe Illustrator, and Adobe Photoshop.

The electronic files that contain your graphic elements fall into two broad categories—**vector objects** and **raster objects**. Vector files contain a mathematical description about how to form the lines, shape, and fill of the graphic. Raster objects (also called **bitmaps**), on the other hand, are patterns made up of thousands of dots called **pixels**. Pixel is a shortened version of the words "picture element."

Publisher comes with a set of ready-made vector files called **AutoShapes**. The collection of AutoShapes includes basic shapes, such as rectangles and circles, plus a variety of lines and connectors, block arrows, flowchart symbols, stars, and banners. Other vector files can be created with drawing or illustration programs, such as Adobe Illustrator, Macromedia FreeHand, and Micrografx Designer. The file extensions for such files are often .eps or .epfs, a file format based on the programming language used by laser printers. Another common vector file extension is .wmf, which is the Microsoft Windows Metafile format. Vector files retain a crisp and clear representation on the page when they are enlarged.

Bitmaps are best for realistic images such as a photograph. The pixels in a bitmap can be black and white, shades of gray, or of varying colors. Your digital camera can be used to capture a bitmap image, or you can create them in paint programs (also called image editing programs), such as Adobe Photoshop and MacromediaxRes. Among the common file extensions for bitmap files are .bmp, .gif, .jpeg, .tif, and .png. Unlike vector images, if bitmap images are enlarged too much, they start to become fuzzy. Bitmap images have a fixed number of pixels, and enlarging a bitmap spreads the pixels further apart. The added white space between the pixels can cause the image to look fuzzy and blurred.

Publication 3A

Trail Announcement

In Activities 3.1–3.9 you will create an announcement for the City of Desert Park's new program to expand the Agave Trail. Your publication will look like Figure 3.1. You will save your publication as *Firstname Lastname-3A Trail Announcement.*

Student Name-3A Trail Announcement

Figure 3.1

Objective 1: Use Rulers, Guides, and Toolbars to Create Lines and Circles

Everything in a publication is an *object*. Recall that an object is any element that can be selected; for example, a graphic frame or text frame. In Publisher, text must be placed inside of a text box (also called a text frame), which is also a type of object. Various graphic objects can be inserted into Publisher, such as a picture, a table, a line, a shape, or *WordArt*. WordArt is an application within Microsoft Office XP that transforms text into a stylized graphic object.

Objects have the following common characteristics:

- ▶ An object can be selected—when you click on an object it displays a frame border and selection handles.
- ▶ An object can be resized and moved.
- ▶ An object can be deleted.
- ▶ An object can be layered in front of, or behind, other objects.
- ▶ An object can *snap to* (automatically line up with guides and other objects).
- ▶ An object can have text wrap around it.

Because the purpose of Publisher is to arrange objects—either text box objects or graphic objects—on a page, various tools are provided to assist you in doing so. Visual guides and measuring tools within Publisher assist you in the precise placement of objects on the page.

Activity 3.1   Selecting Layouts and Color Schemes

❶ **Start** Publisher and display the New Publication task pane. Under Start from a design, be sure that By Publication Type is displayed and, if necessary, click Quick Publications.

The Quick Publications Gallery is displayed.

❷ In the Quick Publications gallery, scroll down, and then click **Blank Quick Publication**.

Activity 3.2   Drawing and Formatting Lines

The pink lines represent the page margins. The blue lines indicate where you should align objects so that you are assured they will not fall outside the margins—they create a safety zone for the margins. Layout guides do not print, they display only on the screen.

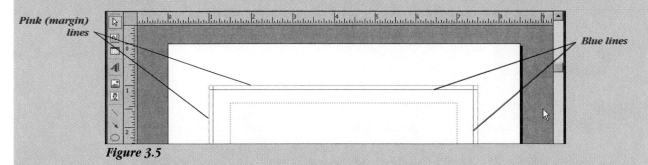

Pink (margin) lines

Blue lines

Figure 3.5

2 At the left side of the Publisher window, locate the Objects toolbar (see Figure 3.6). The Objects toolbar contains the tools you need to get graphic objects and text boxes into your publication by either importing them or creating them yourself. Take a moment to point to each button on the toolbar to view its ScreenTip.

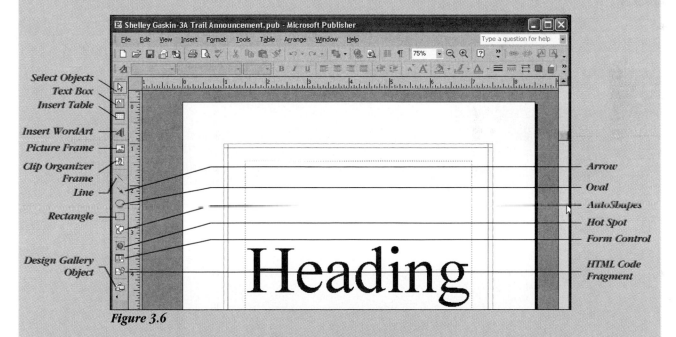

Select Objects
Text Box
Insert Table

Insert WordArt
Picture Frame
Clip Organizer Frame
Line

Rectangle

Design Gallery Object

Arrow
Oval
AutoShapes
Hot Spot
Form Control

HTML Code Fragment

Figure 3.6

3 To the immediate right of the Objects toolbar, position your mouse pointer in the vertical ruler until the double-headed arrow and the ScreenTip "Move Vertical Ruler" display. Hold down the left mouse button, drag the vertical ruler to the right until it is aligned with the first pink dotted line (see Figure 3.7), and then release the left mouse button. Look at the ruler you moved and notice that the horizontal ⇔ pink line is exactly 1 inch from the top edge of the paper.

(Continues)

Activity 3.2   Drawing and Formatting Lines (continued)

When placing objects on a page, sometimes it is convenient to have the ruler close by.

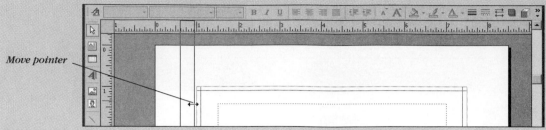

Move pointer

Figure 3.7

4 On the Objects toolbar, click the **Line** button, and then move your mouse pointer into the publication window.

Notice that the pointer is in the shape of a plus sign. This is called the ***crosshair pointer***.

5 Position the crosshair pointer on the left blue dotted guide, at **1.5 inches on the vertical ruler** as shown in Figure 3.8.

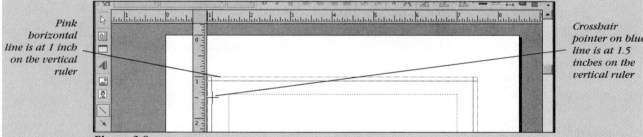

Pink horizontal line is at 1 inch on the vertical ruler

Crosshair pointer on blue line is at 1.5 inches on the vertical ruler

Figure 3.8

6 Press and hold down the (⬆Shift) key, hold down the left mouse button and drag across the page to the blue guide on the right, and then release the mouse button and the (⬆Shift) key.

Holding down the (⬆Shift) key while dragging ensures that you will draw a perfectly straight, not jagged, line. Releasing the mouse button before the (⬆Shift) key ensures that the line remains straight and will not revert to a jagged line. If you are not satisfied with your results, click Undo on the toolbar and begin again.

7 Make sure that the line you just drew displays sizing handles at each end indicating that it is selected (if necessary, click the line to select it). On the menu bar, click **Format**, and then click **AutoShape**.

The Format AutoShape dialog box displays. Publisher considers a line to be an AutoShape for formatting purposes. Recall that an object has two parts—its outside line and its fill area. In this case, however, notice that under the Fill portion of the dialog box, the arrows are ***grayed out*** (unavailable) because a line does not have an inside fill area.

8 Under Line, click the **Color arrow**, and then click the second color block (brown) in the color scheme. Click the **Style arrow**, click the **6 pt** solid line, and then click **OK** to close the dialog box.

The line you created is now a little larger and colored brown.

Activity 3.2   Drawing and Formatting Lines

9 Scroll to view the bottom of the page. On the Objects toolbar, click to select the **Line** tool. Position the crosshair pointer on the left blue guide at **9.5 inches on the vertical ruler**, hold down ◆Shift), and then drag to draw a straight line to the right blue line.

10 With the line selected, move to the Formatting toolbar and click the **Line/Border Style** button as shown in Figure 3.9.

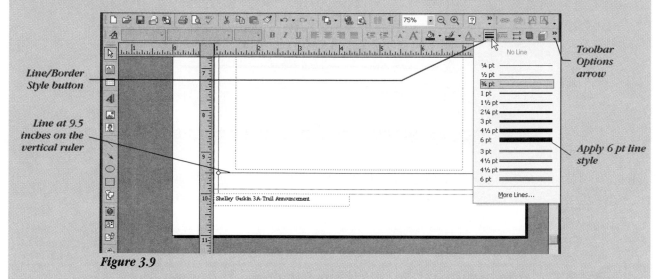

Line/Border Style button

Line at 9.5 inches on the vertical ruler

Toolbar Options arrow

Apply 6 pt line style

Figure 3.9

? Does your screen differ?

If you do not see the Line/Border Style button on your Formatting toolbar, you may have to add it to the toolbar by clicking the Toolbar Options arrow, clicking the Add or Remove Buttons command, and then clicking to place a check mark next to the Line/Border Style button.

11 On the displayed menu, click **6 pt** solid line. On the Formatting toolbar, locate the Line Color button, click the **Line Color arrow** on the button, and then click the second color block (brown). See Figure 3.10.

Recall that toolbar buttons are a one-click method for initiating a command that would otherwise be accomplished from the menu bar and a dialog box. The advantage to using the dialog box is that you can apply more than one command at a time. In the previous step, it was necessary to click two different buttons to achieve the desired effect. Whether you use a dialog box or buttons on a toolbar is a matter of personal preference. Most people use whatever method seems convenient and efficient at the time.

(Continues)

Activity 3.2   Drawing and Formatting Lines (continued)

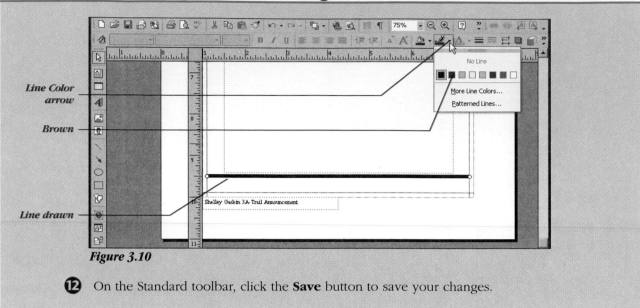

Figure 3.10

⓬   On the Standard toolbar, click the **Save** button to save your changes.

Activity 3.3   Drawing and Formatting Circles

❶   Scroll to view the top portion of the publication. Using the technique you learned in the previous activity, drag the horizontal ruler down and align it with the top pink guide as shown in Figure 3.11.

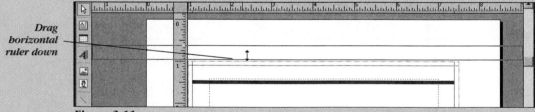

Figure 3.11

❷   Scrolling as necessary, click anywhere in the word "Heading" to select the text frame. Use the upper middle sizing handle to drag the top edge of the frame down to **4 inches on the vertical ruler** (see Figure 3.12).

The word "Heading" aligns at the left.

Activity 3.3   Drawing and Formatting Circles

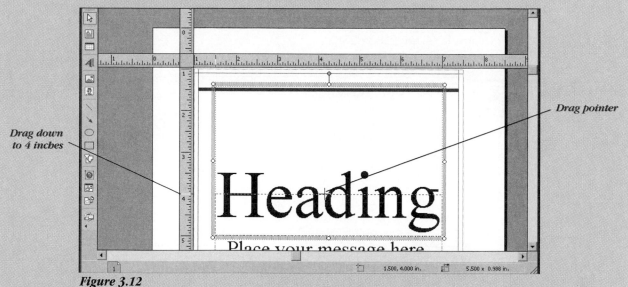

Drag down to 4 inches

Drag pointer

Figure 3.12

❸ On the Objects toolbar, click the **Line** button, and then on the Objects toolbar, click the **Line** button again.

This is a convenient method for "putting back" a tool you no longer want.

❹ On the Objects toolbar, click the **Oval** button, and then using the nearby rulers as your guide, position the crosshair pointer at **1.5 inches on the horizontal ruler** and at **1.25 inches on the vertical ruler** as shown in Figure 3.13.

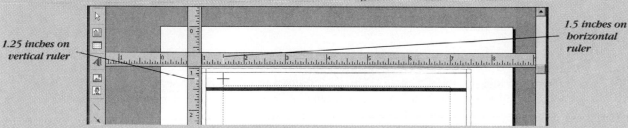

1.25 inches on vertical ruler

1.5 inches on horizontal ruler

Figure 3.13

❺ Hold down the ⬆Shift key and drag the pointer to **2 inches on the horizontal ruler** and **1.75 inches on the vertical ruler** (see Figure 3.14), and then release the left mouse button and ⬆Shift.

Notice that you have created a circle instead of an oval. Holding down the ⬆Shift key while using the Oval tool ensures a perfectly round shape in the same way that holding down the ⬆Shift key while using the Line tool ensures a perfectly straight line.

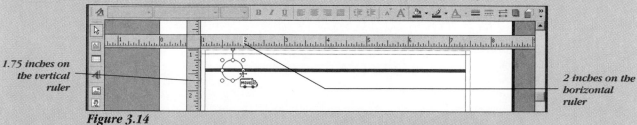

1.75 inches on the vertical ruler

2 inches on the horizontal ruler

Figure 3.14

(Continues)

Activity 3.3   Drawing and Formatting Circles (continued)

6 Position your mouse pointer over the selected circle and double-click.

The Format AutoShape dialog box displays.

 Does your screen differ?

Double-clicking takes a steady hand. It is not the speed of the two clicks that is important, but rather that the mouse remains in the same place between the two clicks. If you have difficulty double-clicking, and many people do, you can right-click to select the object and open the shortcut menu. Click Format AutoShape to open the Format AutoShape dialog box. You might be a good candidate for one of the mouse devices that has an extra button that performs a double-click with just a single click!

7 Under Fill, click the **Color arrow**, and then click the second color block (brown). Notice that under Line, a .75 pt solid black line is automatically applied to the shape.

Recall that an object has two parts—its fill (inside) and its line (outside). Publisher automatically applies a .75 pt solid black line to all shapes, but you can change the size and color of the line, or choose to have no line at all.

8 Click the **Size tab**, and be sure that both the Height and Width of the selected circle is 0.5". If it is not, type or use the spin box arrows to modify the settings.

9 Click **OK** to close the dialog box. Move your mouse pointer away from the selected circle, right-click to display a shortcut menu, point to **Toolbars**, and then click **Measurement**.

The Measurement toolbar displays as a floating toolbar; floating means that it is not **docked** to (aligned with) any other toolbars at the edge of the screen. The top portion of the Measurement toolbar displays the measurements of any selected object. The bottom portion of the Measurement toolbar displays the measurements of selected text, which will be discussed in a subsequent Lesson.

10 If necessary, drag the floating toolbar away from the circle, and then click to select the **circle**. On the Measurement toolbar, point to the spin box to the right of the **x** until the ScreenTip "Horizontal Position" displays. The x is used to denote a horizontal position on a line, like the x-axis of a graph. See Figure 3.15.

Activity 3.3   Drawing and Formatting Circles

The Measurement toolbar displays all of the selected circle's measurements. The brown circle object begins at 1.5 inches from the left edge of the paper.

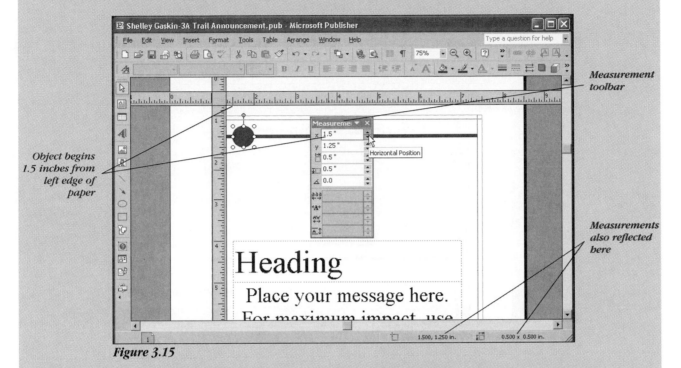

Object begins 1.5 inches from left edge of paper

Measurement toolbar

Measurements also reflected here

Figure 3.15

11 On the Measurement toolbar, point to the spin box to the right of the **y** until the ScreenTip "Vertical Position" displays. The y is used to denote a vertical position on a line, like the y-axis of a graph.

The brown circle object begins 1.25 inches from the top edge of the paper.

 Does your screen differ?

If your x or y measurements differ, type or use the spin boxes to change them accordingly.

12 On the Measurement toolbar, point to the next three spin boxes to view their ScreenTips.

The Width and Height of the object were verified in step 9 when you viewed them in the Format AutoShape dialog box. Currently, there is no rotation applied to the object. All of the measurements shown on the Measurement toolbar are also available from the Size and Layout tabs of the object's Format dialog box. However, the Measurement toolbar conveniently displays them all at once. Additionally, notice that the status bar also indicates the size and position of the selected object (see Figure 3.15).

13 Scroll to view the lower portion of the publication.

(Continues)

Activity 3.3   Drawing and Formatting Circles (continued)

14 On the Objects toolbar, click the **Oval** button and move the crosshair pointer into the publication window. Using your eye as a guide, hold down the (⬆Shift) key, and at the *right* end of the brown line, create a circle similar to the one you created at the top of the page (see Figure 3.16).

Do not be concerned with exact placement or size right now.

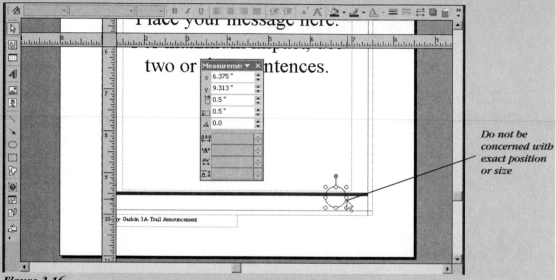

Do not be concerned with exact position or size

Figure 3.16

15 Double-click the circle to display the Format AutoShape dialog box. Under Fill, use the **Color arrow** to fill the shape with the same brown color used for the previous circle and then click **OK** to close the dialog box.

16 With the new circle still selected, move to the Measurement toolbar, and then click to place the insertion point in the x box. Adjust the **x** measurement to **6.5"**. Then, adjust the **y** measurement to **9.25"**, adjust the Width to **0.5"**, and adjust the Height to **0.5"**.

The size and position of the brown circle are now precise.

17 On the Measurement toolbar, click the **X** in the upper right corner to close the toolbar, drag both the vertical and horizontal rulers back to the left and top edges of the screen respectively, and then scroll to position the top portion of the publication in the middle of your screen.

18 On the Standard toolbar, click **Save** to save your changes.

To extend your knowledge...

Changing the Units of Measurement

You can change the units of measurement that Publisher uses by displaying the Tools menu, clicking Options, and then clicking the General tab. In the Measurement units box, select from Inches, Centimeters, Picas, or Points. If you change to a different measurement unit, both the rulers and the Measurement toolbar will use the selected unit of measurement. The default setting is Inches.

Objective 2: Create Ruler Guides

You have seen that Publisher provides many tools to help you create, format, measure, and position graphic objects. Another useful tool is the **Ruler guide**. A ruler guide is a green dotted line that acts as a visual ruler for the purpose of aligning objects when no pink or blue layout guide is close by. You can create ruler guides whenever you need them. They can be placed anywhere on the page and you can create as many of them as you need. When you are done with them, you can easily remove them from the page. Unlike pink and blue layout guides, ruler guides do not appear on every page of the publication. Green ruler guides are activated either from the menu or by dragging from the rulers on the screen.

Activity 3.4   Creating Ruler Guides

1 If necessary, scroll to display the top portion of the publication in the middle of your screen. On the menu bar, click **Arrange**, point to **Ruler Guides**, and then click **Add Horizontal Ruler Guide**.

A dotted green line displays somewhere on the screen.

2 Hold down the (⬆Shift) key, point to the green ruler guide until the Adjust pointer displays, and then drag the line to **1.75 inches on the vertical ruler**.

3 On the menu bar, click **Arrange**, point to **Ruler Guides**, and then click **Add Horizontal Ruler Guide**.

Another green dotted line displays.

4 Using the Adjust pointer, drag the new green ruler guide to **3.5 inches on the vertical ruler** as shown in Figure 3.17.

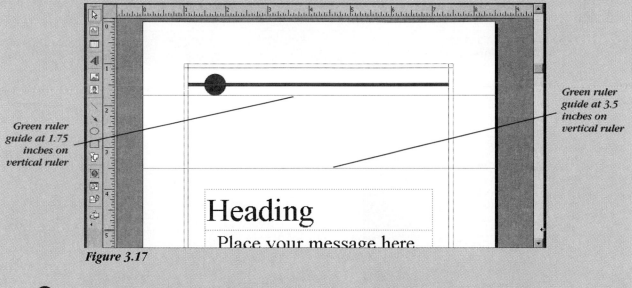

Green ruler guide at 1.75 inches on vertical ruler

Green ruler guide at 3.5 inches on vertical ruler

Figure 3.17

5 Click **Save** to save your changes.

To extend your knowledge...

Creating Ruler Guides

There is a mouse method to create ruler guides. Point to the lower edge of the horizontal ruler (or extreme right edge of the vertical ruler), hold down the (Shift) key until the Adjust pointer displays, and then drag the green dotted ruler guide into your publication.

Objective 3: Insert and Format AutoShapes

Recall that AutoShapes are a type of graphic object. Like other objects they can be resized, flipped, colored, and combined. Many shapes contain a small yellow diamond, called an ***adjustment handle***, that you can use to change the most prominent feature, for example the width of an arm on a star.

Activity 3.5   Inserting and Formatting AutoShapes

 ❶ On the Objects toolbar, click the **AutoShapes** button, and then on the displayed menu, click **More AutoShapes**.

The Insert Clip Art task pane displays.

❷ In the Insert Clip Art task pane, use the scroll bar to scroll to the bottom of the list until the green tree shape displays.

❸ Locate the arrow to the right of the green tree shape, and then click the **arrow** to display a menu. On the displayed menu, click **Insert** (see Figure 3.18).

A green tree shape displays on your screen. The shape is selected (surrounded by handles) and contains a yellow adjustment handle.

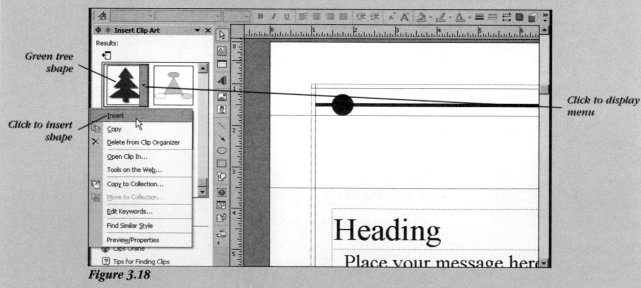

Figure 3.18

❹ At the upper right of the Insert Clip Art task pane, click the **X** to close the task pane.

Activity 3.5   Inserting and Formatting AutoShapes

5 With the tree shape selected, hover the mouse pointer over it until you see the Move pointer. Drag the tree until its top point is aligned with top green ruler guide. Do not be concerned with the horizontal ⇔ position. Then, use the lower left or right resize handles to resize the tree to fit between the two green ruler guides.

The tree shape includes a slight shadow of the tree, which can extend slightly below the green ruler guide.

6 Using the Move pointer and keeping the tree within the two green ruler guides, drag the tree to the left until its bottom left branch is just touching the blue dotted vertical layout guide as shown in Figure 3.19.

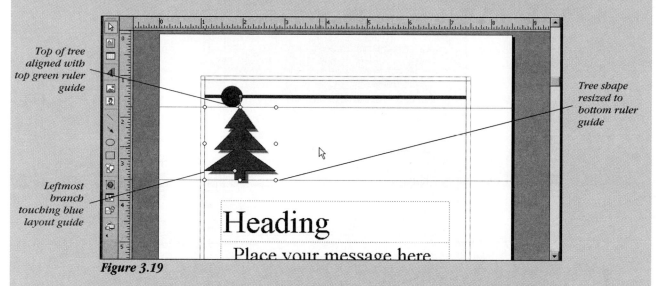

Top of tree aligned with top green ruler guide

Tree shape resized to bottom ruler guide

Leftmost branch touching blue layout guide

Figure 3.19

7 Select the tree shape, if necessary. On the Standard toolbar, click the **Copy** button, and then click the **Paste** button.

A copy of the tree shape displays and is selected.

8 Drag the copy to the right of and slightly overlapping the original as shown in Figure 3.20.

Copy of tree shape

Figure 3.20

(Continues)

Activity 3.5   Inserting and Formatting AutoShapes (continued)

9 With the right tree shape still selected, move the mouse pointer over it, right-click to display a shortcut menu, and then click **Format AutoShape**.

The Format AutoShape dialog box displays.

10 Under Fill, click the **Color arrow**, click **Fill Effects**, and then click the **Tint tab**.

11 Under Tint/Shade, go to the first row and click the last tint color (see Figure 3.21).

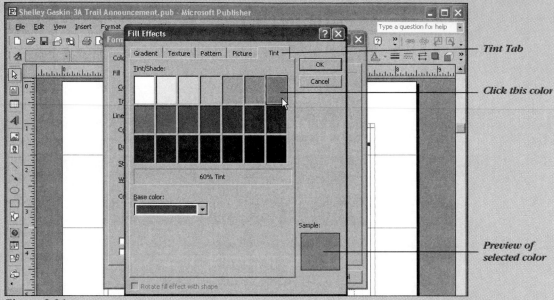

Figure 3.21

12 Click **OK** to close the Fill Effects dialog box, and then click **OK** again to close the Format AutoShape dialog box.

The right tree is a slightly lighter shade of green.

13 Locate the adjustment handle (small yellow diamond) near the trunk of the selected tree. Point to the adjustment handle until your mouse pointer changes to a small white arrowhead, and then drag the handle slightly upward in the center of the tree—about a half inch (see Figure 3.22).

The tree's trunk is lengthened, giving the effect of being a different type of tree.

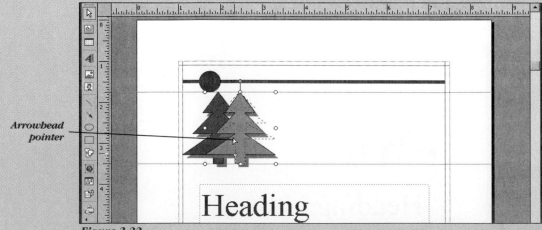

Figure 3.22

14 Click **Save** to save your changes.

Objective 4: Group, Ungroup, and Flip Objects

Grouping is the process of selecting two or more objects and combining them into one object for the purpose of moving, copying, or formatting. Later, you can ungroup the objects, if you want.

Activity 3.6   Grouping, Ungrouping, and Flipping Objects

❶ On the Objects toolbar, click the **Select Objects** button.

❷ Position your mouse pointer in the left margin area and slightly above the upper green ruler guide, hold down the left mouse button, and drag the pointer down and to the right to form a dotted-line box around the two trees as shown in Figure 3.23.

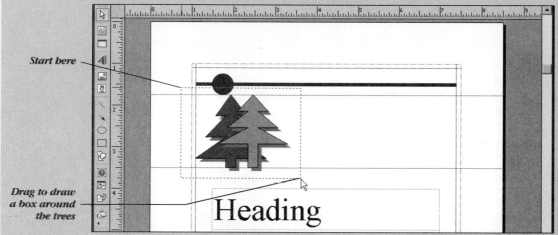

Start here

Drag to draw a box around the trees

Figure 3.23

❸ Release the left mouse button and notice that a small box icon displays under the tree shapes (see Figure 3.24).

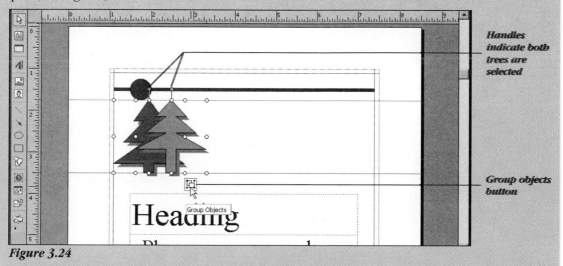

Handles indicate both trees are selected

Group objects button

Figure 3.24

(Continues)

Activity 3.6   Grouping, Ungrouping, and Flipping Objects (continued)

 Does your screen differ?

If you do not see the small box under the tree shapes, it is possible that a small part of one of the tree objects was not included in your selection. Click the Select Objects button and begin again.

4 Point to the button to display the ScreenTip "Group Objects" and then click the **Group Objects** button.

The two trees are now grouped as one object.

5 Hover the mouse pointer over the trees object until the Move pointer displays, and then, keeping the trees object between the two green ruler guides, drag the trees to the right until the rightmost branch just touches the vertical blue layout guide on the right (see Figure 3.25).

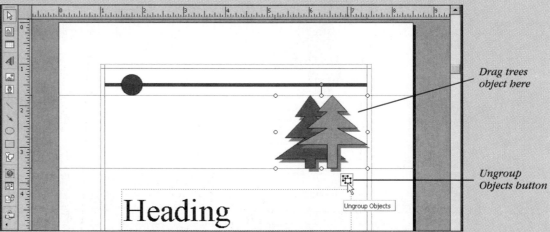

Drag trees object here

Ungroup Objects button

Figure 3.25

6 With the grouped object selected, point to the **Ungroup Objects** button, and click it.

7 Click in the gray scratch area to cancel the selection, and then click on the lighter green tree to select it. Display the **Format AutoShape** dialog box, and change the fill color of the tree to the seventh color (bronze) in the color scheme.

8 With the bronze tree selected, hover the mouse pointer over it, hold down Ctrl, move the mouse pointer slightly, and notice the small plus sign that displays with the pointer. Click the green tree, release the Ctrl key, and then click the **Group Objects** button to regroup the two trees into one object.

9 On the menu bar, click **Arrange**, point to **Rotate or Flip**, and then click **Flip Horizontal**.

The grouped object is flipped and the bronze tree displays on the left.

Activity 3.6   Grouping, Ungrouping, and Flipping Objects

10 Click in the scratch area to cancel the selection, and then click **Save** to save your changes. Compare your screen to Figure 3.26.

Figure 3.26

Objective 5: Add Text to a Shape

Text can be added to most AutoShapes by simply selecting the shape and starting to type. Some AutoShapes, such as lines, connectors, and some freeform drawings, have no space for text, but you can draw a text box near the shape and place your text in it. Additionally, you can draw a text box and move it on top of a shape or draw a text box directly on a shape.

Activity 3.7   Adding Text to a Shape

1 On the Objects toolbar, click the **AutoShapes** button, point to **Block Arrows**, and in the displayed menu, in the fifth row click the second shape—**Notched Right Arrow** (see Figure 3.27).

The crosshair pointer displays.

(Continues)

Activity 3.7   Adding Text to a Shape

Notched
Right Arrow
shape

AutoShapes
button

Figure 3.27

2 Position the crosshair pointer on the upper green ruler guide at **1.5 inches on the horizontal ruler**, and then drag down and to the right to **5 inches on the horizontal ruler**, and positioning the bottom of the arrow on the lower green ruler as shown in Figure 3.28.

Drag to 5
inches on
horizontal
ruler

Drag down to
lower green
ruler guide

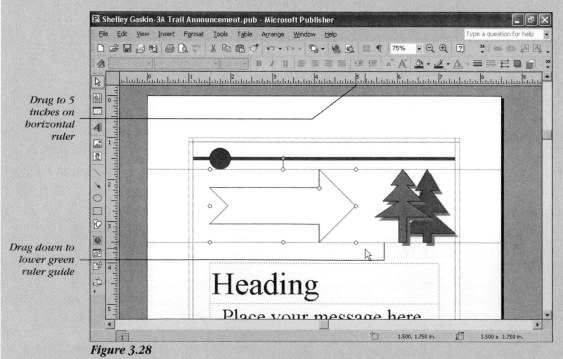

Figure 3.28

Activity 3.7   Adding Text to a Shape

3 With the arrow AutoShape selected, display the **Format AutoShape** dialog box.

4 In the Format AutoShape dialog box, use the **Fill Color arrow** to apply the third color block (gold). Use the **Line Color arrow** to apply the second color block (brown) to the line, and then use the **Line Style arrow** to apply a **3 pt** solid line weight. Click **OK** to close the dialog box.

5 With the arrow AutoShape selected, type Expand the Trail

A frame of diagonal slash marks surrounds the shape indicating a text box, and an insertion point displays within the shape as you type.

6 Use Ctrl + A to select the text you just typed, change the font to **Eras Medium ITC**, and apply **Bold**.

7 With the text still selected, move to the menu bar, click **Format**, point to **AutoFit Text**, and then click **Best Fit**.

8 With the text still selected, move to the Formatting toolbar, click the **Font Color arrow**, and apply the second (brown) color.

9 With the text still selected, move to the menu bar, click **Format**, click **AutoShape**, click the **Text Box tab**, and then use the **Vertical alignment arrow** to center the text vertically in the **Middle** of the shape. Click **OK** to close the dialog box.

10 Click in the gray scratch area to view your changes, and then on the Standard toolbar, click **Save**. Compare your screen to Figure 3.29.

Text and formatting added to the AutoShape

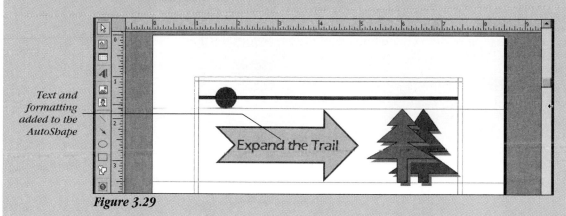

Figure 3.29

Objective 6: Rotate and Nudge an Object

Activity 3.8   Rotating and Nudging an Object

① Click the arrow shape to select it, and then notice the small green ***rotation handle*** above the top center sizing handle (see Figure 3.30).

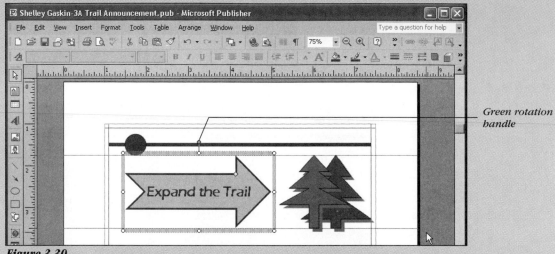

Green rotation handle

Figure 3.30

② Position your mouse pointer over the green rotation handle until it becomes a circle with an arrow. Hold down the left mouse button, and drag slightly to the left until the bottom left point of the dotted image of the arrow touches the lower green ruler guide (see Figure 3.31).

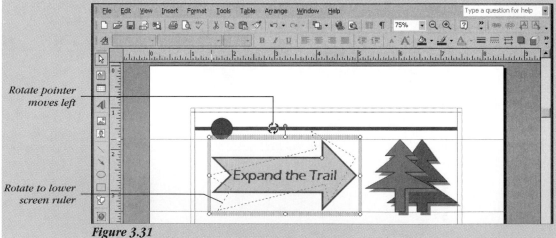

Rotate pointer moves left

Rotate to lower screen ruler

Figure 3.31

Activity 3.8 Rotating and Nudging an Object

3 Be sure the arrow shape is selected. On the menu bar, click **Arrange**, point to **Nudge**, and then hover the mouse pointer over the small lines at the top of the Nudge menu until you see the ScreenTip "Drag to make this menu float." (see Figure 3.32).

Arrange menu

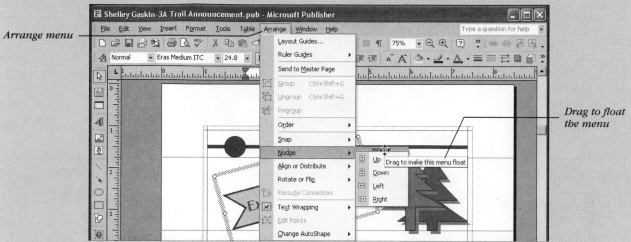

Drag to float the menu

Figure 3.32

4 Drag the menu to the upper right portion of your screen so that it becomes a floating toolbar as shown in Figure 3.33.

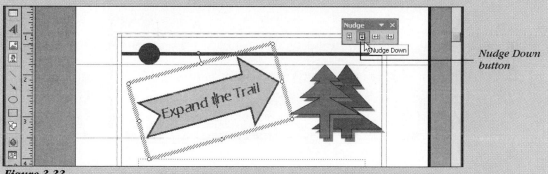

Nudge Down button

Figure 3.33

5 With the arrow shape selected, point to the Nudge Down button on the floating Nudge toolbar, and click it 10 times to **nudge** (move in very small increments) the arrow shape down. Then, hold down Alt and press the ↓ on your keyboard 10–15 more times to nudge downward until the arrow points to the middle branch of the bronze tree. Compare your screen to Figure 3.34.

(Continues)

Activity 3.8   Rotating and Nudging an Object (continued)

Use either method to nudge objects in small increments.

Figure 3.34

6 Close the Nudge toolbar by clicking its **X** button. Scroll the publication down slightly, click the "Heading" placeholder text to select it, and then type Announcement

7 Select the text you just typed, change the font to **Eras Medium ITC**, change the font color to brown, and on the Formatting toolbar, click the **Center** button to center the text horizontally.

Notice that if the Font Color button on the Formatting toolbar displays the color of your choice, you only need to click the Font Color button. It is only necessary to display the color palette if you want to chose a color other than the one displayed on the Font Color button.

8 Click to select the placeholder text that begins "Place your message" and type The Fine Arts and Parks Department is pleased to announce a new community partnership to expand the Agave Trail. Watch for future programs!

9 Use Ctrl + A to select the text you just typed, change the font to **Eras Medium ITC**, apply **Bold**, change the font color to brown, and change the font size to **26**.

10 With the text box still selected, drag the bottom center resize handle up to **7.25 inches on the vertical ruler**. Click in the gray scratch area to cancel all selections, and then compare your screen to Figure 3.35.

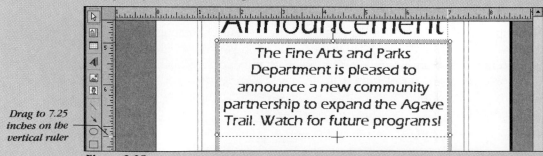

Figure 3.35

11 On the Standard toolbar, click **Save**.

Objective 7: Create and Format WordArt

WordArt is a tool that can transform text into a stylized graphic object. It is best used for titles or short lines of text that you want to enhance to draw the reader's attention. WordArt can be formatted with a texture, a fill color, or a shadowing effect. There are 30 different basic WordArt styles, which can be further modified in shape. After you create a WordArt object, you can flip, stretch, rotate, and angle the words.

Activity 3.9   Creating and Formatting WordArt

1 On the Objects toolbar, click the **Insert WordArt** button.

The WordArt Gallery displays.

2 In the third row, click the first WordArt design (see Figure 3.36) and then click **OK** to accept the design and to open the Edit WordArt Text dialog box.

Click to select this WordArt design

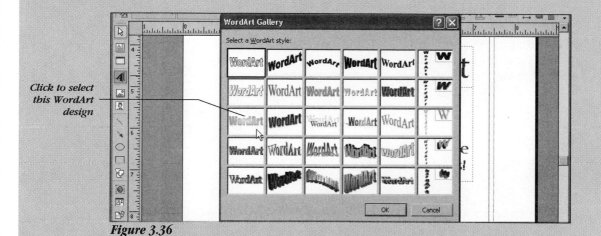

Figure 3.36

3 Type Agave Trail Expansion! and then click **OK** to create the WordArt and return to the publication.

The WordArt is created somewhere on the page and is selected. The WordArt toolbar is displayed as a floating toolbar.

4 Use the Move pointer to drag the WordArt into the empty space below the text box, aligning its top edge at **8 inches on the vertical ruler**, and visually centering it horizontally on the page.

5 Using the left center resize handle, drag to stretch the WordArt to the left blue dotted layout guide. Repeat the process on the right side of the WordArt. Then drag the

(Continues)

Activity 3.9   Creating and Formatting WordArt (continued)

bottom center resize handle down to **9 inches on the vertical ruler**. Compare your screen to Figure 3.37.

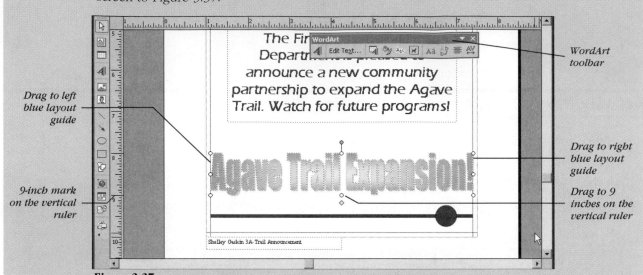

Drag to left blue layout guide

9-inch mark on the vertical ruler

WordArt toolbar

Drag to right blue layout guide

Drag to 9 inches on the vertical ruler

Figure 3.37

6 Take a moment to look at the WordArt toolbar and point to each of its buttons to display the ScreenTips. As you do so, study the following table, which describes each of the buttons on the toolbar.

Button	Description
Insert WordArt	Inserts a new WordArt object into a publication.
Edit Text	Opens the Edit WordArt dialog box so that the text for an existing WordArt object can be modified.
WordArt Gallery	Opens the WordArt Gallery so that a new design can be applied to an existing WordArt object.
Format WordArt	Opens the Format WordArt dialog box so that fill colors, size, position, and layout can be modified.
WordArt Shape	Displays options for changing the shape of an existing WordArt.
Text Wrapping	Displays the text wrapping menu.
WordArt Same Letter Heights	Changes the height of lowercase letters so that they are the same height as uppercase letters.
WordArt Vertical Text	Displays WordArt text vertically.
WordArt Alignment	Applies alignment options to a WordArt object.
WordArt Character Spacing	Adjusts the amount of spacing between WordArt characters.

 7 With the WordArt object selected, move to the WordArt toolbar and click the WordArt Shape button.

A palette of shapes displays.

Activity 3.9   Creating and Formatting WordArt

8 In the first row, click the third shape—**Triangle Up**.

Notice how the shape of the WordArt object changes.

9 On the WordArt toolbar, click the **WordArt Gallery** button, and then in the fourth row, click the third design. Click **OK** to close the WordArt Gallery dialog box.

When a new design is chosen, the default color and shape of the design are applied, and any previous color and shape changes are removed as shown in Figure 3.38.

Figure 3.38

10 On the WordArt toolbar, click the **Format WordArt** button to open the Format WordArt dialog box. If necessary, click the Colors and Lines tab.

11 Use the **Fill Color arrow** to click the seventh (bronze) color. Click the **Fill Color arrow** again, click **Fill Effects**, click the **Gradient tab**, and then under Colors, click the **Two colors** option button.

12 Set **Color 1** to the seventh (bronze) color, and set **Color 2** to the third (gold) color. Under Shading styles, click **Vertical**, and under Variants, accept the default variant (the first variant in the first row). Click **OK** twice to close the dialog boxes.

13 On the WordArt toolbar, click the **WordArt Character Spacing** button.

14 On the displayed menu, click **Tight**.

Notice that the characters appear wider and are spaced closer together.

15 On the WordArt toolbar, click its **X** button to close the toolbar.

16 Scroll to view the top portion of the page. On the menu bar, click **Arrange**, point to **Ruler Guides**, and then click **Clear All Ruler Guides**.

The two green ruler guides that you placed on the page are removed.

17 Click **Save** to save your changes.

(Continues)

Activity 3.9   Creating and Formatting WordArt (continued)

18   **Zoom** to **Whole Page** and click in the gray scratch area to cancel any selections. Compare your screen to Figure 3.39.

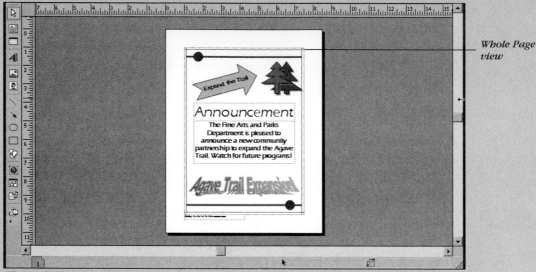

Figure 3.39

19   On the Standard toolbar, click the **Print** button to print one complete copy of the publication, and then **Close** your publication, saving any changes. Publication 3A is complete!

To extend your knowledge...

Removing Ruler Guides

Another way to remove the green ruler guides is to simply drag them back into their respective rulers.

Publication 3B

Trail Brochure

In Activities 3.10–3.19 you will use the brochure wizard to create a brochure announcing a trail building program by the City's Department of Fine Arts and Parks. The front and back of the brochure (two printed sheets of letter-size paper) will look like Figure 3.40. You will save your publication as *Firstname Lastname-3B Trail Brochure.*

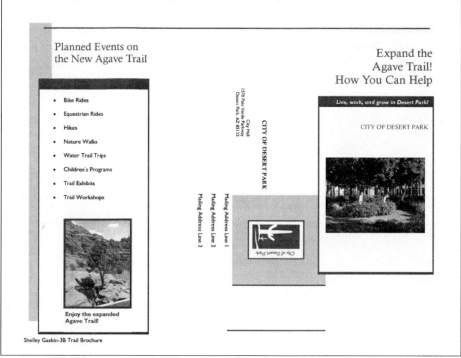

Figure 3.40A

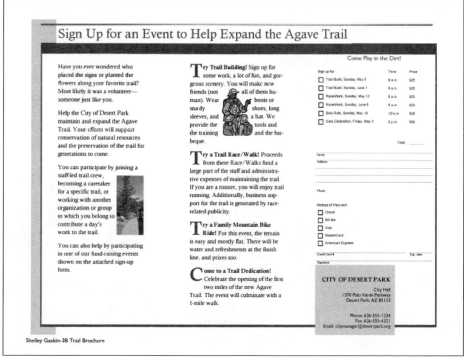

Figure 3.40B

Objective 8: Use a Wizard to Create a Brochure

Recall that a **brochure** is a small pamphlet that describes an event, product, program, or service. A brochure is usually printed in **landscape** (a page orientation in which the paper is wider than it is high) on the front and back of regular letter-size paper, and then folded into thirds. A brochure often includes an **entry blank** (a printed form to be filled out) and sometimes includes space for a mailing label. A brochure does not contain large amounts of text. Rather, it gives the reader brief information and encourages the reader to take further action; for example, buy the product, enroll in the program, or contact the organization for more information.

To assist you in building the brochure from one of Publisher's pre-defined templates, you will activate the brochure wizard, which will enable you to select the features you want to include in the brochure.

Activity 3.10   Using a Wizard to Build a Brochure

① **Start** Publisher and display the New Publication task pane. Under Start from a design, be sure that By Publication Type is displayed, scroll as necessary to click **Brochures**, and then click **Informational**.

② In the Informational Brochures Publication Gallery, scroll as necessary and then click the **Layers Informational Brochure**.

Notice that the Publisher brochure wizard provides several options for the layout of a brochure, including various types of forms that can be included and a mailing address area.

③ In the task pane, if necessary, click Brochure Options. In the Brochure Options task pane, under Page size click **3-panel**, under Customer address click **Include**, and under Form click **Sign-up form** (see Figure 3.41).

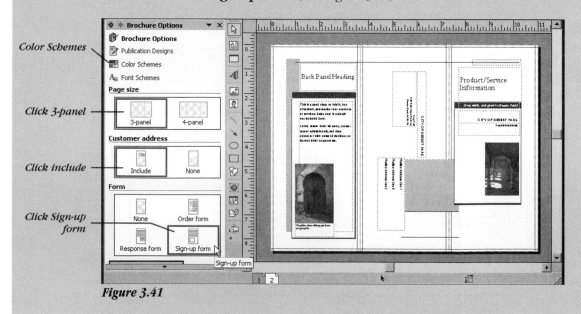

Figure 3.41

Activity 3.10   Using a Wizard to Build a Brochure

④ In the Brochure Options task pane, click **Color Schemes**, and then, if necessary, click **Desert**.

⑤ At the top of the task pane, click the **X** in the upper right corner to close the task pane.

⑥ On the menu bar, click **Edit**, and then click **Personal Information**.

The Personal Information dialog box displays. The brochure templates in Publisher automatically insert organizational information drawn from the personal information set feature. Recall that these information sets are stored on the computer's hard drive. Thus, in a classroom or lab environment, always check to see that the appropriate information is included in your publication.

⑦ Compare your screen to Figure 3.42 and make any corrections or updates to the typed information required so that the Primary Business personal information set matches the Figure.

If the logo does not match the one in the figure, it can be inserted later.

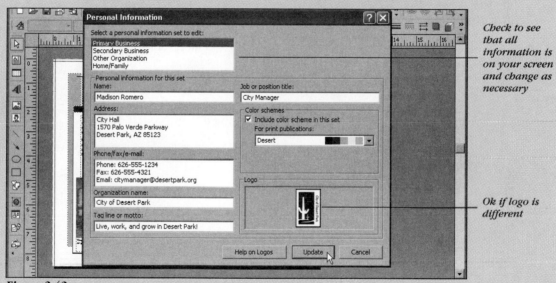

Figure 3.42

⑧ At the bottom of the dialog box, click **Update** to return to the publication.

⑨ On the menu bar, click **View**, and then click **Header and Footer**. Use the Show Header/Footer button on the Header and Footer toolbar to navigate to the footer frame.

Notice that the position of the insertion point within the footer frame is quite close to the edge of the paper.

⑩ Point to the gray scratch area, right-click to display a shortcut menu, point to **Toolbars**, and then click **Measurement**.

Recall that the Measurement toolbar enables you to view and adjust the precise page position and size of a selected object.

(Continues)

Activity 3.10   Using a Wizard to Build a Brochure (continued)

11 Click to select the footer text frame object, and then in the Measurement toolbar, change the **x** measurement to **0.5″**, change the **y** measurement to **8″**, and change the **Width** to **9″**. Press ⏎Enter after typing the final measurement (see Figure 3.43).

Footer frame selected

Measurements changed

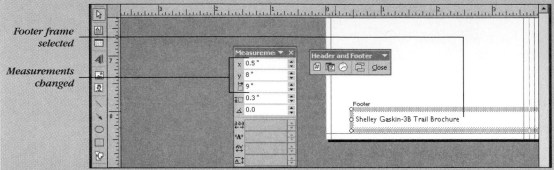

Figure 3.43

12 Click in the footer text frame and type Firstname Lastname-3B Trail Brochure

13 Close the Measurement toolbar. **Close** the Header and Footer toolbar to close the Master page and return to the publication. Click in the **Zoom** box and type 45%, press ⏎Enter, and then scroll so that you can view the entire first page in the center of your screen as shown in Figure 3.44.

Zoom to 45%

Page 1

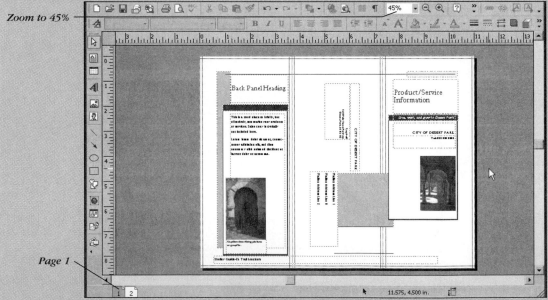

Figure 3.44

14 On the menu bar, click **File**, click **Save As**, and then save the publication in your storage location as *Firstname Lastname-3B Trail Brochure*.

15 On the Standard toolbar, click **Print**, and then put your two printed sheets together with the blank sides facing each other, both sheets right side up.

Activity 3.10   Using a Wizard to Build a Brochure

 With the sheet containing the Sign-Up Form facing you, fold the two sheets into thirds by first folding the right third toward the left, and then folding the left third toward the right. Do not be concerned with extremely precise folding right now.

The result is a folded brochure that opens like a booklet. Use this folded model as a visual guide as you complete this publication.

To extend your knowledge...

The Measurement Toolbar and the Format Dialog Boxes

You have seen that the Measurement toolbar displays the size (width and height) of a selected object and the position (distance from the top and left edges of the paper) of a selected object. This information is also available on the Format AutoShape, Format Text Box, and Format Picture dialog boxes (depending upon the type of object selected). Size measurements are on the Size tab, and position measurements are on the Layout tab. If you are interested only in measurements, the Measurement toolbar is an efficient way to view and, if necessary, change the information.

You can see from your folded model brochure that you have six distinct ***panels*** (paper surfaces) on which to place information—three on page 1 and three on page 2. This is called a ***tri-fold brochure*** because it is folded into thirds. This is the most common size and fold arrangement for a brochure, although there are others. Of course, most brochures will be printed on the front and back of a single sheet of paper, but in terms of composing the brochure, you have two separate pages with which to work.

Activity 3.11   Identifying the Parts of a Brochure

 Using your printed model and Table 3.1, take a few moments to familiarize yourself with the manner in which the six panels are designated by professional designers (see Figures 3.45 and 3.46) and the types of information that should be included in each panel (see Table 3.1).

Because the panel numbering designation is not as logical as you might at first think, you might want to write the panel numbers on your printed model for reference as you complete this publication.

(Continues)

Activity 3.11   Identifying the Parts of a Brochure (continued)

Panel 5

Panel 6

Panel 1

Page 1

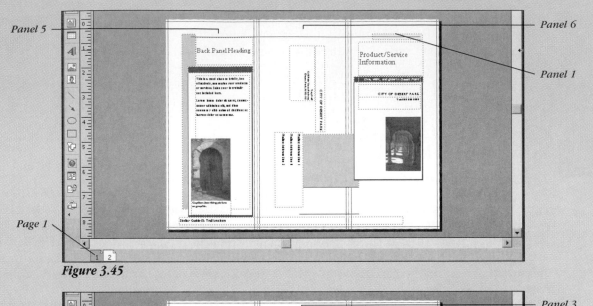

Figure 3.45

Panel 2

Panel 3

Panel 4

Page 2

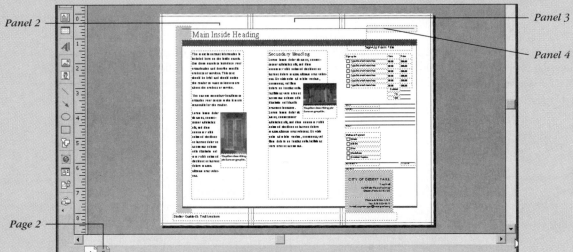

Figure 3.46

TABLE 3.1   PARTS OF A TRI-FOLD BROCHURE

Page 1: The Outside of the Brochure—From Left to Right

Panel 5	After Panel 1, this important panel is probably the next panel that a reader sees. In your folded model, notice that when you open up the "booklet," your eye is drawn to this panel.
	This is a good place to briefly summarize your product or service or to explain the purpose of your brochure. It is also a very good place to put a bulleted list.
Panel 6	This is the panel that is least important because it is usually the last panel that a reader will look at. Normally it contains the organization's contact information and/or a mailing label.
Panel 1	This is the most important panel because it forms the front cover of your brochure. What you place here will determine whether or not a reader is enticed to pick up the brochure and examine its inner contents.

Activity 3.11   Identifying the Parts of a Brochure

Page 2: The Inside of the Brochure—From Left to Right

Panel 2	The most informative details should be included on the three inside panels. Use text and graphics in these panels to introduce your organization and describe specific products, services, or programs. This text should be brief and should entice the reader to seek more information about the product or service or to take some form of action.
Panel 3	You can use secondary headings to organize your text to make it easy for the reader to scan with the eye for additional information. Use additional text and graphics here.
Panel 4	This panel can contain additional text and graphics or a form, such as an entry blank or sign-up form. Frequently the organization contact information is repeated here.

2 In the status bar, use the Page Navigation buttons to navigate to and view page 2 of your publication, and then navigate back to page 1.

Notice that the Publisher design includes suggested positions for graphics, such as pictures and other graphic elements, and that the color scheme and appropriate font scheme have been applied. Additionally, pink (margin) and blue layout guides display.

3 With page 1 displayed, **Zoom** to **66%**, and then scroll to position the top portion of panel 1 (rightmost) in the center of your screen (see Figure 3.47).

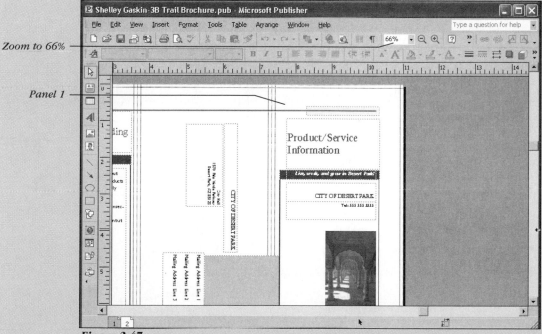

Figure 3.47

4 Click **Save** to save any changes.

Objective 9: Insert and Format Pictures in a Publication

Recall that a photographic image is stored electronically as a bitmap file (a pattern of dots called pixels). A photo is often stored in the *.jpeg* (pronounced JAY-peg) format, a file format created specifically for photographs. The Publisher software includes a feature that lets you use a scanner or a digital camera to capture a picture directly into a publication. More often, you will store your electronic photograph on your computer and then import it directly into your publication.

Activity 3.12   Inserting a Picture in a Publication

1 With panel 1 centered on your screen, click to select the placeholder text beginning "Product/Service" and then, pressing ⏎Enter after each line, type:

    Expand the

    Agave Trail!

    How You Can Help

2 Use Ctrl + A to select the text you just typed, and then on the Formatting toolbar, click the **Align Right** button to align the text at the right.

3 Click to select the text box frame containing the telephone number. If a pattern of slash marks surrounds the text frame, click on the slashed border to display a pattern of dots. Press Del to delete the frame and its text.

Clicking inside a text box selects the text box and generates an insertion point, at which point you can begin to type. If you want to select the text box for the purpose of deleting it, you must click on its border to display the pattern of dots.

4 Select the text "City of Desert Park" and apply **Bold**. On the Formatting toolbar, use the **Font Color arrow** to change the text color to brown, the second color in the color scheme. Then click in the scratch area to cancel the selection. Compare your screen to Figure 3.48.

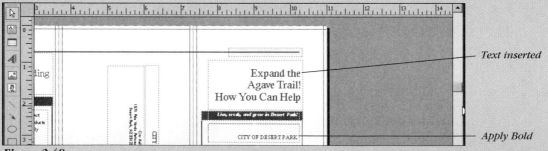

Figure 3.48

5 Scroll down slightly, click on the picture so that sizing handles surround it, and press Del to delete it.

 6 On the Objects toolbar, click the **Picture Frame** button and then move the mouse pointer into the area from which you deleted the picture.

7 Position the crosshair pointer at approximately **7.75 inches on the horizontal ruler** and **3.5 inches on the vertical ruler**, and then drag down and to the right to

Activity 3.12   Inserting a Picture in a Publication

approximately **10.125 (10 1/8) inches on the horizontal ruler** and **5.75 inches on the vertical ruler** (see Figure 3.49) and then release the left mouse button.

The Insert Picture dialog box displays.

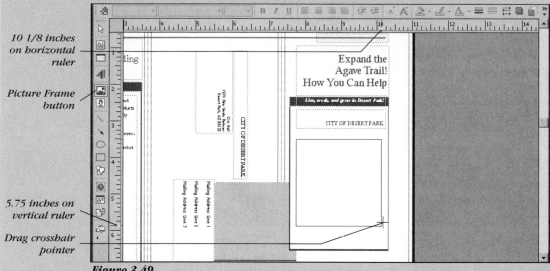

10 1/8 inches on horizontal ruler

Picture Frame button

5.75 inches on vertical ruler

Drag crosshair pointer

Figure 3.49

8 In the Insert Picture dialog box, navigate to the location in which the student files for this textbook are stored, click the file 3B_**Pancl1PIC** and then at the lower right corner of the dialog box, click the **Insert** button.

After you have selected the image, it will display in your publication. Although you created an approximation of where you wanted the picture to display, the frame may automatically resize slightly to accommodate the ***aspect ratio*** of the picture. The aspect ratio is the proportional relationship of the picture's width and height.

9 On the Standard toolbar, click **Save** to save your changes.

To extend your knowledge...

Changing the Size of a Picture

When you want to change the size of a picture, be careful not to change the picture's aspect ratio. There are two ways to do this. You can resize the picture using one of the corner sizing handles. Never use a side handle to resize the picture because only the corner handles will maintain the picture's aspect ratio. You can also use the appropriate Format dialog box to change the picture's size. To do so, simply select the picture, open the Format dialog box, click the Size tab, click to place a check mark in the Lock aspect ratio check box, and then type or use the spin box arrows to change the size. Using either one of these methods will prevent distortion of the picture.

Graphics in your publication can be enhanced by adding a ***caption***—text that briefly describes the graphic. The reader will often read a caption before reading the actual text of your brochure.

Activity 3.13   Changing, Moving, and Adding a Caption to a Picture

① Be sure that page 1 of your publication is displayed and the Zoom is set to either 66% or 75%, whichever is most comfortable for you. Scroll as needed to position panel 5 (leftmost) in the center of your screen.

② Select the placeholder text "Back Panel Heading" and, letting the text wrap, type
Planned Events on the New Agave Trail

③ Click to select the placeholder text that begins "This is a good place" and then type the following list, pressing ⏎Enter after each line:

Bike Rides

Equestrian Rides

Hikes

Nature Walks

Water Trail Trips

Children's Programs

Trail Exhibits

Trail Workshops

④ Use Ctrl + A to select the list you just typed. On the menu bar, click **Format**, and then click **Indents and Lists**.

The Indents and Lists dialog box displays.

⑤ Under Indent settings, click the **Bulleted list** option button, click a small bullet of your choice, and click **OK** to close the dialog box.

Bullets are applied to the list. Notice from the slashed border that the text frame extends over the picture and that the last item in your list is to the right of the picture. Recall that frames can be layered and that when a text frame is positioned on the bottom layer, the text will wrap around the picture, as it does in this instance.

⑥ Scroll down to view the bottom of the panel, and then click the picture of the door to select it (see Figure 3.50).

Notice that sizing handles surround not only the door picture, but also the text box containing the caption underneath the door picture, indicating that the picture and the text

Activity 3.13   Changing, Moving, and Adding a Caption to a Picture

box containing the caption have been grouped into one object. The Ungroup Objects button also displays.

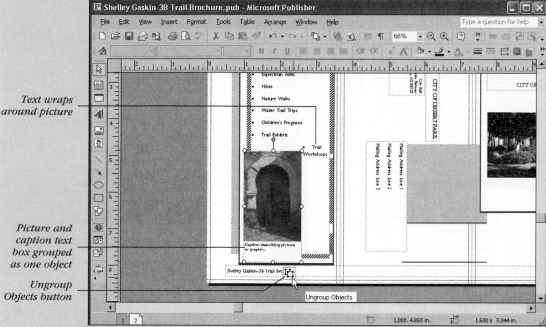

Text wraps around picture

Picture and caption text box grouped as one object

Ungroup Objects button

Figure 3.50

7 Under the selected picture and caption object, click the **Ungroup Objects** button to ungroup, click once in the gray scratch area, and then click the picture to select it.

8 With only the picture selected, hover the mouse pointer over it and right-click. On the displayed shortcut menu, point to **Change Picture**, and then click **From File**.

The Insert Picture dialog box displays. This is another way to insert a picture into your publication—it is especially effective when a picture frame already exists.

9 Navigate to the location in which the student files for this textbook are stored, click **3B_Panel5PIC**, and then click the **Insert** button.

When you insert a picture, Publisher will automatically maintain the original picture's aspect ratio. Thus, this picture is slightly shorter than the picture that it replaced. Your bulleted text now has space to align properly and does not wrap around the picture.

10 With the picture selected, hover the mouse pointer over it, right-click to display a shortcut menu, and click **Format Picture**.

The Format Picture dialog displays. This dialog box is similar to the Format Object dialog box with which you are familiar.

11 Click the **Colors and Lines tab**. Under Line, use the **Line Color arrow** and **Line Style arrow** to apply a brown, **3 pt** solid line to the picture.

12 With the picture selected, hold down the (Ctrl) key and click the text box beneath the picture.

The Group Objects button displays.

(Continues)

Activity 3.13   Changing, Moving, and Adding a Caption to a Picture (continued)

⓭   Click the **Group Objects** button.

The picture and text box with the caption are now grouped as one object.

⓮   Click in the caption text box to select the placeholder text. Press F9 to quickly zoom in on the text and type `Enjoy the expanded Agave Trail!`

⓯   Select the text you just typed and change the font size to **10**.

⓰   Press F9 again to zoom back to your original setting. Hover the mouse pointer over the picture to display the Move pointer, hold down the left mouse button, and drag the picture so that it is centered between the left and right boundaries of the text frame. Use your eye to visually center the object, and maintain the original vertical alignment. Use the Nudge key combination (Alt + a directional arrow key) or display and use the Nudge menu if desired (see Figure 3.51).

Center the picture object between these guides

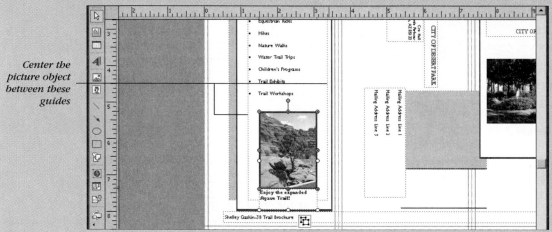

Figure 3.51

⓱   Click in the scratch area to view your changes, and then on the Standard toolbar, click **Save** to save your changes.

Activity 3.14   Using the Picture Toolbar

❶   On the status bar, use the Page Navigation buttons to navigate to **page 2** of your brochure, and then position the upper left portion of the page in the center of your screen.

❷   Click to select the placeholder text "Main Inside Heading" and type `Sign Up for an Event to Help Expand the Agave Trail`

❸   Scroll down slightly, click the picture of the blue door, and then click the **Ungroup Objects** button to ungroup it from its caption.

❹   Click in the gray scratch area to cancel the selection, click the picture to select it only, and then hover and right-click to display a shortcut menu.

Activity 3.14   Using the Picture Toolbar

5 Point to **Change Picture**, click **From File**, navigate to your student files for this textbook, click **3B_Panel2PIC**, and then click the **Insert** button.

6 With the picture selected, hover over it, right-click to display a shortcut menu, and then click **Show Picture Toolbar**. If necessary, drag the toolbar by its title so that it is not covering the picture.

The Picture toolbar displays, floating in the publication window.

7 Take a moment to examine Figure 3.52 and Table 3.2 to familiarize yourself with the commands on the Picture toolbar.

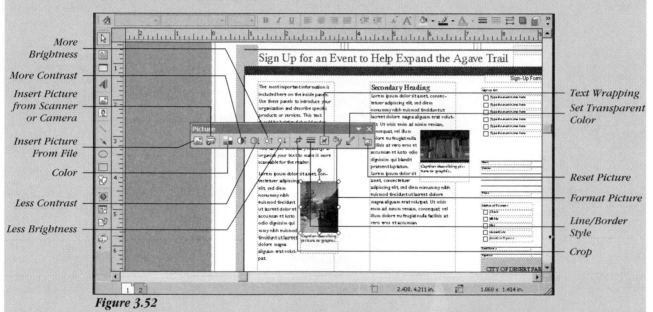

Figure 3.52

Table 3.2 lists and describes the buttons on the Picture toolbar.

TABLE 3.2   BUTTONS ON THE PICTURE TOOLBAR

Button	Description
Insert Picture From File	Displays the Insert Picture dialog box from which you can insert a new picture file.
Insert Picture from Scanner or Camera	Enables the use of a scanner or digital camera to capture a picture directly into the frame. (Installing the software that accompanies the scanner or camera device is usually sufficient to establish it as a system resource, and Publisher will recognize it.)
Color	Displays a menu to change the color of the image to grayscale (shades of gray), Black & White, Washout (faded tones), or Automatic (the original color values of the picture).
More Contrast	Makes light colors lighter and dark colors darker.
Less Contrast	Makes light colors darker and dark colors lighter.
More Brightness	Makes all colors lighter.

(Continues)

Activity 3.14   Using the Picture Toolbar (continued)

Less Brightness	Makes all colors darker.
Crop	Displays the Crop tool with which you can hide parts of a picture.
Line/Border Style	Displays the Line Style menu.
Text Wrapping	Displays the Text Wrapping menu.
Format Picture	Displays the Format Picture dialog box.
Set Transparent Color	Activates the Set Transparent Color pointer with which you can click an area in the picture with the color you want to make transparent. (Not available for pictures in some formats, such as .wmf.)
Reset Picture	Restores the size, cropping, and colors of the picture to their original values.

8   With the picture selected, experiment with some of the buttons on the toolbar.

If you use the Crop tool or the Set Transparent Color tool, you will have to click them again to "put them back." If you experiment with Brightness and Contrast, you can click them numerous times to increase or decrease by small increments.

9   When you are finished experimenting with the Picture toolbar buttons, click the **Reset Picture** button, and close the toolbar.

10   Click to select the caption text box beneath the picture. If necessary, click its border to display a pattern of dots, and then press Del.

The caption text box is deleted.

11   Click to select the picture, and **Zoom** to **100%** so that you can see the picture clearly. Hover and right-click, click **Show Picture Toolbar**, and then move to the displayed Picture toolbar and click the **Crop** button.

Cropping handles—handles that permit you to hide parts of the image—surround the picture.

12   Move your mouse pointer over the center right cropping handle until the mouse pointer also takes the form of a crop mark—called the ***cropping pointer*** (see Figure 3.53).

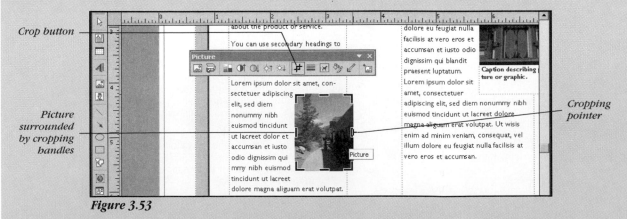

Figure 3.53

13   Drag to the left to crop (hide) the right (building portion) of the picture (see Figure 3.54) and then release the left mouse button.

Activity 3.14 Using the Picture Toolbar

Cropping an image does not delete the cropped part of the picture—it just hides it.

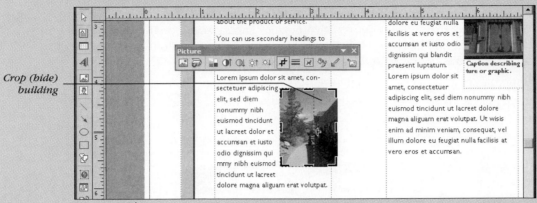

Crop (hide) building

Figure 3.54

14 On the Picture toolbar, click the **Crop** button again to release the cropping tool. Close the Picture toolbar, and then click in the scratch area to cancel the selection and view your changes.

15 On the Standard toolbar, click **Save** to save your changes.

To extend your knowledge...

Cropping Techniques

There are several techniques that you can use to crop images. Crop one side by dragging a center cropping handle on that side. You could also crop two sides evenly at the same time by holding down the Ctrl key as you drag a center cropping handle. To crop all four sides at the same time, hold down the Ctrl key while dragging a corner cropping handle. For precision cropping, display the Picture tab of the Format Picture dialog box and under Crop from, enter exact measurements of the area to be hidden. You can expose the cropped area of an image by dragging the handle out from the center of the image, or restore the image to its original state by clicking Reset Picture on the Picture toolbar.

Objective 10: Combine Text with Graphics

Combining text and graphics on a page with ease is the purpose of Publisher. One way to combine text and graphics is to put text in one frame and graphics in another frame and then place the frames close to each other without touching. However, that technique does not result in a very exciting design.

On the other hand, when you draw a picture frame partially or completely within a text frame, Publisher automatically layers the frames placing the text frame on the bottom, so that the text appears to flow around the graphic image. This results in a more professional and inviting design.

The capability to have text appear to flow around graphic images, even though each is held in different frames, is called ***wrapping***. By default, Publisher has the wrapping feature turned on, although you can turn it off.

Activity 3.15   Arranging Text With Graphics

1 **Zoom** to **75%** and position the top portion of panel 2 (leftmost) in the center of your screen.

2 Click to select the placeholder text that begins "The most important information." On the menu bar, click **Insert**, click **Text File**, and then navigate to the student files that accompany this textbook and click **3B_Panel2Text**.

3 When the message displays indicating that the inserted text will not fit into the selected frame, click **No** so that the text that does not fit in the frame goes into the overflow area. Notice that at the bottom of the frame, the Text in Overflow indicator is active as shown in Figure 3.55.

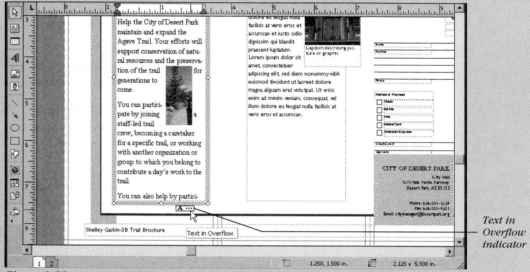

Text in Overflow indicator

Figure 3.55

4 Click anywhere in the inserted text, use Ctrl + A to select the inserted text, and then change the font to **Calisto MT** and the font size to **10**.

The entire text fits into the frame, and the text appears to flow around the picture. The Text in Overflow indicator no longer displays.

Recall that by default, the text wrapping feature is turned on. Thus, inserted text is automatically layered on the bottom. Depending upon how you cropped the picture, the manner in which the text flows around the picture will vary.

5 Click anywhere in the frame to cancel the selection, hover and right-click, point to **Proofing Tools**, and then click **Hyphenation**.

This is another method to display the Language and Spelling tools, collectively called Proofing tools.

6 In the Hyphenation dialog box, click to clear the Automatically hyphenate this story check box, and then click **OK**.

In narrow columns like those in a brochure, it is often advisable to turn off the hyphenation, especially when text is wrapping around a picture.

Activity 3.15   Arranging Text With Graphics

7 Use the Move pointer to move the picture in alignment with the text frame's right boundary (see Figure 3.56), so that the text flows only around the top and left.

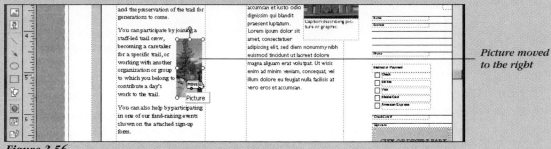

Figure 3.56

8 On the Standard toolbar, click **Save** to save your changes.

Publisher provides five ***wrapping styles***—arrangements by which text can flow around, or position itself relative to, a graphic object. Wrapping styles can be applied from either the Layout tab of the Format Picture dialog box or directly from the Picture toolbar.

The five wrapping styles are:

▶ Square. This is the default style; that is, when you insert a picture into surrounding text, the Square wrapping style is automatically applied. In this style, text wraps around the outside of the image along a square edge.

▶ Tight and Through. These are the two most popular styles, in which the text wraps quite closely around the image. Whether Through or Tight is best depends upon the shape of the image.

▶ Top and Bottom. In this style the text jumps over the image, skipping any white space on either side of the image, and starting again beneath it.

▶ None. In this style the image does not interact with the text at all, and in fact covers the text. This is not a common style; however, you may have seen some magazine covers where part of the image covers a portion of the magazine's title. This would only be done if the magazine was so well recognized that covering part of the title would not prevent one from identifying the magazine.

▶ Edit Wrap Points. This is used for images with quite irregular shapes and will be discussed in a subsequent Lesson.

Activity 3.16   Applying Wrapping Styles to an Object

1 Scroll to position panel 3 (center panel of page 2) in the middle of your screen. Notice the placement of the reddish-orange image.

There are no specific rules about the placement of graphics on a page. It is entirely acceptable to have the image overlap two panels as it does in this instance. Recall that professional graphic designers were used to design Publisher's templates.

2 Click to select the reddish-orange image, click the **Ungroup Objects** button, and then click outside the object to cancel the selection.

(Continues)

Activity 3.16   Applying Wrapping Styles to an Object (continued)

3 Click the caption text box as necessary to display a pattern of dots around it, press the Del key to delete it, and then click the picture again to select it. Right-click over the picture and click **Show Picture Toolbar**.

The Picture toolbar displays.

 4 With the picture selected, point to the **Text Wrapping** button on the Picture toolbar and click it.

The Text Wrapping menu displays.

5 Point to the shaded lines at the top of the displayed menu until the four-headed mouse pointer displays, drag the Text Wrapping menu to the left of your screen, and then close the Picture toolbar (see Figure 3.57).

This will enable the Text Wrapping menu, which is now in the form of a toolbar, to be continuously displayed as you experiment with text wrapping options.

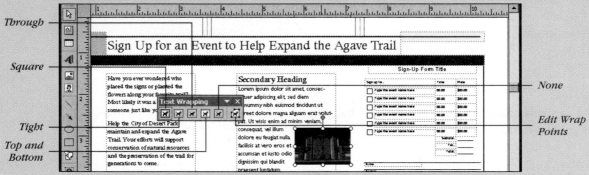

Figure 3.57

6 Notice that the first button on the Text Wrapping menu is selected (surrounded by a black line), and then point to it to display its ScreenTip—Square.

Recall that when pictures are inserted they are layered over existing text frames, and the text in the text box underneath flows around the image in the default square style.

7 Look at the text flow around the bottom of the selected picture, click the second wrapping style button, **Tight**. (Click Yes if a question displays.)

Notice that the text flow around the bottom of the picture is closer and tighter to the image.

8 Click the third wrapping style, **Through**, and if necessary click **Yes** to the question.

Because this is a rectangular image, it is likely that you will see little or no difference between the Tight and Through wrapping styles. An irregularly shaped image would show a more pronounced wrapping.

9 Click the fourth wrapping style, **Top and Bottom**.

This style is obvious and distinctive, although not particularly interesting.

10 Click the fifth wrapping style, **None**.

The picture covers the text. Recall that this is not a commonly used wrapping style, except for highly stylized magazine covers.

Activity 3.16   Applying Wrapping Styles to an Object

The last button—Edit Wrap Points—is best used for images with quite irregular shapes.

11 Click the first wrapping style, **Square**, and then click **X** to close the floating toolbar.

12 Click **Save** to save your changes.

One type of graphic object is *clip art*—predefined images. The Microsoft Office XP software includes many clip art images. You can also purchase clip art from other software vendors. Free clip art is available from various Web sites.

Office Clip Organizer is a program that organizes, finds, previews, and inserts into your documents the contents of *media files* (pictures, movies, or sound recordings) that are stored on your computer and imported into the program. Office Clip Organizer replaces the Microsoft Clip Gallery that was included with previous versions of Microsoft Office.

Activity 3.17   Inserting Clip Art

1 In panel 3 (middle panel) on page 2 of your brochure, click the "Secondary Heading" placeholder text to select it and then press Del to delete it.

2 Click the orange picture to select it and then press Del to delete it.

3 Click to select the placeholder text that begins "Lorem ipsum." On the menu bar, click **Insert**, click **Text File**, navigate to the folder in which your student files are stored, click **3B_Panel3Text**, and then click **OK**.

Because the imported Word file was already in font size 10, no further adjustment to the font size is necessary.

4 On the Objects toolbar, click the **Clip Organizer Frame** button.

(Continues)

Activity 3.17   Inserting Clip Art (continued)

The Insert Clip Art task pane displays as shown in Figure 3.58.

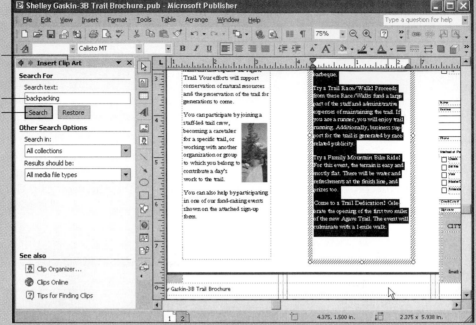

Insert Clip Art task pane

Type here

Search button

Figure 3.58

5 If a message displays regarding setting up the Clip Organizer Program, click Later. At the top of the Insert Clip Art task pane, click to position the insertion point in the box under "Search text" and delete any existing text. Type `backpacking` and then, directly beneath the box, click the **Search** button.

Depending upon the number of media clips that have been imported into the Office Clip Organizer, one or more images display.

6 Locate the clip of the adult and children with backpacks (see Figure 3.59) and click directly on the clip.

The clip displays somewhere on your screen. Although clicking the displayed arrow on the clip displays a menu, you can click directly on the clip to initiate the Insert command.

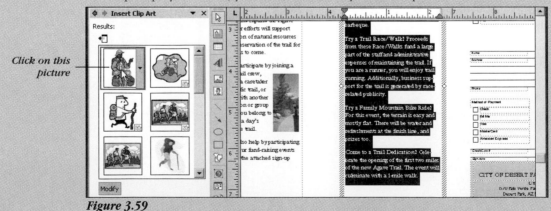

Click on this picture

Figure 3.59

Activity 3.17 Inserting Clip Art

7 Close the Insert Clip Art task pane. Using one of the corner resize handles, resize the picture to about 3/4 inches wide and 1 1/8 inches high. Use the Move pointer to position the clip in the middle of the first paragraph in the frame, and then apply the **Tight** wrapping style. Compare your screen to Figure 3.60, and resize and adjust as necessary; however, the text need not wrap exactly as shown.

Inserted and resized clip

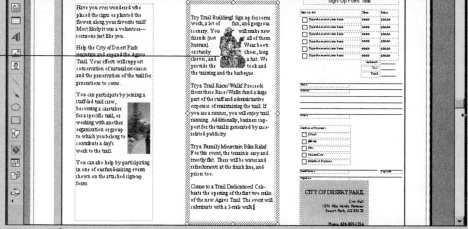

Figure 3.60

8 On the Standard toolbar, click **Save** to save your changes.

To extend your knowledge...

Using the Office Clip Organizer

To access media files from the Office Clip Organizer program, the media file must be imported into the program. When your Office XP software was installed, a small set of media files was automatically imported, and you can import additional media files stored on your local or network drives. Two good sources for additional media clips are the "Media Content" CD that is packaged with the Microsoft XP software and Microsoft's Web site called Design Gallery Live.

A clip art image can be directly inserted from any file location using the Insert Picture command. The advantage to importing images into the Office Clip Organizer program is that the images will be organized in a manner by which you can search for them using a keyword. Once imported, Clip Organizer keeps track of the file's location, description, and keywords. It also provides a thumbnail image of the content so you can see a preview of it.

A **drop cap** is a character effect commonly used in publications. It enlarges a selected letter—usually the first character of an article or paragragh—and lowers the character into the paragraph, raises the character above the paragraph, or suspends the character in the left margin. The drop cap can be further customized by specifying the number of lines into which the character will be dropped, and by applying various other effects to the letter.

Activity 3.18   Applying a Drop Cap

1 **Zoom** to **100%** and position the upper portion of panel 3 (middle) of page 2 in the center of your screen.

2 With your mouse, drag to select the first character, **T**, of the first paragraph in the panel. On the menu bar click **Format** and then click **Drop Cap**.

The Drop Cap dialog box displays.

3 Click the **Custom Drop Cap tab**, and under Select letter position and size, change Size of letters to **2** by either typing or using the spin box. Use the default, Dropped, for the position of the drop cap.

4 Under Select letter appearance, click to clear the Use current color check box. Click the **Color arrow**, and then click the second color (brown) in the color scheme.

5 Click **OK**, and then repeat the process to apply the same drop cap format to the first letter of each of the remaining paragraphs in the frame.

6 Applying the drop cap to each paragraph may have caused some of the text to move into overflow. Click at the top of the frame, and press (Del) to delete the blank line left when the heading was removed (see Figure 3.61).

Click here and then press Delete key to delete blank line

Figure 3.61

7 Scroll to view the upper portion of panel 4 (rightmost) and then **Zoom** to **150%**.

8 Click to select the placeholder text "Sign-Up Form Title" and type Come Play in the Dirt!

9 Select the text you just typed and apply the brown font color and the font **Gill Sans MT**.

10 Click to select the first placeholder text "Type the event name here" and type Trail Build, Sunday, May 5

11 In the "Time" column, click to select the first "00:00" placeholder text and type 8 a.m.

12 In the "Price" column, click to select the first "$00.00" placeholder text and type $25

Activity 3.18   Applying a Drop Cap

13 Fill in the remaining events as follows (see Figure 3.62):

Trail Build, Sunday, June 1	8 a.m.	$25
Race/Walk, Sunday, May 12	8 a.m.	$25
Race/Walk, Sunday, June 8	8 a.m.	$25
Bike Ride, Sunday, May 19	10 a.m.	$30
Gala Dedication, Friday, May 3	8 p.m.	$50

14 To the right of the word "Subtotal:," click on the small line to select the entire object, and press Del to delete it. Repeat with the "Tax" object beneath it.

Normally there is no tax on charitable events such as these.

15 Compare your screen to Figure 3.62 and then click **Save**.

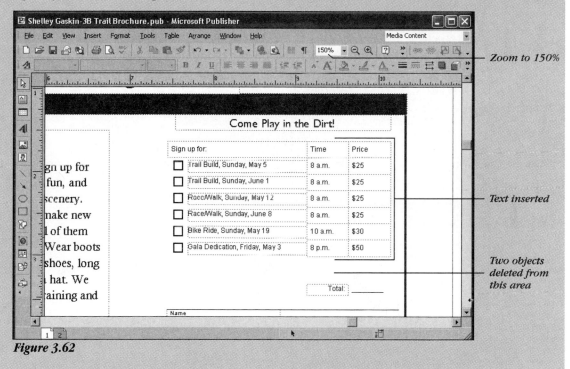

Figure 3.62

Objective 11: Recolor Graphics

Activity 3.19   Recoloring a Graphic

1 Navigate to **page 1**, **Zoom** to **75%**, and then scroll to position the bottom of panel 6 (center) into view.

2 On the Objects toolbar, click the **Picture Frame** button. Inside the gold shape, drag to draw a frame slightly inside (see Figure 3.63) and then release the left mouse button.

The Insert Picture dialog box displays.

(Continues)

Activity 3.19   Recoloring a Graphic (continued)

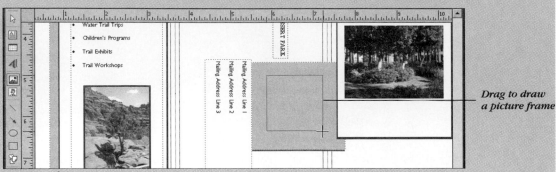

Drag to draw a picture frame

Figure 3.63

3 Navigate to your student files, click **3B_DesertParkLogo**, and then click the **Insert** button.

The logo picture displays within the shape.

4 Hover over the logo, right-click to display a shortcut menu, and then click **Format Picture**.

The Format Picture dialog box displays.

5 If necessary, click the **Picture tab**, and under Image control, click the **Recolor** button.

The Recolor Picture dialog box displays.

6 Click the **Color arrow**, apply the second color (brown) in the color scheme, and be sure the option button for Recolor whole picture is selected.

7 Click **OK** to close the Recolor Picture dialog box, and then click **OK** again to close the Format Picture dialog box.

The logo is recolored in brown.

8 With the logo object still selected, move to the menu bar, click **Arrange**, point to **Rotate or Flip**, and then click **Rotate Right**.

This will align the logo with the text orientation in this panel, which will contain the mailing label.

Activity 3.19   Recoloring a Graphic

9 Use the Move pointer, the corner resize handles, and the Nudge feature as necessary to position and size the image within the gold shape approximately as shown in Figure 3.64.

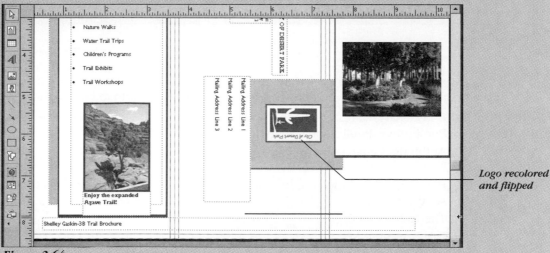

Figure 3.64

10 On the Standard toolbar, click **Save** to save your changes. Then, click **Print Preview**, view two pages side by side, and click **Print** to print your brochure. **Close** the Print Preview, and close the file. Publication 3B Trail Brochure is complete!

Summary

Although text accounts for 80 percent of the content in most publications, it is graphics that gain the reader's initial attention. A graphic is any visual element on the page that is not text. When placing graphics on the page, consider basic design principles and the overall layout of the page.

Publisher 2002 provides many tools to ensure precise size and placement of graphics on a page. Among the tools are layout guides, rulers, ruler guides, and the Measurement toolbar. Once placed on the page, a graphic image can be resized, moved, and rotated.

Graphics can include photographs, clip art, drawings, charts, maps, shapes, lines, and WordArt. A graphic frame can be formatted in various ways by adding borders, fill colors, and fill effects. Additionally, Publisher provides a variety of tools with which you can format images without leaving the Publisher program to access additional software programs. For example, you can recolor an image within the Publisher program.

In this Lesson, you learned about brochures, a very common type of publication. A tri-fold brochure, the most popular form of brochure, contains six distinct panels on which to place text and graphics. Most brochures follow a standard formula for the types of text and graphics placed on each panel.

Because the purpose of Publisher is to arrange text and graphics on a page, Publisher provides various tools by which you can flow text around graphics with ease and precision, and in visually appealing arrangements called wrapping styles.

Using Publisher Help

Scanners are popular additions to a computer. Using Publisher, you can add a picture directly from your scanner into a publication. In this exercise, you will use Help to find out how to use this feature.

1. If necessary, start Publisher and display the New Publication task pane and the Quick Publications Publication Gallery.
2. At the right edge of the menu bar, click in the Ask a Question box and type How can I scan a picture into my publication?
3. Press ⏎Enter and then on the displayed list, click **Add a picture directly from your scanner**.
4. The Help pane displays.
5. If you want to keep a copy of this information, click the **Print** button. It will print on one page, but your name will not print on the document.
6. Click the **Close** button—the **X** in the top right corner of the Help window to close the Help window.

Concepts Assessment

Short Answer

Write the correct answer in the space provided.

1. Although it is graphics that catch the attention of the reader, words comprise approximately _____percent of a typical publication.
2. When placing graphics on a page, consider basic _____ to increase the likelihood of getting people to read your publication.
3. One of the advantages of using Publisher is that basic graphic design has already been created by _____ in graphic design.
4. Rather than an actual image, vector files contain a _____ about how to form an image.
5. Vector files can be created with various types of _____ programs.
6. For realistic images such as photographs, the _____ file format is best.
7. Your digital camera can be used to capture a bitmap image, or images can be created in commercial software programs, such as _____ or _____.
8. The most common size and fold arrangement for a brochure, in thirds, is called a _____ brochure.

9. When double-clicking, it is not the speed of the two clicks that is important, but rather that between the two clicks the mouse remains _____.

10. Text can be added to most AutoShapes by simply selecting the shape and starting to _____.

Matching

Match each term in the second column with its correct definition in the first column. Write the letter of the term on the blank line to the left of the correct definition.

_____ 1. An effect that enlarges the selected character, usually the first character of an article or newsletter, and lowers the character into the paragraph or suspends it in the left margin.

_____ 2. Electronic files consisting of pictures, movies, or sound recordings.

_____ 3. The proportional relationship of a picture's width and height.

_____ 4. A file format created specifically for photographs.

_____ 5. An application within Microsoft Office XP that transforms text into a stylized graphic object.

_____ 6. A small yellow diamond attached to an AutoShape with which you can change the most prominent feature, for example the width of an arm on a star.

_____ 7. Visual arrangements by which text can flow around, or position itself relative to, a graphic object.

_____ 8. Another name for bitmap objects.

_____ 9. The process of selecting two or more objects and combining them into one object for the purpose of moving, copying, or formatting.

_____ 10. Text that briefly describes a photo or graphic.

_____ 11. The ability to have text appear to flow around graphic images, even though each is held in different frames.

_____ 12. A small green handle displayed on a selected image with which the image can be rotated in various directions.

_____ 13. Graphic images whose files contain a mathematical description about how to form the lines, shape, and fill of the graphic.

_____ 14. Anything on the page that is not text.

_____ 15. Graphic files composed of a pattern of thousands of dots (called pixels).

A. Adjustment handle

B. Aspect ratio

C. Bitmaps

D. Caption

E. Drop cap

F. Graphics

G. Grouping

H. jpeg

I. Media Files

J. Raster objects

K. Rotation handle

L. Vector objects

M. WordArt

N. Wrapping

O. Wrapping styles

Skill Assessments

Publication 3C

Building Name

In the following Skill Assessment, you will create an announcement for the City Manager regarding the naming of a new courthouse. Your completed publication will look like the one shown in Figure 3.65. You will save your publication as *Firstname Lastname-3C Building Name.*

Figure 3.65

1. Start Publisher, display the New Publication task pane and the Quick Publications Gallery. Click the Blank Quick Publication.

2. In the Quick Publication Options task pane, under Layout, click the Message only layout. Set the color scheme to Desert, and close the task pane.

3. On the menu bar, click View, and then click Header and Footer. Use the Show Header/Footer button on the Header and Footer toolbar to navigate to the Footer frame, and then type `Firstname Lastname-3C Building Name`

4. Close the Header and Footer toolbar, zoom to 75%, and position the top portion of the page in the middle of your screen.

5. On the menu bar, click File, click Save As, navigate to the location in which you are storing your files for this Lesson, and in the File name box type `Firstname Lastname-3C Building Name`

6. On the left side of the screen, position the pointer over the vertical ruler until the Move Vertical Ruler ScreenTip displays. Drag the ruler to the right to align it with the first vertical pink layout guide. This will assist with positioning some of the objects in this exercise.

7. Click anywhere in the words beginning "Place your message" to select the text box. Use the top center sizing handle to drag the top of the text box down to 2.5 inches on the vertical ruler. Scroll down, and then use the bottom center sizing handle to drag the bottom of the text box up to 5.5 inches on the vertical ruler.

8. Scroll to view the top of the publication. On the Objects toolbar, click the Rectangle button, position the crosshair pointer on the left blue layout guide at 1.25 inches on the vertical ruler. Drag down to 2 inches on the vertical ruler and then across to the right blue layout guide, forming a wide bar across the top of the page.

9. With the rectangle selected, hover and right-click to display a shortcut menu, click Format AutoShape, and then click the Size tab. Confirm that the Height of the selected rectangle is 0.75″ and the Width is 6.3″—make any necessary adjustments.

10. Click the Layout tab of the Format AutoShape dialog box, and under Position on page, confirm that the Horizontal position is 1.1″ from the Top Left Corner and the Vertical position is 1.25″ from the Top Left Corner—make any necessary adjustments. Recall that these measurements can also be viewed by selecting the object and displaying the Measurement toolbar.

11. Click the Colors and Lines tab, use the Fill Color arrow to fill the shape with the third color (gold) in the color scheme, and then click OK to close the Format AutoShape dialog box. Publisher applies the default .75 pt black solid line to the shape.

12. On the Objects toolbar, click the AutoShapes button, point to Basic Shapes, and in the first row, click the fourth shape—Diamond.

13. Position the crosshair pointer on the top edge of the gold bar at 6 inches on the horizontal ruler, and then drag down to the bottom of the gold bar and to the right to 7 inches on the horizontal ruler.

14. With the diamond shape selected, move to the menu bar, click Format, and then click AutoShape. Use the Colors and Lines tab to fill the diamond shape with the seventh (bronze) color in the color scheme.

15. With the diamond shape selected, hold down Ctrl, notice that a plus sign attaches to the mouse pointer, and then click anywhere in the gold bar. This displays the Group Objects button. Click the button to group the bar and the diamond into one object.

16. With the grouped object selected, move to the Standard toolbar and click the Copy button, and then click the Paste button. A copy of the bar displays. Scrolling down as necessary, use the Move pointer to move the copy down to the bottom of the page, positioning it between the blue layout guides, and positioning the top edge at 9 inches on the vertical ruler.

17. In the gray scratch area, right-click to display a shortcut menu, point to Toolbars, and then click Measurement to display the Measurement toolbar. Click the gold bar at the bottom of the page to select it, and confirm that the Horizontal Position is 1.1″ and the Vertical

Position is 9″. The Width and Height have not changed because this object is a copy of the bar at the top.

18. With the bar at the bottom of the page selected, move to the menu bar, click Arrange, point to Rotate or Flip, and then click Flip Horizontal. The diamond shape is on the left side of the bar. Close the Measurement toolbar.

19. If necessary, scroll up slightly to view the bottom boundary of the text frame. On the Objects toolbar, click the Picture Frame button. Beneath the resized text frame, position the crosshair pointer at 1.5 inches on the horizontal ruler and 6 inches on the vertical ruler. Drag down and to the right to 4 inches on the horizontal ruler and 8.5 inches on the vertical ruler.

20. Insert the picture *3C_BLDGPIC*. Display the Format Picture dialog box and click the Size tab. Under Scale, click to select the Lock aspect ratio check box. Under Size and rotate, use the up arrow in the spin box to change the Height to 3.175″—the Width will change proportionately. This is equivalent to dragging a corner sizing handle, but with more precision. Use the Colors and Lines tab to apply a brown 6 pt line style to the picture. Click OK to close the Format Picture dialog box.

21. With the Move pointer, visually center the picture horizontally on the page, and vertically between the text frame and the gold bar as shown in Figure 3.65.

22. Click to select the placeholder text beginning "Place your message" and then type The City is pleased to announce that the new courthouse will be named The Nicholas Black Elk Hall of Justice.

23. Scroll to view the gold bar at the bottom of the page. On the Objects toolbar, click the Text Box button, position the crosshair pointer at 3 inches on the horizontal ruler and 9.25 inches on the vertical ruler, and drag to 7 inches on the horizontal ruler and 9.5 inches on the vertical ruler. This will create a text box over the gold bar.

24. In the text box that you just created, type Nicholas Black Elk served as the mayor from 1988 to 2000.

25. Click in the gray scratch area to view your changes, and then drag the vertical ruler back to the left edge of the screen. On the menu bar, click the Save button to save your changes. On the Standard toolbar, click the Print Preview button to view the page. Then, on the Print Preview toolbar, click the Print button to print one complete copy of your publication.

26. Close the Print Preview. On the menu bar click File, and then click Close. If necessary, click Yes to save any additional changes. Publication 3C is complete!

Publication 3D

Police Brochure

In the following Skill Assessment, you will create a brochure for the City of Desert Park Police Department. Your completed publication will look like the one shown in Figure 3.66. You will save your publication as *Firstname Lastname-3D Police Brochure*.

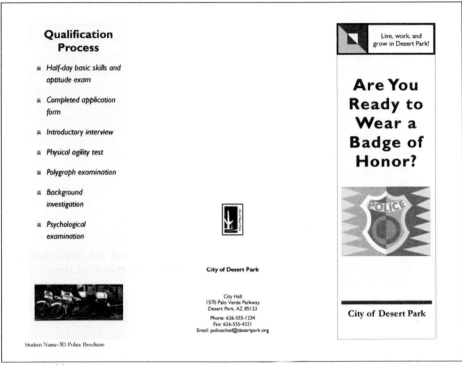

Figure 3.66A

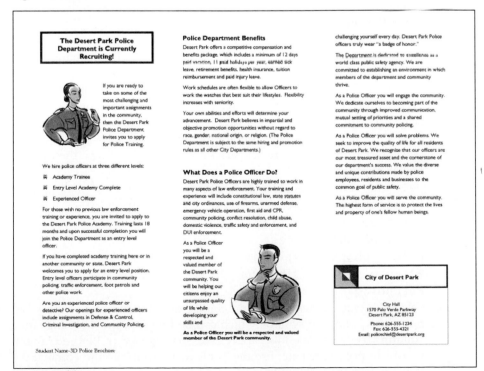

Figure 3.66B

1. Start Publisher and display the New Publication task pane. Under Start from a design, be sure that By Publication Type is displayed. Click Brochures, and then click Informational. In the Informational Brochures Publication Gallery, click the Accent Box Informational Brochure.

2. In the Brochure Options task pane, check to be sure that the following default settings are selected: Under Page size, 3-panel; under Customer address, None; and under Form, None. Check the Color Scheme, and if necessary, set the Color Scheme to Desert. Close the task pane.

3. On the menu bar, click Edit, and then click Personal Information. Be sure that the typed information is for the Desert Park City Manager as shown in Figure 3.42 in Activity 3.10. Do not be concerned if the logo does not match—it can be inserted later. Click Update to close the dialog box.

4. On the menu bar, click View, and then click Header and Footer. Use the Show Header/Footer button on the Header and Footer toolbar to navigate to the Footer frame. Display the Measurement toolbar, click in the footer frame to select it, and then in the Measurement toolbar, change x to 0.5″, change y to 8″, and change Width to 9″. In the footer frame type `Firstname Lastname-3D Police Brochure`

5. Close the Header and Footer toolbar and Zoom to 66%. Close the Measurement toolbar. Save the brochure as *Firstname Lastname-3D Police Brochure* and then print and fold a copy to use as a reference as you work through the exercise. You may want to write the panel numbers on your printed and folded copy.

6. Scroll to position panel 1 into view. Select the "Product/Service" placeholder text and type `Are You Ready to Wear a Badge of Honor?`

7. Click the picture to select it, hover and right-click to display the shortcut menu, point to Change Picture, and then click From File. Navigate to your student files and insert *3D_BADGE*.

8. With the badge selected, hover and right-click, and then click Format Picture. On the Picture tab, click the Recolor button, click the Color arrow, and then click the second color (brown) in the color scheme. Be sure that the Recolor whole picture option button is selected, and then click OK twice to close the dialog boxes.

9. Select the text frame above the badge that contains the brochure title. Drag the bottom center resize handle of the text frame down to 4 inches on the vertical ruler. Select the text, apply Best Fit, and then Center the text horizontally.

10. At the bottom of the panel, delete the entire telephone number text box. In the remaining text box, select the text "City of Desert Park," apply Bold, change the font size to 16, and then center the text horizontally. Click in the scratch area to cancel the selection. Select the line object just above the City's name, and use the Line Color and Line/Border Style buttons on the Formatting toolbar to change it to a brown, 6 pt line.

11. Scroll to display panel 5 (leftmost). Change the "Back Panel Heading" placeholder text to `Qualification Process`. Center the text horizontally and apply Best Fit. Select the placeholder text beginning "This is a good place" and type the following list, pressing (↵Enter) after each line:
    `Half-day basic skills and aptitude exam`
    `Completed application form`
    `Introductory interview`
    `Physical agility test`
    `Polygraph examination`
    `Background investigation`
    `Psychological examination`

12. Select the text you just typed and change the font size to 14. Apply bullets using as the bullet the police car symbol, which can be found in the Webdings font, sixth row, first column. To the bulleted list, apply Line Spacing of 8 pt Before paragraphs. So that the words do not hyphenate, use the Tools menu to locate the command to turn off hyphenation for this text frame.

13. At the bottom of panel 5, click on the picture. Click the Ungroup Objects button to ungroup the picture from its caption. Click in the scratch area to cancel all selections, and then select and delete only the caption frame. Select the picture and display the shortcut menu. Point to Change Picture, and from your student files insert *3D_Panel6PIC*.

14. Press F9 to zoom up to view the picture clearly. With the motorcycle picture selected, display the Show Picture toolbar by displaying the shortcut menu. On the Show Picture toolbar, click the Crop button. Position the cropping pointer over the top center cropping handle, and then drag downward just enough to hide the Exit sign portion at the top of the picture. Click the Crop button again to cancel the crop pointer, and then close the toolbar.

15. On panel 6, in the email address, select "citymanager" and type `policechief` and then click Save to save your changes. If the City of Desert Park logo is not displayed, select the existing logo and use Change Picture to replace it with the file *3D_DesertParkLogo*.

16. Press F9 to return to your original setting. Navigate to page 2 and position panel 2 (leftmost) in view. Select the "Main Inside Heading" placeholder text and type `The Desert Park Police Department is Currently Recruiting!`

17. Select the placeholder text beginning "The most important" and from your student files, insert *3D_Panel2Text*. Click anywhere in the text and turn off hyphenation for this frame. At the top of the panel, select the picture, and then ungroup it from its caption. Click in the scratch area to cancel all selections, and then select and delete the caption text frame.

18. Select the picture and display the shortcut menu. Point to Change Picture, click From File, and from your student files insert *3D_Panel2PIC*. Move the graphic to the top and left edges of the text frame, so that the text wraps as shown in Figure 3.66. In the second paragraph, select the three levels of police officers and apply the police car bullet, which may now display on the dialog box.

19. Scroll to position panel 3 (middle) in view. At the top of the panel, click to select the first "Secondary Heading" placeholder text and type `Police Department Benefits`. Click the placeholder text below the heading you just typed, and insert the file *3D_Panel3Text*. Click anywhere in the inserted text and turn off hyphenation.

20. In the middle of the panel, click to select the second "Secondary Heading" placeholder text, and then type `What Does a Police Officer Do?` Select the placeholder text below the heading you just typed and insert the file *3D_Panel3and4Text*. Notice that this frame is linked to the frame on panel 4, so the text flows over to panel 4.

21. At the bottom of panel 3, ungroup the picture from its caption, select the picture only, and change the picture to *3D_Panel3PIC*. Use the Move pointer to align the picture with the right and bottom edge of the frame. In the caption text frame type `As a Police Officer you will be a respected and valued member of the Desert Park community.`

22. On the menu bar, click the Save button to save your changes. On the Standard toolbar, click the Print Preview button, and then click the Multiple Pages button to view the two pages side by side. Then, on the Print Preview toolbar, click the Print button to print one complete copy of your publication.

23. Close the Print Preview. On the menu bar click File, and then click Close. If necessary, click Yes to save any additional changes. Publication 3D is complete!

Performance Assessments

Publication 3E

Email Announcement

In the following Performance Assessment, you will create an announcement for email training for City employees. Your completed publication will look like the one shown in Figure 3.67. You will save your publication as *Firstname Lastname-3E Email Announcement*.

City of Desert Park

Live, work, and grow in Desert Park!

Date: September 27

Time: 10 a.m.

Learn Email

You have probably heard that the City has implemented a new email system. The Training Department is conducting a two-hour training session for the new system on September 27 at 10 a.m. The training will be conducted by Belle Anderson, our in-house computer instructor. The new system is very fun and easy to use, but there are many new features that you will want to learn about.

Computer Training Room, 3B in City Hall

Call Belle at Ext. 4322

Highlights

◆ Meet new colleagues!

◆ Enjoy a free lunch!

◆ Prizes!

Student Name-3E Email Announcement

Figure 3.67

1. Start Publisher. Click to display the Flyers templates, and then click Event. In the Publication Gallery, click the Ascent Event Flyer. In the Flyer Options task pane, accept the default options under Graphic, Customer address, and Tear-offs, be sure that the Color Scheme is Desert, and then close the task pane. Insert a footer with your first and last name and the file name. Be sure that the Personal Information Set is for the City Manager of Desert Park. Save the file using your first and last name and the file name.

2. Zoom to Whole Page. Click the black and brown bar element and delete it. Along the left blue layout guide, draw a rectangle about .25 inch wide from the top blue layout guide to the bottom blue layout guide. (Hint: Estimate the width visually, then display the Measurement toolbar, select the rectangle, and change the width, which is the third measurement, to exactly .25".)

3. Zoom to 75%. Format the rectangle by applying a two-color gradient fill composed of the fifth (gray) and sixth (purple) colors in the color scheme. Use the Vertical shading style and the first (default) Variant. For the line color, select No Line.

4. Scroll to view the lower portion of the page. At the right, click the border of the text box containing the text "City of Desert Park" to display a pattern of dots, and delete the text box. In the same manner, delete the two text boxes directly below the one you just deleted. (Because this is an internal announcement, this information is not necessary.) Move the Desert Park logo to the left, aligned with the bottom blue layout guide and almost touching the rectangle. (If the logo is not the Desert Park logo, change it using the file *3E_DesertParkLogo*.)

5. Drag the vertical ruler slightly to the right, aligned with the left pink layout guide. Drag the horizontal ruler down, aligned just below the lower blue layout guide. (The footer frame is blocking the view of the lower pink layout guide.) On the Objects toolbar, click the AutoShapes button, point to Basic Shapes and in the first row, click the second shape (Parallelogram). Position the crosshair pointer at 7.5 inches on the horizontal ruler and at 9 inches on the vertical ruler, and then drag down and to the *left* to 6.5 inches on the horizontal ruler and 10 inches on the vertical ruler.

6. With the parallelogram selected, click Copy and then click Paste. With the second (copied) shape selected, format it with the sixth color (purple) in the color scheme as the fill color and No Line. Select the first parallelogram and format it with the fifth color (gray) in the color scheme as the fill color and No Line.

7. On the menu bar, click Arrange, point to Ruler Guides, and then click Add Horizontal Ruler Guide. Point to the green guide, hold down the (Shift) key to display the Adjust pointer, and drag the guide to 8.75 inches on the vertical ruler. Create a second green ruler guide at 10 inches on the vertical ruler. Align the top edge of the gray shape along the top ruler guide, and align the bottom edge of the purple shape along the lower ruler guide. Use the Nudge feature to position the purple shape overlapping about half of the gray shape (refer to Figure 3.67). Use the Arrange menu to clear all ruler guides.

8. Click the Line button on the Objects toolbar, position the crosshair pointer at 9.5 inches on the vertical ruler and 2 inches on the horizontal ruler, hold down the (Shift) key and drag right to the far edge of the second parallelogram. Use the Line Color and Line/Border Style buttons on the Formatting toolbar to apply the seventh color (bronze) and 6 pt solid style to the line. Drag the rulers back to the left and top of the window.

9. Scroll to the top of the page. In the Date box, click on the zeroes and type `September 27`. In the Time box, click on the zeroes and type `10 a.m.` Click to select the placeholder text "Event Title" and then delete the placeholder text. On the Objects toolbar, click the Insert WordArt button. In the second row, click the fourth WordArt style. As the text, type `Learn Email`. With the Move pointer, visually center the WordArt object in the text frame from which you deleted the placeholder text. Use the WordArt toolbar to format the WordArt with the 6th color (purple) in the color scheme, and then stretch each end to fit within the text frame. Apply Tight WordArt character spacing, and then close the WordArt toolbar.

10. Scroll down to view the entire picture. Click to select the picture and then press (Del). If a message displays regarding changing design, click No. (This would select a different template layout.) On the Objects toolbar, click the Clip Organizer Frame button. In the Insert Clip Art task pane, in the Search text box type `computers` and then click the Search button. In the displayed thumbnails, click the picture of the woman seated at a computer as shown in Figure 3.67. If this clip is not available to you, click some other computer picture. Close the task pane, and then use the Move pointer and resize handles to position the clip approximately as shown in the figure.

11. Select the placeholder text that begins "Place text here" and insert the file *3E_Text*. Format the line spacing of the inserted text with 1.5 spaces between lines. In the text box to the right, replace the three bulleted highlights with the following:

    `Meet new colleagues!`
    `Enjoy a free lunch!`
    `Prizes!`

12. Select the placeholder text that begins "Describe your location" and type `Computer Training Room, 3B in City Hall`. For the placeholder text that begins "Contact person" type `Call Belle at Ext. 4322` and then delete the placeholder phone number.

13. Save your changes. Use Print Preview to view the overall look of your publication. Then print the publication, close the Print Preview, and close the publication. Publication 3E is complete!

Publication 3F

Price List

In the following Performance Assessment, you will edit a price list brochure for summer courses being offered by the City's Department of Fine Arts and Parks. The brochure was based on a Publisher price list template. Your completed publication will look like the one shown in Figure 3.68. You will save your publication as *Firstname Lastname-3F Price List*.

Figure 3.68A

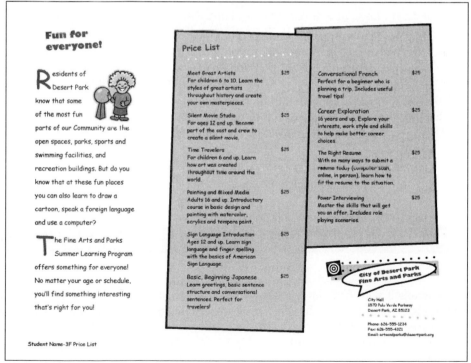

Figure 3.68B

1. Start Publisher. From your student files, open publication *3F_PriceList*. Open the footer frame and change its x measurement to 0.5″, its y measurement to 8″ and its width to 9″. Insert a footer with your first and last name and the file name. Save the file using your first and last name and the file name. Print and fold a copy of the brochure for your reference as you work through the newsletter. Close the Measurement toolbar.

2. Scroll and Zoom as necessary to view panel 1. Replace the "Price List" placeholder text with `Summer Fun Classes Price List`

3. Scroll to view panel 5. Replace the "Back Panel Heading" with `Celebrate Summer!` Click to select the placeholder text beginning "This is a good place" and insert the file *3F_Panel5Text*. Remove hyphenation from this frame. Select the last four lines and apply a small bullet of your choice. In the caption beneath the telephone graphic, type `Call 626-555-ARTS for more information` and change the font size of the caption text to 12.

4. Scroll to view panel 6. Use the Arrange menu to rotate the logo to the right, and recolor it with the 2nd color (brown) in the color scheme.

5. Navigate to page 2, and scroll to view panel 2. Replace the "Main Inside Heading" with `Fun for everyone!` Ungroup the graphic from its caption, and then delete the caption text box. Select the graphic, and then use Change Picture from the shortcut menu to insert the file *3F_Panel2PIC*. Select the placeholder text beginning "Use this space" and replace it with *3F_Panel2Text*. Remove hyphenation from this text. Select the picture and change its wrapping style to Tight. Apply a custom drop cap to the first letter of each of the two paragraphs, using the Dropped position, 2 lines high, in the sixth color (purple) in the color scheme.

6. Scroll to display panel 4. In the third row of the table, click to select the placeholder text that begins "List your product" and type `The Right Resume`. Click to select the placeholder text that begins "Include description" and type `With so many ways to submit a resume today (computer scan, online, in person), learn how to fit the resume to the situation`. Change the font size of the class description text that you just typed to 9. Enter a price of $25

7. In the last row, enter the class title `Power Interviewing` and then the description `Master the skills that will get you an offer. Includes role playing scenarios`. Change the font size of the class description text you just typed to 9. Then enter a price of $25

8. Save your changes. Use Print Preview to view the overall look of your publication. Then print the publication, close the Print Preview, and close the publication. Publication 3F is complete!

On the Internet

"Express yourself with free clip art, photos, animations and sounds from Design Gallery Live." Those are the introductory words at the site from which thousands of additional clip art images are available to you for free. The site is Microsoft's Design Gallery Live. Visit the site at **http://dgl.microsoft.com** (no "www" necessary for this site).

Microsoft provides an easy-to-use form from which you can search for clips by key words. Microsoft is continuously adding new images, and whole new collections of images; for example "Birthday," and you can elect to download the whole collection.

Downloaded clips are stored in the Clip Organizer program on your hard drive, and from there you can use the Clip Organizer program to search for them in the future.

Read Microsoft's "Terms of Use" to be sure that you are using the clips within copyright laws. Clips can be used for personal use, but not in a publication that you plan to sell.

Starting With a Blank Publication

Objectives

In this lesson, you learn how to:

- ✔ Set Document and Sheet Size
- ✔ Change Font Schemes and Color Schemes
- ✔ Use Guides to Align Objects
- ✔ Insert Line Breaks
- ✔ Insert Design Gallery Objects
- ✔ Use the Design Checker
- ✔ Work With Multi-page Publications
- ✔ Create Mirrored Guides
- ✔ Create a WordArt Logo and Save it in the Design Gallery
- ✔ Create Facing Footers
- ✔ Link Text Boxes
- ✔ Create and Apply Text Styles
- ✔ Insert Text in Columns
- ✔ Create Horizontal Rules
- ✔ Create a Folded Publication

Key terms in this Lesson include

- ❏ composite RGB
- ❏ design checker
- ❏ document size
- ❏ embedded graphics
- ❏ font descenders
- ❏ gutters
- ❏ horizontal rules
- ❏ legal size paper
- ❏ letter size paper
- ❏ linked graphics
- ❏ Pack and Go wizard
- ❏ process colors (CMYK)
- ❏ sheet size
- ❏ side fold card
- ❏ smart object
- ❏ style
- ❏ tabloid size paper
- ❏ tent fold card
- ❏ top fold card
- ❏ trapping

Publication Design Tips—Working With a Professional Printing Company

One of the advantages of Microsoft Publisher is the ease with which you can produce attractive publications from your desktop printer; however, you will probably have some publications that require the services of a professional printing company. You need a professional printer when you require a level of quantity, quality, color, or physical characteristics that you cannot produce on your desktop printer.

The Tools menu provides a group of four commands called Commercial Printing Tools that enable you to prepare your publication for commercial printing. Even if you have little knowledge of commercial printing techniques, Publisher assists you by ensuring that an electronic Publisher file provided to a professional printer results in the exact publication that you had in mind.

The first of the four Commercial Printing Tools is Color Printing. In this dialog box, you can decide how the colors in your publication will be printed. The **Process colors (CMYK)** option converts the colors to their CMYK (cyan, magenta, yellow, and black) equivalents—a formula for color formation that is understood by commercial printers. If you intend to distribute the publication only in electronic form (on the Web or on a CD), pick **Composite RGB**—colors that are intended to display on a monitor.

The second Commercial Printing Tool is Trapping. When a commercial printer prints your publication in color, the paper is moved through a printing press at least four times. Slight variations in paper alignment or size can result in some paper showing through where ink was supposed to be. A process called **trapping** is used to compensate for such errors on the printing press. Your printing professional can advise you on how to adjust this setting, depending upon the type of printing press they use.

The third Commercial Printing Tool is the Graphics Manager. Graphics can be either **embedded** in the publication (the graphic becomes part of the publication file) or **linked** to the publication (the graphic exists in a separate file). By default, Publisher embeds all graphics. Ask your printing professional if he or she prefers that you link the graphics files or that you embed them directly into your publication.

The last Commercial Printing Tool is Fonts. To print your publication, your professional printing company must have the same fonts installed on their computer that you used in your publication. If you use the TrueType fonts installed with Publisher, however, it will be easy for your printing service because Publisher can embed them directly into your publication. This could save you time and money because the printer will not have to embed them for you. Rely upon your printing professional to advise you regarding font usage.

Another tool that is frequently used when taking your publication files to a commercial printer is **Pack and Go**. Pack and Go is a wizard (a step-by-step process) that creates **linked graphics** and embeds fonts in your publication so that your printing service has access to the graphics and typefaces you want to use in your publication. The result is a complete file containing all the necessary elements that your professional printer will need to produce your publication on professional printing presses.

Publication 4A

Dog Walk

In Activities 4.1–4.7 you will create an announcement for the Department of Arts and Parks' annual Dog Walk fundraiser. Your completed publication will look like the one shown in Figure 4.1. You will save your publication as *Firstname Lastname-4A Dog Walk*.

Figure 4.1

Objective 1: Set Document and Sheet Size

Up to this point, you have created publications using Publisher's predefined templates. Sometimes the templates will meet all of your publications needs. When they do not, however, Publisher assists you in creating a custom design by beginning with a blank publication.

There are two methods by which you can begin a blank publication in Publisher. From the New Publication task pane, under New, click the By Publication Type arrow and choose By Blank Publications. Here you can choose from among predefined layouts for paper size and fold arrangement, but the layouts contain no predefined graphics or frames.

Sheet size refers to the size of the paper on which you print your publication. The three most common sheet sizes used for creating publications are ***letter size*** (8.5 inches wide and 11 inches tall), ***legal size*** (8.5 inches wide and 14 inches tall), and ***tabloid size*** (11 inches wide and 17 inches tall). Most desktop printers will accommodate letter and legal size paper. For tabloid paper—often used for newsletters—you will need a special printer or the services of a professional copy shop or printing company.

Document size is the area of the sheet that contains your text and graphics and is determined by the margin settings. As you have worked with the predefined templates in this book's activities, you used the default margin settings for the selected template—although these settings can be changed. When you begin with a new blank document in Publisher, the default setting is for a letter size sheet and a document size defined by a 1-inch margin on all four sides.

Activity 4.1   Starting a New Blank Publication

❶ **Start** Publisher and display the New Publication task pane and the Publication Gallery. Under Start from a design, click the **By Publication Type arrow**. From the displayed list, click **By Blank Publications**.

The Blank Full Page publication gallery displays on the right as shown in Figure 4.2. Here you can see a visual representation of the various publications for which predefined sheet size, margins (document size), and fold arrangements have been determined.

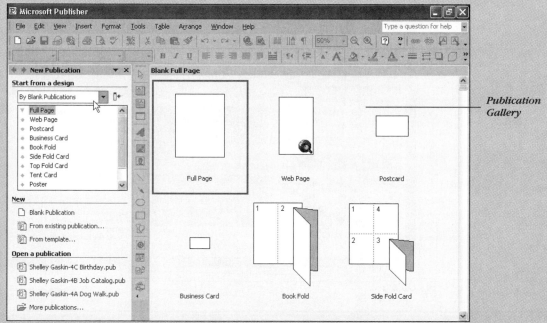

Publication Gallery

Figure 4.2

❷ Scroll down to view the complete array of publications. Scroll back to the top and click **Full Page**.

The page displays with both pink and blue layout guides. Recall that the pink layout guides are the actual margin boundaries of the page, and the blue layout guides indicate where frames should be aligned so that they do not run into each other—they create a safety zone for the margins. The safety zones are referred to as the ***gutters***.

❸ On the menu bar, click **Arrange**, and then click **Layout Guides**.

The Layout Guides dialog box displays. Notice that 1-inch Margin Guides have been set for the Left, Right, Top, and Bottom edges of the sheet.

❹ In the Layout Guides dialog box under Margin Guides, with the Left margin guide highlighted in blue, type .75. Press the Tab↹ key to highlight the Right margin guide and type .75

❺ Use the Tab↹ key to navigate to and then change the Top and Bottom margins to .75.

Activity 4.1   Starting a New Blank Publication

6 In the displayed Layout Guides dialog box, under Grid Guides, use the spin box arrows to change the number of **Columns** to **3** and the number of **Rows** to **2** as shown in Figure 4.3.

Under Preview, the margins, columns, and rows that you selected are pictured.

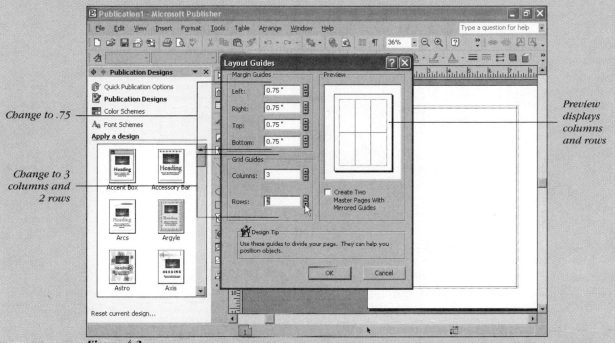

Change to .75

Change to 3 columns and 2 rows

Preview displays columns and rows

Figure 4.3

7 Click **OK** to close the dialog box.

The full page displays in the publication window, showing the guides that will help you position frames on the page.

8 On the menu bar, click **View**, and then click **Header and Footer**. On the Header and Footer toolbar, click the **Show Header/Footer** button to move to the footer frame. In the footer frame, type Firstname Lastname-4A Dog Walk

(Continues)

Activity 4.1   Starting a New Blank Publication (continued)

9 Click the edge of the footer frame to display a pattern of dots, and then use the Move pointer to move the footer frame above and slightly to the right of the blue layout guides as shown in Figure 4.4.

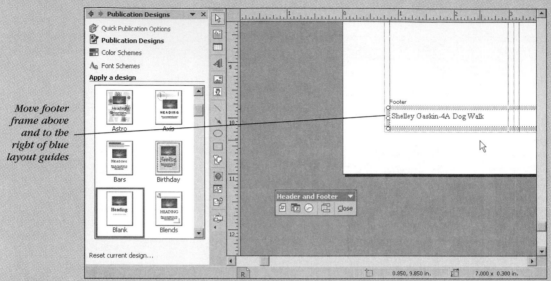

Move footer frame above and to the right of blue layout guides

Figure 4.4

10 On the Header and Footer toolbar, click **Close** to close the Master page and return to the publication.

11 On the menu bar, click **File**, and then click **Save As**. Navigate to the location in which you are storing your publications for Lesson 4, creating a new folder if you want to do so. Save the publication as *Firstname Lastname-4A Dog Walk*.

To extend your knowledge...

Create a blank publication from the New Publication Task Pane

The other method by which you can begin a blank publication is to click Blank Publication, which can be found under New in the New Publication task pane. A blank Full Page publication displays. This is the same as the first publication option that appears in the Blank Full Page publication gallery.

Objective 2: Change Font Schemes and Color Schemes

In the pre-defined publication templates that you used in previous Lessons, the font scheme was provided. Recall from Lesson 2 that professional graphic designers adhere to some specific guidelines regarding the selection of fonts. For example, a serif font is easier to read than a sans serif font. An attractive and easy-to-read arrangement pairs a sans serif font for headings with a serif font for text. From the task pane, you can access a list of font pairs frequently used by professional designers.

Publisher also provides you with a list of professionally assembled color schemes in the same manner. If no Personal Information Set with an accompanying color scheme has been defined on your computer, Publisher's default color scheme is Bluebird. If a Personal Information Set has been defined, the color scheme, if any, for that information set will be automatically applied.

Activity 4.2   Changing Font Schemes and Color Schemes

1 On the task pane, click **Color Schemes**. Under Apply a color scheme, scroll as necessary and click **Mountain**.

In the displayed list, each color scheme is named and the names are in alphabetical order.

2 On the task pane, click **Font Schemes**. Under Apply a font scheme, scroll as necessary and click **Punch**.

In the displayed list, each font scheme is named and the names are in alphabetical order.

3 Close the task pane. On the menu bar, click **File**, and then click **Page Setup**.

The Page Setup dialog box displays.

4 If necessary, click the **Layout tab**, and then under Orientation, click the **Landscape** option button. Click **OK** to close the dialog box.

The publication displays in landscape orientation.

5 On the Standard toolbar, click **Save** to save your changes.

Objective 3: Use Guides to Align Objects

Layout guides are created when you set margins and also when you create columns, rows, or both. The pink guides are the actual boundaries and represent the measurements. The blue guides create extra space so that frames do not bump into each other. Layout guides can be hidden from view, and redisplayed again when you need them. This is accomplished from the menu bar by clicking View, and then clicking Boundaries and Guides.

Activity 4.3   Using Guides to Align Graphics

1 On the Objects toolbar, click the **Picture Frame** button. Position the crosshair pointer in the upper left corner, directly over the intersection of the blue layout guides as shown in Figure 4.5.

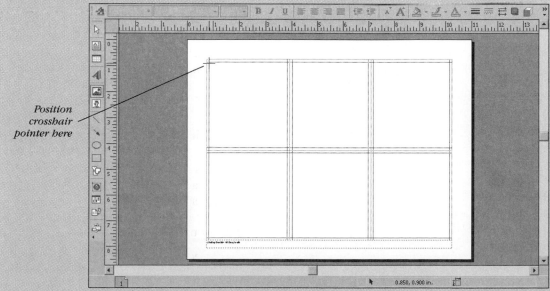

Position crosshair pointer here

Figure 4.5

(Continues)

Activity 4.3   Using Guides to Align Graphics (continued)

2 Hold down the left mouse button and drag to the right to the first blue layout guide. Do not be concerned with how far the lower edge extends. Release the mouse button.

The Insert Picture dialog box displays.

3 Navigate to the location in which your student files for this textbook are stored, click **4A_Dog1**, and then click the **Insert** button.

The dog picture is inserted.

4 With the dog picture selected, hold down the Alt key and press ↑ several times to nudge the upper edge of the picture up and even with the upper blue layout guide as shown in Figure 4.6.

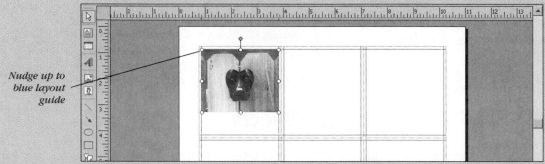

Nudge up to blue layout guide

Figure 4.6

5 With the dog picture selected, display the **Format** menu, click **Picture**, and then click the **Colors and Lines tab**. Under Line, click the **Color arrow**, and then click the first color block—black. Under Line, click the **Style arrow**, and then click **2 1/4 pt** line. Click **OK** to close the dialog box.

6 On the Objects toolbar, click the **Picture Frame** button. Position the crosshair pointer in the second row, middle section, on the upper left corner intersection of the blue layout guides (see Figure 4.7).

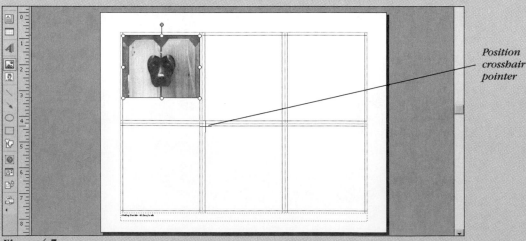

Position crosshair pointer

Figure 4.7

Activity 4.3   Using Guides to Align Graphics

7 Hold down the left mouse button and drag to the column's right blue layout guide as shown in Figure 4.8.

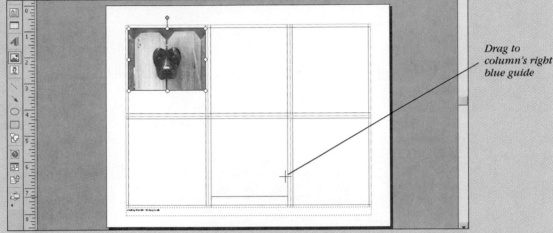

Drag to column's right blue guide

Figure 4.8

8 From the Insert Picture dialog box, insert **4A_Dog2**. Nudge as necessary to align the top of the picture with the upper blue layout guide. Apply a **2 1/4 pt** black line to the picture.

9 On the Standard toolbar, click **Save** to save your changes.

Activity 4.4   Using Guides to Align Text Frames

1 **Zoom** to **66%** and position the upper right portion of the page in the center of your screen.

2 On the Objects toolbar, click the **Text Box** button. Drag to create a text box within the blue layout guides of the second and third blocks in the top row as shown in Figure 4.9.

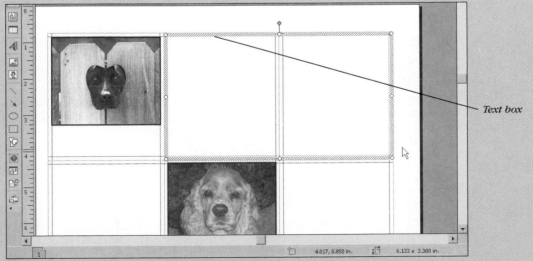

Text box

Figure 4.9

(Continues)

Activity 4.4   Using Guides to Align Text Frames (continued)

3 Within the text box you just created, insert the text file **4A_DogText1**.

4 Use Ctrl + A to select the text, and on the Formatting toolbar, click the **Center** button. Then, display the Format Text Box dialog box, click the **Text Box tab**, and set the Vertical alignment to **Middle**.

5 In the displayed Format Text Box dialog box, click the **Colors and Lines tab**.

6 Under Fill, click the **Color arrow**, and then click **Fill Effects**. Under Colors, click the **Two colors** option button. Click the **Color 1 arrow**, and then click the fourth color block—pale lavender. Click the **Color 2 arrow**, and then click the third color block—gold. Under Shading styles, make sure the **Horizontal** option button is selected, and under Variants, in the first row click the **second variant** as shown in Figure 4.10.

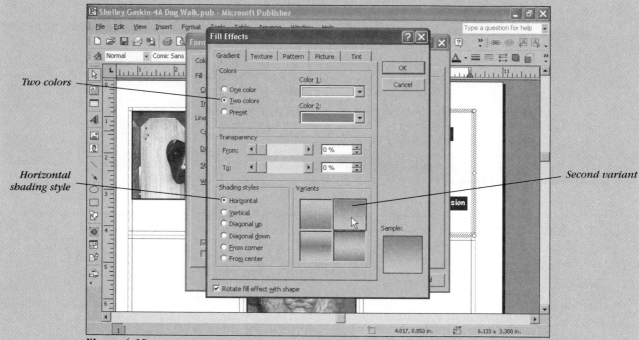

Figure 4.10

7 Click **OK** twice to close the dialog boxes.

8 Click in the gray scratch area to view your changes, and compare your screen to Figure 4.11.

Activity 4.4   Using Guides to Align Text Frames

Note that Cholla may be flagged as a misspelled word because it probably isn't in the Publisher dictionary. This proper noun can either be ignored or added to the dictionary.

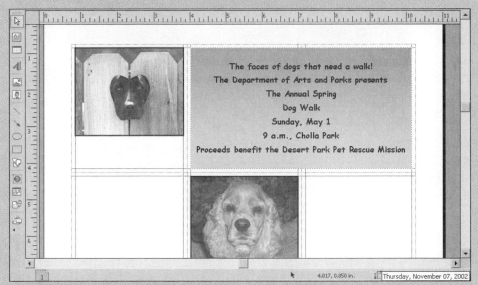

Figure 4.11

9 Position the lower left portion of the page in the center of your screen. As shown in Figure 4.12, create a text box within the blue guides beginning at **3.5 inches on the vertical ruler**.

Text box, beginning at 3.5 inches on the vertical ruler

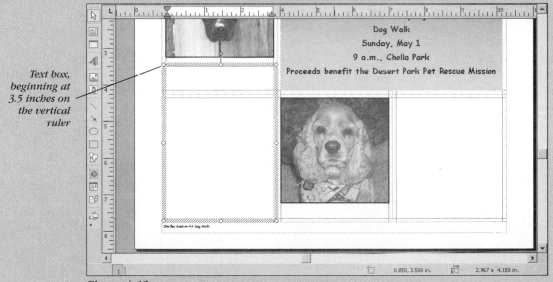

Figure 4.12

10 Insert the text file **4A_DogText2**. Then, select the last four lines of the text and apply a small bullet of your choice.

(Continues)

Activity 4.4   Using Guides to Align Text Frames (continued)

11 In the lower right corner of the page, draw a text box in the last block within the blue layout guides. Insert the text file **4A_DogText3** (see Figure 4.13).

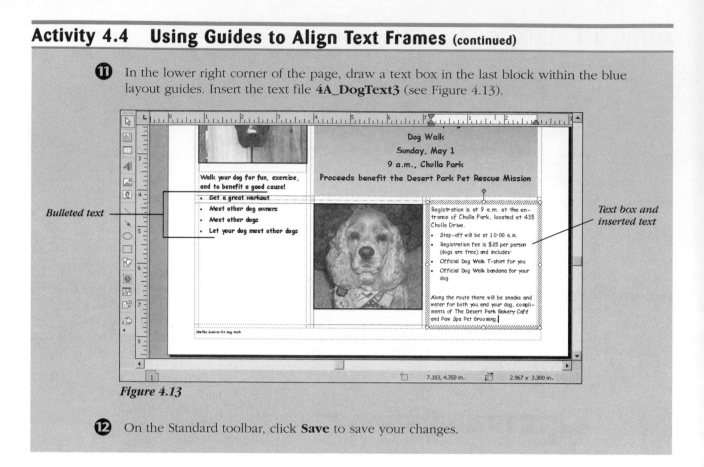

Figure 4.13

12 On the Standard toolbar, click **Save** to save your changes.

Objective 4: Insert Line Breaks

When working with text, each time you press the ⏎Enter key, a new paragraph is created. There are times when you might want to break a line earlier than the word wrap feature does and yet still keep the line within the same paragraph. For example, a line break is convenient when you want to remove hyphenation from a line without removing hyphenation from the entire frame, or at other times when a line simply does not end attractively. To break a line without starting a new paragraph, insert a line break by holding down ⇧Shift and pressing ⏎Enter.

Activity 4.5   Inserting Line Breaks

1 Position the lower right portion of the page in the middle of your screen. On the Standard toolbar, click the **Special Characters** button (to the left of the Zoom button) to display the nonprinting characters that indicate paragraphs and spaces.

2 In the text frame in the lower right corner of the page, in the first line of text, click to position the insertion point in front of the *e* in the word "entrance." Hold down ⇧Shift and press ⏎Enter.

The line is divided and the nonprinting line break character displays.

Activity 4.5   Inserting Line Breaks

3 In the second line of the final paragraph, position the insertion point in front of the *c* in the word "compliments" and then insert a line break as shown in Figure 4.14.

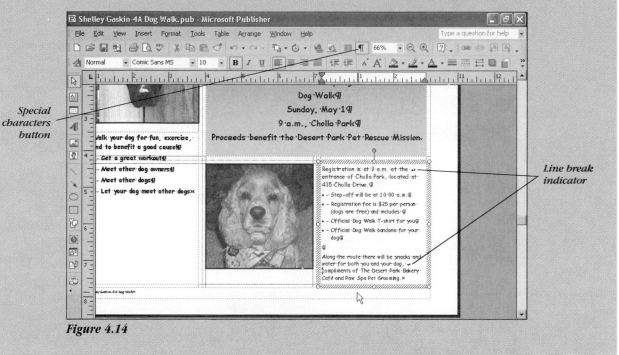

Special characters button

Line break indicator

Figure 4.14

4 On the Standard toolbar, click the **Special Characters** button to turn off their display. Then, on the Standard toolbar, click **Save**.

Objective 5: Insert Design Gallery Objects

Publisher includes a collection of smart objects that you can insert into your publications. A ***smart object*** is a preformatted design element that has a wizard associated with it. The elements include professionally designed logos, headlines, calendars, and mastheads, among many others. These smart objects are stored in the Design Gallery.

Activity 4.6   Inserting Design Gallery Objects

① On the menu bar, click **Insert**, and then click **Design Gallery Object**.

The Design Gallery dialog box displays.

② Under Categories, scroll down the list to view the many different categories of preformatted design elements available (see Figure 4.15).

Categories of Design Gallery Objects

Attention Getters

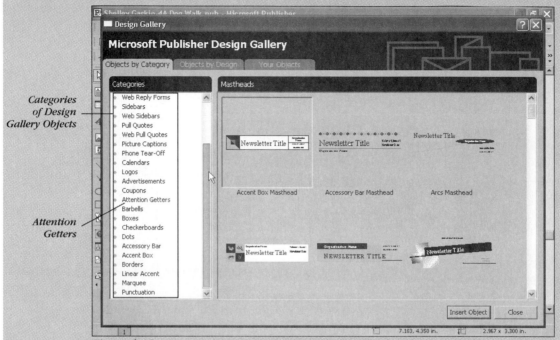

Figure 4.15

③ At the top of the dialog box, click the **Objects by Design tab**. On the left side, under Design Sets, scroll down the list to view the list of design names.

In this tab, the smart objects are filed alphabetically by their design name.

④ Scroll the list and click the **Layers** design, and notice that only a small number of smart objects are available for this design. Then, click the **Bubbles** design, and notice that a much larger number of smart objects are available.

⑤ Click the **Objects by Category tab**. Scroll toward the bottom of the list, and then click **Attention Getters** (see Figure 4.15).

Activity 4.6   Inserting Design Gallery Objects

6 In the Attention Getters window on the right, scroll down to locate and then click the **Shadowed Starburst Attention Getter** as shown in Figure 4.16.

Shadowed Starburst Attention Getter

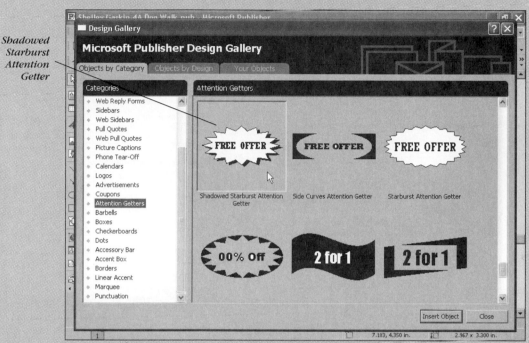

Figure 4.16

7 In the lower right corner, click the **Insert Object** button.

The Attention Getter is inserted onto your page and its wizard button is displayed.

8 Click the **wizard** button.

The Attention Getter Designs task pane opens. From the task pane, you could change to a different Attention Getter design.

9 Close the task pane without changing the design. Then, with the Attention Getter selected, use the Move pointer to position the object below the bulleted list at the

(Continues)

Activity 4.6   Inserting Design Gallery Objects (continued)

lower left side of the page, as shown in Figure 4.17. Visually center the object in the available space.

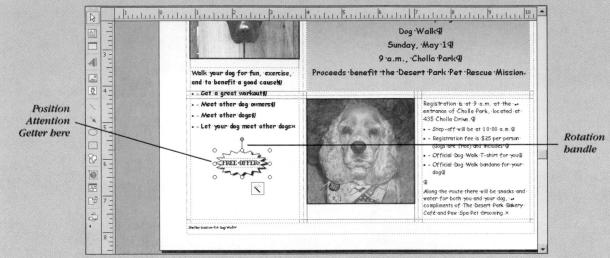

Figure 4.17

🔟 Position the mouse pointer over the green rotation handle, and drag slightly to the left to rotate the Attention Getter as shown in Figure 4.18.

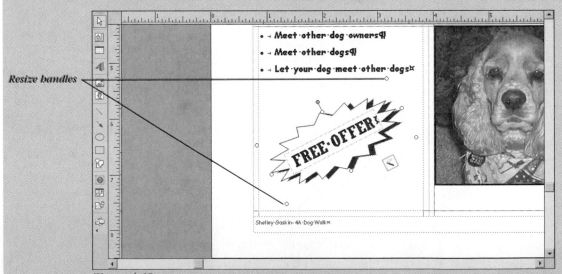

Figure 4.18

⓫ Drag the lower left, upper right, upper middle, and lower middle resize handles to enlarge the Attention Getter approximately as shown in Figure 4.18.

⓬ Click to select the text "Free Offer", change the **Font Size** to **8**, and then change the **Font** to **Comic Sans MS**. Press F9 to zoom in for a better view.

⓭ Type the following text on two lines (see Figure 4.19):

```
Raffle drawing!
Win a Dog Day at the Paw Spa
```

Activity 4.6   Inserting Design Gallery Objects

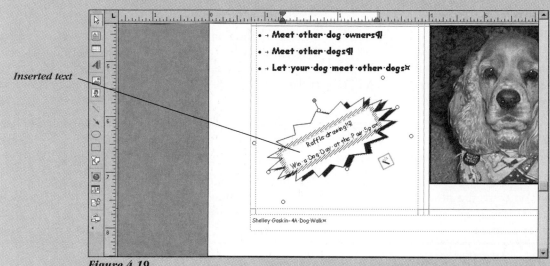

Inserted text

Figure 4.19

⑭ If necessary, enlarge the Attention Getter to accommodate all the text.

⑮ Press (F9) again to zoom out. Display the **Insert** menu, and then click **Design Gallery Object**. Scroll toward the bottom of the list and click **Borders**.

The Borders styles display on the right.

⑯ Click the **Borders Banded Color** style, and then click the **Insert Object** button.

A border displays, but is not sized to fit your landscape page.

⑰ **Zoom** to **Whole Page**. Use the resize handles on each of the four border sides to align the inside edge of each border with the pink layout guide. When adjusting the bottom border, be careful not to hide your footer text. See Figure 4.20.

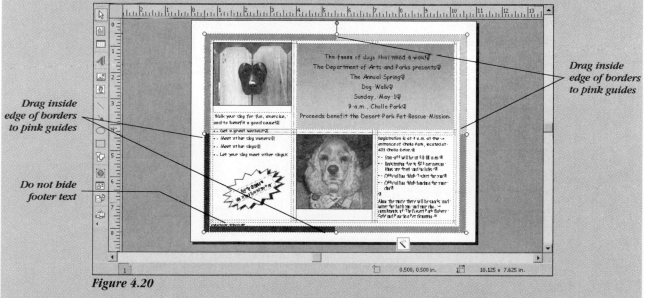

Drag inside edge of borders to pink guides

Drag inside edge of borders to pink guides

Do not hide footer text

Figure 4.20

⑱ On the Standard toolbar, click **Save**.

To extend your knowledge...

Storing Your Own Objects in the Design Gallery

If you create your own graphic elements, you can store them in the Design Gallery and then retrieve them from the area designated by the Your Objects tab. Click to select the object, open the Design Gallery dialog box, and click the Your Objects tab. Click the Options button, and then click Add Selection to Design Gallery. In the Add Object dialog box, type a name for your object, select or add a category, and then click OK.

Your object is saved with the publication that is open, so you will not find it if you open another publication. However, you can open the original publication and use Copy and Paste to place the custom element into the current publication.

Another use for the Your Objects area of the Design Gallery is for the Convert to Web Layout feature. When you convert a newsletter or brochure to Web layout, graphic elements that do not fit precisely on the Web page are stored in the Your Objects area so that you can retrieve them and insert them where appropriate.

Objective 6: Use the Design Checker

With so many features to work with in Publisher, it can be difficult to make sure that you have checked everything. Publisher's **Design Checker** feature will check your publication for errors, such as an empty frame, text left in the overflow area, or an object that is partially covered by another object—among others.

Activity 4.7   Using the Design Checker

❶ On the menu bar, click **Tools**, and then click **Design Checker**.

The Design Checker dialog box displays.

❷ Make sure that under Check which pages? the **All** option button is selected.

❸ On the displayed Design Checker dialog box, click the **Options** button to view the list of specific design elements Publisher can check for you (see Figure 4.21).

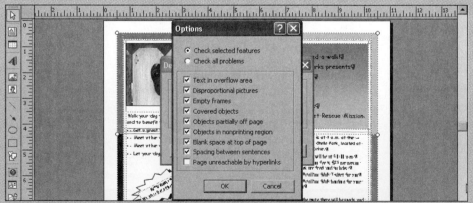

Figure 4.21

❹ Click the **Check all problems** option button.

A check mark displays in each box.

Activity 4.7   Using the Design Checker

5 Click to clear the last check mark (Page unreachable by hyperlinks) because this is not a Web page and no hyperlinks exist.

The Check selected features option button is selected.

6 Click **OK** to close the Options dialog box, and then click **OK** again to begin the check.

Publisher displays a message that a frame is empty as shown in Figure 4.22.

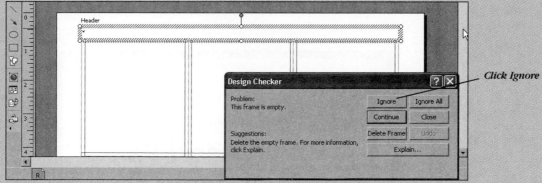

Click Ignore

Figure 4.22

7 Because you have no header in this publication, it is OK to have the header frame empty; click **Ignore** to have Publisher continue checking the publication for errors.

Alternatively, you could click Delete to delete the empty frame.

8 Unless Publisher encounters other errors, a message displays indicating that the check is complete. Click **OK**.

Correct any other errors you may have as necessary.

On the menu bar, click **Print**, and then close the publication, saving any changes. Publication 4A Dog Walk is complete!

Publication 4B

Job Catalog

In Activities 4.8–4.16 you will create a catalog of job descriptions for the City of Desert Park. The eight pages of your completed publication will look like the ones shown in Figure 4.23. You will save your publication as *Firstname Lastname-4B Job Catalog*.

City of Desert Park
Job Guide

This catalog provides descriptions of and information about jobs with the City of Desert Park. It provides information on entry-level clerical and administrative jobs, focusing on occupations that require a high school diploma or some college level courses and knowledge of commonly used business computer applications.

In this guide, business information technology is used to describe occupations that use computer applications to work with information and to solve business problems. These are clerical and administrative support jobs that exist in every department of the City. Today, nearly every job in an office requires the use of a computer. Data entry clerks enter information into computers using database programs. Clerk typists spend much of their day using word processing programs. File clerks use computers to keep track of paper files. Accounting clerks work with spreadsheets. Administrative assistants use word processing, spreadsheet, email and presentation programs. Shipping and receiving clerks use computers to track inventory. It is important for people who do all of these jobs to have the computer skills needed to get a job and to advance within the City.

Clerical and administrative support occupations have traditionally been major entry points for individuals, especially women, who are coming into the workforce for the first time. Even though many other opportunities have opened for women in the past 25 years, women still hold the vast majority of clerical and administrative support positions.

There are a huge number of clerical and administrative support job openings each year in Desert Park and in the state of Arizona. More than 174,000 job openings in these occupations will occur in the state between 1999 and 2006. This offers many opportunities for starting on a career path that can lead in many directions. Most clerical and administrative support positions are entry-level jobs that require only a high school diploma with no additional training or experience. They tend to be lower paying jobs, but many offer good opportunities for advancement for employees who have good skills and show initiative and a willingness to learn.

Student Name–4B Job Catalog   Page 1

Figure 4.23A

require much contact with people outside the accounting department. However, some jobs in billing, accounts receivable or accounts payable include frequent telephone contact with people outside the City.

Entry level wages range from $10 to $12 per hour. Experienced accounting clerks earn from $11 to $20 per hour. The usual work week is 40 hours, Monday through Friday. Overtime is common in some departments at the end of the fiscal year, when preparing taxes or during audits. About 25% of accounting clerks are employed on a part-time basis.

Benefits for full-time employees usually include paid holidays, vacations and sick leave, health, dental and life insurance and retirement plans. Some departments offer bonuses. Part-time employees may earn some benefits, depending on the number of hours worked.

Entry-level accounting clerk positions require a high school diploma or GED. High school classes in business math, computers and data entry are useful. Entry-level positions may require six months experience in clerical, cash handling (such as bank teller), or customer service positions. Specialized positions, such as billing clerk, accounts receivable and accounts payable generally require one to two years experience as an accounting clerk. Some departments require college courses or an Associate degree in business or accounting.

Knowledge of spreadsheet and word processing programs are required for these jobs and most positions also require knowledge of computer databases. Ability to use a 10-key calculator and accurate data entry skills are also essential.

Accounting clerks must have good math skills and be detail oriented, since a small mistake in data entry or calculation can create a big problem for the City. Workers must be willing to do repetitious and routine work. Accounting clerks must be able and willing to comply with City policies and procedures and government regulations. Department heads also want employees who are honest and trustworthy, since accounting clerks often handle cash and checks, and may have access to confidential records.

Community college courses that teach the computer skills used by accounting clerks include introduction to computers, keyboarding, Windows, word processing, spreadsheet and database. Courses that teach other business skills used in this occupation include business English and business math.

Employment for accounting clerks will remain steady; most job openings will be as a result of people leaving the City. Billing clerk positions will grow by 6.7 percent.

- **Knowledge of accounting principles**
- **Spreadsheet skills**
- **Detail oriented**
- **Able to do repetitive work**
- **Oral and writing skills**

City Jobs

Figure 4.23C

Job Title: Accounting Clerk

Accounting clerks help the City keep track of money. They record all the money coming into or going out. This is a good job for people who like working with numbers, are good with computers, and are detail oriented. Accounting clerks use computers to track money and also do much of the clerical work related to accounting and bookkeeping. They open mail to look for checks or bills, prepare bank deposits, write bills, receipts or invoices, file and make copies.

Computer spreadsheet programs or specialized accounting software are used by accounting clerks to record debits and credits and enter data. Accounting clerks perform a wide range of calculations using 10-key calculators or computers, such as balancing accounts and preparing purchase orders, sales tickets, charge slips or bank deposits. They compute interest charges on loans or purchases and check loans and accounts to make sure payments are up to date. Some contact City residents to check on late payments. They also use word processing programs to create letters or reports and email programs. More experienced clerks use computers to create financial statements, track inventory, handle payroll, and prepare balance sheets or monthly payroll. They also compare computer records to paper records to ensure accuracy.

In smaller departments, accounting clerks often do a wide variety of tasks. However, in larger departments, the tasks of accounting clerks are usually divided among several specialties. These include accounts payable (AP) clerks, accounts receivable (AR) clerks, auditing clerks and billing clerks.

Accounts payable clerks work with the accounts of money that the City owes to other businesses or individuals. *Accounts receivable clerks* are responsible for keeping track of money coming into the City. In many departments accounts receivable and accounts payable are handled by the same person. *Auditing clerks* check records of other clerks' work to make sure they are accurate. This position usually requires a high level of accounting clerk experience so that they can catch and correct errors and find other problems.

Billing clerks prepare bills, invoices and statements. In most departments billing is done on a computer, though some departments use a calculator. Billing clerks may answer questions from residents about bills, or this may be done by customer service staff. They create bills based on standard fees, hourly charges or the percentage of work completed.

Accounting clerks usually work in an office environment. The job generally requires sitting at a desk for most of the day, and usually includes many hours working at a computer. Most positions do not

- Great field for people who like to calculate and work with numbers
- Uses spreadsheet and other computer software
- Training easily obtained at a community college

City Jobs

Figure 4.23B

Job Title: Administrative Assistant

Administrative assistant is a job that is halfway between a clerical and a professional occupation. Administrative assistants do a range of clerical tasks, such as answering phones, word processing, ordering supplies and bookkeeping. But they also carry out many administrative tasks that require skills at writing, planning, management and coordination. This job requires a person who is well educated, has previous office experience and is able to make decisions on their own.

Administrative assistants need excellent computer skills to carry out their varied duties. They use computer spreadsheet programs to create budgets, word processors to write reports, database programs to track information and desktop publishing programs to create annual reports. They use graphics programs to create presentations and email to communicate within their organization and with other organizations. Because most professionals now do their own word processing on a desktop computer, administrative assistants no longer routinely handle dictation or typing.

As office automation has increased, administrative assistants have taken on tasks that were once performed by managers or professional staff. For example, administrative assistants may develop project budgets, manage projects, and direct the work flow of a unit or department. They might also train new staff members or conduct research on the Internet. They write letters or reports, interact with outside clients or people in other departments and make decisions on administrative issues. Administrative assistants often supervise other office staff and handle personnel activities such as timesheets, travel reimbursement or tracking vacations. Other common responsibilities of administrative assistants include arranging and coordinating meetings, making travel arrangements and handling correspondence and telephone calls.

In general, administrative assistants perform fewer purely clerical tasks than secretaries and perform many tasks independently, under the general supervision of a professional staff member. Administrative assistants perform more activities related to the actual work of an organization or department. For example, an administrative assistant working for a public relations department would be responsible for editing and submitting press releases, while a secretary would format releases written by someone else. Therefore, administrative assistants need to gain a wide knowledge of all the programs, activities, and people within the organization.

Administrative assistants usually work in offices, and may spend many hours each day working at a computer. They may feel stress

- Wide variety of responsibilities keeps job interesting
- A job for highly skilled and experienced workers
- Positions available in many City departments
- Usually requires Associate or Bachelor's degree

Figure 4.23D

---

because they deal with many different people and may support high-level executives or managers.

Entry level wages range from $12 to $14 per hour Experienced administrative assistants earn from $14 to $24 per hour. Administrative assistants usually work a standard 40-hour week, Monday through Friday. Overtime may be necessary during particularly busy times. There are part-time positions available in many departments.

Benefits for full-time employees usually include paid holidays, vacations and sick leave, health, dental and life insurance and retirement plans. Some departments offer bonuses. Part-time employees may earn some benefits, depending on the number of hours worked.

Most departments prefer administrative assistants to have an Associate degree. Some require a Bachelor's degree. Some prefer business degrees; however other departments prefer a degree related to the main activity of the department. In addition, at least two to four years of related experience are usually required. Some department heads will substitute experience for education.

Administrative assistants need a high level of computer skills. They frequently use word processing, spreadsheet, database, presentation and email programs. Administrative assistants need good communication skills and must have good grammar, spelling and writing skills. They must prioritize tasks and deal with interruptions and still be able to keep projects on schedule. Most work independently and with a good deal of responsibility. Administrative assistants may also need accounting knowledge and project management skills.

Testing and certification for office computer applications is available through the Microsoft MOUS (Microsoft Office User Specialist) program offered at many community colleges. These certificates indicate to a Department Head that an individual has met an acceptable standard of knowledge for a specific computer application. Testing and certification for entry-level office skills is available through the International Association of Administrative Professionals. Community college courses that teach the computer skills used by administrative assistants include introduction to computers, keyboarding, Windows, word processing, spreadsheet, presentation graphics, database, Internet search skills and email/office collaboration. Courses that teach other business skills used in this occupation include business communications, business English, business math, business records skills, office machines and office procedures.

- *Keyboarding skill*
- *Major software applications*
- *Business writing*
- *Office machine skills*
- *Ability to work under pressure*
- *Prioritize tasks and deal with interruptions*

Figure 4.23E

Job Title: Human Resources Assistant

Human resources assistants work at a variety of clerical tasks in human resources or personnel departments. They act as a link between current, past and future employees and the City's management. Human resources assistants may work in a variety of areas related to personnel matters such as recruiting new employees, payroll, benefits, training and general administration.

Human resources assistants use computers for a wide variety of tasks such as tracking job applicants, preparing correspondence and paychecks, posting job listings and tracking employee benefits. They need skills with word processing, spreadsheet, database and email programs.

Entry-level human resources assistants usually do a variety of clerical tasks in a department such as opening mail, filing, data entry, word processing, updating employee records and mailing out job announcements. They also schedule meetings and appointments for job interviews. They answer phones from employees and job applicants and answer routine questions about job openings or benefits. They help new employees with paperwork and prepare routine correspondence.

More experienced human resources assistants may screen applications and refer them for testing or interviews, check references and prepare job descriptions. They also administer employment tests and orient new employees when they are hired. They may conduct preliminary interviews for some job candidates. Human resources assistants may also explain the City's policies to new employees, and inform job applicants by telephone or letter of their acceptance or rejection for employment.

Some human resources assistants specialize in employee benefits. They help employees who have questions about their medical plan, insurance, retirement, tuition reimbursement and other benefits. They track and file forms related to these benefits and assist employees in completing required forms. Some human resources assistants work as payroll and timekeeping clerks. They review time cards and make sure that pay is calculated correctly and that deductions are correct. This work is done using computer database or spreadsheet programs.

Human resources assistants usually work in an office environment. They generally work at a desk and some spend many hours each day using a computer. The job may involve lifting heavy files up to twenty pounds or more.

Entry-level wages range from $11 to $13 per hour. Experienced human resources assistants earn from $12 to $20 per hour. Human resources assistants usually work a standard 40-hour work week,

- Interesting job if you enjoy working with lots of different people
- Expanding job responsibilities
- Good job in which to learn about other jobs
- Salary $11 to $20 per hour

City Jobs

Page 6 Student Name-4B Job Catalog

Figure 4.23F

Monday through Friday. Some part-time positions are available. Benefits for full-time employees usually include paid holidays, vacations and sick leave, health, dental and life insurance and retirement plans. Some departments offer bonuses. Part-time employees may earn some benefits, depending on the number of hours worked.

Entry-level human resources assistant positions generally require a high school diploma or GED and one to three years clerical experience. Higher level positions often require an Associate or Bachelor's degree with a major in business.

Human resources assistants need good computer skills including keyboarding, spreadsheet, word processing, database, scheduling and email programs. Human resources assistants use a variety of office machines such as faxes, copiers, printers and postage meters. They need excellent communication skills and an interest in helping the employees of the City. Department heads look for detail-oriented people with the ability to work as a team and to prioritize many tasks. Those working in benefits and payroll positions need good math ability and general bookkeeping knowledge. The ability to keep information confidential is important because human resources assistants deal with personal information about employees of the City.

Community college courses that teach the computer skills used by human resources assistants include introduction to computers, keyboarding, Windows, word processing, spreadsheet, database, email/collaboration and Internet search skills. Courses that teach other business skills used in this occupation include payroll and tax accounting, business English, business math, human relations in business, business records skills, office machines and office procedures.

Entry-level human resources assistants may advance by specializing in payroll, benefits or recruitment. In larger departments, human resources assistants usually have the opportunity to rotate among the various areas within the department to learn about each area. They may move to other clerical and administrative positions such as bookkeeper, secretary or administrative assistant. Advancement to professional level human resources positions generally requires a Bachelor's degree. Many colleges and universities offer degrees in human resource management or organizational behavior, which would be beneficial to career advancement.

Many departments are moving toward giving payroll responsibilities to secretaries, bookkeepers or general office clerks. Many positions will be available as people advance into other human resources positions from this entry-level job.

- *Able to maintain confidential information*
- *Computer skills, especially word processing and database*
- *Telephone skills*
- *Oral and writing skills*

City Jobs

Student Name-4B Job Catalog Page 7

Figure 4.23G

What City Employers Are Looking For

City Department Heads look for a variety of skills and knowledge when hiring employees. In clerical and administrative positions, basic reading, writing, oral communication and math skills are essential. Department Heads want people who can speak, read and write English clearly with good grammar. They also require knowledge of basic math, including addition, subtraction, multiplication, percentages and fractions. Many Departments test these basic skills before hiring. High school level courses should provide the level of skills needed. Job seekers who need to improve these skills can take free or low-cost classes at Desert Park Community College or adult education programs.

Computer skills are essential to all of the jobs covered in this guide. Nearly all jobs require word processing and many also require knowledge of spreadsheets, database, presentation and email programs. Applicants who have completed the Microsoft Office User Specialist tests would have a good chance of qualifying for the jobs described in this guide. Job seekers who need to acquire or improve these skills

can enroll in classes at Desert Park Community College or in the adult education programs at Desert Park High School.

Personal skills are extremely important, and Department Heads often find that younger or inexperienced applicants lack knowledge of the importance of these "soft" skills. These include basic skills that allow employees to get along with each other in the work place, such as honesty, communication, responsibility and cooperation.

Department Heads also value skills that help employees to take on new tasks and solve problems on the job such as problem solving, ability to learn new things, decision-making, reasoning, and creative thinking. Workers are also expected to show up on time every day for work, dress appropriately, treat other workers with respect, and concentrate on their job during working hours. These may seem obvious, but they are the basic skills that the City looks for in addition to the specific skills needed for a particular job. People hiring new workers want to choose employees that will be easy to get along with on the job.

Page 8   Student Name-4B Job Catalog

Figure 4.23H

Objective 7: Work With Multi-page Publications

Publications such as technical publications, directories, annual reports, and catalogs usually have numerous pages. Publisher assists you in creating and managing long documents, and provides several features, such as the Master page and page numbering, to help you do so.

Activity 4.8   Create a Multi-page Publication

1 **Start** Publisher and display the New Publication task pane and the Publication Gallery. In the New Publication task pane, under New, click **Blank Publication**.

The Full Page format displays and the task pane closes. Recall that the Full Page format is also available from the By Blank Publications menu.

2 On the menu bar, click **Arrange**, and then click **Layout Guides**.

The Layout Guides dialog box displays.

3 Under Grid Guides, use the spin box arrows to change the number of **Columns** to **2** and the number of **Rows** to **2**.

Under Preview, the layout guides that you have selected display.

4 Click **OK** to close the Layout Guides dialog box.

5 On the menu bar, click **Insert**, and then click **Page**.

The Insert Page dialog box displays.

6 Change the Number of new pages to **7** so that you will have a total of 8 pages. Be sure that the **After current page** option button is selected. Under Options, be sure that the **Insert blank pages** option button is selected. Click **OK** to close the dialog box.

Page 2 of your publication displays, and a total of eight pages display on the page navigation bar as shown in Figure 4.24.

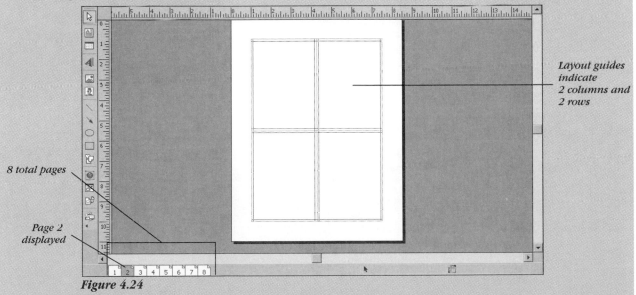

Layout guides indicate 2 columns and 2 rows

8 total pages

Page 2 displayed

Figure 4.24

7 On the menu bar, click **File**, and then click **Save As**. Navigate to the location in which you are storing your publications for Lesson 4. Save the publication as *Firstname Lastname-4B Job Catalog*.

Objective 8: Create Mirrored Guides

Every publication has two parts—the actual publication pages and the underlying Master page. Recall that the Master page is where you can place repeating elements. For example, the footer with your name and file name that you have placed on all of your publications is an element that repeats on every page.

Think about a magazine or a book. When you open it, there is a page on the left and a page on the right. When page numbering is applied, pages on the right have odd numbers (1, 3, 5, and so on) and pages on the left have even numbers (2, 4, 6, and so on). By default, Publisher's Master page is a right-facing page. Because this is a multi-page document, you will need to create a separate Master page for the left-facing pages. This is easily accomplished using Publisher's Mirrored Guides feature.

Activity 4.9   Creating Mirrored Guides

1 Be sure that you are on **page 2** of your publication. On the menu bar, click **View**, and then click **Master Page**.

On the page navigation bar, "R" displays, indicating that this is the Master page for the right-facing pages of the multi-page document.

2 Hold down the ⬆Shift key and position the mouse pointer over the pink center vertical layout guide until the **Adjust pointer** displays.

3 Drag the vertical guide to the left to **2.5 inches on the horizontal ruler** as shown in Figure 4.25.

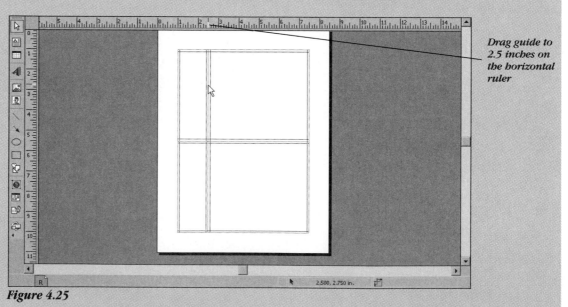

Drag guide to 2.5 inches on the horizontal ruler

Figure 4.25

Activity 4.9   Creating Mirrored Guides

4 On the menu bar, click **Arrange**, and then click **Layout Guides**. On the displayed Layout Guides dialog box, under Preview, click to place a check mark in the **Create Two Master Pages With Mirrored Guides** check box (see Figure 4.26).

Changed from Left and Right to Inside and Outside

Two-page spread view

Click here to create mirrored guides

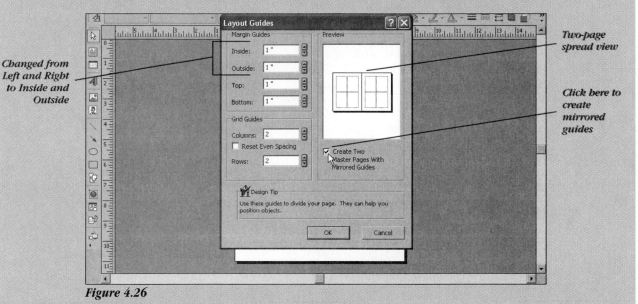

Figure 4.26

5 Look under Margin Guides and notice that the Margin Guides for Left and Right have changed to Inside and Outside, and that the Preview displays a two-page spread as shown in Figure 4.26.

Having a wider inside margin on two facing pages allows for some space that may be taken up by binding or, in the case of information inserted in a three-ring binder, for hole punching. For this publication, no change is necessary for the Inside margin.

6 Click **OK** to close the dialog box. On the menu bar, click **View**, and then click **Master Page** to close the Master Page view.

The Master Page view is closed, and the page navigation bar indicates all 8 pages of your publication, with page 2, the current page, highlighted.

7 On the menu bar, click **View**, and then click **Two-Page Spread**.

(Continues)

Activity 4.9   Creating Mirrored Guides (continued)

Pages 2 and 3 are displayed in the Two-Page Spread view. Notice how the guides on the left-facing and right-facing pages are mirror images of each other (see Figure 4.27).

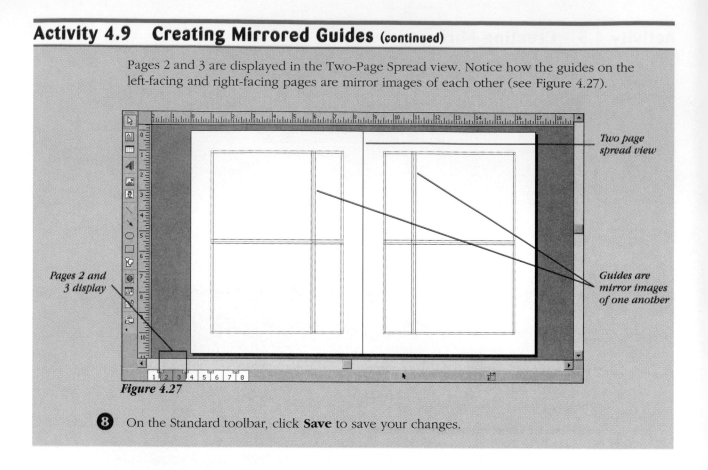

Two page spread view

Pages 2 and 3 display

Guides are mirror images of one another

Figure 4.27

8   On the Standard toolbar, click **Save** to save your changes.

Objective 9: Create a WordArt Logo and Save it in the Design Gallery

If your organization or department does not have its own logo, it is easy to create a logo using WordArt and clip art. After created, you can store the logo in the Design Gallery and use it in other publications.

Activity 4.10   Create a WordArt Logo

1   Navigate to **page 1** of your publication.

Page 1 displays as a single page because as the first page of the publication, it has no left-facing page.

2   Drag the **horizontal scroll box** to the right so that you have a large portion of gray scratch area visible on the right side of your screen as shown in Figure 4.28.

Activity 4.10   Create a WordArt Logo

You can use the gray scratch area to create, and also to temporarily store, objects.

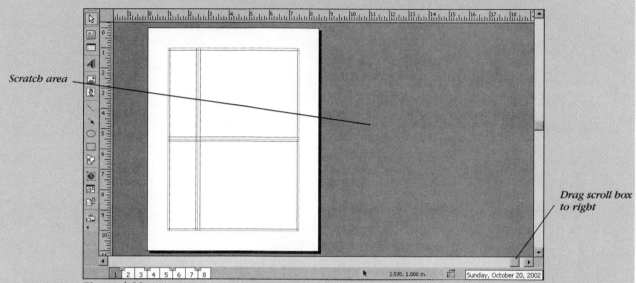

Scratch area

Drag scroll box to right

Figure 4.28

❸   On the Objects toolbar, click the **Insert WordArt** button.

The WordArt Gallery dialog box displays.

❹   In the WordArt Gallery dialog box, in the **first row** click the third WordArt style (see Figure 4.29).

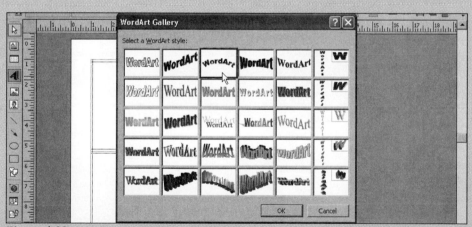

Figure 4.29

❺   Click **OK** to display the Edit WordArt Text dialog box.

❻   Type `City Jobs` to replace the highlighted "Your Text Here." Under Font, be sure that **Arial Black** is indicated. Click the **Size arrow**, and change the font size to **10**. Click **OK** to close the dialog box.

(Continues)

Activity 4.10   Create a WordArt Logo (continued)

The WordArt object displays somewhere on your screen.

7 **Zoom** to **100%** and close the WordArt toolbar. Hover the mouse pointer over the WordArt object until the Move pointer displays, and then drag the WordArt into the gray scratch area. Click in the gray scratch area so that the WordArt object is no longer selected (see Figure 4.30).

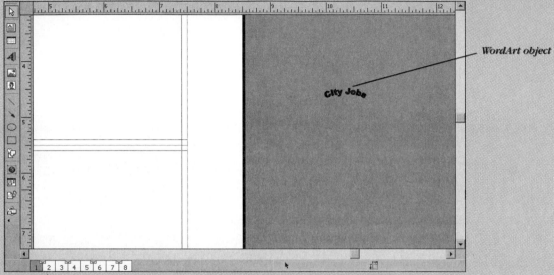

Figure 4.30

8 On the menu bar, click **Insert**, point to **Picture**, and then click **From File**.

The Insert Picture dialog box displays.

9 Navigate to the folder in which the student files for this textbook are stored, and insert **4B_CityHallPIC**.

The City Hall drawing displays somewhere on your screen.

10 Use the Move pointer, the corner resize handles, and the Nudge feature as necessary to size and position the City Hall drawing approximately as shown in Figure 4.31.

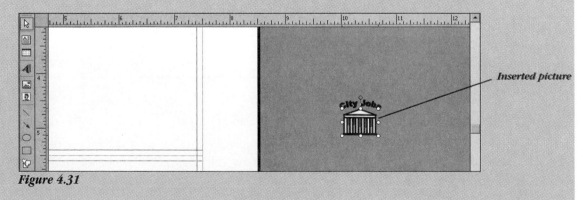

Figure 4.31

Activity 4.10   Create a WordArt Logo

11 With the City Hall drawing selected, hold down Ctrl, move the mouse pointer toward the WordArt object so that a small plus sign (+) displays with the arrow pointer, and then click the WordArt object.

The Group Objects button displays.

12 Click the **Group Objects** button to group the drawing and the WordArt together as one object.

13 Display the **View** menu, point to **Toolbars**, and then click **Measurement**.

The Measurement toolbar displays.

14 Be sure the newly created object is selected. On the Measurement toolbar, change the **Width** to **0.45″** and change the **Height** to **0.35″** (see Figure 4.32). Be sure to press ↵Enter to lock in the measurements, and then close the Measurement toolbar.

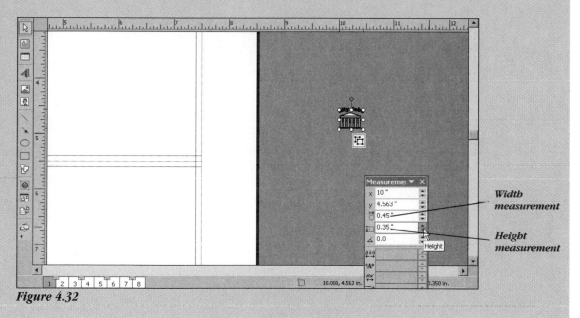

Figure 4.32

Activity 4.11   Save a Logo in the Design Gallery

1 With the City Jobs object selected, move to the menu bar, click **Insert**, and then click **Design Gallery Object**.

The Design Gallery dialog box, with its three tabs, displays.

2 Click the **Your Objects tab**. In the lower left corner, click the **Options** button, and then click **Add Selection to Design Gallery**.

The Add Object dialog box displays.

3 In the Add Object dialog box, in the box under Object name, type Jobs Logo. In the box under Category type Logos as shown in Figure 4.33. In the lower right corner,

(Continues)

Activity 4.11   Save a Logo in the Design Gallery (continued)

click **OK**, and then in the lower right corner of the Design Gallery dialog box, click the **Close** button.

The logo is stored with this publication in the Design Gallery. To use this logo in other publications, open this publication and use the Copy and Paste feature to place a copy in another publication.

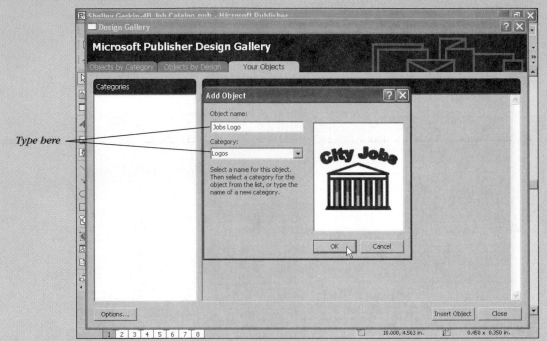

Type here

Figure 4.33

4 With the object still selected, press Del.

You do not need to keep the object in the scratch area because it is now available to you from the Design Gallery.

5 On the Standard toolbar, click **Save** to save your changes.

Objective 10: Create Facing Footers

In professionally produced books, magazines, and reports, the headers at the top of the page, and the footers at the bottom of the page, are usually mirror images of each other. Thus, although they contain the same information, the header or footer for even numbered pages is different than the header or footer for odd numbered pages. These are referred to as facing headers or facing footers.

Activity 4.12   Creating Facing Footers

1 Navigate to **page 2** of your publication, and **Zoom** to **Whole Page**.

Pages 2 and 3 display in the Two-Page Spread view.

2 On the menu bar, click **View**, and then click **Header and Footer**. On the Header and Footer toolbar, use the **Show Header/Footer** button to navigate to the Footer frame.

Activity 4.12   Creating Facing Footers

3 Move the **Horizontal scroll box** to the left so that you are viewing the footer on the left-facing Master page (see Figure 4.34).

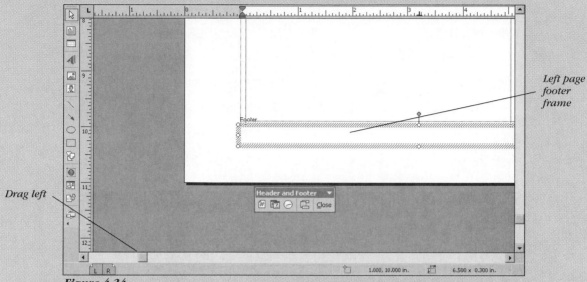

Figure 4.34

4 Display the Measurement toolbar, select the Footer frame, and then change the **Height** of the frame to **0.5″.**

5 With the insertion point blinking at the left edge of the Footer frame, type Page and then press Spacebar once. On the Header and Footer toolbar, click the **Insert Page Number** button as shown in Figure 4.35.

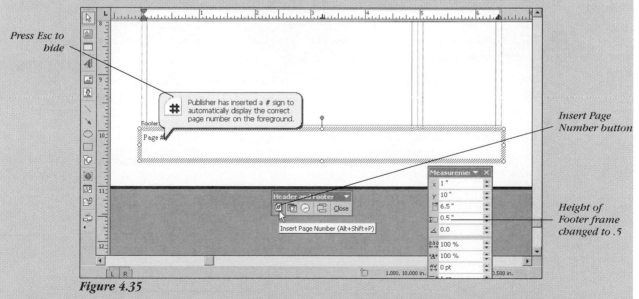

Figure 4.35

6 If a yellow box displays explaining the symbol that you inserted, press Esc to close it.

The # symbol indicates a code that will automatically insert the correct page number.

(Continues)

Activity 4.12   Creating Facing Footers (continued)

7 After the # symbol, press Spacebar three times, and then type `Firstname Lastname-4B Job Catalog`

8 On the menu bar, click **Insert**, and then click **Design Gallery Object**. Click the **Your Objects** tab.

9 Click the **Jobs Logo** and then in the lower right corner, click the **Insert Object** button.

The Jobs Logo is inserted somewhere in the Footer frame.

10 Use the Move pointer and Nudge feature as necessary to position the logo approximately as shown in Figure 4.36.

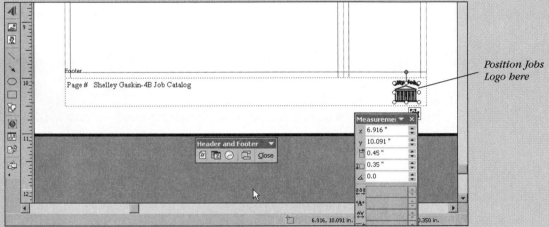

Figure 4.36

11 Drag the **Horizontal scroll box** to the right to view the Footer frame on the right-facing page.

12 Click inside the frame, and then use the displayed Measurement toolbar to change the **Height** to **0.5″**. Close the Measurement toolbar.

13 On the menu bar, click **Insert**, click **Design Gallery Object**, and then click the **Your Objects** tab. Click the **Jobs Logo**. At the lower right corner, click **Insert Object** to insert the Jobs Logo and close the dialog box.

14 Use the Move pointer to position the Jobs Logo approximately as shown in Figure 4.37.

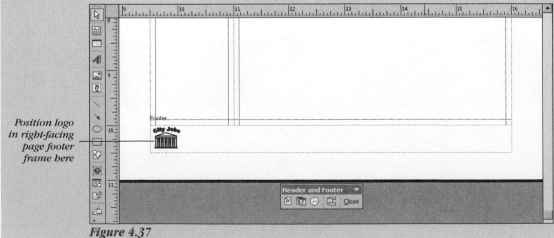

Figure 4.37

Activity 4.12   Creating Facing Footers

15 Click just to the right of the inserted logo to display the insertion point, and then press `Tab⇆` two times to position the insertion point at the far right edge of the frame. Type `Firstname Lastname-4B Job Catalog` and then press `Spacebar` three times.

16 Type `Page` and then press `Spacebar` one time. Then, on the Header and Footer toolbar, click the **Insert Page Number** button. Compare your screen to Figure 4.38.

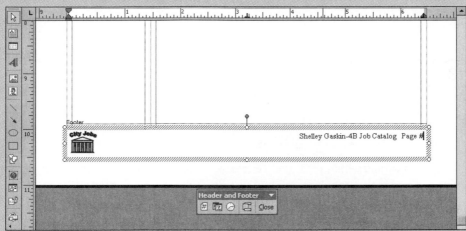

Figure 4.38

17 On the Header and Footer toolbar, click **Close**.

18 **Zoom** to **Whole Page**.

Notice that the footers are mirror images of each other (see Figure 4.39).

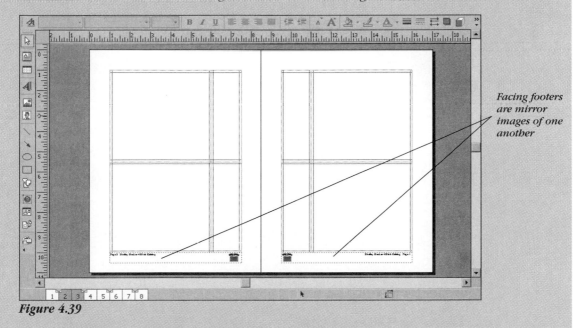

Facing footers are mirror images of one another

Figure 4.39

19 On the Standard toolbar, click **Save** to save your changes.

Objective 11: Link Text Boxes

When you worked with newsletters and brochures in Lesson 2, the predefined templates included text boxes that were linked in a logical manner. For example, if a story that began on page 1 of a newsletter was too long to fit in the page 1 space, a link was provided to a text box on another page, into which you could place the remaining text.

In a blank publication that has no predefined frames, you can still have text flow automatically into a linked frame. This is accomplished by linking frames manually using the buttons on the Connect Frames toolbar.

Activity 4.13   Linking Text Boxes

1 Be sure that **pages 2 and 3** of your 4B Job Catalog publication are displayed, and that **Zoom** is set to **Whole Page**.

Because the Two-Page Spread view is active, both pages 2 and 3 display.

2 On the Objects toolbar, click the **Text Box** button. Using the blue layout guides to assist you, create a text box on the left side of page 2 as shown in Figure 4.40.

Draw text box within blue guides

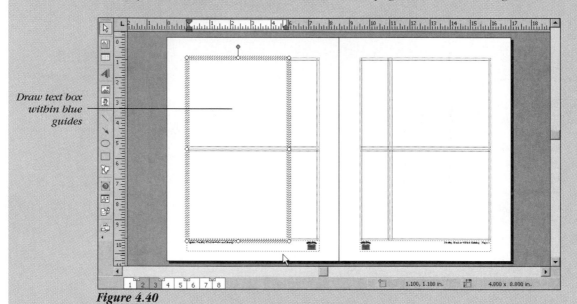

Figure 4.40

Activity 4.13   Linking Text Boxes

3 Create a similar text box on the right side of page 3. See Figure 4.41.

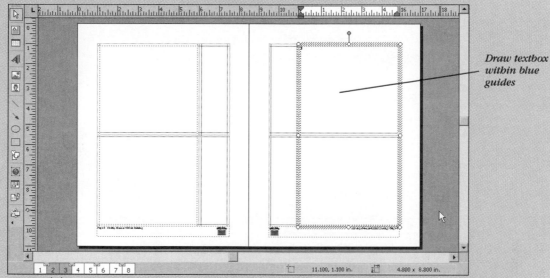

Draw textbox within blue guides

Figure 4.41

4 On the left, click to select the text box on page 2. On the Connect Frames toolbar, click the **Create Text Box Link** button. See Figure 4.42.

Your mouse pointer, when positioned over the text box on page 2, takes the shape of a cup.

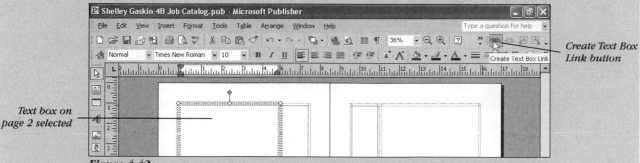

Text box on page 2 selected

Create Text Box Link button

Figure 4.42

5 Move the mouse pointer over the text box on page 3, and notice that the mouse pointer takes the shape of a cup with letters pouring out, as shown in Figure 4.43.

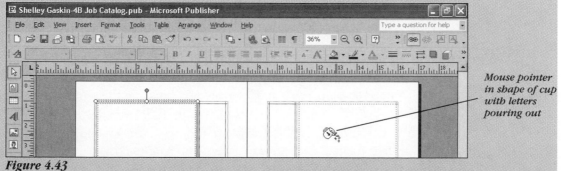

Mouse pointer in shape of cup with letters pouring out

Figure 4.43

(Continues)

Activity 4.13   Linking Text Boxes (continued)

6 Click anywhere in the text box on page 3.

A Go to Previous Frame button displays at the top of the text box on page 3.

7 Click anywhere in the text box on page 2, and notice that a Go to Next Frame button displays at the bottom of the text box.

The text boxes on pages 2 and 3 are linked, as evidenced by the Go to Next Frame and Go To Previous Frame buttons.

8 With the text box on page 2 selected, insert the text file **4B_JobText2**. Right-click anywhere within the text, point to **Proofing Tools**, and then click **Hyphenation**. Click to clear the check mark from the check box so that hyphenation is removed from the story.

The text flows from the first text box into the second (see Figure 4.44).

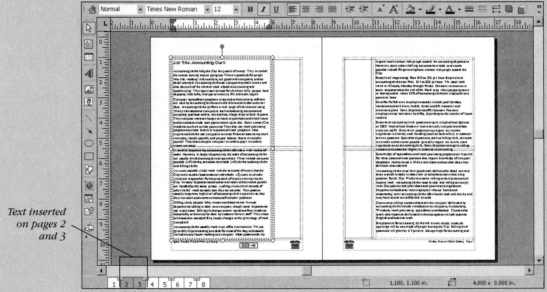

Text inserted on pages 2 and 3

Figure 4.44

9 Navigate to **page 4**, and make sure that you are zoomed to **Whole Page**. Create a text box on pages 4 and 5 in the same manner that you did for pages 2 and 3, using the blue layout guides to guide your eye.

10 Select the text box on page 4. On the Connect Frames toolbar, click the **Create Text Box Link** button, and then click the text box on page 5 to connect the two frames.

11 Select the text box on page 4 and insert the text file **4B_JobText3**. Remove hyphenation from the story.

12 Navigate to page 6. On pages 6 and 7, create text boxes in the same manner that you did for pages 2 and 3. Link the two text boxes, insert the text file **4B_JobText4**, and then remove hyphenation from the story.

13 On the Standard toolbar, click **Save** to save your changes.

Objective 12: Create and Apply Text Styles

When you create a publication such as a catalog, you often use the same text formatting instructions repeatedly. For example, if a bulleted list formatted in Arial, 14 point, and bold is placed on a page, you will likely want similar bulleted lists on other pages formatted in the same manner.

Publisher provides an easy way to apply an entire group of formatting instructions to various portions of text by using *styles*. A style is a group of formatting instructions that are stored by Publisher with a specific name, and which you can quickly retrieve and apply to text in a publication.

Activity 4.14   Creating and Applying Text Styles

1 Navigate to **page 2**. Draw a text box in the upper half of the second column, as shown in Figure 4.45.

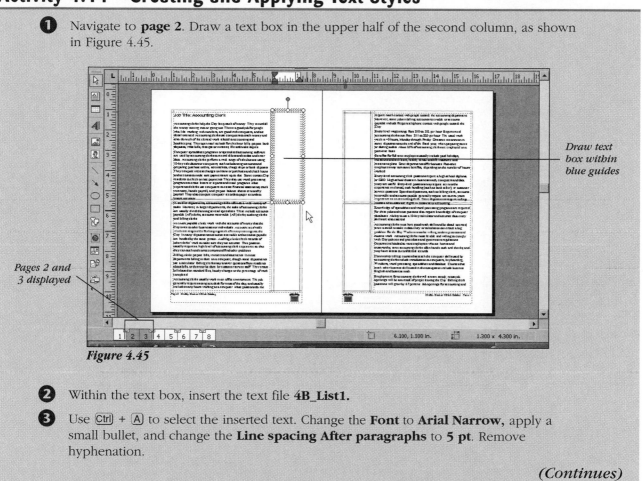

Draw text box within blue guides

Pages 2 and 3 displayed

Figure 4.45

2 Within the text box, insert the text file **4B_List1**.

3 Use Ctrl + A to select the inserted text. Change the **Font** to **Arial Narrow,** apply a small bullet, and change the **Line spacing After paragraphs** to **5 pt**. Remove hyphenation.

(Continues)

Activity 4.14   Creating and Applying Text Styles (continued)

4 With the formatted list still selected, move to the Formatting toolbar and click the **Style box** (see Figure 4.46).

Click here to highlight the word "Normal"

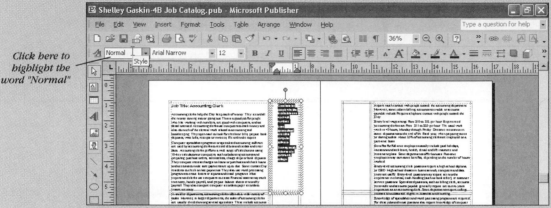

Figure 4.46

5 In the Style box, replace the highlighted text by typing `Info Text`—the name that you will use to identify this set of formatting commands—and then press `↵Enter`.

The Create Style By Example dialog box displays, indicating the various formats you have applied (see Figure 4.47). Notice that removing hyphenation is *not* part of the stored style.

All the formatting choices are stored, with the exception of hyphenation

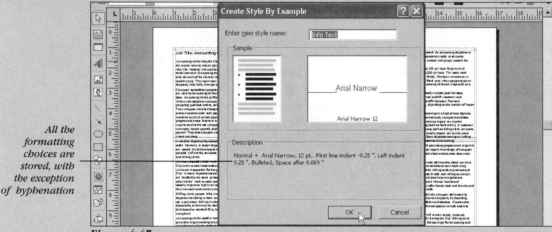

Figure 4.47

6 Click **OK** to close the Create Style By Example dialog box. On the Formatting toolbar, click the **Style arrow** to display the list of styles, and notice that your newly created style displays on the list as shown in Figure 4.48.

Style arrow

The style you created

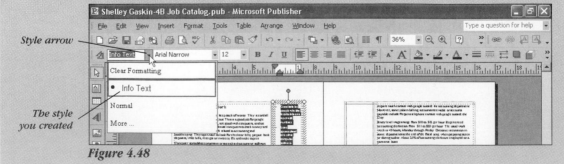

Figure 4.48

Activity 4.14   Creating and Applying Text Styles

7 On page 3, draw a text box in the lower half of the first column as shown in Figure 4.49.

Draw text box within blue guides

Figure 4.49

8 Insert the text file **4B_List2**. Select the text, change the **Font** to **Forte,** apply a diamond shaped bullet, and then change the **Line spacing After paragraphs** to **5 pt**. Remove hyphenation.

9 With the formatted list still selected, move to the Formatting toolbar and click the **Style box**.

10 In the Style box, replace the highlighted text by typing `Skill Text`—the name that you will use to identify this set of formatting commands—and then press **⏎Enter**.

The Create Style By Example dialog box displays, indicating the various formats you have applied.

11 Click **OK** to close the dialog box. Navigate to **page 4**. Draw a text box in the upper half of the second column, and insert the text file **4B_List3**.

12 Use **Ctrl** + **A** to select the inserted text. Remove hyphenation. On the Formatting toolbar, click the **Style arrow** (see Figure 4.50). From the displayed list, click **Info Text**.

(Continues)

Activity 4.14   Creating and Applying Text Styles (continued)

The Info Text style is applied to the text.

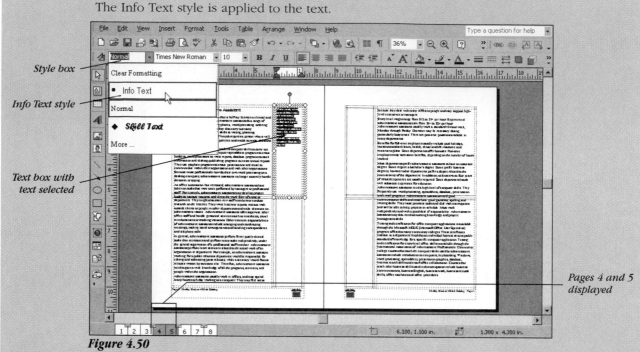

Figure 4.50

⓭ On page 5, draw a text box in the lower half of the first column, and insert the text file **4B_List4**.

⓮ Select the inserted text and remove hyphenation. On the Formatting toolbar, click the **Style arrow**, and then from the displayed list, click **Skill Text**.

The Skill Text style is applied to the text.

⓯ Navigate to **page 6**. In the upper half of the second column, draw a text box, insert the file **4B_List5**, select the inserted text, remove hyphenation, and then format it with the **Info Text** style.

⓰ On **page 7**, in the lower half of the first column, draw a text box, insert the file **4B_List6**, select the text, remove hyphenation, and then format the text with the **Skill Text** style.

⓱ On the Standard toolbar, click **Save** to save your changes.

Objective 13: Insert Text in Columns

Have you ever thought about why the text in magazines and newspapers is arranged in columns? It is not to save space; in fact, separating text into columns actually uses more space on the page. Rather, it is because text in columns is easier for the human eye to read. The eye quickly tires of moving back and forth over a wide span. Text broken into columns allows the eye to rest at the end of each short line.

Activity 4.15   Inserting Text in Columns

1 If necessary, open your publication 4B Job Catalog. Navigate to **page 1** and **Zoom** to **Whole Page**.

2 On the Objects toolbar, click the **Text Box** button, and then, using the blue layout guides, create a text box in the upper half of the page as shown in Figure 4.51.

Do not be concerned about creating a frame over top of guides. Recall that guides do not print, and serve only to divide the page for convenience.

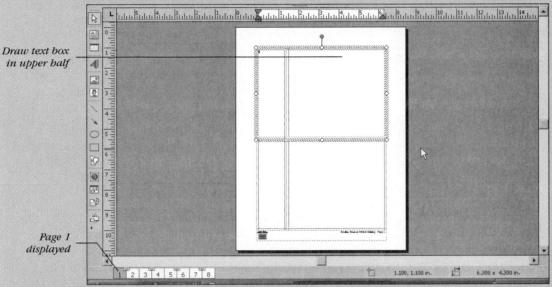

Draw text box in upper half

Page 1 displayed

Figure 4.51

3 Press F9 to zoom in, and then type on two lines:

```
City of Desert Park
Job Guide
```

4 Select the text and center it in the frame horizontally by clicking the **Center** button on the Formatting toolbar. Change the **Font** to **Arial Rounded MT Bold** and the **Font Size** to **36**. Display the Format Text Box dialog box, click the **Text Box tab**, and then change the **Vertical alignment** to **Middle**. Click **OK** to close the dialog box.

5 Press F9 to zoom back to Whole Page view. From the **Format** menu, display the Format Text Box dialog box again. From the **Colors and Lines tab**, apply the **Southwest** border to the text frame.

(Continues)

Activity 4.15   Inserting Text in Columns (continued)

6 On the Objects toolbar, click the **Text Box** button, and then, using the blue layout guides, create a text box in the lower half of the page as shown in Figure 4.52.

Draw text box

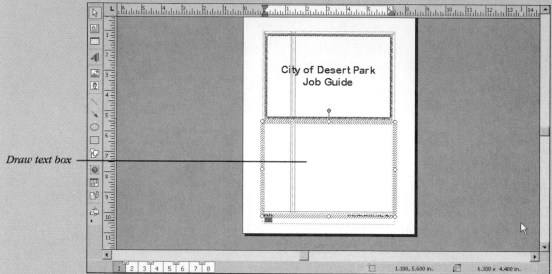

Figure 4.52

7 On the menu bar, click **Format**, and then click **Text Box**. On the displayed Format Text Box dialog box, click the **Text Box tab**.

8 At the lower right corner of the Text Box tab, click the **Columns** button.

The Columns dialog box displays.

9 In the Columns dialog box, use the spin box arrow to increase the number of columns to **2** (see Figure 4.53). Click **OK** to close the Columns dialog box, and then click **OK** to close the Format Text Box dialog box.

A dotted vertical line divides the frame.

Click and increment to 2

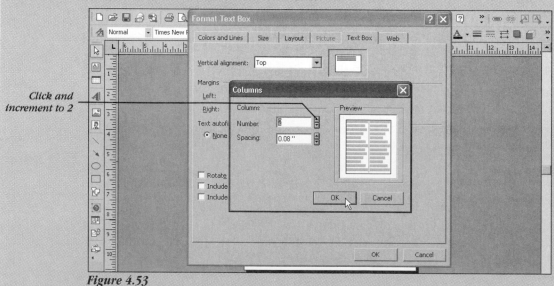

Figure 4.53

Activity 4.15   Inserting Text in Columns

10 In the frame, insert the Text File **4B_JobText1**.

The text flows automatically from the bottom of the first column to the top of the second column. Note that this is not the same as two connected frames. This is simply one frame with two columns.

11 On the menu bar, click **Tools**, point to **Language**, and then click **Hyphenation**. Clear the check box so that hyphenation is removed from the story. To balance the columns, move the lower center resize handle of the frame up to **9.25 inches on the vertical ruler** as shown in Figure 4.54.

If you shorten the frame too much, the Text in Overflow symbol displays. If that happens, drag the frame border down slightly to accommodate the text.

One frame with two columns

Move lower boundary up to 9.25 inches on the vertical ruler

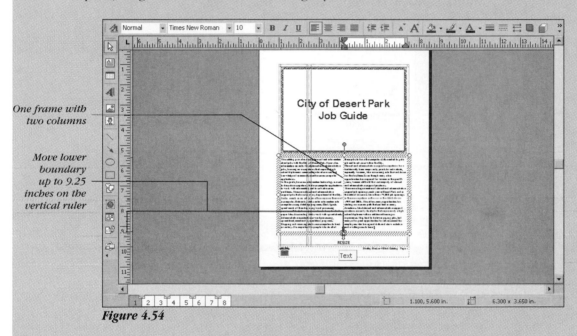

Figure 4.54

12 On the Standard toolbar, click **Save** to save your changes.

Objective 14: Create Horizontal Rules

The ***Horizontal Rules*** feature formats a horizontal line under text or between paragraphs and is an alternative to using the Underline style. Applying the Underline style to text has the disadvantage of cutting off ***font descenders***—the lower parts of letters, such as p and g. Additionally, using the Underline style does not provide any flexibility as to the size, position, or appearance of the underline because it places all underlines in the same position. The Horizontal Rules feature has none of these disadvantages, and offers much more flexibility in the size, position, and appearance of the underline.

Activity 4.16   Creating Horizontal Rules

1 Navigate to **page 8**. On the Objects toolbar, click the **Text Box** button. Using the outer blue layout guides as an outline, draw a text box covering the entire page (see Figure 4.55).

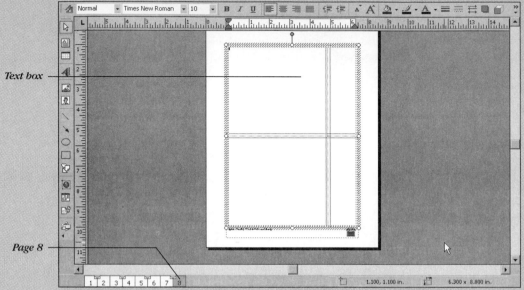

Text box

Page 8

Figure 4.55

2 From the **Format** menu, click **Text Box**, and then click the **Text Box tab**. Click the **Columns** button, and set **2** Columns. In the Spacing box, click the spin box up arrow once to set the spacing to **0.18″**. Click **OK** two times to close the dialog boxes.

3 Insert the text file **4B_JobText5**, and remove hyphenation from the story.

The text flows from the first column to the second.

4 **Zoom** to **50%**, and position the top portion of the page in the middle of your screen. On the Objects toolbar, click the **Text Box** button. Beginning in the upper left corner of the text box, draw another text box over the existing text from the left margin to the right margin, and down to **3.5 inches on the vertical ruler** (see Figure 4.56).

The text in the columns moves down to accommodate the new text box.

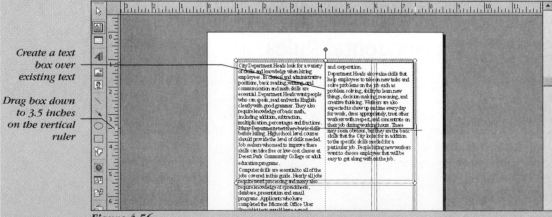

Create a text box over existing text

Drag box down to 3.5 inches on the vertical ruler

Figure 4.56

Activity 4.16   Creating Horizontal Rules

5 With the insertion point blinking in the smaller text box at the top of the page, type on two lines:

What City Employers
Are Looking For

6 Select the text you just typed. On the Formatting toolbar, click the **Center** button to center the text horizontally. Change the **Font** to **Forte**, and then change the **Font Size** to **48**.

7 With the text still selected, click the **Underline** button on the Formatting toolbar, and then click in the gray scratch area to view your changes.

Notice how the Underline style cuts through the bottom of letters that extend below the line as shown in Figure 4.57.

Underline style button

Line cuts through lower portion of letters

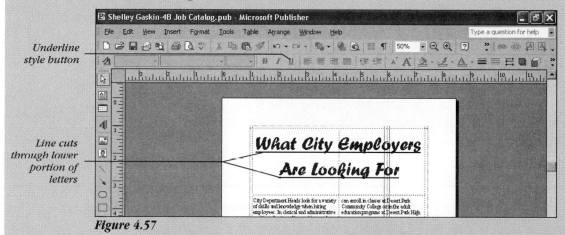

Figure 4.57

8 Select the text again and click the **Underline** button again to remove the Underline style. With the text still selected, display the **Format** menu, and then click **Horizontal Rules**.

The Horizontal Rules dialog box displays.

9 In the middle of the dialog box, click to place a check mark in the **Rule after paragraph** check box. Under Appearance, click the **Thickness arrow**, change the size to **2 pt** (see Figure 4.58). Click **OK** to close the dialog box, and then click in the gray scratch area to view your changes.

(Continues)

Activity 4.16   Creating Horizontal Rules (continued)

Notice that the Horizontal Rules method does not cut through the font descenders.

Places the rule after the paragraph

Set rule thickness to 2 pt

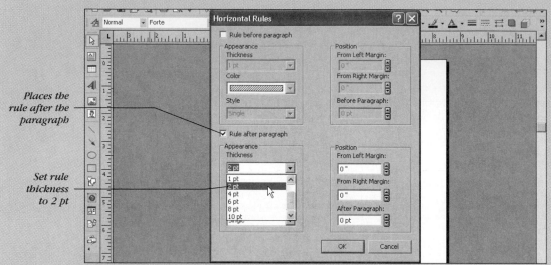

Figure 4.58

🔟 On the Standard toolbar, click **Save** to save your changes. Print your eight-page publication, and then close it. Publication 4B is complete!

To extend your knowledge...

It may be desirable to hide the Master page background for a single page. For example, in some booklets or reports, it is customary to hide the header or footer on the first page. To hide the repeating elements on the Master page for a single page within the publication, display the page, and then from the View menu, click Ignore Master Page.

Publication 4C

Birthday

In Activity 4.17, you will create a birthday card for the City Manager of Desert Park. Your completed publication will result in one sheet, folded two times in the manner of a greeting card, and will look like the one shown in Figure 4.59. You will save your publication as *Firstname Lastname-4C Birthday*.

Figure 4.59

Objective 15: Create a Folded Publication

Publisher provides several blank publication layouts that print on a single 8.5-inch by 11-inch sheet, and which are folded to create two or four pages. The ***Side Fold Card*** results in four pages and is folded in the style of a greeting card. The ***Top Fold Card*** results in four pages and is folded in the style of a personal note card. The ***Tent Fold Card*** results in two pages folded in the style of a tent card. A tent card is commonly used in meetings to display, in large letters, the name of each person seated around a table. This is convenient when members of a group may not know one another very well, or are meeting each other for the first time.

Activity 4.17   Creating a Folded Publication

1 **Start** Publisher and display the New Publication task pane and the Publication Gallery. Under Start from a design, click the **By Publication Type arrow**. From the displayed list, click **By Blank Publications**.

2 In the Publication Gallery, scroll down and click **Side Fold Card**. When a message displays asking if you want to automatically insert pages, click **Yes**.

Page 1 of your publication displays, and a total of four pages display on the page navigation bar as shown in Figure 4.60.

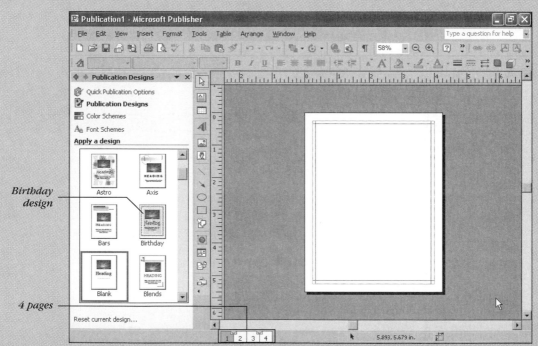

Figure 4.60

3 In the task pane, under Apply a design, click **Birthday** (see Figure 4.60).

A birthday design is applied to page 1 of your publication.

4 In the task pane, click **Color Schemes**, and then click the **Lagoon** color scheme.

5 In the task pane, click **Font Schemes**, and then click the **Deckle** font scheme. Close the task pane.

6 On the Objects toolbar, click the **Insert WordArt** button. In the first row, click the second WordArt style, and then click **OK** to close the WordArt Gallery dialog box.

The Edit WordArt Text dialog box displays.

Activity 4.17   Creating a Folded Publication

7 In the Edit WordArt Text dialog box, type Happy Birthday and then press ⏎Enter.
Type Madison! and then change the font **Size** to **24**. Click **OK** to close the Edit
WordArt Text dialog box.

The WordArt displays on the page.

8 Use the Move pointer to position the WordArt approximately as shown in Figure 4.61.

*Position
WordArt*

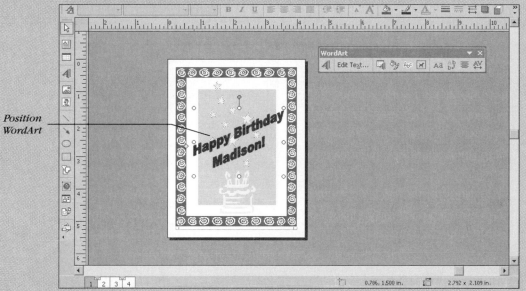

Figure 4.61

9 **Zoom** to **100%**. Position the lower portion of the page in the center of your screen.
Draw a small text box approximately as shown in Figure 4.62, change the **Font Size** to
8, and then type Firstname Lastname-4C Birthday

*Text box with
your name
and file name*

Figure 4.62

10 Click on the outer edge of the green border to select it, and then on the Formatting
toolbar, click the **Copy** button.

11 **Zoom** to **66%**, and then navigate to **page 2**. On the Formatting toolbar, click the **Paste**
button.

(Continues)

Activity 4.17   Creating a Folded Publication (continued)

The Two-Page Spread view displays pages 2 and 3, and the pasted border displays on page 3.

12 Click the **Paste** button again to paste another copy of the border, and then move it to page 2. Use the Move pointer and the Nudge feature as necessary to position the two borders as shown in Figure 4.63.

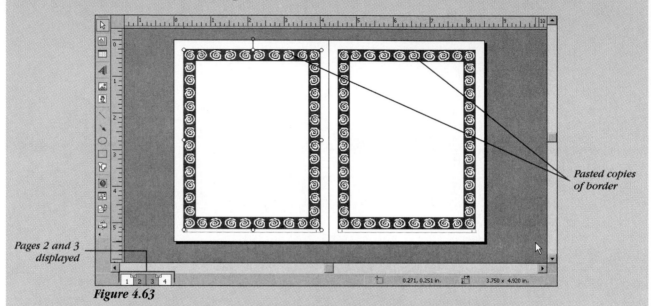

Pasted copies of border

Pages 2 and 3 displayed

Figure 4.63

13 On pages 2 and 3, draw text boxes, and then insert and **Center** text approximately as shown in Figure 4.64.

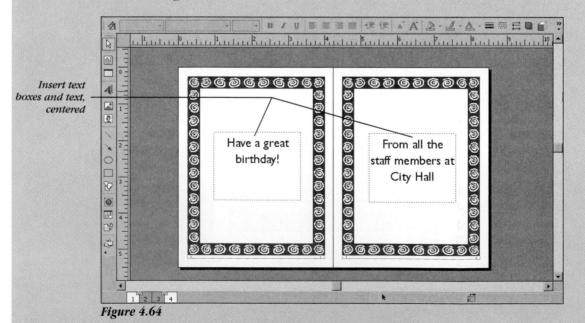

Insert text boxes and text, centered

Have a great birthday!

From all the staff members at City Hall

Figure 4.64

14 Navigate to **page 4**. On the Objects toolbar, click the **Picture Frame** button. Draw a frame beginning at **1.25 inches on the horizontal ruler** and **2 inches on the**

Activity 4.17   Creating a Folded Publication

vertical ruler. Drag down and to the right to **3 inches on the horizontal ruler** and **3.75 inches on the vertical ruler**.

The Insert Picture dialog box displays.

15 Navigate to your student files and insert **4C_Cake**.

16 On the menu bar, click **File** and then click **Save As**. Save the publication in your storage location as *Firstname Lastname-4C Birthday*.

17 On the menu bar, click **File**, and then click **Print**. In the displayed Print dialog box, under Print range, be sure that the **All** option button is selected. Click **OK** to print your publication.

18 Hold your printed sheet so that the panel with your name is in the lower right corner. Fold the top half of the page back. Then, with the panel containing your name still facing you, fold the left half of the page back. Your folded publication should open like a greeting card, with the picture of the cake on the back.

19 Close the publication, saving any changes. Publication 4C is complete!

Summary

There will be occasions when you need a level of quantity, quality, or features that you cannot produce on your desktop printer. Publisher 2002 provides a number of tools to help you prepare your electronic file for delivery to a professional printing company. From the Tools menu, you can select from among four specific tools that ensure that the file you provide to a professional printer results in a perfect publication.

Although Microsoft Publisher 2002 provides hundreds of preformatted designs from which you can create a publication, there may be times when you need to begin with a blank publication. It is easy to create a custom publication using the techniques you have learned in previous lessons. Layout guides, which can be placed on the page, are a convenient way to align the frames you create on a blank publication. You can also create custom graphic objects and store them in the Design Gallery for future use.

Lengthy publications, such as catalogs and reports, are easily managed and produced with Publisher. The Connect Frames toolbar provides a method by which you can connect text frames so that long passages of text can automatically flow in a manner you choose. The ability to create text styles ensures that you can apply the same set of formatting characteristics to numerous pages.

Publisher includes a number of blank publication layouts that print on one sheet, and which can be folded to produce a greeting card, a personal note card, or a tent card.

Using Publisher Help

Spot color is a less expensive method of adding color to a publication. With spot color you can add a second color to a regular black print job. The Publisher Help system contains information about setting up your publication for professional spot color printing.

1. If necessary, **Start** Publisher and display the New Publication task pane and the Quick Publications Publication Gallery.
2. On the menu bar, click **Help** and then click **Microsoft Publisher Help**. The Office Assistant character displays.
3. In the Office Assistant's text box, type:
   How can I prepare for spot color printing?
   and then click **Search**.
4. On the displayed list, click **Set up a publication for spot- or process-color printing**.
5. At the top of the displayed Help pane, click **Show All** to display all of the Help information. If you want to keep a copy of this information, click the **Print** button.
6. Click the **Close** button—the **X** in the top right corner of the Help window—to close the Help window.

Concepts Assessment

Short Answer

Write the correct answer in the space provided.

1. To print your publication, a professional printing company must have the same _____ installed on their computer that you used in your publication.
2. If you use the _____ fonts installed with Publisher, it will be easier for your printing service because Publisher can embed them directly into your publication.
3. Most desktop printers will accommodate _____ size and _____ size paper.
4. In Publisher, margin boundaries display as a _____ dotted line.
5. An attractive and easy-to-read font arrangement pairs a sans serif font for _____ and a serif font for _____.
6. Publisher's default color scheme is _____.
7. Smart objects are stored for your use in the _____.
8. Text arranged in columns is easier for the _____ to read.
9. A tent card with an individual's name is commonly used in a _____.
10. To prevent a repeating element from printing on a single page within a publication, display the page, and then from the View menu click _____.

Matching

Match each term in the second column with its correct definition in the first column. Write the letter of the term on the blank line to the left of the correct definition.

_____ **1.** Colors that are intended to display on a monitor.

_____ **2.** A Publisher option that converts colors to their CMYK (cyan, magenta, yellow, and black) equivalents—a formula for color formation that is understood by professional printing organizations.

_____ **3.** A process used on professional printing presses to compensate for errors on the printing press that result from paper being moved on the press.

_____ **4.** Graphics that are stored as part of a publication's file.

_____ **5.** Graphics that are part of a publication, but which are stored as separate electronic files.

_____ **6.** A process that creates linked graphics and embeds fonts in your publication, so that your printing service has access to the graphics and typefaces you want to use in your publication.

_____ **7.** The size of the paper on which you print your publication.

_____ **8.** The area of a sheet of paper that contains the text and graphics and that is determined by the margin settings.

_____ **9.** A preformatted design element that has a wizard associated with it.

_____ **10.** A Publisher feature that checks your publication for errors, such as an empty frame, text left in the overflow area, broken hyperlinks, or an object that is partially covered by another object.

_____ **11.** A group of formatting instructions that are stored by Publisher with a specific name, and which you can quickly retrieve and apply to text in a publication.

_____ **12.** The lower parts of letters, such as p and g, that extend slightly below the line of text.

_____ **13.** A sheet arrangement which, when folded, results in four pages in the style of a greeting card.

_____ **14.** A sheet arrangement which, when folded, results in two pages in the style of a tent card—commonly used at a meeting table to display the names of people in large letters.

_____ **15.** A Publisher feature that formats a horizontal line under text or between paragraphs, and which, unlike the Underline style, does not cut through font descenders.

A. Composite RGB

B. Design checker

C. Document size

D. Embedded graphics

E. Font descenders

F. Horizontal rules

G. Linked graphics

H. Pack and Go Wizard

I. Process colors (CYMK)

J. Sheet size

K. Side fold card

L. Smart object

M. Style

N. Tent fold card

O. Trapping

Skill Assessments

Publication 4D

City Services

In the following Skill Assessment, you will create a press release announcing the results of an annual survey of City residents. Your completed publication will look like the one shown in Figure 4.65. You will save your publication as *Firstname Lastname-4D City Services*.

Residential Trash Collection Top-Rated Service for Second Consecutive Year!

At today's City Council meeting, City Manager Madison Romero recognized City of Desert Park departments and programs that were highly rated in the City's annual survey of Resident Satisfaction.

For the second year in a row, the highest-rated City service was residential trash collection, with a 96 percent satisfaction rating.

For Immediate Release

From the Public Information Office

Top-Rated City Departments Recognized as City Council Annual Resident Survey Gives City High Ratings

The latest annual survey showed that 85 percent of City residents rated Desert Park's quality of life as good or excellent and 95 percent are satisfied with the City's services overall.

"These results show continued high satisfaction with the quality of life and City services," City Manager Romero said. "The survey is a continuing annual indication of what citizens think about our work, and it gives me great pride in the dedicated men and women who serve our citizens so well."

Other services receiving a 90 percent or higher rating included Police Services (92 percent), Library Services (95 percent), City-provided home recycling service (94 percent), Fire Emergency Response (94 percent), quality of parks and recreation facilities (98 percent), and the City's web site (92 percent).

Citizens rated the clarity and collection process of water and sewer bills as the most-improved City service, up 17 percentage points from last year.

Desert Park Community Bank sponsors the annual awards program. The survey was conducted in October of last year by the Behavior Center for Community Research. It involved 500 in-depth telephone surveys to obtain statistically significant results with a demographic mix comparable to the actual population of the City. This is the seventh year the survey has been taken.

Most Improved City Service!

Student Name-4D City Services

Figure 4.65

1. Start Publisher and display the New Publication task pane and the Publication Gallery. Under Start from a design, click the By Publication Type arrow. From the displayed list, click By Blank Publications.

2. In the Blank Full Page publication gallery, click Full Page. From the Arrange menu, click Layout Guides. Change each of the four margin settings to .75 inches, and then under Grid Guides, set 2 Columns and 3 Rows.

3. From the View menu, click Header and Footer, switch to the Footer frame. Change the Font to Agency FB and change the Font Size to 12. Type `Firstname Lastname-4D City Services` and close the Header and Footer toolbar. Then, save the file in your storage location as *Firstname Lastname-4D City Services*.

4. From the Publication Designs task pane, change the Font Scheme to Verbatim and the Color Scheme to Vineyard. Close the task pane.

5. Zoom to Whole Page. On the Objects toolbar, click the Picture Frame button. Draw a frame in the first block of the first row beginning in the upper left corner and extending from the top blue guide to the bottom blue guide of the block—do not be concerned with the right edge of the frame. Insert the file 4D_Trash. Use the Nudge feature to visually center the picture in the block, both vertically and horizontally.

6. Click the Picture Frame button, and then draw a frame in the second block of the second row beginning in the upper left corner and extending from the top blue guide to the lower blue guide of the block—do not be concerned with the right edge of the frame. Insert the file 4D_Police. Use the Nudge feature to visually center the picture in the block, both vertically and horizontally.

7. Using the same technique as steps 5 and 6, draw a picture frame in the first block of the third row, and then insert and center the file 4D_Payments. Compare your screen to Figure 4.66.

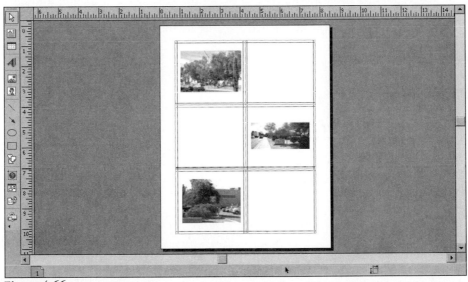

Figure 4.66

8. Select each picture, and apply a 6 pt line using the seventh block in the color scheme.

9. On the Objects toolbar, click the Text Box button. Draw a text box within the blue guides of the second column, beginning at the upper left corner of the top block, extending down to just slightly above the Police picture. Insert the Text File 4D_TrashText.

10. Draw another text box to fill the first block in the second row, using the blue layout guides to assist in your placement. Insert the text file 4D_Awards. When the message displays regarding autoflow, click No. Then, drag the lower boundary of the text box down slightly to accommodate the text in overflow.

11. Draw another text box in the second column, beginning just below the Police picture, and extending down to the blue guide at the bottom of the page. Insert the text file 4D_Other.

12. On the Standard toolbar, click the Special Characters button to view the characters that represent spaces, paragraphs, and other formatting codes. Press F9 to zoom to 100%. In the text below the Police picture, at the end of the first line, click in front of the *i* in the word *included*. Hold down ⬆Shift and press ↵Enter to insert a line break so that the word is no longer hyphenated. At the end of the third line from the bottom, click in front of the *a* in *actual* and insert a line break.

13. In the text to the left of the police picture, at the end of the third line, click in front of the *A* in *Annual* and insert a line break. On the Standard toolbar, click the Special Characters button again to turn off their display. Zoom to 66% and position the lower portion of the page in the middle of your screen. Click Save to save your changes.

14. From the Insert menu, click Design Gallery Object. In the Categories list, click Attention Getters, and then scroll as necessary and click the Plaque Attention Getter. Click Insert Object.

15. With the Attention Getter selected, display the Format menu, click Object, and then change the fill color to the third block in the color scheme. Use the move pointer to position the Attention Getter in the upper left portion of the Payments picture, and rotate it slightly to the left as shown in Figure 4.65.

16. Click inside the Attention Getter to select the text. Change the Font to Agency FB and change the Font Size to 12. Type Most Improved City Service!

17. From the Design Gallery, click Borders and then click Borders Open Border. Zoom to Whole Page and adjust the borders so that their inside edges align with the outer pink layout guides.

18. From the Tools menu, click Design Checker, check All pages, and Ignore or correct any design problems. Save your changes, print, and close the publication. Publication 4D City Services is complete!

Publication 4E

City Information

In the following Skill Assessment, you will create an Information Booklet for the City Manager. Your completed publication will look like the one shown in Figure 4.67. You will save your publication as *Firstname Lastname-4E City Information*.

Figure 4.67B

Figure 4.67A

Figure 4.67C

Desert Park

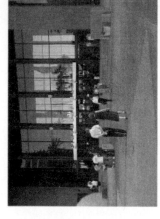

schools, 10 middle schools, six high schools and many private and charter schools. The city is home to Desert Park Community College and Desert Park State University with a graduate college and 11 undergraduate colleges: Arts and Sciences, Business Administration, Communications, Ecosystem Science and Management, Engineering and Technology, Education, Health Professions, Hotel and Restaurant Management, Museum Facility of Fine Arts, Performing Arts, and Social and Behavioral Sciences.

Desert Park has an extensive array of medical facilities and resources in the areas of traditional, integrative and alternative healthcare. Desert Park Medical Center is the Arizona regional referral center for trauma, cancer, rehabilitation, cardiac, high-risk maternal/fetal, MRI/CT scan, and more. More than 300 physicians are on active staff at the hospital, representing 50 medical specialties. There are 40 financial institutions

(banks and credit unions) with 120 local branch offices. Also, Desert Park businesses are eligible for assistance in financing fixed assets through the Finance Division, Arizona Department of Commerce. Information on private activity bonds within the city may be obtained from the same source or from the Industrial Development Authority.

The City of Desert Park is governed by a mayor, six council members and a city manager. There also is a police department, sheriff's department and fire department.

Desert Park prides itself on its Fine Arts and Parks Department, which was created in 1930 as an independent government agency with a mission to promote the fine arts, protect local natural resources, and to provide outdoor recreation for residents of and visitors to Desert Park.

The agency is funded by a one-mill, 15-year levy that was passed by voters in Desert Park in 1996. Funds are used to acquire additional land for preservation.

Figure 4.67D

Desert Park

Every year Desert Park hosts dozens of festivals, conventions and events. The following is a partial listing of this year's events, courtesy of the Greater Desert Park Convention & Visitors Bureau. To see a full listing, please visit the City's web site.

Desert Park Race for the Cure
May 18, Desert Park Community College

Rhythm & Food Festival
May 25-27, Botanical Garden

Native American Festival
May 25-26, Washington Park

Desert Park Arts Festival
June 6-9, City Hall Plaza

Desert Park Rose Festival
June 9-10, Park of Roses behind City Hall

Festival Latino
June 21-22, Mariposa Park

Red, White & Blue!
July 3, City Hall Plaza

Desert Park Jazz & Rib Fest
July 19-21, City Hall Plaza

Village Oktoberfest
October 4-6, Historic District
Located at Sycamore and Verde Streets

Desert Park Marathon
October 20, Downtown

Desert Park International Festival
November TBA, Veterans Memorial Hall

First Night Desert Park
December 31, Downtown, City Hall Plaza

Community Block Party
April 27, various communities

Halloween Costume Parade
October 24, City Hall Plaza

1. Start Publisher and display the New Publication task pane and the Publication Gallery. In the New Publication task pane, under New, click Blank Publication. From the Arrange menu, click Layout Guides. Under Grid Guides, use the spin box arrows to change the number of Columns to 2 and the number of Rows to 2. Click OK to close the dialog box.

2. From the Insert menu, click Page, and then change the Number of new pages to 3 so that you will have a total of 4 pages. Be sure that both the After current page and Insert blank pages option buttons are selected. Click OK to close the dialog box.

3. From the File menu, click Save As, and store the publication in your storage location as *Firstname Lastname-4E City Information*.

4. Navigate to page 2, if necessary. From the View menu, click Master Page. Hold down the ⬆Shift key and position the mouse pointer over the pink center vertical layout guide to display the Adjust pointer. Drag the vertical guide to the left to 3.5 inches on the horizontal ruler. Using the same technique, drag the pink center horizontal guide up to 4 inches on the vertical ruler.

5. From the Arrange menu, click Layout Guides, and click to place a check mark in the Create Two Master Pages With Mirrored Guides check box. Click OK. From the View menu, click Master Page to close the Master Page view. From the View menu, click Two-Page Spread to display pages 2 and 3. Compare your screen to Figure 4.68.

Mirrored guides

Total of 4 pages

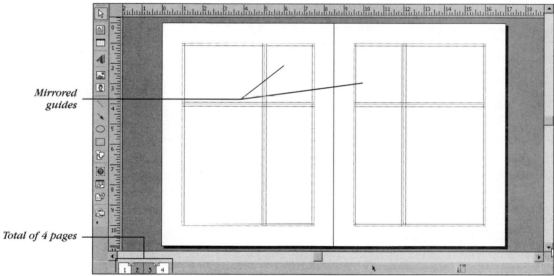

Figure 4.68

6. Navigate to page 1, and then drag the horizontal scroll box to the right to widen the gray scratch area. On the Objects toolbar, click the Insert WordArt button, and then in the first row, click the fourth style. Click OK. Type Desert Park and change the font size to 10. Click OK.

7. Zoom to 100% and close the WordArt toolbar. Move the WordArt object into the center of the gray scratch area, and click so that it is not selected. From the Insert menu, point to Picture, and then click From File. Insert 4E_Cactus. Use the Move pointer, the corner-resize handles and the Nudge feature to size and position the drawing approximately as shown in Figure 4.69.

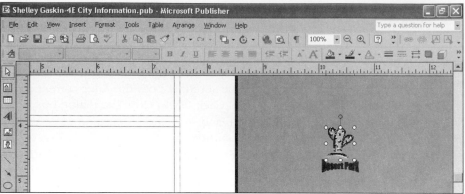

Figure 4.69

8. With the cactus selected, hold down Ctrl and click the WordArt. Click the Group Objects button. From the View menu, point to Toolbars, and then click Measurement. With the object selected, change the Width to 2.15″ and change the Height to 2.65″. Press ↵Enter to lock in the measurements. Close the Measurement toolbar.

9. Make sure the object is selected. From the Insert menu, click Design Gallery Object. Click the Your Objects tab, and in the lower left corner, click the Options button. Click Add Selection to Design Gallery. Name the object Info Logo, and place it in the Logos Category. Click OK, and then click Close. Press Del to delete the cactus object from the gray scratch area.

10. Navigate to page 2, and Zoom to Whole Page. From the View menu, click Header and Footer. Switch to the Footer frame. Move the horizontal scroll box to the left and make sure that you are viewing the left-facing page. In the footer frame, type Page and then press Spacebar once. On the Header and Footer toolbar, click the Insert Page Number button. If necessary, press Esc to close the yellow information box. Press Spacebar three times and then type Firstname Lastname-4E City Information

11. Move the horizontal scroll box to the extreme right so that you are viewing the bottom of the right-facing page. Click inside the footer frame, and then press Tab⇄ two times to move the insertion point to the right edge of the footer frame. Type Firstname Lastname-4E City Information and then press Spacebar three times. Type Page and then press Spacebar once. Click the Insert Page Number button on the Header and Footer toolbar.

12. Close the Header and Footer toolbar, and navigate to page 1. Zoom to Whole Page. From the Insert menu, click Design Gallery Object, click the Your Objects tab, and then click Info Logo. Click the Insert Object button. Position the logo in the first row of the first column— the upper left corner of the page.

13. In the upper block of the second column, draw a picture frame, beginning in the upper left corner of the block and extending to the lower blue guide of the block. Insert 4E_PIC1. Nudge the picture into the uppermost left corner of the block, and then use the lower right resize handle to size it so that it fits the block as shown in Figure 4.70.

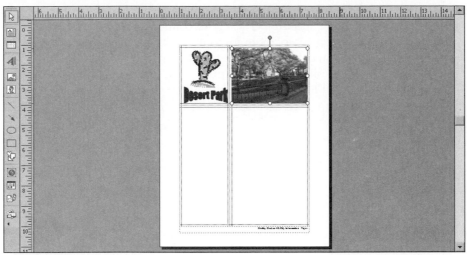

Figure 4.70

14. Using the blue guides in the lower portion of the page, draw a text box across both columns. From the Format menu, click Text Box, and then click the Text Box tab. Click the Columns button, and set two columns, and then increase the spacing between the columns to 0.18″. Insert the text file 4E_Text1 and remove hyphenation.

15. Use Ctrl + A to select all the text you just inserted. Change the font to Century Schoolbook. From the Format menu, click Line Spacing, and then change the Line spacing Before paragraphs to 5 pt. Click OK to close the dialog box. With the text still selected, click inside the Style box and replace the highlighted word "Normal" with City Info and then press ↵Enter. When the Create Style By Example dialog box displays, click OK.

16. To balance the columns, drag the upper center resize handle of the text box down to 4.5 inches on the vertical ruler. Check to see that text was not moved into overflow. If it did, drag the upper boundary of the text box up slightly so that no text is in overflow. On the Standard toolbar, click Save to save your changes.

17. Navigate to page 2 to display pages 2 and 3 in the two-page spread view. From the Insert menu, click Design Gallery Object and insert the Info Logo. Position it on page 2, in the upper block of the second column. On page 3, insert and position the same Design Gallery object in the upper block of the first column, creating a mirrored image of the two objects on the facing pages.

18. On page 2, create a picture frame in the upper block of the first column, insert 4E_PIC2, and position and size it to fit the block. On page 3, create a picture frame in the upper block of the second column, insert 4E_PIC3, and position and size it to fit the block.

19. On page 2, create a text box, within the blue guides, across the entire lower portion of the page. Format the text box with two columns spaced 0.18″ apart. Create an identical text box, with two columns, on page 3. Click in the text box on page 2, and on the Connect Frames toolbar, click the Create Text Box Link button. Move the mouse pointer over the text box on page 3, and click to connect the two text boxes.

20. Click in the text box on page 2. Insert the text file 4E_Text2. Because you connected the text boxes on pages 2 and 3, the text flows from one column to the next, and into the connecting text box. Remove hyphenation from the story. Use Ctrl + A to select all of the text, which will select the text in both text boxes. On the Formatting toolbar, click the Style arrow, and apply the style City Info. Click Save.

21. Navigate to page 4. In the upper block of the first column, draw a picture frame and insert the picture 4E_PIC4. Position and resize the picture to fit into the block. Insert the Design Gallery object that you created and position it in the upper block of the second column.

22. Draw a text box covering the lower portion of the page and format it with two columns. Do not change the spacing between the columns. Insert the text file 4E_Text3. Remove hyphenation. Press F9 to zoom in. In the first paragraph, drag to select the last line of text. From the Format menu, click Horizontal Rules, and then click in the second check box— Rule after paragraph. Change the Appearance Thickness to 2 pt. Click OK. Press F9 to zoom back to Full Page view. Click in the gray scratch area to view your changes.

23. On the Standard toolbar, click Save. Print the publication. Publication 4E City Information is complete!

Publication 4F

Thanks

In the following Performance Assessment, you will create a thank-you note for the City Manager. Your completed publication will look like the one shown in Figure 4.71. You will save your publication as *Firstname Lastname-4F Thanks*.

Figure 4.71

1. Start Publisher and display the New Publication task pane and the Publication Gallery. Under Start from a design, click the By Publication Type arrow. From the displayed list, click By Blank Publications.

2. In the Publication Gallery, scroll down and click Top Fold Card. When a message displays asking if you want to automatically insert pages, click Yes. From the File menu, click Page Setup, and click the Layout tab. Under Orientation, click Landscape, and then click OK. Although Landscape is not the default orientation for the Top Fold Card, it is common to see it in the Landscape orientation.

3. In the task pane, under Apply a design, scroll down and click Triangles. In the task pane, click Color Schemes and then click Moss. Click Font Schemes, and then click Fusion. Close the task pane.

4. On the Objects toolbar, click the Insert WordArt button. In the first row, click the second WordArt style, and then click OK. Type `Thanks!` and then change the font size to 40. Click OK. Visually center the WordArt object in the middle of the decorative border. Close the WordArt toolbar and click in the gray scratch area.

5. Zoom to 100%. Position the lower portion of the page in the center of your screen. Draw a small text box in the lower *right* corner, just above the border, change the font size to 8, and then type `Firstname Lastname-4F Thanks`. Size the text box as needed to accommodate your name and the file name on one line.

6. Click on the outside edge of the decorative border making sure that white selection handles surround all four sides, and then on the Standard toolbar, click Copy. Navigate to page 2 and zoom to 50% to view both pages 2 and 3, which display with one on top and one below. Click the Paste button. In most cases, the pasted border will be on the lower page. Click the Paste button again, and size and position the pasted border on the remaining page.

7. On the upper page, draw a text box just inside the decorative border. Type `Thanks for a great birthday party!` Select the text and change the font size to 36, and then center the text in the frame horizontally (from the toolbar) and vertically (from the Text Box tab of the Format Text Box dialog box).

8. On the lower page, create a text box just inside the decorative border and type on two lines:
   `Sincerely,`
   `Madison Romero`

9. Select the text, change the font size to 28, and center it vertically and horizontally. Navigate to page 4. Draw a picture frame in the middle of the page, approximately 2 inches high and 2 inches wide. Insert 4F_PIC1. Visually center the picture on the page.

10. From the File menu, click Save As, and save the publication in your storage location as *Firstname Lastname-4F Thanks*. Click Print. Hold your printed sheet so that the panel with your name is in the lower right corner. Fold the left half back, and then fold the top half back. Your folded publication should open like a personal note card, with the fold at the top, and the picture of the flower on the back. Publication 4F is complete!

Performance Assessments

Publication 4G
Jazz

In the following Performance Assessment, you will create an announcement for the next concert in the outdoor concert series at the Desert Park Botanical Garden. Your completed publication will look like the one shown in Figure 4.72. You will save your publication as *Firstname Lastname-4G Jazz*.

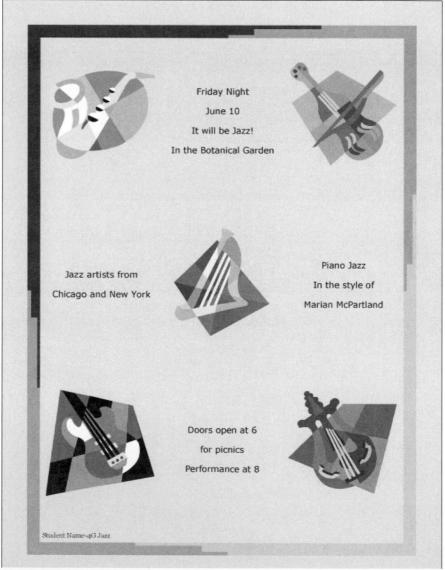

Friday Night
June 10
It will be Jazz!
In the Botanical Garden

Jazz artists from
Chicago and New York

Piano Jazz
In the style of
Marian McPartland

Doors open at 6
for picnics
Performance at 8

Student Name-4G Jazz

Figure 4.72

1. Start Publisher and display the New Publication task pane and the Publication Gallery. Under Start from a design, click the By Publication Type arrow. From the displayed list, click By Blank Publications.

2. In the Blank Full Page publication gallery, click Full Page. From the Layout Guides dialog box, change each of the four margin settings to .75 inches and set Grid Guides for 3 Columns and 3 Rows.

3. Save the publication in your storage location with your name and the file name. Change the Font Scheme to Binary and the Color Scheme to Mountain. Close the task pane. Create a footer with your name and the file name.

4. Zoom to Whole Page. In the block representing the first row of the first column, use the blue layout guides and create a picture frame beginning in the upper left corner and extending to the right to the first blue layout guide—the frame will not extend all the way to the bottom of the block. Insert 4G_PIC1, and then use the Nudge feature to visually center it within the block formed by the blue guides.

5. In the block representing the first row and the third column, insert 4G_PIC2. In the block representing the second row and second column, insert 4G_PIC3. In the block representing the third row and the first column, insert 4G_PIC4. In the block representing the third row and the third column, insert 4G_PIC5. Use the Nudge feature to visually align each of the five pictures in the center of its block.

6. From the Format menu, click Background. Under Apply a background, click the third block (tan), and then under More colors, click the second block in the first row (30% tint of Accent 2). Close the task pane. Draw a text box in the block representing the first row, second column. Press F9 to zoom in. Type on four lines:

Friday Night
June 10
It will be Jazz!
In the Botanical Garden

7. Select the text, change the font size to 12, change the Font to Verdana, and then center the text horizontally and vertically. In the block representing the second row and the first column, insert a text box and type on two lines:

Jazz artists from
Chicago and New York

and then format the text in the same manner as the first text box. Center the text horizontally and vertically.

8. In the block representing the second row, third column, insert a text box, type, and then format in the manner above:

Piano jazz
In the style of
Marian McPartland

9. In the empty block in the third row, insert a text box, type the text indicated below, and then format as above:

Doors open at 6
for picnics
Performance at 8

10. Zoom to Whole Page. From the Design Gallery, insert the Borders Interlocking Color border, and arrange it attractively around the page. Use caution not to cover your footer with the border. Run the Design Checker to check for any incorrect elements. Save your changes and print. Publication 4G Jazz is complete!

Publication 4H

Job Fair

In the following Performance Assessment, you will create a booklet for an upcoming Job Fair. Your completed publication will look like the one shown in Figure 4.73. You will save your publication as *Firstname Lastname-4H Job Fair*.

Find a Job

City of Desert Park Job Fair

How to Find a Job

The first step in finding a job is to gain the skills needed for that job. Community colleges and adult education programs offer many classes that teach the necessary skills. Even for entry-level jobs, the basic skills are required.

Clerical and administrative employees work in every industry and in every size business. Job seekers can take advantage of this variety to find a job in an industry that is of special interest to them. It can be a way to get a "foot in the door" in an industry while pursuing higher education in order to enter a professional job. Once employed, workers can usually advance within a business from an entry-level job on a variety of career paths.

Many job seekers have a tendency to only look for jobs at large companies with which they are familiar. However, one in three jobs in is in a company that employs fewer than 50 employees. These companies may be less obvious places to look and may be more difficult to find, but they offer many opportunities. They are great places to start a career and often offer a wider variety of job tasks than are found in a job at a larger company. Smaller companies often have a more relaxed working environment and a less formal application process. Small business owners may be more likely to give a first job to someone who has fewer skills but has good personal qualities.

Student Name–4H Job Fair   Page 1

Figure 4.73A

Find a Job

Nearly every job requires:

- Basic reading, writing, and math skills
- Computer skills
- Enthusiasm
- Good communication skills
- Positive attitude
- Willingness to learn
- Workforce skills

Companies employing 250 or more people employ 36 percent of America's workers. Larger companies tend to offer better benefits than smaller businesses. They may also have a more structured career path. They sometimes offer better starting pay, but may also have higher requirements for education and experience. Competition for jobs with larger companies is often stiffer than for jobs in smaller organizations.

Larger organizations have formal procedures for job applicants. However, knowing someone in the company, even if they are not responsible for the hiring, often helps an applicant get an interview and a job. Often an informational interview can be helpful to introduce yourself and gain access to information and referrals. It helps to speak with employers who are not currently hiring and ask when they will be hiring. Most companies have a good idea of when they will be adding employees well into the future. Job seekers should learn as much as they can about companies with current job openings. Most large companies have Web sites that tell about their products, corporate culture, benefits packages and current job openings. Read the information about the company. Job seekers who know about a company always

make a better impression in an interview and have a better chance of getting the job. Useful Web sites for job seekers are listed on the last page of this booklet.

Students may take advantage of internships or volunteer opportunities to gain experience before entering the paid workforce. These are excellent ways to get experience as a student, and some internships are paid positions. Both internships and volunteer work count as work experience and should be included on job applications and resumes. Internships and volunteer work help in two ways. First, they give a student experience. Second, if the intern or volunteer does a good job, they may be hired when they complete their education. Employers always prefer to hire people they know over strangers. Internships and volunteer work are a great ways to get a foot in the door.

It pays to be assertive in tracking down employers and jobs. Remember: employers need good employees as much as job seekers need the job. Recruiters want applicants. Although job announcements sometimes state "no phone calls," human resource professionals may be willing to speak with counselors, instructors and others who can help send them good job candidates.

Page 2   Student Name–4H Job Fair

Figure 4.73B

Find a Job

City of Desert Park Job Fair

General Career Sites

www.jobstar.org
Jobstar is an excellent site sponsored by public libraries that includes links to career guides, job listings, salary surveys and much more. This is a great place to begin an internet job search. The site has specific information for Los Angeles, Sacramento, San Francisco and San Diego areas.

www.ajb.dni.us
America's job bank offers a huge number of job listings throughout the country. It is sponsored by the United States Department of Labor and state employment development departments.

www.bls.gov/oco
The Occupational Outlook Handbook at the U.S. Bureau of Labor Statistics site gives a detailed description of just about every occupation in the country including skills, training, wages, and employment trends. This is an excellent source of general career information.

www.careercity.com
Career City offers job listings, a career center, resume samples and interview strategies.

www.careers.org
Careers.org offers a huge list of links to internet job and career sites.

www.dol.gov
The United States Department of Labor offers a wealth of information on all types of issues related to employment.

www.hoovers.com
This is an excellent general business site and a good place to learn background information about companies or industries. It has links to companies by name or by industry.

Page 4   Student Name–4H Job Fair

Figure 4.73D

Find a Job

Find a job through:
- Career fairs
- Employment agencies
- In-house promotion
- Internet job listings
- Newspaper ads
- Referrals from colleges

A job seeker should use as many job search resources as possible. More job leads mean more applications. More applications lead to more interviews and finding a job more quickly. A common mistake job seekers make is "putting all the eggs in one basket." They apply to a job that looks just perfect and do not continue to apply for other positions while they are waiting for an interview. It is important to keep looking and applying for jobs while waiting for interviews. Here are some of the best ways to find employers and job openings.

Networking: The best advice job seekers can get is, "Tell everyone you know that you are looking for a job." Probably the most effective way of finding a job is to find job leads through friends, acquaintances and relatives. Even if they do not know of current job leads, personal contacts can often lead to meeting people who know of job openings. Friends, acquaintances, members of community organizations and relatives can often refer job seekers to someone who can help. College and high school instructors often have contacts in industry. Ask them for leads. Speaking with people working in an occupation will help job seekers learn about the job and about current or future job openings.

Referrals from Current Employees:
Employers like to hire new workers that are referred by current employees. Current employees are often the first to know when positions are open at their company. Ask people you know if openings exist at their company.

Newspapers: The classified ads are the most well-known source of job listings. They are the only source of job listings that many people use. However only about 20 percent of all job openings are listed in a newspaper, so it is advisable to use other sources as well. Newspaper advertisements usually result in a large number of job applicants, which creates lots of competition for the position that is listed. Job seekers may have more luck applying to jobs listed in local papers rather than large regional newspapers.

The business section of a newspaper contains valuable information about companies that are increasing staffing, opening new facilities, getting big contracts, growing or moving. Even if they do not list jobs in the paper, these companies are well worth contacting. Major newspapers sometimes have special sections on jobs or information about job fairs.

Student Name–4H Job Fair   Page 3

Figure 4.73C

1. Start Publisher and display the New Publication task pane and the Publication Gallery. In the New Publication task pane, under New, click Blank Publication. From the Layout Guides dialog box, create Grid Guides for 2 Columns and 2 Rows.

2. Insert 3 new blank pages after the current page. Save the publication with your name and the file name. Navigate to page 2 and display the Master Page. With the Adjust pointer (hold down ⬆Shift) and point to guide), drag the vertical pink guide to the right to 5 inches on the horizontal ruler, and the horizontal pink guide up to 4 inches on the vertical ruler.

3. From the Layout Guides dialog box, click to place a check mark in the Create Two Master Pages With Mirrored Guides check box. Close the Master Page view. From the View menu, click Two-Page Spread.

4. Navigate to page 1. Scroll to view a larger gray scratch area. Create a WordArt using the third style in the first row. Type Find a Job and change the font size to 10. Close the WordArt toolbar and zoom to 100%. If necessary, move the WordArt into the gray scratch area, and then click so that the WordArt is no longer selected. Insert the picture 4H_Desk. Move and resize the picture so that it fits under, and is no wider than, the arc formed by the WordArt. Group the two objects, display the Format Object dialog box, and on the Size tab, set the Height to 2.65″ and the Width to 2.15″. On the Colors and Lines tab, set the Line color to No Line. Store the object in the Design Gallery with the name Job Logo in the Logos category. Delete the object from the scratch area.

5. Navigate to page 2. Create facing footers on the left and then on the right in the same manner as you did in Publication 4E City Information.

6. Navigate to page 1 and zoom to Whole Page. In the second block of the first row, insert the Design Gallery Object Job Logo. Use Move and Nudge as necessary to visually center it in the block formed by the guides. In the lower portion of the page, draw a text box covering both columns. Use the Text Box tab of the Format Text Box dialog box to set two columns within the text box. Insert the text file 4H_Text1 and remove hyphenation. Select all of the text, change the font to Bookman Old Style, and then change the Line Spacing Before paragraphs to 5 pt.

7. In the block representing the first row and first column, draw a text box, type on two lines
   City of Desert Park
   Job Fair
   Format the text to 28 pt Arial Rounded MT Bold and center the text horizontally and vertically. Place a 3 pt black line around the text box.

8. Navigate to page 2. In the block representing the first row and second column, insert the Design Gallery Object Job Logo. Insert it again on page 3 in the block representing the first row, first column. Visually center each within its block. On page 2, in the block representing the first row and the first column, draw a text box and insert 4H_List1.

9. Press F9 to zoom in on the inserted list text. Select the lines following "Nearly every job requires:" and change the font to Arial, apply a small round bullet, and set the Line Spacing After paragraphs to 3 pt. With the text selected, move to the style box, type List Text and then press ↵Enter. When the Create Style By Example dialog box displays, check it to make sure all the formatting you applied is listed, and then click OK. Format the text box with a 3 pt black line.

10. On page 3, in the block representing the first row and the second column, draw a text box, and insert the file 4H_List2. Select the lines following "Find a job through:" and apply the List Text style. Format the text box with a 3 pt black line.

11. Zoom to Whole page. On page 2, and again on page 3, draw a text box across the entire lower portion of the page and set each one with two text columns. Click in the text box on page 2, and then use the Create Text Box Link button on the Connect Frames toolbar to connect the two text large boxes. Insert the text file 4H_Text2 in the text box on page 2—it will flow over to page 3. Remove hyphenation from the story.

12. Navigate to page 4. Insert the Job Logo from the Design Gallery and position it in the block representing the first row, first column. Draw a text box across the lower portion of the page and insert two text columns. Insert the text file 4H_Text3. In the first column, select

the text "General Career Sites," format it with Bold, center it horizontally, and then place a 4 pt Thickness Horizontal Rule under it. From page 1, select the text box at the top of the page, copy it, and then on page 4, paste and position it in the block representing the first row and the second column. Save your changes and print the publication. Publication 4H is complete!

Publication 4I

Name

In the following Performance Assessment, you will create a name tent for a meeting attendee. Your completed publication will look like Figure 4.74. You will save your publication as *Firstname Lastname-4I Name*.

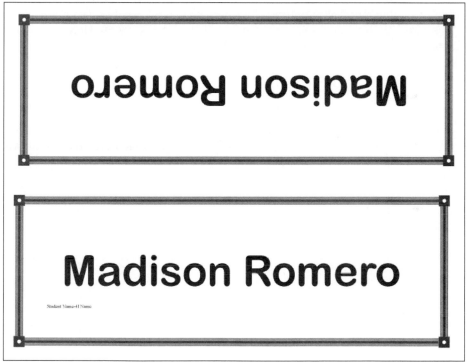

Figure 4.74

1. Start Publisher and display the New Publication task pane and the Publication Gallery. Under Start from a design, click the By Publication Type arrow. From the displayed list, click By Blank Publications, and then click Tent Card. Click Yes to automatically insert pages.

2. From the File menu, display the Page Setup dialog box, and change the Orientation to Landscape. From the task pane, change the Color Scheme to Waterfall. Close the task pane.

3. From the Insert menu, display the Design Gallery dialog box. Scroll down the Categories list, click the Borders category, and click Borders Accent Corners. Drag each side of the four borders so that the outside edge is aligned with the pink layout guide. With the border selected, click the Copy button.

4. Draw a text box just inside the border. Change the font to Arial Rounded MT Bold, and change the font size to 72. Type Madison Romero. Center the text horizontally and vertically. In the lower left corner, just above the border, insert a small text box, press F9 to zoom in, change the font size to 8, and type Firstname Lastname-4I Name

5. Navigate to page 2, zoom to 50%, and then click the Paste button. If necessary, align the pasted border on the page just inside the pink layout guides. Insert Madison Romero's name in the same manner as the previous step. It is common to have the name display on both sides of the card.

6. Save the completed publication in your storage location with your name and the file name. Print, and then fold the paper in half lengthwise. Heavy card stock works well for a publication of this type. Publication 4I is complete!

On the Internet

Microsoft can help you find a professional printing organization in your area that specializes in producing quality publications from Publisher files. Visit the Publisher site at **www.microsoft.com/office/publisher** and look for the heading Printing Services. Here you can find a printer in your local area, and professional printers can access various resources.

Design Sets, Tables, and Mail Merge

Objectives

In this lesson, you learn how to:

✔ Use Design Sets
✔ Attach a Logo to a Personal Information Set
✔ Create a Postcard Using a Design Set
✔ Create Business Forms Using a Design Set
✔ Edit a Table Within a Design Set Publication
✔ Create a Letterhead Using a Design Set
✔ Create a Table
✔ Format a Table
✔ Create a Mail Merge

Key terms in this Lesson include

- ❏ bulk mail
- ❏ cell
- ❏ cell diagonal
- ❏ columns
- ❏ crop marks
- ❏ data source
- ❏ design set
- ❏ field
- ❏ field code
- ❏ Grow to Fit Text
- ❏ letterhead
- ❏ mail merge
- ❏ mass mailing
- ❏ master set
- ❏ printer's marks
- ❏ purchase order
- ❏ record
- ❏ rows
- ❏ Table AutoFormat
- ❏ table
- ❏ trim size

Publication Design Tips—Choosing Paper for Your Publications

Paper makes an impression. Think about the feel of the heavy glossy paper in a high quality magazine as opposed to the feel of the paper used for newspapers. After you have taken care and time to create your publications, you will want to give thought to the paper on which they will be printed. The look and feel of your paper—its color, texture, weight, and crispness—contributes to the impression you are creating when people pick up your publications and read them.

Paper has various characteristics including its size, weight, *finish* (smoothness), *opacity* (degree of transparency), *brightness* (how well it reflects light), *grain* (the direction in which the majority of the paper fibers run), and color. All of these characteristics impact the way people will view your publication. If you are taking your publication to a copy shop or professional printer, they will be able to advise you on various papers.

Your first consideration is the printing process that will be used. Will you be printing from your desktop laser printer, taking paper copies to a local copy shop for duplication, or having a professional printing company produce your publication? Any paper that works on a photocopier will likely work well in a desktop laser printer because the printing process is similar. Other papers are made specifically for professional printing presses.

Your second consideration is the content. If your publication contains photographs, you should use glossy, coated paper. Photos produced on laser or ink jet printers are usually not visually appealing. An uncoated or matte coated paper works well for drawings, maps, charts, and illustrations.

Your third consideration is cost. Some publications, such as flyers, do not require expensive paper, whereas others require quality. For example, your business letterhead and envelopes should be on good quality paper. Brochures present the best impression using a heavier (and more costly) paper, but you can offset the higher paper costs by using the brochure as a self-mailer with a printed address or label instead of mailing it in an envelope. The paper may cost more, but you will save the cost of the envelope, postage, and the labor of inserting the brochures into the envelopes.

Your fourth consideration is the function of the publication. A flyer is a time-sensitive publication that will be quickly discarded. A business card or brochure, on the other hand, is often kept for reference and requires a better quality paper.

Finally, consider the occasion and the tone you want to convey. For example, an award certificate is an important publication. Use a quality, heavy, and formal paper in white, cream, or gray. Conversely, a flyer to announce the annual summer barbeque should have a lighthearted feel. You can choose a brightly colored, inexpensive paper.

Publisher includes templates for use with special papers from PaperDirect, a company that produces paper for desktop publishing and printing on laser printers. When you open these templates, you will see the design on the screen. You can create your document around the design, but the design itself does not print. The design is on the paper that must be purchased from the company. You can visit PaperDirect's Web site at www.paperdirect.com.

Publication 5A

PIO Postcard

In Activities 5.1–5.3 you will create an informational postcard for the Public Information Officer (a title that is often abbreviated as PIO) for the City of Desert Park. The Public Information Officer for an organization interacts with the public and the media on behalf of the organization he or she represents. The two pages of your completed postcard, which represent the front and back of an actual printed postcard, will look similar to Figure 5.1. You will save your publication as *Firstname Lastname-5A PIO Postcard*.

Figure 5.1A

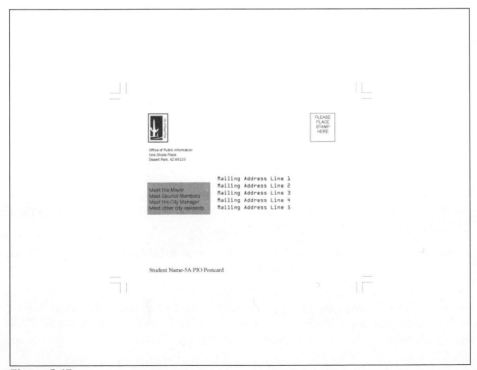

Figure 5.1B

Objective 1: Use Design Sets

Before desktop publishing programs were available, it was difficult and expensive to produce *business stationery* (letters, envelopes, postcards, business cards, and other business forms). A professional print shop was needed to not only print but also design the stationery. Desktop publishing programs in general, and Publisher in particular, have made the process so easy that anyone can design and then produce their own business stationery on a desktop printer.

Think about the kinds of paper you encounter in an average week—a letter you received, a bill for something you purchased, a business card with a telephone number, or a postcard with an important meeting reminder. These are all examples of business stationery that can be easily created with Publisher.

Publisher's pre-formatted design templates are grouped in two ways—by publication type (brochures, flyers, newsletters, for example) and by design set. *Design set* refers to a group of pre-formatted publications that share the same graphic design elements and font formatting. For example, recall that the first tri-fold brochure you produced was based on the "Layers" design for a brochure. The "Layers" brochure can be found grouped with other brochure designs under "By Publication Type." It can also be found under Design Sets, along with all the other types of publications that share the "Layers" design and formatting. The use of similar design elements—colors, fonts, and graphics—across all of your publications creates a professional image for your organization.

Activity 5.1   Viewing Publisher's Design Sets

①   **Start** Publisher and display the New Publication task pane and the Publication Gallery. Under Start from a design, click **By Publication Type**, if necessary.

In this display, all the templates are grouped by type, as shown in Figure 5.2. For example, all the Quick Publications, Newsletters, and Brochures are grouped together.

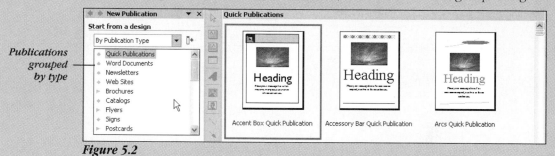

Publications grouped by type

Figure 5.2

②   Click **Newsletters**.

In the Newsletters Publication Gallery at the right, notice the first three newsletter design names—Accent Box Newsletter, Accessory Bar Newsletter, and Arcs Newsletter. The newsletter designs are in alphabetical order by design name.

③   In the New Publication task pane, click the **Start from a design** arrow to display the drop-down list, and then click **By Design Sets**.

As shown in Figure 5.3, Master Sets is highlighted and a list of design names displays. Notice the first three design names. They are the same names you viewed in the list of newsletter designs in Step 2—for example, Accent Box, Accessory Bar, and Arcs. A

Activity 5.1   Viewing Publisher's Design Sets

master set is a complete set of pre-formatted publications that are available for the design name—for example Accent Box.

List of Master Sets in alphabetical order by design name

Figure 5.3

4 Scroll down to the end of the list.

The last Master Set, entitled Waves, is followed by several more design sets for specific functions. For example, Restaurant Sets contain designs for various menu styles.

5 Scroll back up in the list of Master Sets and click **Layers**. In the Layers Publication Gallery, scroll down to view the 30 different types of business documents preformatted with the Layers design. They are arranged alphabetically—everything from a Business Card to a Word Document.

6 Move back to the New Publication task pane. In the Master Sets list scroll down and click **Straight Edge**.

In the Publication Gallery, the preformatted documents in the Straight Edge design set display in alphabetic order.

7 In the Publication Gallery, scroll down and click the **Straight Edge Informational Postcard** (see Figure 5.4).

The Straight Edge Informational Postcard pre-formatted design displays, using the color scheme of the Primary Business information set. The default layout includes a logo. If no

(Continued)

Activity 5.1 Viewing Publisher's Design Sets (continued)

logo is attached to the Primary Business information set, a default Publisher logo with the word "Organization" displays.

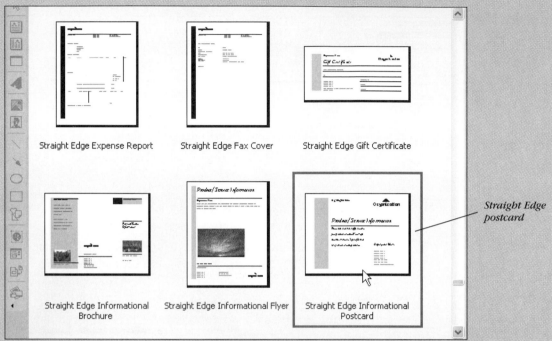

Figure 5.4

8 In the Postcard Options task pane there are some choices you must make about the format of your postcard. Under Size, accept the default **Quarter-page**; under Side 2 information, use the scroll bar to view all of the choices, and then click **Promotional text**. Under Copies per sheet, accept the default **One**.

In Microsoft Publisher, page size refers to the size of your publication, not to the paper size used for printing. The Promotional text option provides space on the address side of the postcard to include additional information.

9 Close the task pane. On the menu bar, click **View**, and then click **Header and Footer**. On the Header and Footer toolbar, click the **Show Header/Footer** button to navigate to the footer frame, and type `Firstname Lastname-5A PIO Postcard`

10 **Close** the Header and Footer toolbar. On the menu bar, click **File**, and then click **Save As**. Navigate to the location in which you are storing your publications for this Lesson, creating a new folder if you want to do so. Save the file as *Firstname Lastname-5A PIO Postcard*.

The postcard zooms to 100%.

Objective 2: Attach a Logo to a Personal Information Set

Many organizations use a logo—a letter, symbol, or sign used as an identifying statement by an organization—on their business stationery. When you create a publication where the design includes a logo, Publisher automatically inserts whatever logo is attached to one of Publisher's information sets so that you do not have to do it manually. If no logo is attached, Publisher will use a placeholder logo.

In the following Activity, you will attach a logo to the information set of the Office of Public Information. Recall that the information sets are stored on the hard drive of the computer on which they are created; they are not stored with the publication.

Activity 5.2   Attaching a Logo to a Personal Information Set

1 On the menu bar, click **Edit**, click **Personal Information**, and in the Personal Information dialog box, under Select a personal information set to edit, click **Other Organization**.

The information displayed will depend upon previous use of the computer at which you are working. In Lesson 1, this information set was configured for Gloria French, the Public Information Officer for the City of Desert Park.

2 Compare your screen to Figure 5.5, and change the information on your screen as necessary to match the figure.

If another student has completed a similar exercise at the computer at which you are working, a logo may display.

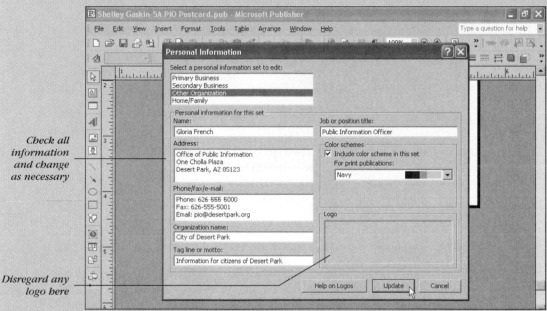

Check all information and change as necessary

Disregard any logo here

Figure 5.5

3 After making any necessary changes, move to the bottom of the Personal Information dialog box, and then click the **Update** button to close the dialog box.

The Navy color scheme for the Public Information Officer's information set is applied to the postcard.

4 Click to select the logo.

Depending upon what was stored on your computer's hard drive, this could be the placeholder logo or some other logo design (see Figure 5.6).

(Continues)

Activity 5.2   Attaching a Logo to a Personal Information Set (continued)

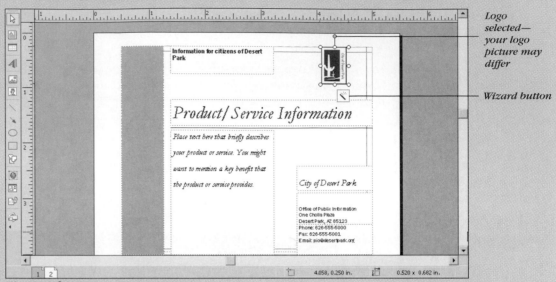

Logo selected— your logo picture may differ

Wizard button

Figure 5.6

5 Click the **Wizard** button.

The Logo Designs task pane displays at the left.

6 In the Logo Designs task pane, click **Logo Options**, click **Inserted picture**, and then click the **Choose picture** button.

The Insert Picture dialog box displays.

7 Navigate to the student files for this textbook, click **5A_PIO_Logo**, and then at the bottom right of the dialog box, click the **Insert** button.

A dark blue version of the City of Desert Park logo is inserted. Handles that are gray and contain an x indicate that this particular object is composed of more than one object (a drawing, a frame, and words). Click outside of the object and click to select it again to see only the white handles.

8 Close the task pane. Use the Move pointer and the Nudge feature to position the logo picture in the upper right corner, as shown in Figure 5.7.

Position logo here

Figure 5.7

Activity 5.2   Attaching a Logo to a Personal Information Set

9 On the Standard toolbar, click the **Save** button. If a message displays asking if you want to save the logo with the information set (see Figure 5.8), click **Yes**.

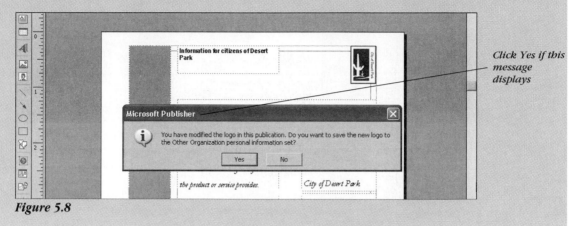

Click Yes if this message displays

Figure 5.8

Objective 3: Create a Postcard Using a Design Set

Business stationery includes all of the publications that an organization uses for mailing, communicating, and conducting everyday business transactions. One example of business stationery is a postcard. Postcards are used by organizations to mail brief messages, such as meeting reminders, event announcements, thank you notes, and invitations. Postcards require less postage than a letter, and have a good chance of being read by the person receiving it because there is no envelope to open.

Activity 5.3   Formatting a Postcard

1 At the top of the postcard, click to select the text box containing the words "Information for citizens of Desert Park." Then use the center right resize handle to make the text box wider so that the text displays on one line (see Figure 5.9).

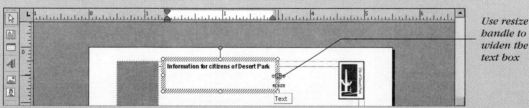

Use resize handle to widen the text box

Figure 5.9

2 Click to select the placeholder text "Product/Service Information" and type Public Swearing-In Ceremony

3 Select the placeholder text beginning "Place text here" and type the following (see Figure 5.10): Residents of Desert Park are invited to attend the Swearing-In Ceremony for Mayor David Parker on the City Hall steps, 1570 Palo Verde Parkway, at 7:00 p.m. on May 12. A reception with refreshments will follow in the City Hall lobby.

(Continues)

Activity 5.3   Formatting a Postcard (continued)

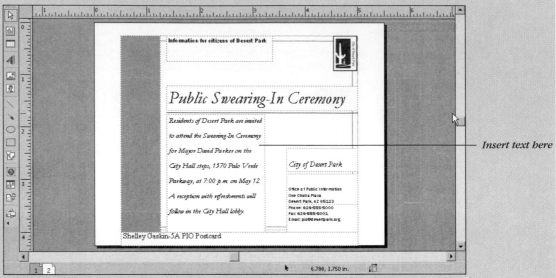

Figure 5.10

4 Use the page navigation buttons to navigate to page 2—the back of the postcard.

5 Select all of the placeholder text beginning "List items here" and type the following, pressing `↵Enter` after each line:

Meet the Mayor
Meet Council Members
Meet the City Manager
Meet other city residents

6 Select the text you just typed, change the **Font Size** to **9**, change the **Font** to **Franklin Gothic Book**, and then use the lower center resize handle to decrease the size of the text box slightly, as shown in Figure 5.11.

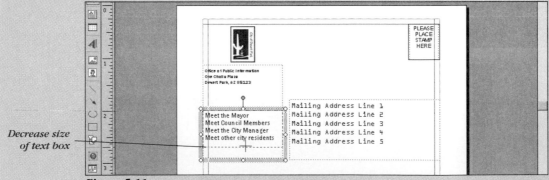

Figure 5.11

 Does your screen differ?

If the Text in Overflow button displays after shrinking the text box, it means you decreased its size too much. Drag the resize handle down a little to readjust.

Activity 5.3   Formatting a Postcard

7 With the text box selected, hover your mouse pointer over it, right-click to display a shortcut menu, and then click **Format Text Box**.

8 Display the **Colors and Lines tab** and apply a **Fill Color** using the third color (lavender) in the color scheme. Display the **Text Box tab** and set the Vertical alignment to **Middle**.

9 Click the outer edge of the object with the placeholder text "00% OFF" and press ⌈Del⌉ to delete the entire object.

10 Use the Move pointer and the Nudge feature as necessary to position the logo as shown in Figure 5.12.

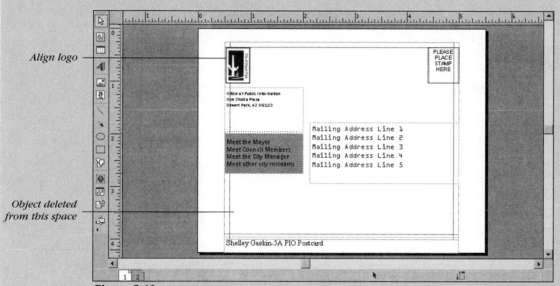

Align logo

Object deleted from this space

Figure 5.12

11 Compare your screen to Figure 5.12. On the Standard toolbar, click **Save** to save your changes.

12 Click the **Print Preview** button and use the **Multiple Pages** button to view the two pages of your postcard side by side.

In the Print Preview screen, notice the markings at the outer corners of the postcard (see Figure 5.13). These are *crop marks* and they are lines that appear when your publication is smaller than a piece of paper. They define the *trim size*, or actual size, of the document—where the paper would be cut.

(Continues)

Activity 5.3   Formatting a Postcard (continued)

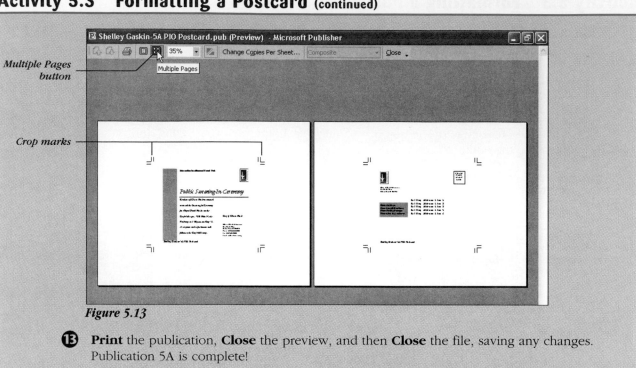

Multiple Pages button

Crop marks

Figure 5.13

13 **Print** the publication, **Close** the preview, and then **Close** the file, saving any changes. Publication 5A is complete!

To extend your knowledge...

Printing Postcards

In your classroom or lab, you will probably not have access to the type of paper used for printing postcards. For your own organization, however, card stock for postcards is readily available at office supply stores and is easy to use.

In Microsoft Publisher, page size refers to the size of your publication, not to the paper size used for printing. Thus, when printing a publication on paper that is larger than the actual card, crop marks print on the paper, indicating where you should cut the paper to make it the right size. Crop marks are part of a collection of marks, called **_printer's marks_**, which direct a printing press operator at a commercial print shop as to the size, alignment, and color of your publication.

Crop marks can be turned off. To do so, on the File menu, click Print, and then click the Advanced Print Settings button. In the Publications Options dialog box, under Printer's marks, clear the Crop marks checkbox.

Publication 5B

Purchase Order

In Activities 5.4–5.7 you will create a business form for the City's Finance Director. Your completed publication will look similar to Figure 5.14. You will save your publication as *Firstname Lastname-5B Purchase Order*.

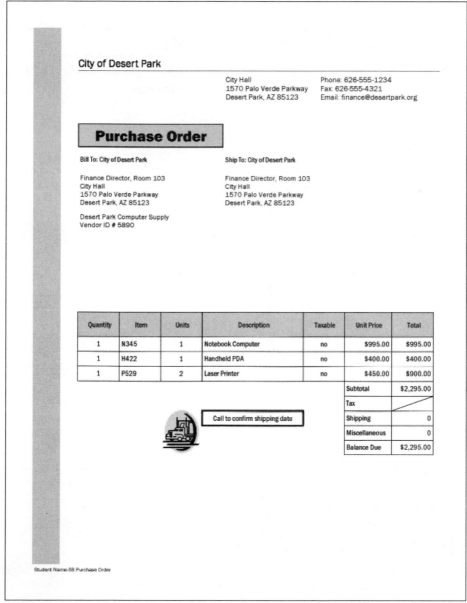

Figure 5.14

Objective 4: Create Business Forms Using a Design Set

Each of Publisher's Master Sets includes not only basic business stationery, such as letterhead, envelopes, and business cards, but also includes many pre-designed forms for basic business transactions and activities.

For example, there are forms for inventory sheets, invoices, expense reports, and ***purchase orders***. A purchase order is a business form generated when an organization makes a request to buy goods or services from a vendor and to be billed for the amount.

Activity 5.4   Formatting a Purchase Order

1 **Start** Publisher and display the New Publication task pane. Click the **Start from a design arrow**, click **By Design Sets**, and then under Master Sets, scroll down and click **Straight Edge**.

2 In the Straight Edge Publication Gallery, scroll down to locate the Straight Edge Purchase Order.

Notice that within a Master Set, some publications are formatted without color, as shown in Figure 5.15. Forms used for everyday business transactions, and those that are not intended to make a public impression or create a mood, are normally produced in low-cost black and white.

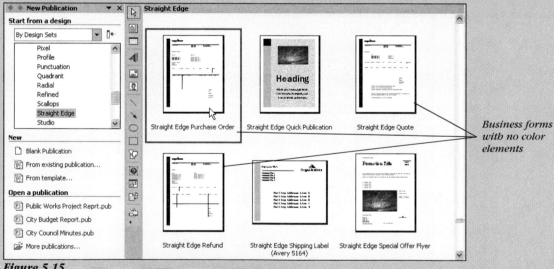

Business forms with no color elements

Figure 5.15

3 Click the **Straight Edge Purchase Order**.

The black and white purchase order displays on the right and the Business Form Options task pane displays on the left as shown in Figure 5.16.

Activity 5.4   Formatting a Purchase Order

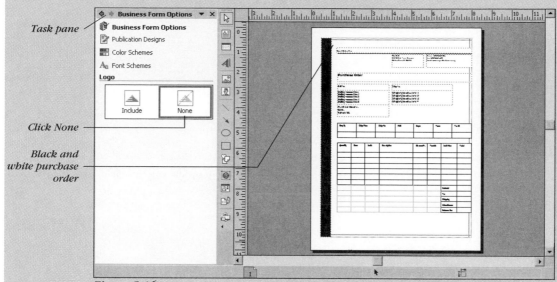

Figure 5.16

4 In the Business Form Options task pane under Logo, click **None**.

Some organizations include their logo on business forms, others do not. Whether or not to do so is optional. Organizations with elaborately colored logos often opt not to include them on everyday business forms because they are expensive to produce.

5 Close the task pane.

6 On the menu bar, click **View**, and then click **Header and Footer**. On the Header and Footer toolbar, click the **Show Header/Footer** button to navigate to the Footer frame, and type Firstname Lastname-5B Purchase Order

7 **Close** the Header and Footer toolbar. In your storage location, save the file as *Firstname Lastname-5B Purchase Order*.

8 In the **Zoom** box, type 85% and press ↵Enter. At the top of the purchase order form, click to select the text box containing the words "City of Desert Park." Select the text, change the **Font Size** to **14** and apply **Bold**.

9 In the two text boxes with the City Hall address and phone numbers, change the **Font Size** to **10**. In the email address, delete "citymanager" and type finance

10 In the text box containing "Purchase Order," select the text and apply **Best Fit**. Display the Format Textbox dialog box and apply a **Fill color** using the fifth color (gray) and apply a **1 pt** black line. Shorten the text box by dragging the right center resize handle to **4 inches on the horizontal ruler**. On the Formatting toolbar, click **Center** to center the text horizontally.

11 In both the text box containing "Bill To" and the text box containing "Ship To" click to place the insertion point after the colon, press the Spacebar once, and then type City of Desert Park

(Continues)

Activity 5.4   Formatting a Purchase Order (continued)

12 Select the placeholder text beginning "Mailing Address" and type the following on four lines:

```
Finance Director, Room 103
City Hall
1570 Palo Verde Parkway
Desert Park, AZ 85123
```

13 Select the text you just typed, and then on the Standard toolbar click the **Copy** button. Click to select the placeholder text beginning "Shipping Address," and then on the Standard toolbar click the **Paste** button.

14 Click within the text in the "Purchase Order #:" text box to select all of the placeholder text, and then press Del. On two lines type:

```
Desert Park Computer Supply
Vendor ID # 5890
```

15 Click to select the black bar graphic element on the left side of the page. Display the Format AutoShape dialog box and change the **Fill color** from black to the fifth color (gray) in the color scheme. (This will conserve ink or toner on your printer.)

16 Compare the upper portion of your publication to Figure 5.17, and then click **Save** to save your changes.

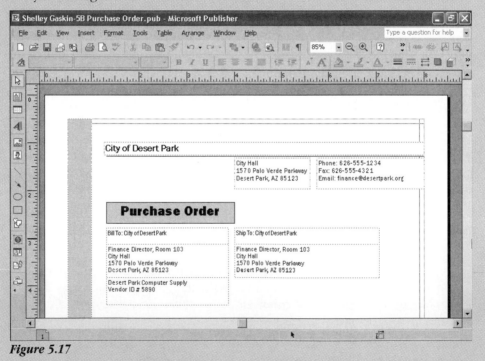

Figure 5.17

Objective 5: Edit a Table Within a Design Set Publication

Tables organize information using an arrangement of vertical ⇕ *columns* and horizontal ⇔ *rows*. The intersection of a column and a row in a table is a *cell*. Within a cell, you can insert text, numbers, or graphics.

On the Objects toolbar, the Insert Table button is useful for creating tables within a publication. In a Master Set form such as a purchase order, tables have already been created for you. A table looks similar to a spreadsheet in a program such as Microsoft Excel, but note that Publisher will not perform calculations on numbers in a table.

Within the purchase order form, there are two pre-designed tables—a two-row table followed by a larger table.

Activity 5.5   Editing a Table Within a Business Form

1 In the two-row table shown in Figure 5.18, click in any cell.

The table is surrounded by a pattern of slashes.

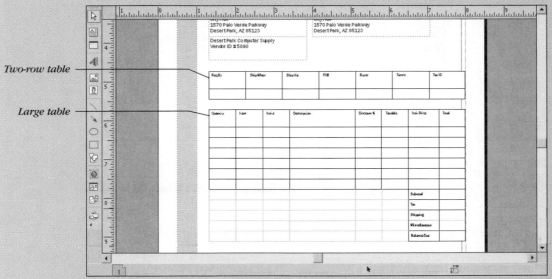

Figure 5.18

2 Click anywhere on the slashed border of the table to display a pattern of dots, and then press Del.

The entire two-row table is deleted.

3 In the table cell containing the word "Quantity," click to place the insertion point in the cell.

4 On the menu bar, click **Table**, point to **Select**, and then click **Row**.

All of the cells in the first row of the table are selected.

5 On the Formatting toolbar, click the **Center** button to horizontally center the text in each cell.

6 With the first row still selected, display the **Format** menu, and then click **Table**.

The Format Table dialog box displays.

7 Click the **Cell Properties tab**, click the **Vertical alignment arrow**, and then click **Middle**. Click **OK** to close the dialog box and apply the formatting.

The text is vertically centered in the selected cells.

(Continues)

Activity 5.5   Editing a Table Within a Business Form (continued)

8 In the second table row, click to position the insertion point in the first cell (under "Quantity") and type 1

9 Drag down to select the cell you just modified and the two cells under it (see Figure 5.19).

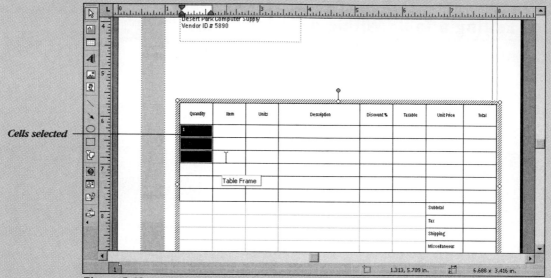

Figure 5.19

10 With the three cells selected, display the **Table** menu, and then click **Fill Down.**

The number 1 is inserted in all of the selected cells. This is a convenient feature that can save you from typing the same text numerous times.

11 In the "Discount %" column of the table, click in any cell. On the menu bar, click **Table**, point to **Delete**, and then click **Columns**.

The column is deleted, and the width of the table is decreased accordingly.

12 Drag the right center resize handle of the table to the right pink guide (see Figure 5.20).

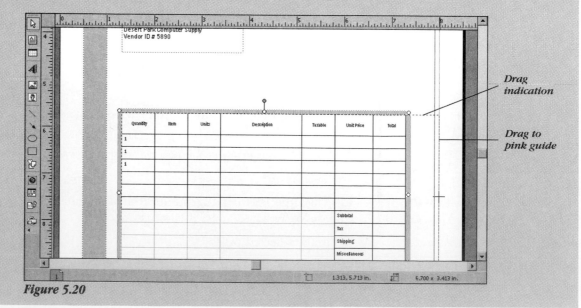

Figure 5.20

Activity 5.5   Editing a Table Within a Business Form

13 Click in any cell of the table. On the menu bar click **Table**, point to **Select**, and then click **Table**. With the entire table selected, change the **Font Size** to **10**.

14 Click outside of the table to cancel the selection and view your changes, and then on the Standard toolbar, click **Save** to save your changes.

Activity 5.6   Entering Data Into a Table

1 Fill in the remaining cells in rows 2, 3, and 4 as shown in Figure 5.21. You can use the (Tab) key to move from cell to cell, and the key combination of (Shift) + (Tab) to move backward one cell at a time. Zoom to a setting in which you can comfortably enter the text in the cells.

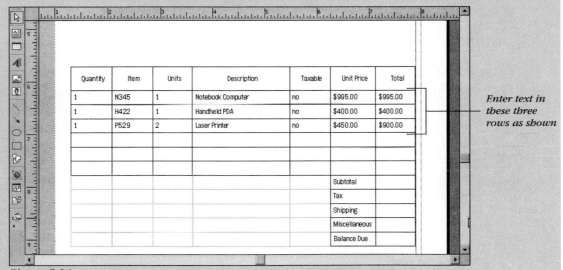

Enter text in these three rows as shown

Figure 5.21

2 Select the six cells containing dollar amounts. On the Formatting toolbar click **Align Right**, and then horizontally **Center** the information you typed in the Quantity, Units, and Taxable columns.

3 In the Quantity column, select the three empty cells below the data (rows 5–7; be sure you do not include the row with the word Subtotal). On the menu bar, click **Table**, point to **Delete**, and then click **Rows**.

The three empty rows are deleted.

4 In the last column, click to select the cell to the right of the word "Tax." On the menu bar, click **Table**, and then click **Cell Diagonals**.

The Cell Diagonals dialog box displays.

(Continues)

Activity 5.6   Entering Data Into a Table (continued)

5 Click the **Divide up** option button, and then click **OK** to close the dialog box.

The *Cell Diagonal* feature is a convenient way to indicate that a cell is not to be used or that the content of the cell is not applicable. For example, in most states, public entities, such as a city, do not pay sales tax. By including the cell diagonal, it is clear that the tax cell was not overlooked; it simply does not apply. Applying the Cell Diagonal, however, does not prevent you from entering text into the cell. In fact, it converts the cell into two usable portions.

6 With your mouse pointer, move to the left of the first row, point to the row until the mouse pointer becomes a right-pointing arrow, (see Figure 5.22.) and then click to select the entire row.

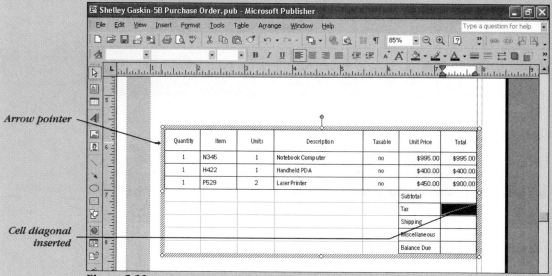

Figure 5.22

7 Hover over the selected row, right-click to display a shortcut menu, and then click **Format Table**.

8 From the **Colors and Lines tab,** apply a **Fill color** to the selected row, using the fifth color (gray) in the color scheme. Click **OK** to close the dialog box.

9 Fill in the remainder of the table as shown in Figure 5.23, and use **Align Right** to align the cells containing numbers.

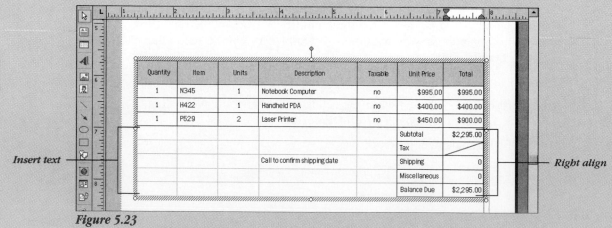

Figure 5.23

Activity 5.6   Entering Data Into a Table

10   Click in the cell containing the text "Call to confirm shipping date." On the Formatting toolbar, click **Center** to center the text horizontally in the cell.

11   Display the Format Table dialog box. Click the **Colors and Lines tab** if necessary.

Under Preview, notice that the preview pane shows no border on this cell.

12   Click the **Line Color arrow** and then click the first color (black) in the color scheme.

Under Preview, a border surrounds the cell.

13   Use the spin box arrow to change the **Weight** of the border to **2 pt**. Compare your screen to Figure 5.24.

Increase to 2

Cell border previewed

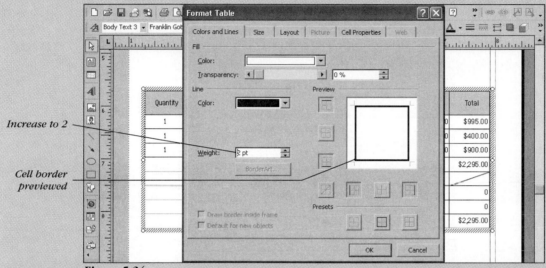

Figure 5.24

14   Click **OK** to close the dialog box. On the Standard toolbar, click **Save** to save your changes.

Activity 5.7   Merging Cells and Inserting Graphics in a Table

1   In the Units column, select the cells in rows 7, 8, and 9 (see Figure 5.25).

Select cells

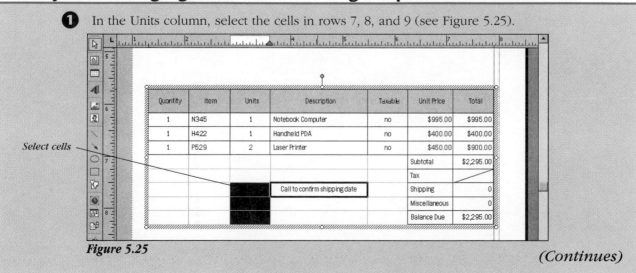

Figure 5.25

(Continues)

Activity 5.7   Merging Cells and Inserting Graphics in a Table (continued)

2 On the menu bar, click **Table**, and then click **Merge Cells**.

The three cells are merged into one large cell.

3 With the merged cell selected, on the menu bar click **Insert**, point to **Picture**, and then click **From File**.

The Insert Picture dialog box displays.

4 Navigate to your student files and insert **5B_PIC**.

A graphic of a truck displays on your screen.

5 Use one of the corner resize handles to decrease the size of the graphic to the approximate size of the merged cell, and then use the Move pointer to position it in the cell as shown in Figure 5.26.

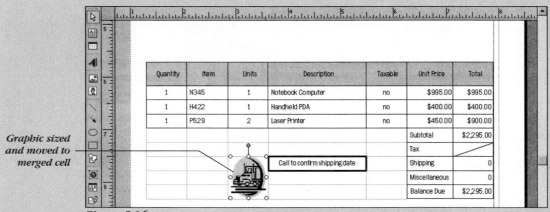

Graphic sized and moved to merged cell

Figure 5.26

6 With the truck graphic selected, hover over it and right-click to display a shortcut menu, and then click **Format Picture**.

The Format Picture dialog box displays.

7 On the **Picture tab**, click the **Recolor** button. In the Recolor Picture dialog box, click the **Color arrow**, and then click the first color (black) in the color scheme. Click the **Leave black parts black** option button, and then click **OK** twice.

8 On the menu bar, click **Save**, and then click **Print Preview** to view a preview of the completed purchase order. On the Print Preview menu bar, click **Print**. **Close** the preview window, and then close the file, saving any changes. Publication 5B is complete!

Publication 5C

PIO Letter

In Activities 5.8–5.13 you will use a Design Set letterhead from the Master Sets list to create a letter, insert a table into the letter, and then conduct a mail merge operation to produce a letter for each of the five members of the City Council. Your completed publication will look similar to Figure 5.27. You will save your publication as *Firstname Lastname-5C PIO Letter*.

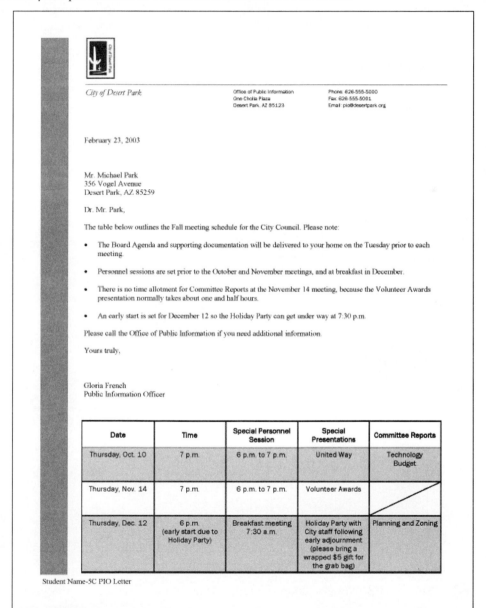

Figure 5.27

Objective 6: Create a Letterhead Using a Design Set

Letterhead refers to paper printed with the name, address, and contact information of an organization or individual and used to produce letters. A logo is usually included on the letterhead of an organization. A letterhead creates an impression of the organization. Using Publisher's Master Design Sets to produce a letterhead ensures a professional and consistent appearance.

Activity 5.8   Creating a Letterhead from a Design Set

1 **Start** Publisher and display the New Publication task pane. Click the **Start from a design arrow**, click **By Design Sets**, and then under Master Sets, click **Straight Edge**.

2 In the Straight Edge Publication Gallery, scroll down to locate and click the **Straight Edge Letterhead**.

The Straight Edge letterhead displays using the information from the Primary information set stored on the computer's hard drive. The Letterhead Options task pane displays on the left.

3 In the Letterhead Options task pane, under Logo, be sure that **Include** is selected, and then close the task pane.

4 On the menu bar, click **Edit**, click **Personal Information**, and in the Personal Information dialog box, under Select a personal information set to edit, click **Other Organization**.

5 Compare your screen to Figure 5.28. If necessary, change the typed information on your screen to match the Figure, and then click the **Update** button.

The color scheme, and logo if any, for the information set is applied to the letterhead.

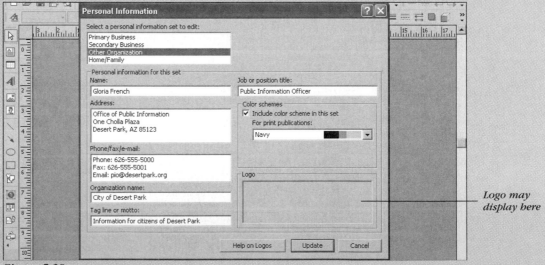

Figure 5.28

6 **Zoom** to **75%** and position the top portion of the letterhead in the center of your screen.

Look at the logo, and if it is not the blue City of Desert Park logo used by the Public Information Office, click it to display the Wizard button. Click the Wizard button, and

Activity 5.8   Creating a Letterhead from a Design Set

then use the Logo Options command on the task pane to insert the logo picture 5C_PIO_Logo.

7 If necessary, close the task pane. Create a footer and in it type Firstname Lastname-5C PIO Letter and then save the publication in your storage location as *Firstname Lastname-5C PIO Letter*. If a message displays regarding saving the logo, click **Yes**.

8 **Zoom** to **75%** and position the top portion of the page in the middle of your screen. Use the Move pointer and the Nudge feature to align the logo as shown in Figure 5.29.

Position logo here

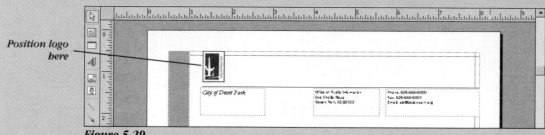

Figure 5.29

9 On the Standard toolbar, click **Save** to save your changes.

Objective 7: Create a Table

A table is a useful format for organizing information. Some publications within the Master Set designs include pre-formatted tables—for example, the purchase order that you created in Publication 5B. When needed, a table can be created in any publication by either using the Insert Table button on the Objects toolbar, or by displaying the Table menu and clicking Insert.

Activity 5.9   Creating a Table Using the Objects Toolbar

1 Position the bottom portion of the letterhead in view.

2 On the Objects toolbar, click the **Insert Table** button, and move the mouse pointer into the letterhead.

The mouse pointer takes the shape of a crosshair pointer.

3 Position the crosshair pointer at **1.25 inches on the horizontal ruler** and **6.5 inches on the vertical ruler**, and then drag down to **9 inches on the vertical ruler** and over to the **right blue layout guide** (see Figure 5.30).

(Continues)

Activity 5.9   Creating a Table Using the Objects Toolbar (continued)

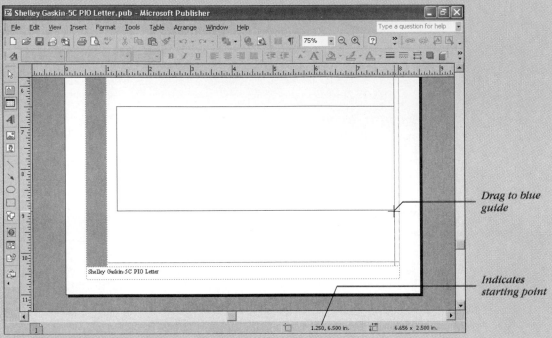

Figure 5.30

④ Release the left mouse button.

The Create Table dialog box displays. From this dialog box you can select the number of rows and columns that you want in your table. Additionally, if you want, you can select from one of Publisher's pre-designed table formats, which consist primarily of various arrangements for bordering and shading the cells.

⑤ In the Create Table dialog box, either type or use the spin boxes to create a table with **4 rows** and **5 columns**. Under Table format, click **None**, and then click **OK** to close the dialog box.

The table displays within the area you defined with the mouse, and the insertion point is positioned in the first cell (see Figure 5.31).

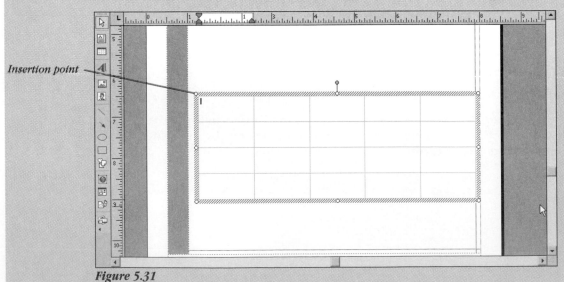

Figure 5.31

Activity 5.9 Creating a Table Using the Objects Toolbar

6 Using Figure 5.32 as your guide, type the text into the cells as shown in the figure. Where shown, insert a cell diagonal. You may want to zoom up to 100% or more for easy text entry. Recall that the (Tab⇄) key moves the insertion point from cell to cell and (⬆Shift) + (Tab⇄) moves the insertion point backward one cell.

Insert text as indicated

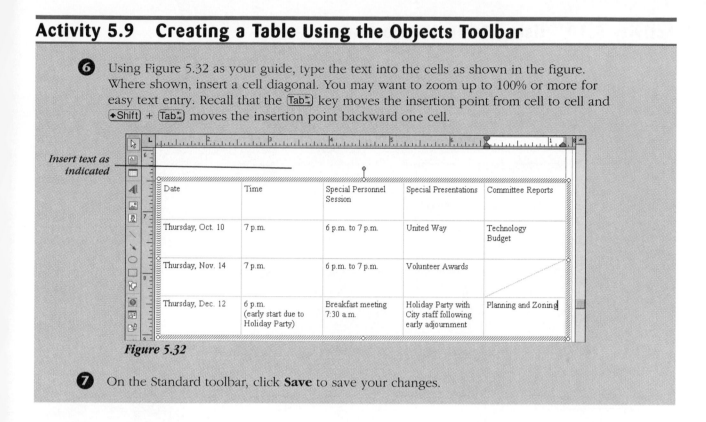

Date	Time	Special Personnel Session	Special Presentations	Committee Reports
Thursday, Oct. 10	7 p.m.	6 p.m. to 7 p.m.	United Way	Technology Budget
Thursday, Nov. 14	7 p.m.	6 p.m. to 7 p.m.	Volunteer Awards	
Thursday, Dec. 12	6 p.m. (early start due to Holiday Party)	Breakfast meeting 7:30 a.m.	Holiday Party with City staff following early adjournment	Planning and Zoning

Figure 5.32

7 On the Standard toolbar, click **Save** to save your changes.

Objective 8: Format a Table

Tables have three basic elements with which you work—rows, columns, and cells. To format a table, select various table elements and apply formatting to them. By default, tables created from the Objects toolbar (or alternatively from the Insert command on the Table menu) have no formatting—including no cell borders. Although you can see faint cell borders on the screen, unless you apply a line to the cells using the Color and Lines tab of the Format Table dialog box, cell borders will not print.

To distinguish various table elements, Publisher provides a number of pre-designed formats, which makes tables easier to read. The **Table AutoFormat** command can quickly and easily apply a pre-defined format to a table.

Activity 5.10   Using Table AutoFormat

1 Click anywhere in the table. On the menu bar click **Table**, and then click **Table AutoFormat**.

The Auto Format dialog box displays.

2 At the bottom of the dialog box, click the **Options** button to expand the menu.

As you view the various formats, you can further customize the formats by clearing the check marks from one or more of the check boxes under Formats to apply.

3 Under Table format, click **Checkbook Register**, and notice that in the Sample box, the cells containing numbers are right aligned.

Because the table you created contains only text, and not numbers, right alignment is not appropriate.

4 At the bottom of the dialog box, click to clear the check mark from the **Text alignment** check box.

In the Sample box, all the numerical text has changed to left alignment as shown in Figure 5.33.

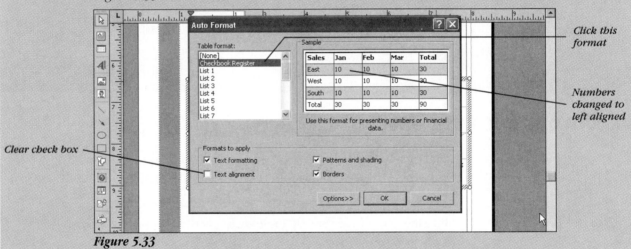

Figure 5.33

5 Click **OK** to close the Auto Format dialog box, and click **Save** to save your changes.

To extend your knowledge...

Disabling the Grow to Fit Text feature

By default, a cell in a Publisher table will expand to accommodate your typing. This feature, called **Grow to Fit Text**, can be turned off by clicking to remove its checkmark from the Table menu.

Activity 5.11 Formatting a Table

1 Click the cell containing the cell diagonal, and then on the Standard toolbar, click the **Print Preview** button.

Notice that although the Table AutoFormat feature applied borders to all the cells, it did not define the cell diagonal (see Figure 5.34).

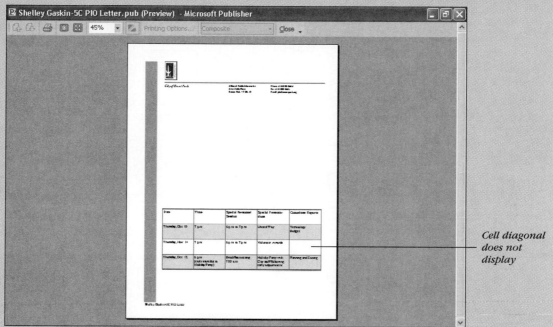

Cell diagonal does not display

Figure 5.34

2 **Close** the Print Preview. Be sure that the cell with the diagonal is still selected. On the menu bar, click **Format** and then click **Table**.

The Format Table dialog box displays.

3 On the **Colors and Lines tab**, under Preview, click the box with a diagonal line. Under Line, click the **Color arrow** and click the first color (black) in the color scheme. Use the spin box to set the **Weight** of the line to **1 pt** (see Figure 5.35).

(Continues)

Activity 5.11   Formatting a Table (continued)

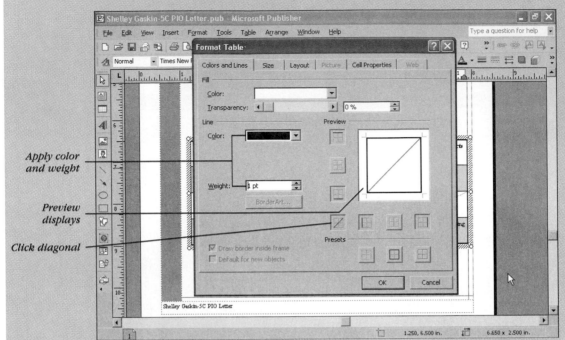

Apply color and weight

Preview displays

Click diagonal

Figure 5.35

4 Click **OK** to close the dialog box.

The black color is applied to the cell diagonal line.

5 On the menu bar, click **Table**, point to **Select**, and then click **Table**. With the entire table selected, change the **Font** to **Franklin Gothic Book**, and then click the **Center** button to horizontally center the text in every cell.

6 Click to position the insertion point in the first cell of the first row. On the menu bar click **Table**, point to **Select**, and then click **Row**. Hover over the selected row, right-click to display a shortcut menu, and then click **Format Table**.

The Format Table dialog box displays.

7 Click the **Cell Properties tab**, and then use the **Vertical alignment arrow** to vertically center the text in the **Middle**. Click **OK** to close the dialog box.

8 Hover over the table and right-click to display a shortcut menu, point to **Proofing Tools**, and then click **Hyphenation**. Click to clear the check mark from the Automatically hyphenate this story check box, and then click **OK** to close the dialog box.

The hyphenation is removed from the text in the first row.

9 Position the mouse pointer over the lower border of row 1 until the adjust pointer displays (see Figure 5.36) and then drag the lower border up slightly to **7 inches on the vertical ruler**.

Adjust pointer

7-inch mark

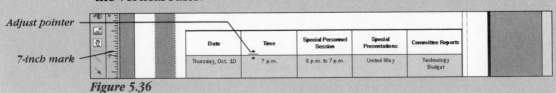

Figure 5.36

Activity 5.11   Formatting a Table

10 In the last cell in the Special Presentations column, click to position the insertion point after the word "adjournment," press ⏎Enter, and then type (please bring a wrapped $5 gift for the grab bag)

The cell expands to accommodate your typing because the Grow to Fit Text feature is active by default.

11 On the Standard toolbar, click the **Print Preview** button to view the letterhead, and notice the position of the table as shown in Figure 5.37.

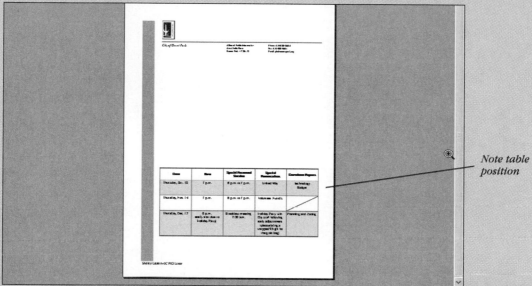

Note table position

Figure 5.37

12 **Close** the Print Preview. Click anywhere in the table, hover and right-click to display a shortcut menu, and then click **Format Table**.

13 In the Format Table dialog box, click the **Layout tab**, and under Position on page, change the vertical position to **7.5"**.

14 Click **OK** to close the dialog box, and then use **Print Preview** to view your changes. Compare your screen to Figure 5.38.

Notice that the lower edge of the table aligns with the lower edge of the graphic element on the left.

(Continues)

Activity 5.11   Formatting a Table (continued)

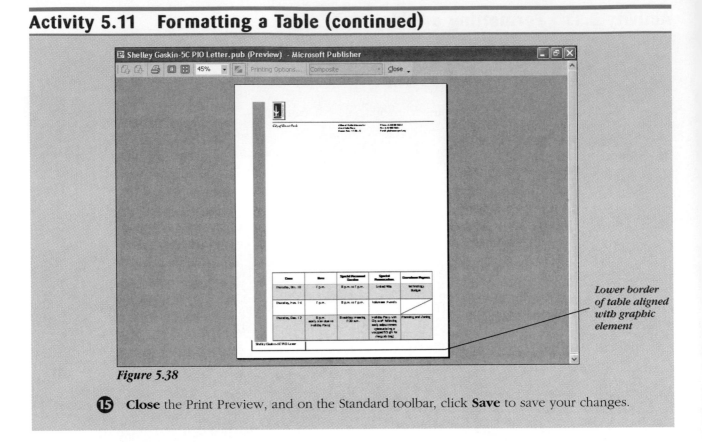

Figure 5.38

15   **Close** the Print Preview, and on the Standard toolbar, click **Save** to save your changes.

Objective 9: Create a Mail Merge

Mail merge is the process of combining a *data source* with a publication to print a group of individually customized publications. A data source is an electronic file where you store the names, addresses, and other contact information about individuals who will receive a copy of the publication. Within a data source, each person's information is a *record*. Within individual records, each piece of information—for example, the name, street address, city name—is called a *field*. Thus, a group of related fields comprise a record, and a group of records comprise a data source.

The mail merge feature is used to personalize publications, for example, by adding people's names. Mail merge is also used to create a *mass mailing*—mailing the same publication to many people. For example, recall that some of the brochures you created in Lesson 3 had space for mailing information. Using a list of residents and their addresses, the City of Desert Park could merge the list (the data source) with the brochure publication to produce hundreds of individually addressed brochures.

The mail merge feature includes some features found in database programs such as Microsoft Access. For example, mail merge can sort the addresses in your data source by ZIP Code. Pre-sorting mail in this manner enables you to take advantage of lower postal rates provided by the United States Postal Service under its *bulk mail* (presorted mail) program.

The basic steps in the mail merge process are: 1) create the publication, 2) create or obtain the data source, 3) merge the publication with the data source, and 4) print and distribute the merged publications.

Activity 5.12   Creating a Data Source

1 With your publication 5C PIO Letter containing the table displayed, **Zoom** to **66%**, and then position the top portion of the letterhead in the center of your screen.

2 On the Objects toolbar, click the **Text Box** button, and then move the mouse pointer into the middle of the page.

The mouse pointer takes the shape of a crosshair pointer.

3 Position the crosshair pointer at **1.25 inches on the horizontal ruler** and **2.25 inches on the vertical ruler** and then drag over to the **right blue layout guide** and down to **7.25 inches on the vertical ruler**.

A text box is created on your letterhead.

4 On the menu bar, click **Tools**, point to **Mail Merge**, and then click **Mail Merge Wizard**.

The Mail Merge task pane displays.

5 In the task pane, under Select recipients, click the **Type a new list** option button. Then, under Type a new list, click **Create**.

The New Address List dialog box displays as shown in Figure 5.39.

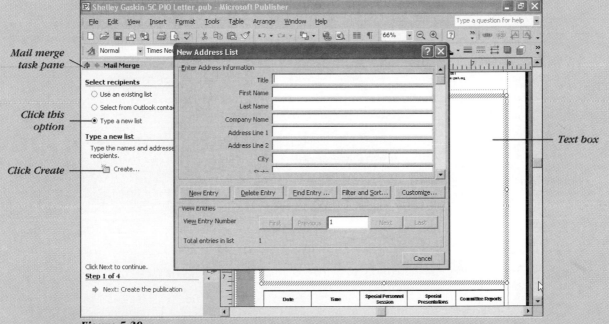

Figure 5.39

6 In the New Address List dialog box, use the following table and Figure 5.40 to enter the information for Mr. Michael Park, the first of five City Council members.

Notice that no Company Name is necessary for these personal addresses. Use Tab to move from field to field, and use the scroll bar at the right to scroll down to view the fields for the City, State, and ZIP Code.

(Continues)

Activity 5.12   Creating a Data Source (continued)

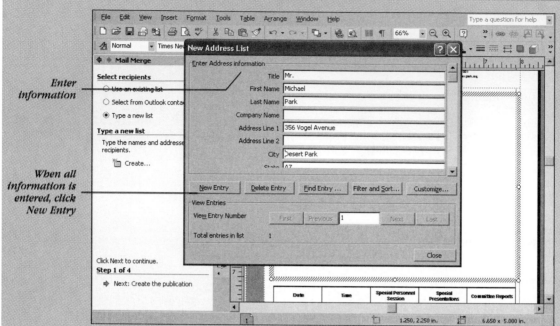

Figure 5.40

	Member #1	Member #2	Member #3	Member #4	Member #5
Title	Mr.	Ms.	Dr.	Mr.	Dr.
First Name	Michael	Pauline	Raj	Donald	Betty
Last Name	Park	McPherson	Singh	Kelley	Perez
Company Name					
Address Line 1	356 Vogel Avenue	1489 Cactus Road	One Desert Circle	955 Tumbleweed Court	47 Hidalgo Drive
Address Line 2					
City	Desert Park	Desert Park	Desert Park	Desert Park	Desert Park
State	AZ	AZ	AZ	AZ	AZ
ZIP Code	85259	85259	85259	85259	85259

7 When you have finished adding Mr. Park's information, click the **New Entry** button to store the information and display a new blank form for the second record.

8 Fill in a form for each of the remaining City Council members, clicking the New Entry button after each addition. After filling in Dr. Perez's information form (see Figure 5.41), move to the bottom of the dialog box and click **Close**.

The Save Address List dialog box displays.

Activity 5.12   Creating a Data Source

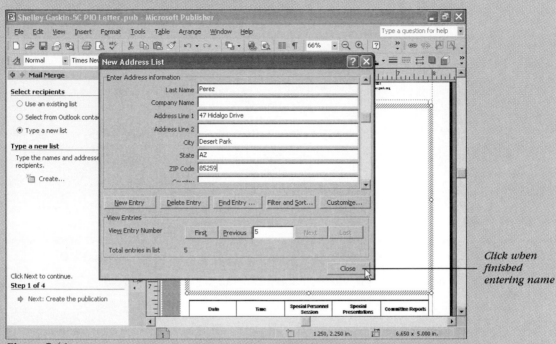

Figure 5.41

9 Use the **Save in arrow** to navigate to the location where you are storing your files for this Lesson. In the File name box type 5C Council List and then click **Save**.

The Mail Merge Recipients dialog box displays. See Figure 5.42.

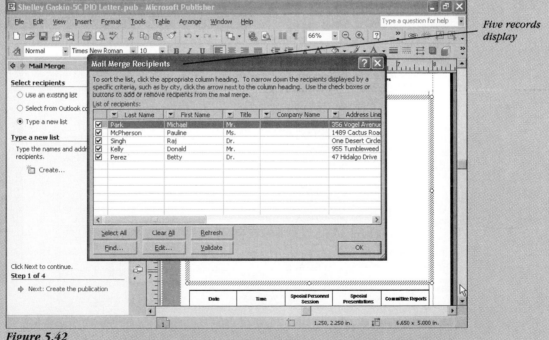

Figure 5.42

(Continues)

Activity 5.12   Creating a Data Source (continued)

10 Take a moment to read the information at the top of the Mail Merge Recipients dialog box, which describes a number of useful methods to manipulate the records in your data source, such as sorting your records by ZIP Code to qualify for the lower postage rate.

11 If necessary, edit any of the records by clicking on the record and then clicking the Edit button.

The Address List form will display providing you a place to make any needed changes.

12 At the bottom of the Mail Merge Recipients dialog box, click **OK**.

13 Click **Save** to save your changes.

Activity 5.13   Connecting a Publication to a Data Source

1 At the bottom of the Mail Merge task pane, click **Next: Create the publication**.

Instructions for creating the publication display in the task pane. In this instance, you have already created your publication—the letterhead.

2 In the text box you created in the letterhead, be sure that the insertion point is blinking at the top of the text box. Then, type today's date and press **Enter** four times as shown in Figure 5.43.

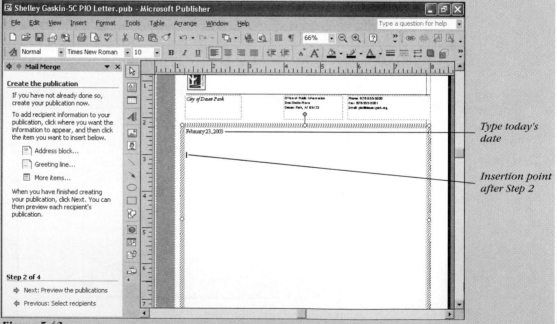

Figure 5.43

3 In the middle portion of the task pane, click **Address block**.

The Insert Address Block dialog box displays. See Figure 5.44. Here you can change the format of your address block in a variety of ways; however, for this Activity use the default settings.

Activity 5.13   Connecting a Publication to a Data Source

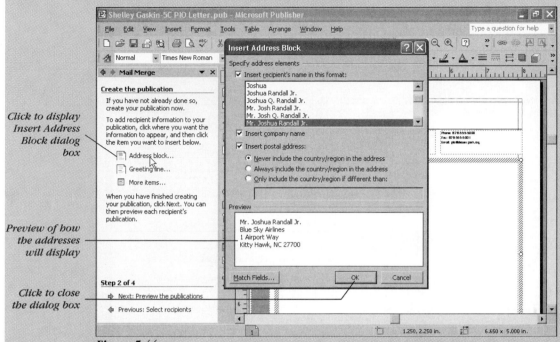

Figure 5.44

4 At the bottom of the Insert Address Block dialog box, click **OK**.

The *field code* for the Address Block is inserted in the text box. A field code is a place-holder for data that changes with each publication.

5 Press [↵Enter] twice, and then, in the task pane, click **Greeting line**.

The Greeting Line dialog box shown in Figure 5.45 displays. Here you can vary the format of the greeting line.

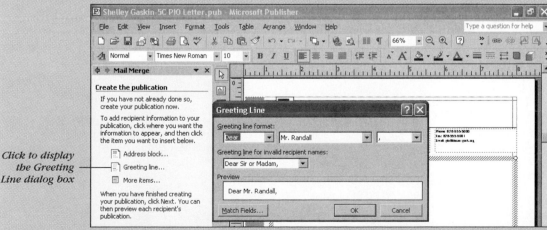

Figure 5.45

6 In the Greeting Line dialog box, click **OK** to accept the default settings.

(Continues)

Activity 5.13   Connecting a Publication to a Data Source (continued)

The Greeting Line field code displays in the letter.

7 Press **⏎Enter** twice. On the menu bar, click **Insert**, click **Text File**, navigate to your student files, and then click **5C_LetterText**.

The body of the letter is inserted into the text box (see Figure 5.46).

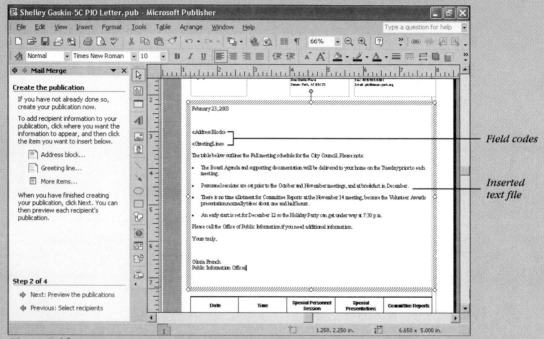

Figure 5.46

8 At the bottom of the task pane, click **Next: Preview the publications**.

The letter to the first recipient, Mr. Park, displays. In the upper portion of the task pane, arrows that permit you to scroll through the group of five letters to view each one display as shown in Figure 5.47. Additionally, the task pane displays a method by which you could exclude (discard) any of the displayed letters.

Activity 5.13   Connecting a Publication to a Data Source

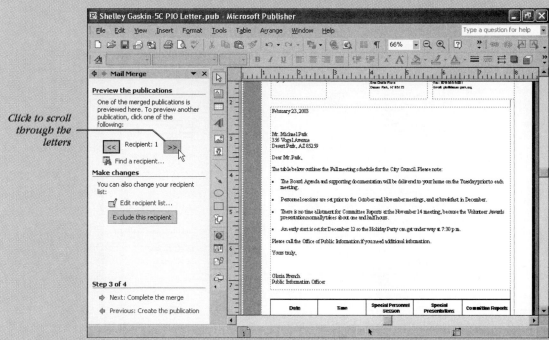

Figure 5.47

9 At the bottom of the task pane, click **Next: Complete the merge**, and then at the top of the task pane, under Merge, click **Print**.

The Print Merge dialog box displays as shown in Figure 5.48. Here you can elect to print all five of the letters, print only some of the letters, or print only one of the letters as a test.

(Continues)

Activity 5.13   Connecting a Publication to a Data Source (continued)

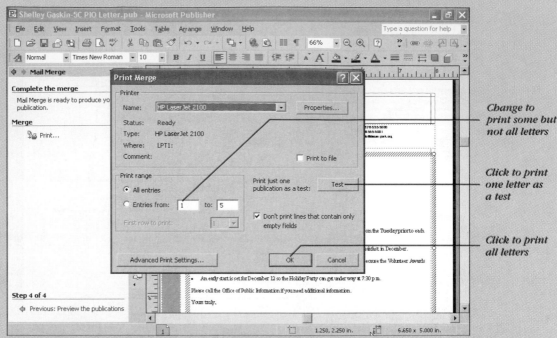

Figure 5.48

10 Unless otherwise directed by your instructor or lab coordinator, click **OK** to print all five letters.

11 Close the task pane. On the Standard toolbar click **Save**, and then **Close** your file. Publication 5C is complete!

To extend your knowledge...

When you open a publication that is a mail merge, the window will display the publication with the merge codes. However, if you print the document, you will print the actual merged publications. You can display the Print Merge dialog box again by displaying the File menu, and then clicking Print Merge.

Summary

When you are ready to print your publications, there are a number of things to think about when choosing the paper. You will need to consider the printing process you plan to use, the content of the publication, the cost of the paper, the function (objective) of the publication, and the overall mood of the publication.

With Publisher, it is easy to produce a complete set of business stationery for your organization that includes not only letterhead, envelopes, and business cards, but also forms for completing everyday business transactions. For example, Publisher provides forms for expense reports, invoices, and purchase orders. The Master Sets within Publisher ensure that all of your business documents display an attractive graphic design and layout and do so in a consistent manner.

Because many kinds of information are best presented in a table format, Publisher includes tables within some of its predesigned forms. Additionally, tables can be created in any publication. Whether predesigned or created by you, tables are easy to format in a variety of distinctive ways.

Publications, especially letters, newsletters, and brochures, are frequently mailed to a large group of individuals. The mail merge feature within Publisher provides an efficient means by which you can create a data source and merge it with a publication to produce a mass mailing.

Using Publisher Help

Publisher's mail merge feature can filter the records in a data source file. For example, the City of Desert Park could apply a filter to the data source of residents to produce letters only for residents who live on Pine Street. Then, residents of the street could be notified of upcoming street repairs.

Use Publisher Help to find out how to filter records in a data source.

1. If necessary, start Publisher and display the New Publication task pane and the Quick Publications Publication Gallery.
2. At the right edge of the menu bar, click in the Ask a Question box and type How can I filter a data source?
3. Press ⏎Enter, and then on the displayed list, click **Narrow the list of recipients in a Mail Merge**.
   The Help pane displays.
4. In the upper right corner, click **Show All** so that all of the information is displayed.
5. If you want to keep a copy of this information, click the **Print** button. It will print on one page, but your name will not print on the document.
6. Click the **Close** button—the X in the top right corner of the Help window—to close the Help window.

Concepts Assessment

Short Answer
Write the correct answer in the space provided.

1. The smoothness of paper is referred to as its _____.

2. The direction in which the majority of the paper fibers run in paper is referred to as its _____.

3. Publisher groups its pre-formatted publications by both publication type and by _____.

4. A publication mailed by organizations for brief messages, event announcements, thank you notes, and invitations is a _____.

5. In Publisher, page size refers to the size of the publication, not to the size of the _____.

6. The three elements that you work with when formatting a table are _____, _____, and _____.

7. Unlike a spreadsheet in Microsoft Excel, Publisher cannot perform _____ on numbers in a table.

8. A program provided by the United States Postal Service that provides lower rates for presorted mail is known as _____.

9. Within a data source, each person's information is called a _____.

10. Within a mail merge operation, a placeholder for data that will change in each printed publication is called a _____.

Matching

Match each term in the second column with its correct definition in the first column. Write the letter of the term on the blank line to the left of the correct definition.

_____ **1.** Letters, envelopes, postcards, business cards, and other business forms.

_____ **2.** A group of preformatted publications that share the same graphic design elements and font formatting.

_____ **3.** A Publisher command that can quickly and easily apply a pre-defined format to a table.

_____ **4.** Lines that print when your publication is smaller or larger than a piece of paper.

_____ **5.** The actual size of a publication after the paper is cut.

_____ **6.** A collection of marks that direct a printing press operator at a commercial print shop as to the size, alignment, and color of a publication.

_____ **7.** A business form generated when an organization makes a request to buy goods or services from a vendor and to be billed for the amount.

_____ **8.** An arrangement of information in columns and rows.

_____ **9.** The intersection of a column and a row in a table.

_____ **10.** A feature that draws a diagonal line through a cell in a table.

_____ **11.** The process of combining a data source with a publication to print a group of individually customized publications.

_____ **12.** A Publisher feature that expands a cell to accommodate your typing.

_____ **13.** An electronic file where you store the names, addresses, and other contact information about individuals who will receive a copy of a publication.

_____ **14.** The process of mailing the same publication to many people.

_____ **15.** Paper printed with the name, address, and contact information of an organization or individual.

A. Business stationery
B. Cell
C. Cell diagonal
D. Crop marks
E. Data source
F. Design set
G. Grow to Fit Text
H. Letterhead
I. Mail merge
J. Mass mailing
K. Printer's marks
L. Purchase order
M. Table AutoFormat
N. Table
O. Trim size

Skill Assessments

Publication 5D

Envelope

In the following Skill Assessment, you will create an envelope for the Office of Public Information. Because you may not have blank envelopes available in your classroom or lab, you will print your envelope on regular letter-size paper. Your printed page will look similar to the one shown in Figure 5.49. You will save your publication as *Firstname Lastname-5D Envelope*.

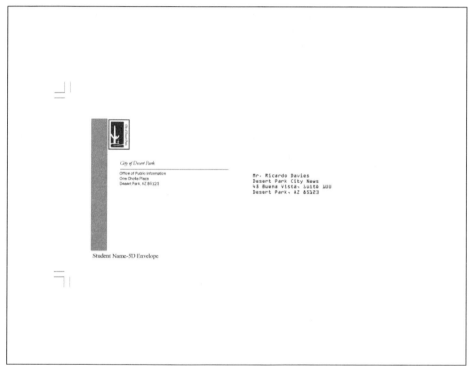

Figure 5.49

1. Start Publisher, display the New Publication task pane and the Publication Gallery. Click the Start from a design arrow, and then click By Design Sets.
2. Under Master Sets, click Straight Edge. In the Straight Edge Publication Gallery, click the Straight Edge Envelope. In the Envelope Options task pane, under Logo, be sure that Include is selected. Under Size, click #10. (A #10 envelope is the standard business-size envelope measuring 9.5 inches wide and 4.13 inches high.)
3. Close the task pane. On the menu bar, click Edit, and then click Personal Information. In the Personal Information dialog box, under Select a personal information set to edit, click Other Organization.

4. Compare your screen to the information for the Public Information Officer as shown in the steps for Publication 5A Postcard (Figure 5.5), and make any necessary changes. Click the Update button.

5. Zoom to 75% and position the envelope in the middle of your screen. If the logo is not the blue City of Desert Park logo used by the Office of Public Information, click to select it, and then use the Wizard button to insert the logo picture 5D_PIO_Logo. Close the task pane.

6. Use the Move pointer and the Nudge feature as necessary to position the logo so that its top edge is aligned with the pink guide. Align the left edge along the edge of the bar graphic element.

7. Click to select the placeholder text beginning Mailing Address and type the following four-line address:
Mr. Ricardo Davies
Desert Park City News
45 Buena Vista, Suite 100
Desert Park, AZ 85123

8. Look at the font used for the address. This is a special font that can be read by Postal Service scanners. On the menu bar, click View, and then click Header and Footer. Use the Show Header/Footer button on the Header and Footer toolbar to navigate to the Footer frame, and then type Firstname Lastname-5D Envelope

9. Close the Header and Footer toolbar. On the menu bar, click File, click Save As, navigate to the location in which you are storing your files for this Lesson, and in the File name box type Firstname Lastname-5D Envelope

10. If a message displays regarding the logo, click Yes. On the Standard toolbar, click the Print Preview button to view the page. Recall that you are printing on regular paper, so your envelope displays in the upper left position of a sheet of paper in landscape orientation. On the Print Preview toolbar, click the Print button to print one complete copy of your envelope.

11. Close the Print Preview. On the menu bar click File, and then click Close. If necessary, click Yes to save any additional changes. Publication 5D is complete!

Publication 5E

Inventory

In the following Skill Assessment, you will edit and format an Inventory List that lists all of the computer equipment in the Office of Public Information. The list is based on one of the business forms within the Straight Edge Master Set. Your completed publication will look similar to the one shown in Figure 5.50. You will save your publication as *Firstname Lastname-5E Inventory List*.

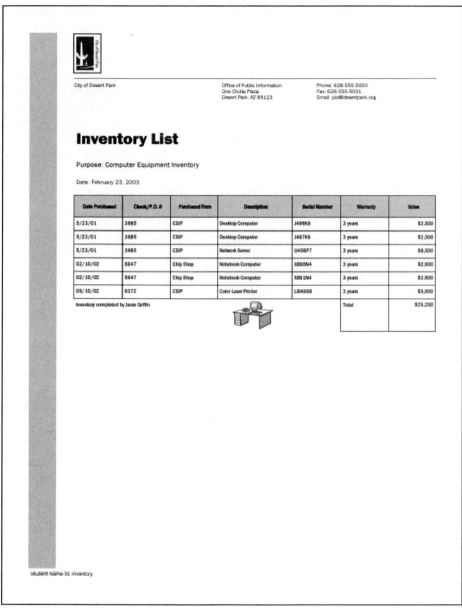

Figure 5.50

1. Start Publisher, display the New Publication task pane and the Publication Gallery. From your student files, open the publication 5E_InventoryList.

2. On the menu bar, click View, and then click Header and Footer. Use the Show Header/Footer button on the Header and Footer toolbar to navigate to the Footer frame, and then type `Firstname Lastname-5E Inventory`

3. Close the Header and Footer toolbar. On the menu bar, click File, click Save As, navigate to the location in which you are storing your files for this Lesson, and in the File name box type `Firstname Lastname-5E Inventory`

4. Zoom to 100% and position the top portion of the publication in the middle of your screen.

5. Select the text "Inventory List" and apply Best Fit. Click after the text "Purpose:" and press the (Spacebar) once. Then, type `Computer Equipment Inventory`

6. In the next text box, position the insertion point after "Date:" and press the (Spacebar) once. Type today's date.

7. Click after the text "Date Purchased." On the menu bar, click Table, point to Select, and then click Row. With the row selected, click the Center button, and then apply Bold. Hover over the selected row, and then right-click to display a shortcut menu. Click Format Table. Display the Cell Properties tab, and then vertically align the text in the middle of the cells. Display the Colors and Lines tab, and then apply a Fill color to the row, using the fifth color (gray) in the color scheme.

8. Select the black bar graphic element along the left side of the page, display the Format AutoShape dialog box, and then change its Fill color to the fifth color (gray) in the color scheme.

9. Zoom to 75%. In the Warranty column, select all the empty cells (the cells between "3 years" and "Total"). On the menu bar, click Table, point to Delete, and then click Rows. All the empty rows are deleted.

10. Zoom back to 100%. In the last cell in the Value column, type $25,200 and then right align all the cells with dollar amounts. In the last row, select the first three cells (the cell borders are light gray because they have no line color applied to them).

11. On the menu bar, click Table, and then click Merge Cells. In the enlarged cell type
Inventory completed by Janie Griffin

12. Position the pointer on the lower boundary of the table until the Adjust pointer displays, and then drag down to 6 inches on the vertical ruler.

13. In the Description column, click in the newly enlarged cell at the bottom. On the menu bar, click Insert, point to Picture, and then click From File. Navigate to your student files and insert 5E_PIC. Use a corner resize handle to decrease the size of the picture to a size that will fit in the cell, and then use the Move pointer and the Nudge feature to center it in the cell.

14. On the Standard toolbar, click to Save, and then click the Print Preview button to view the page. On the Print Preview toolbar, click the Print button to print one complete copy.

15. Close the Print Preview. On the menu bar click File, and then click Close. If necessary, click Yes to save any additional changes. Publication 5E is complete!

Publication 5F

Brochure Mailing

In the following Skill Assessment, you will merge an existing data source with a brochure to create a mass mailing. Page 2 of your completed brochure will look similar to the one shown in Figure 5.51. You will save your publication as *Firstname Lastname-5F Brochure Mailing*.

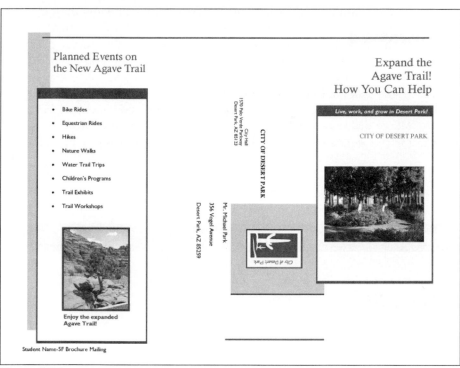

Figure 5.51

1. Start Publisher, display the New Publication task pane and the Publication Gallery. From your student files, open the publication 5F_Brochure.

2. On the menu bar, click View, and then click Header and Footer. Use the Show Header/Footer button on the Header and Footer toolbar to navigate to the Footer frame, and then type `Firstname Lastname-5F Brochure Mailing`

3. Close the Header and Footer toolbar. On the menu bar, click File, click Save As, navigate to the location in which you are storing your files for this Lesson, and in the File name box type `Firstname Lastname-5F Brochure Mailing`

4. Zoom to 75%. On the menu bar, click Tools, point to Mail Merge, and then click Mail Merge Wizard.

5. In the Mail Merge task pane, under Select recipients, be sure that the Use an existing list option button is selected. Then, under Use an existing list, click Browse. The Select Data Source dialog box displays.

6. Use the Look in arrow to navigate to your student files, and then click 5F_MailingList. At the lower right corner, click Open. The Mail Merge Recipients dialog box displays. The list contains the names and addresses of the City Council members, all of whom will receive a copy of the brochure. Click OK.

7. In the publication window, scroll to position panel 6 (middle panel) in the center of the window. Click to select the placeholder text that begins "Mailing Address" and then press Del to delete the placeholder text. Be sure that the insertion point is blinking in the empty text box. Because you will not have to type in this text box, do not be concerned with your sideways view of the textbox.

8. At the bottom of the Mail Merge task pane, click Create the publication. Then, in the upper portion of the task pane, click Address block. The Insert Address Block dialog box displays. Click OK to accept the default format. The Address Block field code is inserted in the text box.

9. At the bottom of the Mail Merge task pane, click Preview the publications. The first address in the data source is placed in the mailing area of the brochure.

10. In the Mail Merge task pane, under Preview the publications, click the arrows to scroll through and look at the individual publications. Then, at the bottom of the task pane, click Complete the merge.

11. In the task pane, under Merge, click Print. In the Print Merge dialog box, click Test. This will print just one copy (two pages) of the merged brochure. Click Cancel to close the Print Merge dialog box without printing the remaining brochures.

12. On the Standard toolbar, click Save to save your changes, and close the publication.

Performance Assessments

Publication 5G

Park Purchase

In the following Performance Assessment, you will create a purchase order for the Fine Arts and Parks Department. Your completed publication will look similar to the one shown in Figure 5.52. You will save your publication as *Firstname Lastname-5G Park Purchase*.

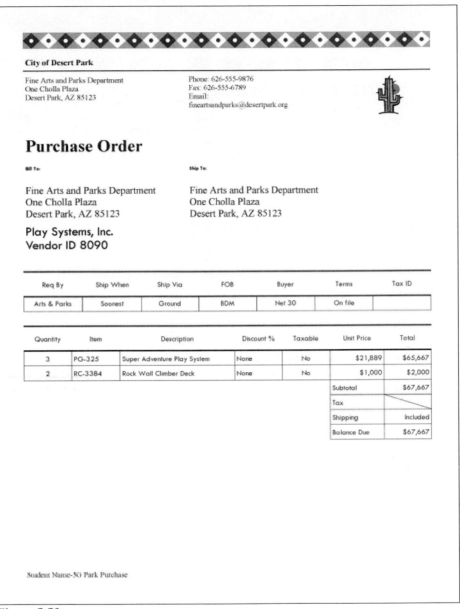

Figure 5.52

1. Start Publisher. Under Master Sets, click Accessory Bar and display the Accessory Bar Purchase Order. Include a logo, and change the Color Scheme to Mountain. Close the task pane.

2. Change the personal information set to Secondary Business, which is for the Fine Arts and Parks Department using the Mountain color scheme. If this information set has been changed on your computer, use Figure 5.53 to fill in the appropriate information. If the cactus/sun logo shown in the figure does not display, insert 5G_ParksLogo. Move and size it as shown in the figure.

Fill in information if necessary

Move and resize text boxes as necessary

Insert from file if necessary

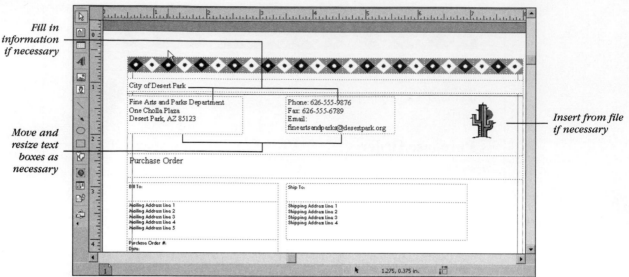

Figure 5.53

3. Insert a footer with your first and last name and the file name, and then save the file as *Firstname Lastname-5G Park Purchase.* If a message displays regarding the logo, click Yes.

4. Move and resize the two text boxes to the left of the logo as shown in Figure 5.53.

5. Apply Bold and Best Fit to the text boxes containing "City of Desert Park" and "Purchase Order." In the Mailing Address text box, copy the address of the Fine Arts and Parks Department from the text box near the top of the page, and then Paste it into this text box. Apply Best Fit. Copy this text, and then Paste it into the Shipping Address text box. Apply Best Fit to the copied address.

6. Delete the placeholder text in the "Purchase Order #" text box, type the Vendor Information text as shown in Figure 5.54, and apply Best Fit. Enter the data into the two tables in the purchase order and format them as shown in Figure 5.54. Delete columns and rows as necessary. In both tables, change all the cells to Font Tw Cen Mt, the Font Size to 10, and remove any Italic formatting. After deleting the column in the second table, resize the table by dragging the right center handle to the right pink layout guide.

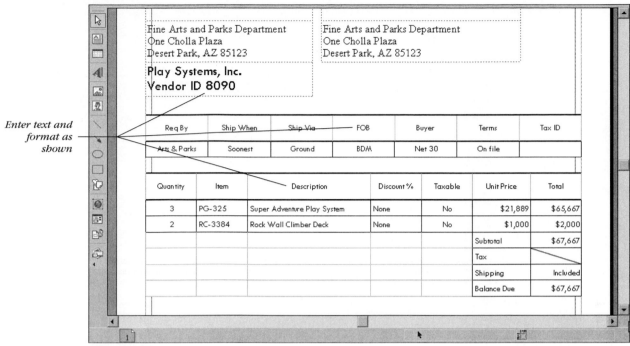

Enter text and format as shown

Figure 5.54

7. On the Standard toolbar, click Save, and then click the Print Preview button to view the page. On the Print Preview toolbar, click the Print button to print one copy.

8. Close the Print Preview. On the menu bar click File, and then click Close. If necessary, click Yes to save any additional changes. Publication 5G is complete!

Publication 5H

Fine Arts Letter

In the following Performance Assessment, you will create a data source and merge it with a Press Release letter. Additionally you will create a table within the letter. Your completed publication will look similar to the one shown in Figure 5.55. You will save your publication as *Firstname Lastname-5H Fine Arts Letter.*

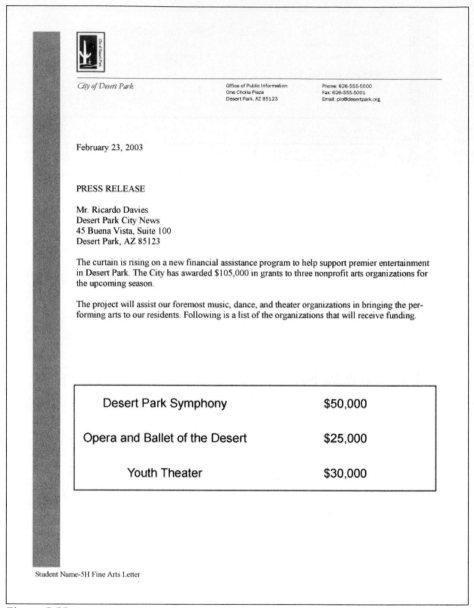

Figure 5.55

1. Start Publisher. Create a letterhead using the Straight Edge design and include a logo. Use the personal information set for the Public Information Officer. If necessary, update this information from the Figure in Publication 5A. If necessary, insert the logo of the Office of Public Information using 5H_PIO_Logo. Position the logo as shown in Figure 5.55.

2. Insert a footer with your first and last name and the file name, and then save the file as *Firstname Lastname-5H Fine Arts Letter*. If a message displays regarding the logo, click Yes.

3. Zoom to 75%. Close the task pane and display the lower portion of the letterhead. Use the Insert Table button on the Objects toolbar to draw a table beginning at 1.25 inches on the horizontal ruler and 7 inches on the vertical ruler and drag down to 9 inches on the vertical ruler and over to the right blue layout guide. Insert 3 rows and 2 columns, and click None for the Table format. Type the following information into the table.

   ```
   Desert Park Symphony                    $50,000
   Opera and Ballet of the Desert          $25,000
   Youth Theater                           $30,000
   ```

4. Select the table, Center the text horizontally, change the Font Size to 16, and change the Font to Arial. With the table selected, display the Format Table dialog box. On the Colors and Lines tab, apply a .75 black line around the table. Display the Cell Properties tab and center the text vertically in the cells.

5. Click in the gray scratch area to cancel the selection of the table and view your changes. On the Standard toolbar, click Save. On the menu bar, click Tools, point to Mail Merge, and then click Mail Merge Wizard. Under Select recipients, click Type a new list, and then under Type a new list, click Create. Add the following two records into the data source.

	RECORD #1	RECORD #2
Title	Mr.	Ms.
First Name	Ricardo	Angie
Last Name	Davies	Lee
Company Name	Desert Park City News	County News Weekly
Address Line 1	45 Buena Vista, Suite 100	27 Fifth Avenue
Address Line 2		
City	Desert Park	Desert Park
State	AZ	AZ
ZIP Code	85123	85123

6. After adding the two records, click Close, navigate to your storage location, and then save the data source as *5H Media List*. Make any necessary corrections in the Mail Merge Recipients dialog box, and then click OK to close the dialog box.

7. Zoom to about 50% so that you can see both the letterhead and the task pane. Position the upper portion of the letterhead in the center of the window. Use the Text Box button on the Objects toolbar to draw a text box beginning at 1.25 inches on the horizontal ruler and 2.5 inches on the vertical ruler and then drag down and over to the right blue layout guide and to 6.5 inches on the vertical ruler.

8. With the insertion point blinking at the top of the text box, press F9 to zoom in, type today's date, and then press ⏎Enter four times. Type PRESS RELEASE and then press ⏎Enter two times. Press F9 to zoom back to 50%.

9. At the bottom of the task pane, click Create the publication. Because you have just created the publication, move to the middle of the task pane and click Address block. On the Insert Address Block dialog box, click OK to accept the default address format. Press ⏎Enter twice.

10. Insert the text file 5H_ArtsAward. Select all the text in the text box and change the font size to 12.

11. At the bottom of the task pane, click Preview the publications. The first merged publication, to Mr. Davies, displays. In the task pane, click the arrow to view the second merged publication.

12. At the bottom of the task pane, click Complete the merge, and then in the middle of the task pane, click Print. Click OK to print a copy of both publications.

13. On the Standard toolbar, click Save, and then close the file. Publication 5H is complete!

On the Internet

The United States Postal Service has a feature on its Web site called Mail 101. Here you can learn more about how to prepare publications for bulk (presorted) mail. Visit their site at **www.usps.com**.

Using Publisher for the Web

Objectives

In this lesson, you learn how to:

✔ Create a Web Site from a Wizard
✔ Insert Pages in a Web Site
✔ Format a Home Page
✔ Format a Calendar Page in a Web Site
✔ Insert Hyperlinks in a Web Site
✔ Format a Story Page in a Web Site
✔ Format a Price List Page in a Web Site
✔ Insert a Related Links Page with a Hot Spot
✔ Add Background Color to a Web Site
✔ Preview a Web Site in Internet Explorer
✔ Print a Web Site
✔ Convert a Print Publication to a Web Site

Key terms in this Lesson include

❏ browser
❏ Convert to Web Layout
❏ form
❏ form controls
❏ home page
❏ horizontal navigation bar
❏ hot spot
❏ hyperlink
❏ Hypertext Markup Language

❏ Internet
❏ navigation bar
❏ navigation structure
❏ subsidiary pages
❏ topic pages
❏ URL
❏ vertical navigation bar
❏ Web pages
❏ Web Sites Wizard
❏ World Wide Web

Publication Design Tips—Using Publisher for Web Sites

Businesses and organizations use printed publications to communicate with customers, employees, and others who seek information about them. In addition to printed publications, the **World Wide Web** is also used to communicate with customers, employees, and others. The World Wide Web, or "the Web" as it is usually called, is the multimedia branch of the **Internet**. The Internet is the worldwide network of computers that connects other, smaller networks of computers.

The Internet was used as early as 1969 to communicate plain text without graphics or color. In 1989, a scientist named Tim Berners-Lee developed **Hypertext Markup Language**, known as **HTML**. HTML is a programming language that communicates color and graphics in a format that all computers can understand. Information coded in HTML can be viewed on the Web using software known as a **browser**. The two most commonly used browsers are Microsoft Internet Explorer and Netscape Navigator.

With Microsoft Publisher, you can easily create simple Web sites for yourself or for your organization. Using one of Publisher's wizards, you lay out the pages using the same frame techniques you learned to create printed publications, enter the content (your text and graphics), and then Publisher converts your publication to HTML.

In addition to the wizards, there are several other ways to use Publisher to create a Web site. For example, you can create a Web site by starting with a blank publication. Another way to create a Web site is to use the **Convert to Web Layout** option, which is available within the Newsletter and Brochure Wizards. Finally, the Save As Web Page command begins the process of converting any publication to a Web site, whether it was created with the wizard or started from a blank publication.

Planning for Web publication begins with the same planning process used for a printed publication; that is, determine the purpose of your publication and identify the audience. After that, however, the Web brings some additional considerations. For example, it is more difficult to read text on a computer screen than on paper, so keep your Web pages short and concise. Organize the pages in a way that readers can quickly find the information they are looking for. Do not use so many graphics that it takes a long time for your pages to display on the average computer user's screen. Finally, remember that readers will probably not read the pages of your site in sequential order. Thus, each page should be able to stand on its own, and each page should provide a way to move to other pages.

Although Publisher is a convenient tool for creating simple Web sites for an individual, small business, or small department, if you need to create and maintain a complex Web site for an organization, choose Microsoft FrontPage. FrontPage is a tool designed specifically for Web site development and management.

Publication 6A

Parks Web

In Activities 6.1–6.12 you will create a Web site for the Department of Fine Arts and Parks. The pages of your completed Web site will look like Figure 6.1. You will save your publication as *Firstname Lastname-6A Parks Web*.

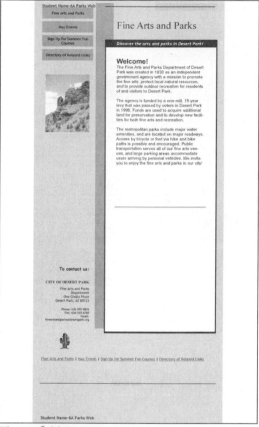

Figure 6.1A

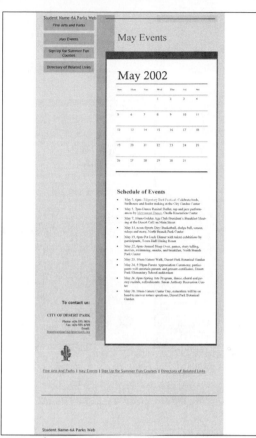

Figure 6.1B

Figure 6.1C

Figure 6.1D

Figure 6.1E

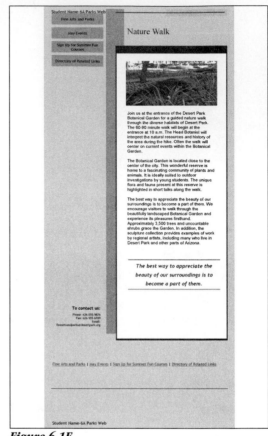

Figure 6.1F

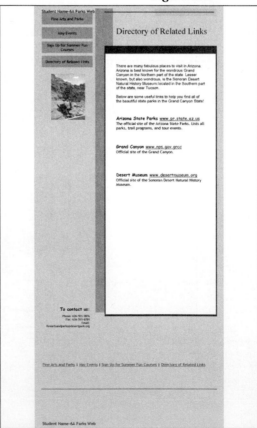

Figure 6.1G

Objective 1: Create a Web Site from a Wizard

The easiest way to create a Web site using Microsoft Publisher is to use the Web Sites wizard. Recall that a wizard is a tool that takes you step by step through the process of building a publication.

A Web site has one or more **Web pages**—documents that contain the text and graphics of the Web site. A Web page is similar to a page in a book, but it can be of any length. However, if you have long Web pages, the viewer will have to scroll to see information at the bottom of the page. Thus, take care not to make pages too long. It might be better to add an additional page instead.

When developing a Web site, the most important task is deciding upon the **navigation structure** of the site. The navigation structure defines the order in which the pages will be arranged, and how viewers of your Web site will navigate (move from one page to another) within the site.

The best arrangement for a site is a tree structure similar to the one shown in Figure 6.2. In a tree structure, the first page is the **Home Page**—the first page of any Web site. The Home Page is the doorway to your site. Under the Home Page you can have any number of **topic pages**. Topic pages are the Web pages to which the Home Page links directly. Then, branching from the topic pages— like the branches of a tree—you can add any number of **subsidiary pages**. A subsidiary page is a subset of the topic page. In terms of navigation, a subsidiary page is usually not accessible directly *from* the Home Page, although a subsidiary page should provide a link *back* to the Home Page.

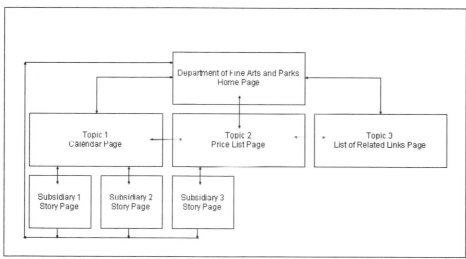

Figure 6.2

Microsoft Publisher includes the **Web Sites wizard**, which helps you quickly and easily create Web sites. You will create Publication 6A using this wizard. Figure 6.2 shows the navigation structure that you will use. This is a small, simple Web site. Large Web sites can have hundreds, or even thousands of pages, but the basic tree structure for navigation remains the same for any size site.

Activity 6.1   Creating a Web Site from a Wizard

① **Start** Publisher and display the New Publication task pane and the Quick Publications Gallery. Under By Publication Type, click **Web Sites**.

The Web Sites publication gallery displays on the right.

② In the Web Sites publication gallery, scroll as necessary, and then click the **Layers Web Site** (see Figure 6.3).

(Continues)

Activity 6.1 Creating a Web Site from a Wizard (continued)

The first page of the Web site displays in the publication window on the right, and the Web Site Options task pane displays on the left. Because Web site pages are intended to be viewed on a computer monitor, not printed on paper, the pages are preset to 6 inches wide and 14 inches tall. This format allows easy viewing on most computer monitors.

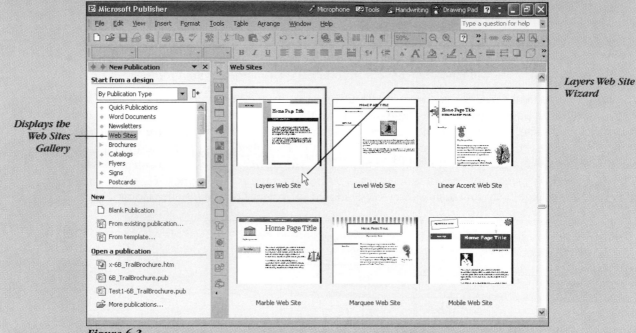

Displays the Web Sites Gallery

Layers Web Site Wizard

Figure 6.3

3 On the menu bar, click **Edit**, and then click **Personal Information**. In the Personal Information dialog box, under Select a personal information set to edit, click **Secondary Business**.

4 Compare your screen to Figure 6.4, and make any necessary changes to the typed information. Include the Mountain color scheme. If the logo does not display, you can insert it later.

Activity 6.1   Creating a Web Site from a Wizard

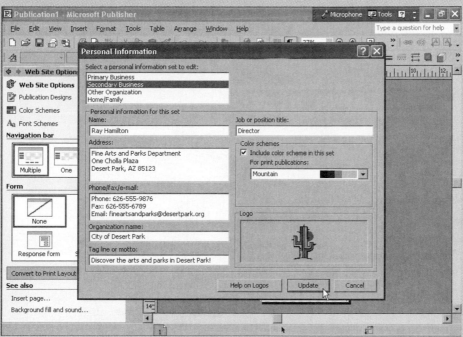

Figure 6.4

5 At the bottom of the Personal Information dialog box, click the **Update** button to update any information and return to the publication.

6 In the Web Site Options task pane, under Navigation bar, be sure that **Multiple** is selected.

The *navigation bar* is one of the methods by which visitors to your site can move among the pages of the site. A navigation bar is an area on a Web page containing a set of *hyperlinks* to other pages in the Web site. A hyperlink is text or graphics that you click, the result of which is that your computer is directed to display a different Web page.

When you select "Multiple" under Navigation bar, Publisher places both a vertical navigation bar on the left side of every page, and a horizontal navigation bar at the bottom of every page. Changes you make to the vertical bar at the top are automatically reflected in the horizontal bar at the bottom.

7 Under Form, be sure that **None** is selected.

Forms enable your Web site to be instantly interactive. You can insert a form into your site that visitors can use to communicate with you by email, to order a product or service, or to request more information.

8 On the menu bar, click **View**, and then click **Header and Footer**. With the insertion point positioned at the left edge of the Header frame, type Firstname Lastname-6A Parks Web

(Continues)

Activity 6.1   Creating a Web Site from a Wizard (continued)

9 Use the Move pointer or the Nudge feature as necessary to move the Header frame so that your name is aligned below and to the right of the blue layout guides (see Figure 6.5).

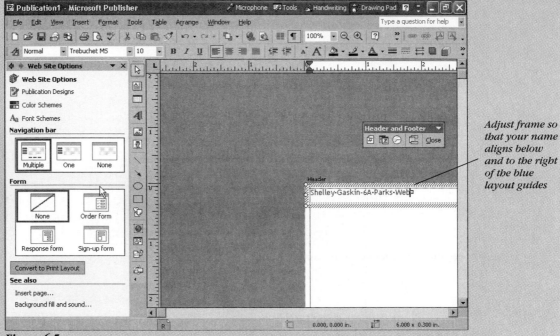

Figure 6.5

10 On the Header and Footer toolbar, click the **Show Header/Footer** button to move to the footer frame. With the insertion point positioned at the left edge of the Footer frame, type `Firstname Lastname-6A Parks Web` and then use the Move pointer or the Nudge feature as necessary to move the frame so that your name is aligned above and to the right of the blue layout guides.

When you print Web pages on regular letter-size paper, each page will require two sheets of paper. Adding both a header and footer will ensure that you can identify all of your pages when they print.

11 **Close** the Header and Footer toolbar.

12 On the menu bar, click **File**, and then click **Save As**. To save the publication as a Web page, move to the bottom of the Save As dialog box, and click the **Save as type arrow**. Scroll the displayed list as necessary, and then click **Web Page** (see Figure 6.6).

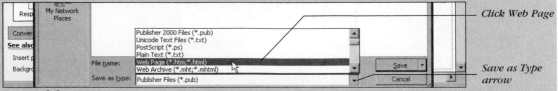

Figure 6.6

13 At the top of the dialog box, use the Save in arrow to navigate to the location in which you are storing your files for this lesson, creating a new folder if you want to do so.

Activity 6.1   Creating a Web Site from a Wizard

Then, at the bottom of the dialog box in the File name box, delete the existing text, type `Firstname Lastname-6A Parks Web` and click the **Save** button.

Your publication is saved as a Web, and the Web site name displays in the title bar. The publication zooms to 100%.

Objective 2: Insert Pages in a Web Site

Publisher is used to create quick and easy Web sites. Therefore, a number of pre-formatted Web pages are provided so that you do not have to design them yourself. The pre-formatted pages include those that are most frequently used in Web sites.

Activity 6.2   Inserting Pages in a Web Site

1 Be sure that your Web site named 6A Parks Web is displayed, and that the Web Site Options task pane is displayed. **Zoom** to **75%** and position the top of the page in the middle of your screen. If necessary, click the **Special Characters** button to display the characters for paragraph marks and spaces.

Displaying the special characters, as shown in Figure 6.7, makes it easier to see where lines end. Recall that these marks do not print.

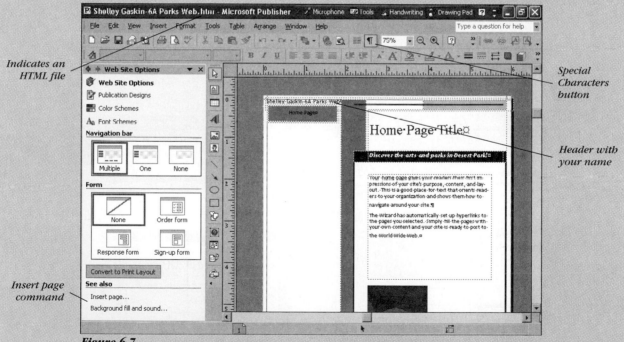

Figure 6.7

2 At the bottom of the Web Site Options task pane, under See also, click **Insert page**.

The Insert Page dialog box displays.

3 Look back at the Web site structure shown in Figure 6.2.

Notice that this Web site will contain a Home Page plus six additional pages. At the topic level, there will be three pages—a Calendar page, a Price List page, and a Related Links

(Continues)

Activity 6.2   Inserting Pages in a Web Site (continued)

page. At the subsidiary level, there will be three Story pages—two under Topic 1, and one under Topic 2.

4 In the Insert Page dialog box, click the **Available page types arrow** (see Figure 6.8).

Available page types arrow

Click Calendar

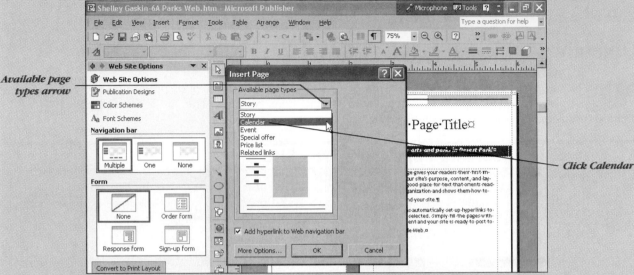

Figure 6.8

5 On the displayed list, click **Calendar**, and notice the preview of the layout. Then, click **OK** to close the dialog box.

In the status bar, page 2 has been added to your Web site, "Calendar" is added to the vertical navigation bar, and the inserted Calendar page displays in the publication window as shown in Figure 6.9.

Calendar hyperlink added to the vertical navigation bar

The current month and year will display here

Page 2 added

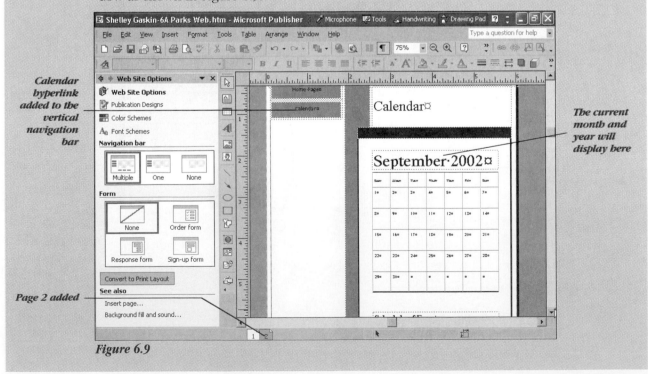

Figure 6.9

Activity 6.2   Inserting Pages in a Web Site

6 In the task pane, click **Insert page** again.

In the Insert Page dialog box, "Story" is the default page type. Notice the preview layout of the Story page.

7 At the bottom of the Insert Page dialog box, click to **clear (remove) the check mark** from the Add hyperlink to Web navigation bar check box (see Figure 6.10).

Clear the check box

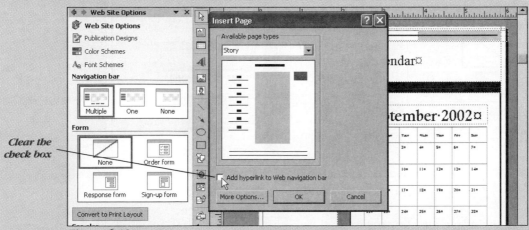

Figure 6.10

8 Click **OK** to close the dialog box, and notice page 3, the Story page, is added to your Web site. Also notice that no link for this page was added to the navigation bar, because you cleared the check box in the previous step.

When creating Web sites, it is not practical or logical to link every single page directly to the Home Page.

9 From the task pane, click **Insert page** again. With Story as the page type, **clear the check box** at the bottom of the dialog box. Then click **OK** to insert this Story page as page 4 of your Web site.

10 Using the Insert Page dialog box, insert a **Price list** page, leave the check box checked so that a direct link to the page is placed on the navigation bar, and then click **OK**.

The Price List page is inserted as page 5, and a link for it displays on the navigation bar as shown in Figure 6.11.

(Continues)

Activity 6.2   Inserting Pages in a Web Site (continued)

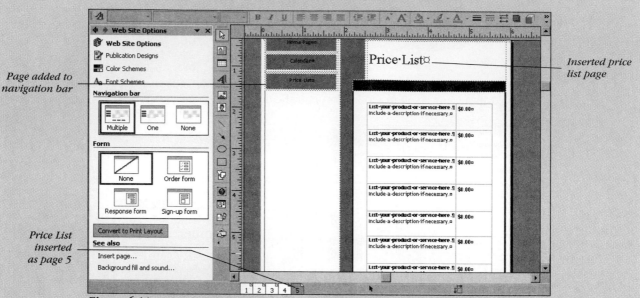

Page added to navigation bar

Inserted price list page

Price List inserted as page 5

Figure 6.11

⓫ On the menu bar, click **Insert**, and then click **Page**, which is an alternative method to display the Insert Page dialog box. Leave the page type as **Story**, and then **clear the check box**. Click **OK**.

The Story page is inserted as page 6 of your Web site.

⓬ On the Standard toolbar, click **Save** to save your changes.

A brief Working message displays indicating that HTML files are being exported.

⓭ On the menu bar, click **File**, and then click **Close**.

The file is closed.

⓮ On the Standard toolbar, click the **Open** button, and then, if necessary, navigate to the storage location in which you saved the Web site.

Notice that the Web site is stored differently than regular publications. A Publisher icon, superimposed over a Web icon, displays along with a folder as shown in Figure 6.12. The folder above it contains a file for each page of your Web site, numerous image files, and a master list of all the files in the folder. When you want to open an existing Web site in Publisher, click the file with the overlapping icons, located *outside* of the folder.

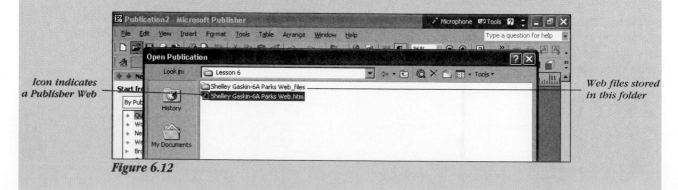

Icon indicates a Publisher Web

Web files stored in this folder

Figure 6.12

Activity 6.2   Inserting Pages in a Web Site

 On the displayed list, click the file with the icons and then click the **Open** button.

A Working message displays briefly indicating that HTML files are being imported, and then page 1 of the Web site displays in the publication window. Use this technique to open an existing Web site in Publisher.

Objective 3: Format a Home Page

The Home Page is the most important page in your Web site. It presents a first impression for visitors to your site. The Home Page must look professional and attractive, and must convey three things. First, the Home Page should provide the site's purpose. This would include the organization's name and contact information. Second, the Home Page should tell visitors about the kind of information contained within the site. Finally, the Home Page should convey to visitors how to access the information they want to find.

Activity 6.3   Formatting a Home Page

1 Be sure that **page 1**, the Home Page, is displayed in the Publication window, and then close the task pane. **Zoom** to **75%** and position the top portion of the page in the center of your screen.

2 On the left side of the Home Page, notice the boxes indicating the names of the pages to which a visitor can link directly from this page.

This is the **vertical navigation bar**, as shown in Figure 6.13. The wizard has automatically set up hyperlinks to these pages as you requested on the Insert Page dialog box.

A visitor can click here to move to one of these pages

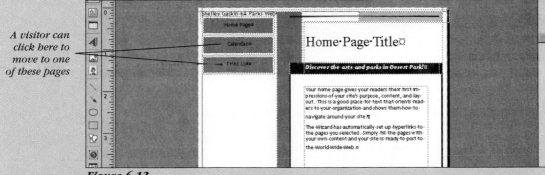

Figure 6.13

3 Scroll to view the bottom of the home page, and locate the names, in blue, of the pages you inserted to which you requested a direct link from the Home Page.

This is the **horizontal navigation bar** (see Figure 6.14). Any changes you make to the vertical navigation bar at the top will be automatically changed in the horizontal navigation bar at the bottom. Having both a vertical navigation bar at the top and a horizontal navigation bar at the bottom provides visitors to your site with the convenience of navigating to other pages from either the top of the page or the bottom of the page—depending upon what portion of the page they are viewing.

(Continues)

Activity 6.3   Formatting a Home Page (continued)

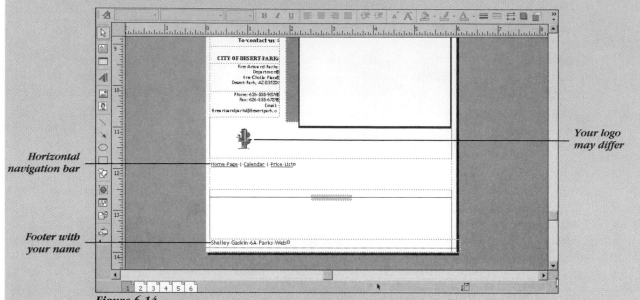

Horizontal navigation bar

Footer with your name

Your logo may differ

Figure 6.14

4   Scroll up to once again view the top portion of the page. Click anywhere in the text box "Home Page Title" and use Ctrl + A to select the text. Type `Fine Arts and Parks`

5   Click in the text box with the placeholder text that begins "Your home page." Take a moment to read the placeholder text, which offers good tips about the type of information best suited for a home page. Then, use Ctrl + A to select all of the placeholder text in the text box.

6   With your mouse pointer positioned over the selected text, right-click to display a shortcut menu, point to **Change Text**, and then click **Text File**.

The Insert Text dialog box displays.

7   Navigate to the location in which the student files for this textbook are stored, and insert **6A_HomePageText**.

8   When the message regarding text flow displays, click **No**.

Text is inserted, and the Text in Overflow indicator displays at the bottom of the text box, as shown Figure 6.15.

Activity 6.3   Formatting a Home Page

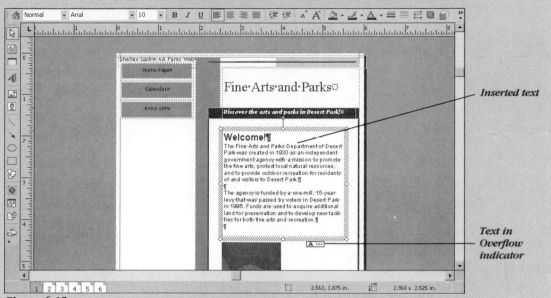

Inserted text

Text in Overflow indicator

Figure 6.15

9 Scroll down the page as necessary and click the picture to select it. Use the Move pointer to position the picture to the left of the gold bar shape with its top edge at approximately **2.5 inches on the vertical ruler**, as shown in Figure 6.16. Select the main text box again, and then drag the bottom center resize handle of the text box down to **6 inches on the vertical ruler** to enlarge the text box to fit the text.

The Text in Overflow indicator is removed.

10 Select all the text in the main text box. On the Formatting toolbar, click the **Font Color arrow** and change the font color to the second color in the color scheme (dark navy), as shown in Figure 6.16.

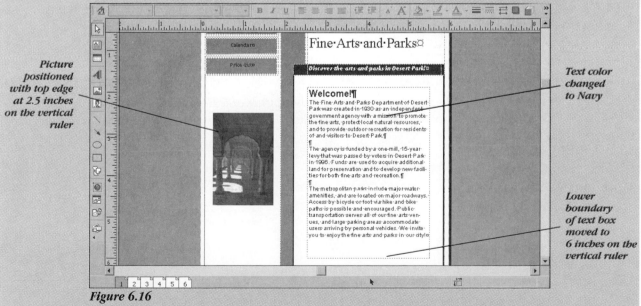

Picture positioned with top edge at 2.5 inches on the vertical ruler

Text color changed to Navy

Lower boundary of text box moved to 6 inches on the vertical ruler

Figure 6.16

(Continues)

Activity 6.3   Formatting a Home Page (continued)

⑪ Click to select the picture, and then hover and right-click to display a shortcut menu. Point to **Change Picture**, and then click **From File**.

⑫ Navigate to your student files, click **6A_Park**, and then click the **Insert** button at the lower right corner of the dialog box.

The new picture is inserted on the Home Page.

⑬ Scroll to view the bottom of the Home Page. If the logo for the Department of Fine Arts and Parks (a cactus with a sun) is not displayed, click whatever logo image is displayed, and use the Wizard button to insert the picture 6A_ParksLogo. Resize and reposition the inserted logo as necessary.

⑭ Close the task pane if it is displayed. In the text box containing the phone and email information, select all the text and change the font size to **7**.

⑮ On the Standard toolbar, click **Save** to save your changes. If a message displays regarding the logo, click Yes.

Objective 4: Format a Calendar Page in a Web Site

A calendar page within a Web site is useful for informing visitors about upcoming events. If you decide to include calendar pages in your Web site, remember to keep them up to date—adding new pages and deleting old ones as appropriate. Visitors to your site will be disappointed if old months are still displayed and future months are missing.

Activity 6.4   Formatting a Calendar Page in a Web Site

❶ Use the Page Navigation buttons on the status bar to navigate to **page 2** of your Web site publication. Position the top portion of the page in the middle of your screen.

❷ At the top of the page, replace the text "Calendar" with May Events and then click in the gray scratch area. Look at the vertical navigation bar, and then scroll down and look at the horizontal navigation bar.

By changing "Calendar" to "May Events," both the vertical navigation bar and the horizontal navigation bar at the bottom are immediately updated with the new page name.

❸ Click on any date in the calendar portion of the page to display the Wizard button.

Notice that the calendar will display the current month and year (see Figure 6.17).

Activity 6.4   Formatting a Calendar Page in a Web Site

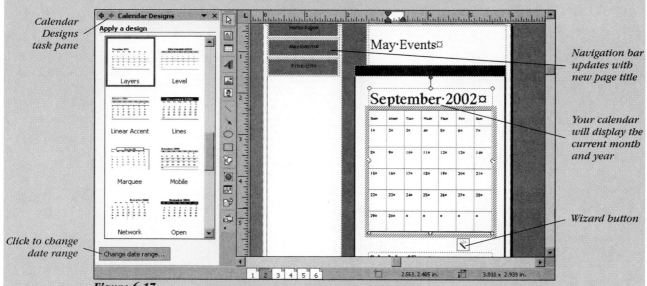

Calendar Designs task pane

Click to change date range

Navigation bar updates with new page title

Your calendar will display the current month and year

Wizard button

Figure 6.17

4 Click the **Wizard** button to display the Calendar Designs task pane, and then at the bottom of the task pane, click the **Change date range** button.

The Change Calendar Dates dialog box displays.

5 In the Change Calendar Dates dialog box, click the **Start date arrow**, and from the displayed list, scroll as necessary and click **May**. Leave the year as the current year, and then click **OK**.

6 Close the Calendar Designs task pane. Scroll as necessary to view the large text box with the placeholder text beginning "Date."

7 Click anywhere inside the large text box, and then use Ctrl + A to select the text. From your student files, insert the text file **6A_MayEvents**.

The new text is inserted as shown in Figure 6.18.

(Continues)

Activity 6.4   Formatting a Calendar Page in a Web Site (continued)

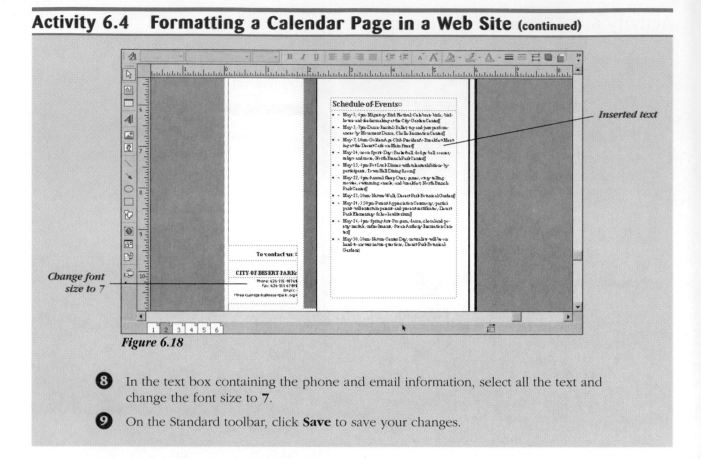

Change font size to 7

Inserted text

Figure 6.18

8 In the text box containing the phone and email information, select all the text and change the font size to **7**.

9 On the Standard toolbar, click **Save** to save your changes.

Objective 5: Insert Hyperlinks in a Web Site

Recall that a hyperlink is text or graphics that you click, the result of which is that your computer is directed to display a different Web page. The hyperlink acts like a button that, when clicked, takes the visitor to the place it describes. Hyperlinked text is usually in a different color than the surrounding text and is underlined. Most Web development tools, including Publisher, change the color of the hyperlink after a visitor to the site has clicked it once. This color change lets the visitor know that he or she has used the hyperlink at least once during this visit. A hyperlink can take a visitor to another page in your Web site, to another Web site, or to a form, such as an email form.

Activity 6.5   Inserting Hyperlinks in a Web Site

1 **Zoom** to **100%**. Be sure that **page 2**, the May Events page, is displayed, and then use your mouse to select the text "Migratory Bird Festival" in the first line of the event descriptions (see Figure 6.19).

Activity 6.5   Inserting Hyperlinks in a Web Site

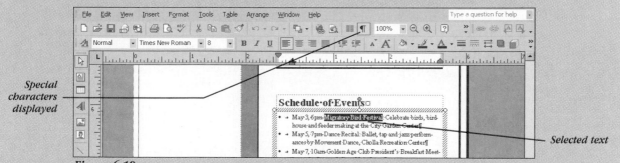

Special characters displayed

Selected text

Figure 6.19

2 On the Standard toolbar, click the **Insert Hyperlink** button. Alternatively, you can display the Insert menu and click Insert Hyperlink.

The Insert Hyperlink dialog box displays.

3 In the Link to bar on the left side of the dialog box, click **Place in This Document**. Then, under Select a place in this document, click **Page 3, Story Page** (see Figure 6.20).

Recall that a hyperlink is text or graphics that you click to take you somewhere else. In this case, clicking the text "Migratory Bird Festival" will take the visitor to the Story page in which you will insert additional information about the Festival.

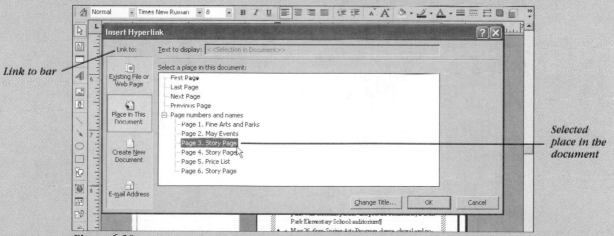

Link to bar

Selected place in the document

Figure 6.20

4 At the bottom of the dialog box, click the **Change Title** button.

The Enter Text dialog box displays. Text you enter here will display on the title bar of the browser software as the name of the Web page.

5 Type `Migratory Bird Festival`, click **OK** to close the Enter Text dialog box, and then click **OK** again to close the Insert Hyperlink dialog box.

The text you selected is changed to blue and is underlined, indicating a hyperlink. When visitors to the site click on this hyperlink, the Story page containing information about the Migratory Bird Festival will be displayed.

(Continues)

Activity 6.5   Inserting Hyperlinks in a Web Site (continued)

6 In the fourth line of the events text, select the text "Movement Dance." Display the **Insert Hyperlink** dialog box, and in the Link to bar, click **Place in This Document**. Then, insert a hyperlink in this document, on **Page 4, Story Page**.

7 Click the **Change Title** button. Type the title Movement Dance and then close the dialog boxes.

In the Schedule of Events, the text "Movement Dance" is blue and underlined, indicating a hyperlink.

8 Scroll to the bottom. In the text box containing the phone and email information, select the text "fineartsandparks@desertpark.org" and then display the **Insert Hyperlink** dialog box.

9 In the Link to bar, click **E-mail Address**, and then in the E-mail address box type fineartsandparks@desertpark.org

As you begin to type, Publisher automatically inserts "mailto:" in front of your typing.

10 In the Subject box, type Fine Arts and Parks Request for Information

If a visitor to your site clicks this hyperlink, his or her email system automatically generates a message with this subject line. The visitor is freed from having to type a subject and address. It also assists you in determining that incoming messages with this subject line were likely generated by visitors looking at your Web site.

11 Compare your screen to Figure 6.21, and then click **OK** to close the dialog boxes.

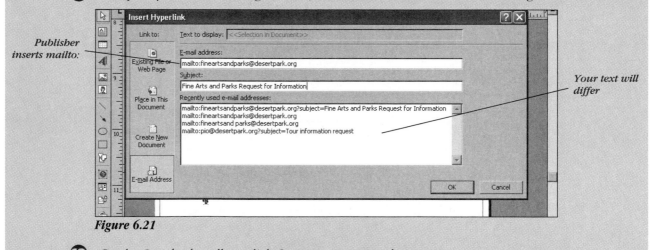

Publisher inserts mailto:

Your text will differ

Figure 6.21

12 On the Standard toolbar, click **Save** to save your changes.

Objective 6: Format a Story Page in a Web Site

Use a Story page to present detailed information about a subject. For example, in the previous Activity, you created a hyperlink to a Story page regarding the Migratory Bird Festival and a hyperlink to a Story page regarding the Movement Dance Company. Now you will fill in those two Story pages with detailed information about the Festival and the dance company.

Activity 6.6   Formatting a Story Page in a Web Site

1 If necessary, open your file 6A Parks Web, and then navigate to **page 3**.

2 At the top of the page, select the text "Story Page Heading" and then type Migratory Bird Festival

3 Select the picture and ungroup it from its caption. Click in the gray scratch area, and then click to select the picture only.

4 Hover over the picture and right-click, point to **Change Picture**, and then click **From File**. Navigate to your student files and insert **6A_Bird**.

5 In the caption text box to the right of the picture, replace the placeholder text with Witness the spectacular migration and then change the font size of the caption text to **10**.

6 Drag the right center resize handle of the text box to the right so that the text you just typed displays on one line as shown in Figure 6.22.

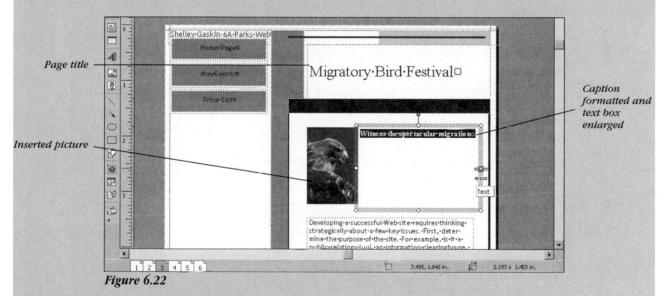

Page title

Inserted picture

Caption formatted and text box enlarged

Figure 6.22

7 In the large text box beginning "Developing," select the placeholder text and replace it with the text file **6A_BirdText**. Remove hyphenation from the story. Shorten the bottom boundary of the text box to approximately **9 inches on the vertical ruler**.

8 At the bottom of the page, in the pull quote, replace the placeholder text with The Festival offers non-stop birding activities that are sure to entertain you and your family!

9 Use the move pointer to position the pull quote text box directly below the large text box. In the text box with the phone and email information, select all the text and change the font size to **7**. Compare your screen to Figure 6.23.

(Continues)

Activity 6.6   Formatting a Story Page in a Web Site (continued)

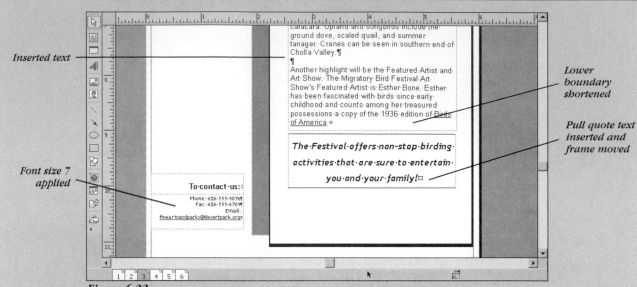

Inserted text

Font size 7 applied

Lower boundary shortened

Pull quote text inserted and frame moved

Figure 6.23

10 Navigate to **page 4**. At the top of the page, replace the text "Story Page Heading" with `Movement Dance`

11 At the top of the page, select the picture and ungroup it from its caption. Click in the gray scratch area, and then click the picture only. Display the shortcut menu, and use the **Change Picture** command to insert the picture **6A_Dance** from your student files. Delete the caption text box.

12 Select the picture, display the **Format** menu, and then click **Picture**. In the Format Picture dialog box, click the **Size tab**. In the **Height** box, delete the existing text and type `1.5"`. In the **Width** box, delete the existing text and type `1"`. Compare your screen to Figure 6.24. Click **OK** to close the dialog box.

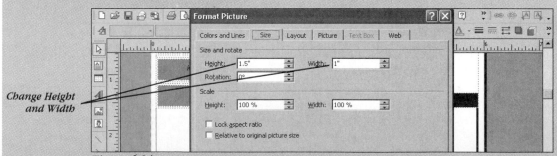

Change Height and Width

Figure 6.24

13 In the large text box, select the placeholder text. Replace it with the text file **6A_DanceText**. Remove hyphenation, and then shorten the lower boundary of the text box to approximately **7.75 inches on the vertical ruler**.

14 In the text box containing the phone and email information, select all the text and change the font size to **7**.

15 Delete the text box containing the pull quote.

16 On the Standard toolbar, click **Save** to save your changes.

Objective 7: Format a Price List Page in a Web Site

Organizations frequently use their Web site to sell products or services. Thus, one of the pre-formatted Web pages provided by Publisher is a Price List page. The Price List page includes tables into which you can import information.

Activity 6.7   Formatting a Price List Page in a Web Site

1 If necessary, open your file 6A Parks Web, and then navigate to **page 5**.

2 At the top of the page, replace the placeholder text "Price List" with Sign Up for Summer Fun Courses

3 Click in the first cell beginning "List your product." Scroll down and notice that this table contains eight rows, and that another table of four rows follows it.

4 With your mouse, drag to select the first two rows of the top table as shown in Figure 6.25. Then, on the menu bar, click **Table**, point to **Delete**, and then click **Rows**.

The top table is reduced to six rows.

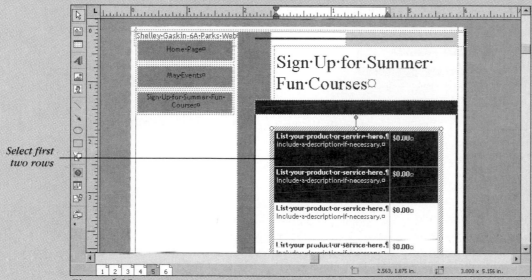

Select first two rows

Figure 6.25

5 Scroll to the bottom, click the border of the smaller four-row table to display a pattern of dots, and then press Del to delete the entire table. Click the remaining table, and drag its lower boundary down to **7.5 inches on the vertical ruler**.

6 Use your **Start** button and the **All Programs** menu to open **Microsoft Word**. Within Word, navigate to your student files and open **6A_Prices**. Click to position the insertion point anywhere in the table.

7 On the menu bar in Word, click **Table**, point to **Select**, and then click **Table**.

The Word table is selected.

(Continues)

Activity 6.7   Formatting a Price List Page in a Web Site (continued)

8 On the menu bar in Word, click the **Copy** button (see Figure 6.26). Then, close the Word document and close Word.

Word closes and your publication displays.

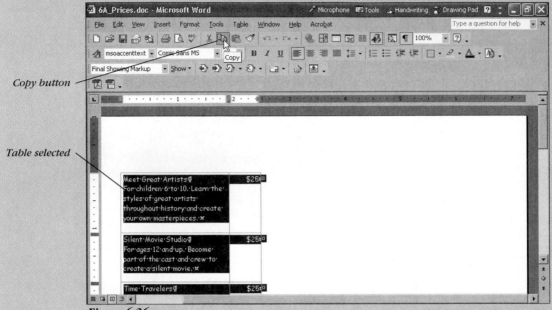

Figure 6.26

9 Click anywhere in the table. On the menu bar, click **Table**, point to **Select**, and then click **Table**. Then, on the Formatting toolbar, click the **Paste** button.

The table you copied from the Word document is copied into the Publisher table.

10 **Zoom** to **66%** and click in the gray scratch area to cancel the selection. Scroll to view the empty portion of the screen below the table. On the Objects toolbar, click the **Picture Frame** button, and position the crosshair pointer at **2.5 inches on the horizontal toolbar** and **8 inches on the vertical ruler**. Drag down and to the right to **5 inches on the horizontal ruler** and **10.5 inches on the vertical ruler**.

The Insert Picture dialog box displays.

11 Navigate to your student files and insert **6A_FunPIC**.

12 Change the font size of the phone and email text box to **7**. Compare your screen to Figure 6.27.

Activity 6.7   Formatting a Price List Page in a Web Site

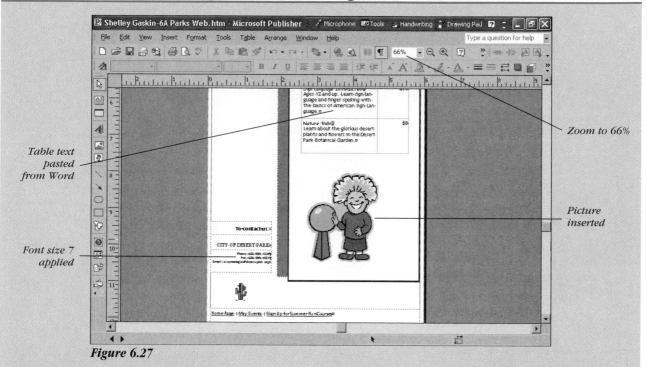

Figure 6.27

13 In the Price List table, navigate to the last course name and select the text "Nature Walk." Move your mouse pointer over the highlighted text, right-click to display a shortcut menu, and then click **Hyperlink**.

The Insert Hyperlink dialog box displays.

14 In the Link to bar, click **Place in This Document**. Under Select a place in this document, click **Page 6, Story Page**.

15 Click the **Change Title** button, change the title to Nature Walk, and then click **OK** two times to close both dialog boxes.

16 Navigate to **page 6**. Replace "Story Page Heading" with Nature Walk and **Zoom** to **75%**.

17 Ungroup the caption from its picture and then select only the picture. From the shortcut menu, use the **Change Picture** command to insert the picture **6A_NaturePIC**. Delete the caption text box.

18 Select the picture, display the Format Picture dialog box, click the **Size tab**, and change the **Height** to **1.5″** and the **Width** to **3″**.

19 In the large text box beginning "Developing," replace the placeholder text with the text file **6A_Nature**. Remove hyphenation from the story. Shorten the lower boundary to **8.25 inches on the vertical ruler**. Move the pull quote text box up so that it is positioned directly beneath the text box.

(Continues)

Activity 6.7   Formatting a Price List Page in a Web Site (continued)

20 In the third paragraph of text, select the sentence "The best way to appreciate the beauty of our surroundings is to become a part of them." Then, on the Standard toolbar, click the **Copy** button.

21 In the pull quote text box, select the placeholder text, and then click the **Paste** button to insert the copied text.

A Paste Options button displays as shown in Figure 6.28.

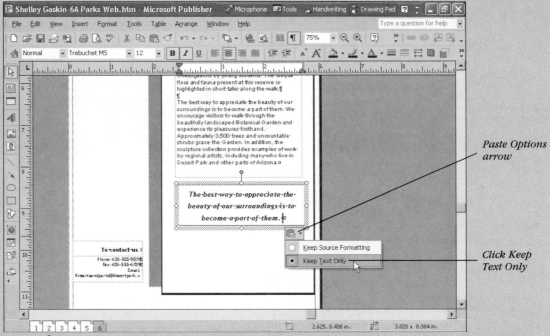

Figure 6.28

22 Point to the displayed Paste Options button, click the **Paste Options arrow**, and then click **Keep Text Only**.

This will ensure that the pull quote text retains the formatting of font Trebuchet MS, 12 pt, in Navy.

23 In the text box containing the phone and email information, select the text and change the font size to **7**.

24 On the Standard toolbar, click the **Save** button to save your changes.

Objective 8: Insert a Related Links Page with a Hot Spot

To the extent possible, you want to keep visitors to your site within your own site. That is how you get them to view the information about your products and services. However, it is also useful to your visitors to provide them with hyperlinks to other Web sites that relate to yours. It is appropriate to ask the owners of sites to which you link to do the same for you; that is, ask them to include your site on their list of related hyperlinks.

A list of related links should include both the Uniform Resource Locator or **URL**—the electronic address of a Web site—to which a *link* has been added and some information about the site. Link is the word commonly used to mean hyperlink.

Activity 6.8   Inserting a Related Links Page

1 If necessary, open your file 6A Parks Web, and then navigate to **page 6**.

2 On the menu bar click **Insert**, and then click **Page**. On the displayed Insert Page dialog box, click the **Available page types arrow**, click **Related links** and then click **OK**.

Notice that the new page becomes page 7.

3 **Zoom** to **100%**. Select the placeholder text beginning "Hyperlinks are electronic connections" and replace it with the text file **6A_Links**. Remove hyphenation.

4 Click the first occurrence of "Web site name and address hyperlink" to select this placeholder text, and type Arizona State Parks www.pr.state.az.us

5 If Publisher flagged your typing as a spelling error, right-click on the wavy red line and click Ignore All.

Removing the spelling flags makes it easier to view your text.

6 In the same text box, click to select the placeholder text that begins "Briefly summarize" and then type The official site of the Arizona State Parks. Lists all parks, trail programs, and tour events.

7 Using Figure 6.29 as a guide, fill in the remaining two URLs and descriptions.

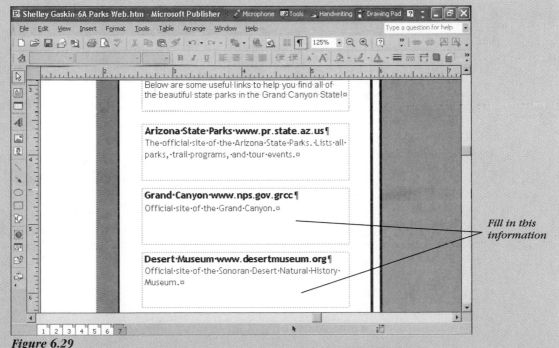

Figure 6.29

(Continues)

Activity 6.8   Inserting a Related Links Page (continued)

8 Use your mouse to select the Web address in the first text box, and then, on the Standard toolbar, click the **Copy** button. With the address still selected, move to the Standard toolbar and click the **Insert Hyperlink** button.

The Insert Hyperlink dialog box displays.

9 In the Link to bar, click **Existing File or Web Page.**

Notice that the insertion point is positioned in the Address text box.

10 Use the Ctrl + V keyboard shortcut to paste the copied Web address into the text box as shown in Figure 6.30. Click **OK** to close the dialog box.

The selected text is blue and underlined indicating that it is a hyperlink.

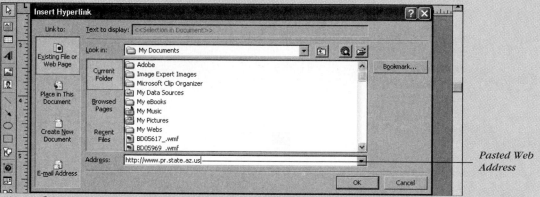

Figure 6.30

11 Repeat Steps 8–11 selecting the second and then the third URLs.

12 Delete the remaining three link text boxes, and then scroll to position the top of the page in the middle of your screen. Then, on the Objects toolbar, click the **Picture Frame** button. Draw a picture frame beginning at **0.25 inches on the horizontal ruler** and **2.25 inches on the vertical ruler**. Drag down and to the right to **1.75 inches on the horizontal ruler** and **3.75 inches on the vertical ruler**.

13 From your student files, insert the picture **6A_Tree**.

14 On the Standard toolbar, click **Save** to save your changes.

A ***hot spot*** is an area of an object that is a hyperlink. Creating a hyperlink for an object, such as a picture, turns that picture into a single hot spot. You can also create several hot spots on one object. For example, if you have an object picturing a group of people, you could create a hot spot over each person's face. Clicking on the hot spot would take the visitor to another page containing information about that person.

Activity 6.9   Creating a Hot Spot

1 Display **page 7** of your 6A Parks Web. With your mouse, select the text "www.nps.gov.grcc" and then, on the Standard toolbar, click **Copy**.

2 On the Objects toolbar, click the **Hot Spot** button as shown in Figure 6.31.

The Insert Hyperlink dialog box displays.

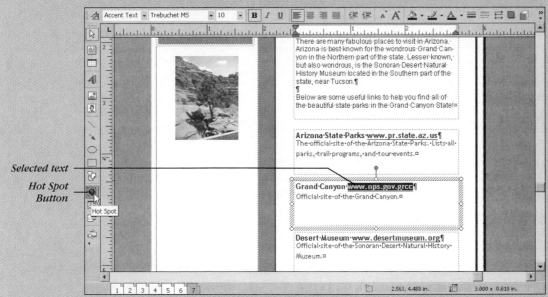

Figure 6.31

3 In the Insert Hyperlink dialog box, be sure that in the Link to bar, **Existing File or Web Page** is selected, and under Look in, **Current Folder** is selected. Then, with the insertion point blinking in the Address text box, use Ctrl + V to paste the URL into the box. Click **OK** to close the dialog box.

An AutoShape displays somewhere on your screen, as shown in Figure 6.32.

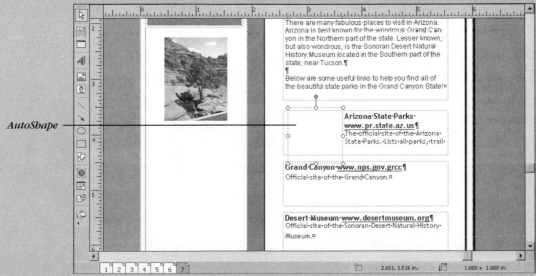

Figure 6.32

(Continues)

Activity 6.9   Creating a Hot Spot (continued)

4 Using the Move pointer, move the AutoShape over the picture, and then resize the shape to the approximate size of the tree picture (see Figure 6.33).

When a visitor to the site positions the pointer over the tree, he or she will be able to link to the Grand Canyon Web site. The dotted image of the AutoShape will not display when the pages are displayed with browser software on the Web.

AutoShape positioned and resized

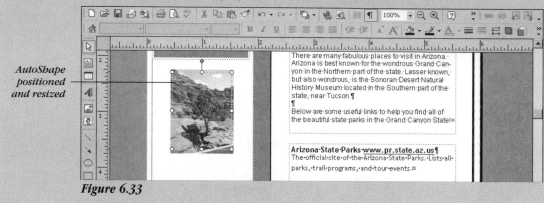

Figure 6.33

5 **Save** your changes.

Objective 9: Add Background Color to a Web Site

Color and graphics create visual appeal for your Web site and keep the reader interested. You must balance that knowledge with the fact that the more color and graphics you add, the longer it will take for your Web pages to open on the average viewer's computer screen. Thus, add color and graphics in moderation.

Based on the need for visual appeal, you will probably want some type of color background for your Web site. You can apply fill effects to the background of Web sites in much the same manner as you can for text boxes. You can use gradients, textures, patterns, pictures, or tints. Use the Web Site Options task pane to apply a background.

Activity 6.10   Changing the Background of a Web Page

1 Navigate to **page 1** of your 6A Parks Web. On the menu bar, click **Format**, and then click **Web Site Options**.

The Web Site Options task pane displays on the left.

2 At the bottom of the task pane, click the small arrow if necessary, and then click **Background fill and sound**.

The Background task pane displays.

3 Using the scroll bar in the task pane, scroll down, locate the blue flowered box, point to it, and then click its **arrow** as shown in Figure 6.34.

Notice that you have the option to apply this background to the displayed page, or to all pages in the Web site.

Activity 6.10   Changing the Background of a Web Page

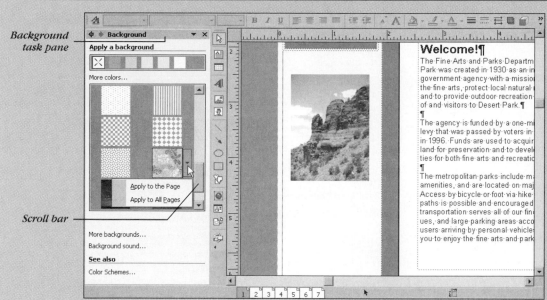

Background task pane

Scroll bar

Figure 6.34

④ Click Apply to the Page.

The blue flowered background displays on the page. While this is a distinctive background, it is probably not appropriate for this Web site.

⑤ At the top of the task pane, under Apply a background, click the second box (pale lavender). Then, if necessary, use the scroll bar to scroll to the top of the More colors box.

⑥ In the More colors box, point in the second row to the first box to display the ScreenTip "14% tint of Accent 1." Click its down arrow, and then click **Apply to All Pages** (see Figure 6.35).

The pale lavender tint is applied to all the pages in the Web site.

(Continues)

Activity 6.10   Changing the Background of a Web Page (continued)

Figure 6.35

7 Close the task pane. On the Standard toolbar, click **Save** to save your changes.

To extend your knowledge...

Audio Files

Audio files of good quality can be a valuable part of your Web site. Sound can create a mood or supply information, such as pronunciation. There are two important things to consider when using sound. First, consider that in many work and educational environments, the sound feature of computers is disabled to avoid disturbing others close by. Thus, because many visitors to your site will never actually hear your sound files, do not depend on sound to deliver key information. Second, consider that audio files add additional download time. Visitors could become impatient waiting for too much information to download.

Objective 10: Preview a Web Site in Internet Explorer

Before you actually publish your site to the Internet, either through your organization's own Web server or by contracting with a Web presence provider who will publish it for you, you should preview the site. Previewing the site in browser software enables you to see what your visitors will see when they access your site from their Internet connection.

Publisher makes it easy for you to preview your site by using the Web Page Preview command, which is accessed from the File menu or by clicking the Web Page Preview button on the Formatting toolbar.

Activity 6.11   Previewing a Web Site in Internet Explorer

1 Display **page 1** of your 6A Parks Web. On the Formatting toolbar bar, click the **Web Page Preview** button. Alternatively, you can display the File menu and click Web Page Preview.

The Web Page Preview dialog box displays. See Figure 6.36.

Web Page Preview button

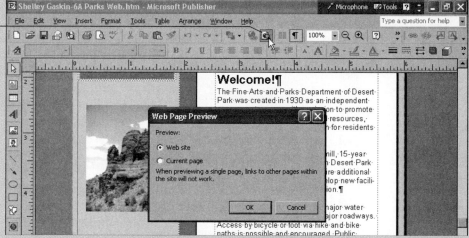

Figure 6.36

2 In the Web Page Preview dialog box, click the **Web site** option button if necessary, and then click **OK**.

Microsoft Internet Explorer opens, and Working Offline may display in the title bar.

3 On the vertical navigation bar, click **May Events**.

The May Events page displays.

4 On the May Events page, scroll down to view the event information. Point to the hyperlink for **Migratory Bird Festival** and click.

The story page with the festival information displays.

5 At the top of the Festival page, click the **May Events** button on the vertical navigation bar.

The May Events page displays.

6 On the May Events page, scroll down to view the event information. Point to the hyperlink for **Movement Dance** and click.

7 Scroll to the bottom of the Movement Dance page, and in the horizontal navigation bar, click **Sign Up for Summer Fun Courses**.

The Summer Fun Courses page displays.

8 At the bottom of the Summer Fun page, click the hyperlink for **Nature Walk** (see Figure 6.37).

The Nature Walk page displays.

(Continues)

Activity 6.11   Previewing a Web Site in Internet Explorer (continued)

Indicates that you are not currently connected to the Internet

Hyperlink pointer

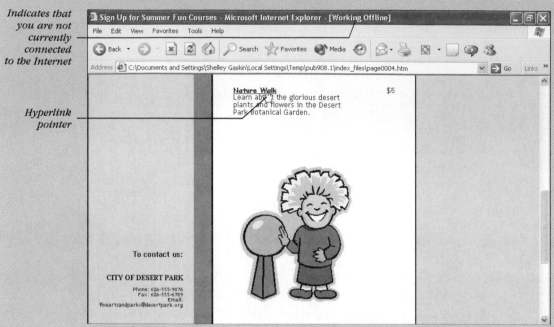

Figure 6.37

9 On the vertical navigation bar, click the **Directory of Related Links** hyperlink.

The Related Links page displays.

10 Point to the tree picture and notice that the Pointing Hand icon displays, indicating that the picture is a hyperlink.

It is not necessary to link to these sites at this time. If you have an Internet connection, you may want to try them later.

11 On the menu bar, click **File**, and then click **Close**.

The Web Page Preview browser software is closed and your publication displays.

12 On the Standard toolbar, click **Save**.

Objective 11: Print a Web Site

The pages of a Web site are intended to be viewed on a computer screen, not printed on paper. You will, of course, want to print your Web pages to review and proofread the content. Recall that Web pages are preset to 6 inches wide and 14 inches tall to accommodate easy viewing on most computer monitors.

One way to print Web pages is to use legal size paper, which is 8 inches wide and 14 inches tall. However, extremely long Web pages would exceed even legal size paper. Assuming that your classroom or lab printer has regular 8.5-inch by 11-inch letter-sized paper, you will need to make an adjustment on the Page Layout dialog box to print your pages properly.

Activity 6.12   Printing a Web Site

1 If necessary, display your 6A Parks Web. On the menu bar, click **File**, and then click **Page Setup**.

The Page Setup dialog box displays.

2 In the Page Setup dialog box, click the **Printer & Paper tab**.

Your default printer displays under Printer, and under Paper, the Size is set to Legal.

3 Under Paper, click the **Size arrow**, and then click **Letter** as shown in Figure 6.38.

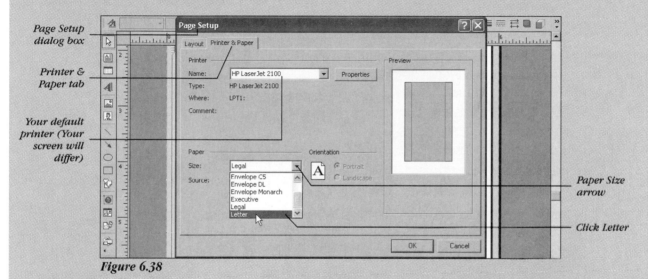

Page Setup dialog box

Printer & Paper tab

Your default printer (Your screen will differ)

Paper Size arrow

Click Letter

Figure 6.38

4 Click **OK** to close the Page Setup dialog box. On the Standard toolbar, click the **Print** button.

Fourteen sheets will print—two sheets for each Web page. The cut marks will display. Because you inserted both a header and footer with your name, all pages will have your name.

5 **Save** and close your publication. Publication 6A Parks Web is complete!

To extend your knowledge...

Publishing Your Web site

To have visitors actually visit your Web site via the World Wide Web, you must publish it on a Web server that is connected to the Internet. If your organization does not have a Web server connected to the Internet, you can rent server space from various Internet service providers (ISPs) or from a Web Presence Provider. After you have the URL for the server where your Web folder can be saved, display the File menu and click Save As. Click My Network Places, and then double-click Add Network Place. The Add Network Place Wizard will guide you through the steps to store your Web folder on the Web server.

Publication 6B

Trail Web

In Activities 6.13–6.15 you will convert a brochure that was created in Publisher to a Web site. The pages of your completed Web site will look like Figure 6.39. You will save your publication as *Firstname Lastname-6B Trail Web*.

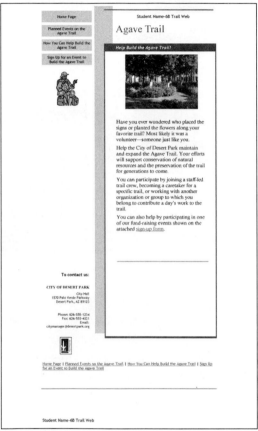

Figure 6.39A

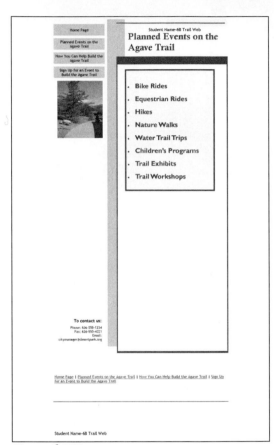

Figure 6.39B

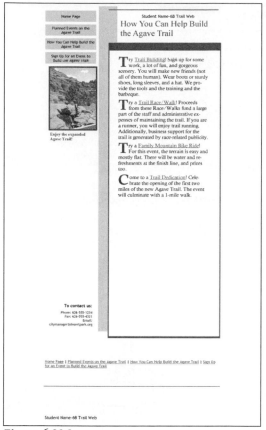

Figure 6.39C

Figure 6.39D

Objective 12: Convert a Print Publication to a Web Site

Recall that within Publisher you have several ways to create a Web site. You can design a Web site from a blank publication, in which case you would lay out the design and insert the Web elements yourself. Or, as you have done in the previous Activities, you can use Publisher's Web Sites Wizard and its accompanying formats. Finally, you can convert an existing publication into a Web site.

An option available in the Newsletter and Brochure Wizards is the capability to convert a Publisher-designed newsletter or brochure to a Web site. This feature is especially useful because Web users often seek the type of information contained in newsletters and brochures. Recall that a newsletter is used to distribute news and information to a specific group, and a brochure describes an event, product, program, or service.

There are two advantages to providing these types of information on the Web. You can easily change and add to the information without the expense of printing. Also, users of the information do not have to wait to receive the printed publication or find a location where they can obtain the printed publication.

Activity 6.13   Converting a Publication to Web Layout

❶   **Start** Publisher. On the Standard toolbar, click the **Open** button, and then navigate to the student files for this textbook. Click **6B_TrailBrochure**, and then click **Open**.

The Trail Brochure displays in the Publication window.

❷   On the menu bar, click **Format**, and then click **Brochure Options**.

The Brochure Options task pane displays as shown in Figure 6.40.

Brochure Options task pane

Convert to Web Layout command button

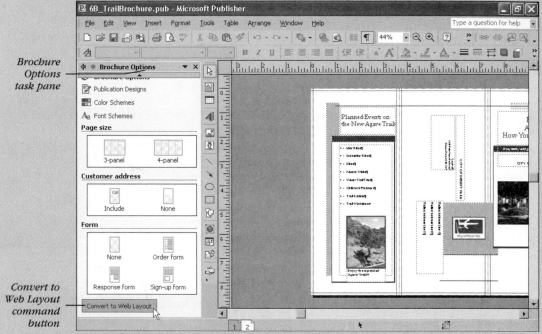

Figure 6.40

❸   At the bottom of the Brochure Options task pane, click **Convert to Web Layout**.

A brief message displays indicating that the conversion is taking place. In the publication window, the first page of the newsletter displays in Web page layout and the Web Site Options task pane displays on the left. Because of the difference in page lengths and layouts, the conversion is not necessarily precise. Pictures or graphics may spill over into the gray scratch area. In general, brochure conversion results in three or four Web pages. Color and font schemes carry over. Graphic and text frames are either displayed or stored for optional insertion.

❹   On the Web Site Options task pane, be sure that under Navigation bar, **Multiple** is selected. Under Form, be sure that **Sign-up form** is selected.

❺   Compare your screen to Figure 6.41. Then, close the task pane.

Activity 6.13   Converting a Publication to Web Layout

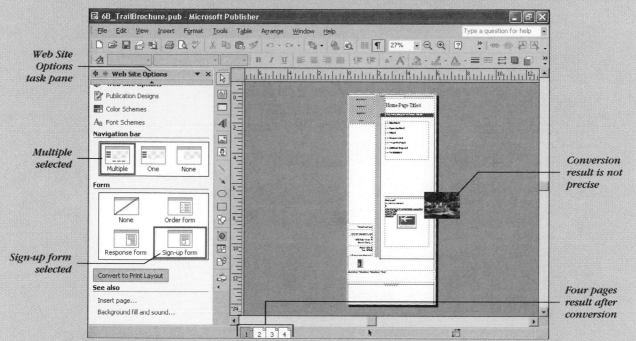

Web Site Options task pane

Multiple selected

Sign-up form selected

Conversion result is not precise

Four pages result after conversion

Figure 6.41

6 On the menu bar, click **View**, and then click **Header and Footer**. With the insertion point positioned at the left edge of the Header frame, type Firstname Lastname-6B Trail Web

7 **Zoom** to **50%**. Display the Measurement toolbar. If necessary, click to select the Header frame, and in the first four boxes of the Measurement toolbar, change the Horizontal position to **3.25″**, the Vertical position to **0.313″**, the Width to **2.525″**, and the Height to **0.3″** as shown in Figure 6.42.

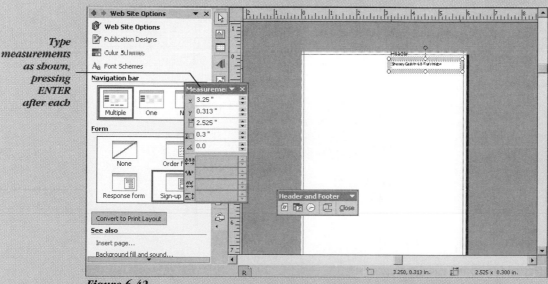

Type measurements as shown, pressing ENTER after each

Figure 6.42

(Continues)

Activity 6.13   Converting a Publication to Web Layout (continued)

8 On the Header and Footer toolbar, click the **Show Header/Footer** button to move to the footer frame. If necessary, shorten the Footer frame to fit between the blue vertical layout guides. Type `Firstname Lastname-6B Trail Web`. Use the Move pointer or the Nudge feature to move the Footer frame so that your name is aligned just above the lower blue layout guide and its left edge is aligned with the left blue layout guide.

9 **Close** the Header and Footer toolbar. On the menu bar, click **File**, and then click **Save As**. To save the publication as a Web page, move to the bottom of the Save As dialog box, locate the Save as type box, and then click the **Save as type arrow**. Scroll the displayed list as necessary, and then click **Web Page**.

10 At the top of the dialog box, use the Save in arrow to navigate to the location in which you are storing your files for this lesson. Then, at the bottom of the dialog box, in the File name box, delete the existing text, type `Firstname Lastname-6B Trail Web` and click the **Save** button.

11 When the message displays regarding your form on page 4, click **No**. (You will process the form later in this Lesson.)

Your publication is saved as a Web, and the Web site name displays in the title bar.

Conversion from print publication to Web publication is not a precise operation. During the conversion process, Publisher inserts some objects and stores some objects in the Extra Content tab of the Design Gallery.

Activity 6.14   Editing and Arranging Objects on a Converted Publication

1 If necessary, close the Measurement toolbar and the Web Site Options task pane and then **Zoom** to **66%**. On page 1, change "Home Page Title" to `Agave Trail`. Replace the text "Live, work, and grow in Desert Park!" with `Help Build the Agave Trail!` Select the frame with the bulleted items, and then move the frame into the gray scratch area for use later. Move the picture of the trail up positioning it just slightly below the brown bar element, and visually center it as shown in Figure 6.43.

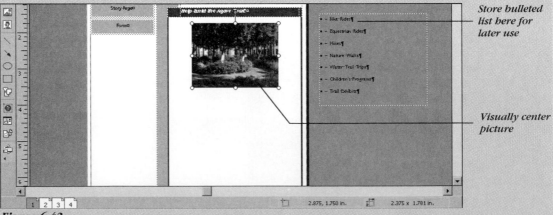

Figure 6.43

2 Navigate to **page 2**. Select the frame with the text and clip art, and shorten its lower boundary to **7.5 inches on the vertical ruler** as shown in Figure 6.44.

Activity 6.14   Editing and Arranging Objects on a Converted Publication

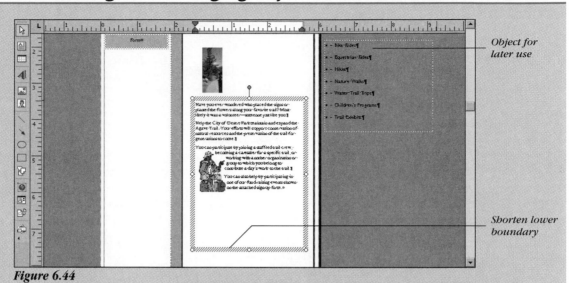

Object for later use

Shorten lower boundary

Figure 6.44

3 Click the small clip art to select it, hold down Ctrl, and click the frame border to select it also. Click the **Group Objects** button to group the clip art and the text frame into one object. On the Standard toolbar, click the **Cut** button to place the object on the Office Clipboard.

The text box and clip art are removed from the page and placed on the Office Clipboard.

4 Navigate back to **page 1**, and move to the bottom of the page. In the frame with the text beginning "Features," click the frame border to display a pattern of dots, and then press Del to delete the entire frame. Then select and delete the brown logo.

5 Select the brown line object and move it down to **8.5 inches on the vertical ruler**.

6 On the Standard toolbar, click the **Paste** button. Click anywhere in the text of the pasted text box, and click the **Ungroup Objects** button to ungroup the text and the clip art. Click in the gray scratch area, and then click to select only the clip art. Move it directly beneath the vertical navigation bar.

7 Select the pasted text and change the font size to **12**. Move and size the frame as necessary to position it as shown in Figure 6.45.

(Continues)

Activity 6.14   Editing and Arranging Objects on a Converted Publication (continued)

Stored for later use

Clip Art moved

Position frame and apply font size 12

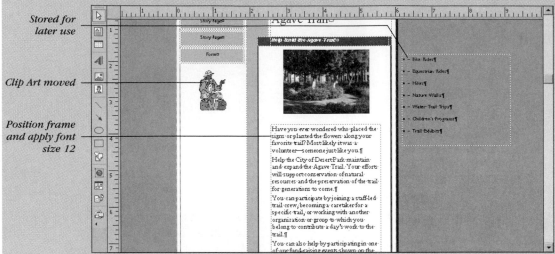

Figure 6.45

8   In the last line of text, select the words "sign-up form" and then click the **Insert Hyperlink** button.

The Insert Hyperlink dialog box displays.

9   In the Link to bar, click **Place in This Document**. Under Select a place in this document, click **Page 4, Form**. Click **OK** to close the dialog box.

10   Navigate to **page 2**. Move the picture so that its upper left corner is just below the left edge of the vertical navigation bar. Then use the lower right resize handle to enlarge the picture to the approximate width of the navigation bar as shown in Figure 6.46.

Move picture here

Resize picture to here

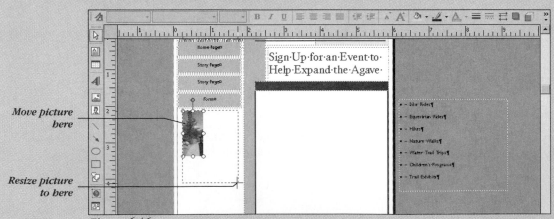

Figure 6.46

11   From the gray scratch area, move the text box with the bulleted items directly below the brown bar element beneath the page title. To make the text visible, move to the menu bar, click **Arrange**, point to **Order**, and then click **Bring to Front**.

Activity 6.14   Editing and Arranging Objects on a Converted Publication

12 Drag the lower boundary of the frame down to **5.75 inches on the vertical ruler**. Format the text box with a **3 pt brown** border and **yellow** fill color.

13 Select the bulleted item text. Change the font size to **16**, apply **Bold**, and change the font color to **brown**. Use the **Text Box tab** of the Format Text Box dialog box to vertically align the text in the **Middle** of the frame.

14 Change the page title to Planned Events on the Agave Trail and then click in the gray scratch area.

The new page title displays on both the vertical and horizontal navigation bars.

15 At the bottom of the page, delete the pull quote frame.

16 Navigate to **page 3**. Change the page title to How You Can Help Build the Agave Trail and then move the text frame up directly beneath the brown bar element. Select the text and change the font size to **12**.

17 On the Objects toolbar, click the **Design Gallery Object** button. Click the **Extra Content tab**, locate and click the picture of the tree. At the bottom of the dialog box, click the **Insert Object** button. Move and resize the picture and its caption, as shown in Figure 6.47.

Position picture and caption here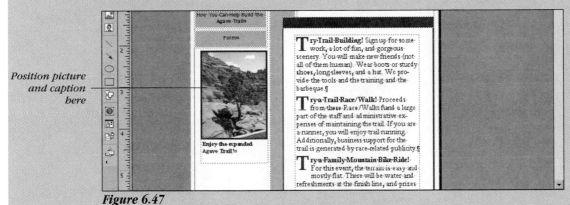

Figure 6.47

18 In the large text box, select the bold text "Trail Building." Insert a hyperlink to the Form page on page 4. Repeat this process for the bold text "Trail Race/Walk," "Family Mountain Bike Ride," and "Trail Dedication."

19 Delete the pull quote frame at the bottom of the page. On the Standard toolbar, click **Save** to save your changes. Click **No** in response to the displayed message.

A **form** is a structured document with spaces reserved for entering information. **Form controls** are the individual boxes and buttons with which a Web site visitor enters information. Publisher supports several types of form controls within a Web site, including a check box and a submit button.

Activity 6.15   Editing a Web Form

❶ Navigate to **page** 4. Change the page title to Sign Up for an Event to Build the Agave Trail. Select the text "Come Play in the Dirt!" and then change the font size to **16** and apply **Bold**. Delete the small text box containing the word Time.

❷ In the middle of the page, click to select and then delete all the objects except the Submit and Reset buttons as shown in Figure 6.48.

You can select and delete each one separately or hold down Ctrl and click each object, group them into one object, and then delete the entire object.

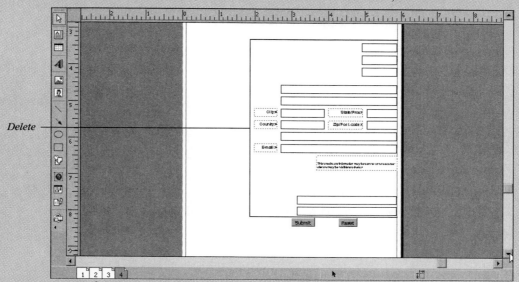

Delete

Figure 6.48

❸ On the Objects toolbar, click the **Form Control** button.

❹ On the displayed menu shown in Figure 6.49, click **Checkbox**.

A small check box with an accompanying text box is inserted on the page.

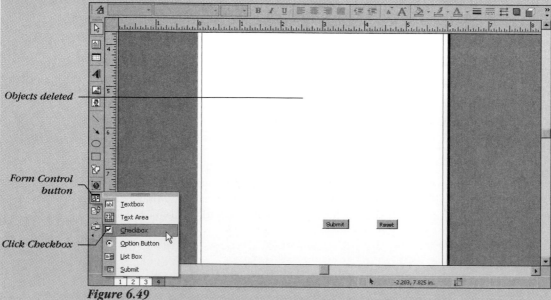

Objects deleted

Form Control button

Click Checkbox

Figure 6.49

Activity 6.15   Editing a Web Form

5 Position and enlarge the check box approximately as shown in Figure 6.50.

Figure 6.50

6 With the object selected, click the **Copy** button. Then, click the **Paste** button three times, and arrange the four objects as shown in Figure 6.51.

The keyboard method of using the Nudge feature is convenient for this operation. Select one of the objects, hold down Alt, and then use the arrow keys to move the object into the desired position. You can actually hold down an arrow key and "drive" the object into the position you want.

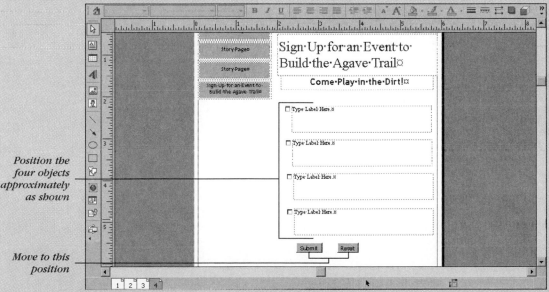

Figure 6.51

7 Move the Submit and Reset buttons as shown in Figure 6.51.

8 Using Figure 6.52 as a guide, insert text into each of the four text boxes, and then format the text in **12 pt Arial Narrow** and apply **Bold**. Use F9 to zoom in and out as necessary.

(Continues)

Activity 6.15   Editing a Web Form (continued)

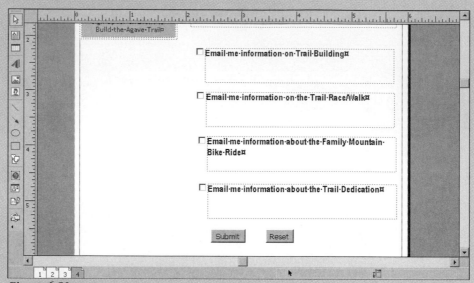

Figure 6.52

9 Click the dotted edge of the first check box object to select it as shown in Figure 6.53.

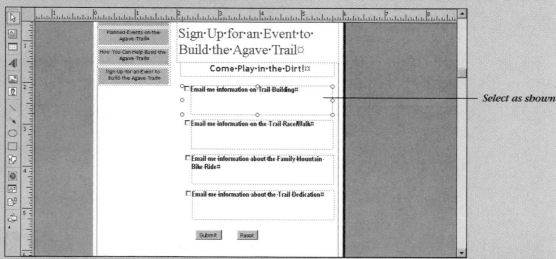

Select as shown

Figure 6.53

10 On the menu bar, click **Arrange**, and then click **Ungroup**. Repeat the process for the three remaining check box objects.

This will ungroup the text box from the tiny check box.

11 Select the first check box as shown in Figure 6.54.

Activity 6.15   Editing a Web Form

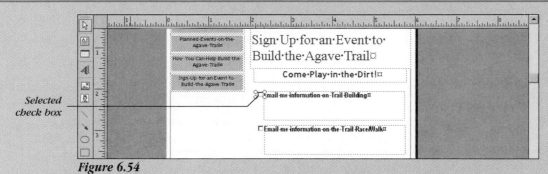

Selected check box

Figure 6.54

12 On the menu bar, click **Format**, and then click **Form Properties**.

The Checkbox Properties dialog box displays.

13 At the bottom of the Checkbox Properties dialog box, click the **Form Properties** button.

The Form Properties dialog box displays.

14 In the displayed Form Properties dialog box, under Data retrieval method, click the **Send data to me in e-mail** option button.

15 Under Data retrieval information, in the Send data to this address text box, type rhamilton@cityofdesertpark.org (see Figure 6.55) and then click **OK** twice to close the dialog boxes.

If a visitor to the Web site checks the box and then clicks the Submit button at the bottom of the form, his or her form responses are sent to the email address you just typed.

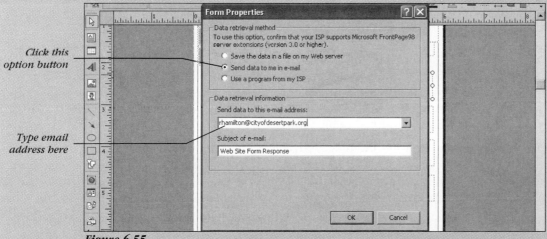

Click this option button

Type email address here

Figure 6.55

16 Repeat steps 11–15 for the second, third, and fourth check boxes. You will not have to retype the information, because Publisher will remember it.

17 Click the **Submit** button to select it. On the menu bar, click **Format**, and then click **Form Properties**. (Alternatively, you can double-click the Submit button.)

(Continues)

Activity 6.15   Editing a Web Form (continued)

The Command Button Properties dialog box displays.

18 At the bottom of the dialog box, click the **Form Properties** button. Compare your screen to Figure 6.55 and make any necessary changes. Then, click **OK** twice to close the dialog boxes.

19 On the Standard toolbar, click **Save** to save your changes.

20 Display the **File** menu and then click **Page Setup**. Click the **Printer & Paper tab** and change the Paper size to **Letter**. Click **OK** to close the dialog box, and then click the **Print** button on the Standard toolbar.

Eight sheets will print.

21 Display the **File** menu, click **Web Page Preview,** and view your Web site in the browser. Check the hyperlinks to be sure that they work properly.

You can click the check boxes to place a check mark in each one. If you click the Submit button, nothing will happen because you are working offline. But if a visitor to your site clicked the Submit button, his or her email software would generate an email message to you at the email address you typed in the Properties dialog box.

22 **Close** the browser and close the publication. Publication 6B Trail Web is complete!

Summary

Organizations can communicate with customers, employees, and others who seek information through either printed or electronic publications. A Web site on the World Wide Web offers some advantages over printed publications. A Web site is easily changed and therefore can always present the most up-to-date information. Additionally, it is usually cheaper to maintain a Web site than it is to produce large quantities of printed publications.

You can easily create a Web site in Publisher using the basic techniques of creating and arranging frames and objects. Publisher can also convert your printed publications to hypertext markup language. Hypertext markup language, called HTML, is the programming language that permits the viewing of text and graphics on most computers.

When designing publications for the Web, there are a number of considerations. Because individuals will read Web information in a different manner than a printed publication, you will need to consider page content, page length, and the arrangement of the pages. Also, while color and graphics make a Web site interesting, you must balance the use of such features with the knowledge that they add to the display time on some computers.

Using Publisher Help

Although color and graphics make a Web site visually appealing, they can also make the Web files too large to download on the average computer user's screen.

Use Publisher Help to find out how to add graphics efficiently.

1. If necessary, start Publisher and display the New Publication task pane and the Quick Publications Publication Gallery.
2. At the right edge of the menu bar, click in the Ask a Question box and type How can I use Web graphics efficiently?
3. Press ⏎Enter and then on the displayed list, click **About Web graphics**. The Help pane displays.
4. Here there are many good tips on how to add graphics to your Web pages. If you want to keep a copy of this information, click the **Print** button. It will print on one page, but your name will not print on the document.
5. Click the **Close** button—the X in the top right corner of the Help window—to close the Help window.

Concepts Assessment

Short Answer

Write the correct answer in the space provided.

1. In addition to printed publications, most organizations also communicate with employees, customers, and others using the _____.
2. The two most commonly used browsers are _____ and _____.
3. Most people find it easier to read text on paper than on a _____, which is why you should keep your Web pages short and concise.
4. Planning for Web publication begins with the same planning process used for a _____ publication.
5. Although Publisher is a good tool for creating a quick and simple Web site for an individual or a small organization, complex Web sites would be better developed in the Microsoft application called _____.
6. The most important page in your Web site is the _____.
7. Visitors to your Web site will find it useful if you provide a navigation bar at both the top of the page and at the _____ of the page.
8. If you include Calendar pages in your Web site, it is important to keep them _____.
9. Most Web development tools, including Microsoft Publisher, change the _____ of a hyperlink after it has been clicked once to signal the visitor that he or she has used the hyperlink at least once during this visit.
10. Because organizations often use their Web site to sell products or services, one of the pre-formatted Web pages provided in Publisher is a _____ page.

Matching

Match each term in the second column with its correct definition in the first column. Write the letter of the term on the blank line to the left of the correct definition.

_____ **1.** The abbreviation for Uniform Resource Locator, which is the electronic address of a Web site.

_____ **2.** The multimedia branch of the Internet.

_____ **3.** Also known as HTML, a programming language that communicates color and graphics in a format that all computers can understand.

_____ **4.** The scientist who created hypertext markup language (HTML).

_____ **5.** Documents in your Web site that enable interaction between you and the visitors to the Web site.

_____ **6.** Software used to view information coded in hypertext markup language.

_____ **7.** An option available in Microsoft Publisher that enables you to convert either a newsletter or a brochure to a Web publication.

_____ **8.** The worldwide network of computers that connects other, smaller, networks of computers.

_____ **9.** A tool that takes you step by step through the process of creating a Web site in Publisher.

_____ **10.** The order in which the pages of a Web site will be arranged.

_____ **11.** The first page of a Web site.

_____ **12.** Documents that contain the text and graphics of a Web site.

_____ **13.** The subset of a topic page in a Web site.

_____ **14.** Text or graphics that you click, the result of which is that your computer is directed to display a different Web page.

_____ **15.** An area on a Web site, arranged vertically or horizontally, indicating the names of the pages to which a visitor can link directly from the page.

A. Browser

B. Convert to Web Layout

C. Forms

D. Home Page

E. Hyperlink

F. Hypertext Markup Language

G. Internet

H. Navigation bar

I. Navigation structure

J. Subsidiary page

K. Tim Berners-Lee

L. URL

M. Web pages

N. Web Sites Wizard

O. World Wide Web

Skill Assessments

Publication 6C

Mayor Web

In the following Skill Assessment, you will create a Web site for the Mayor's Office. Your pages will look like Figure 6.56. You will save your publication as *Firstname Lastname-6C Mayor Web.*

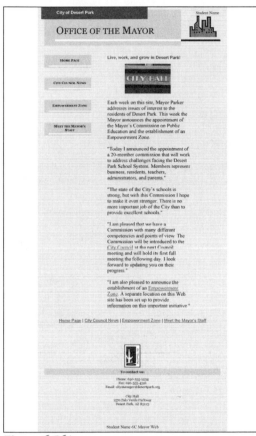

Figure 6.56A

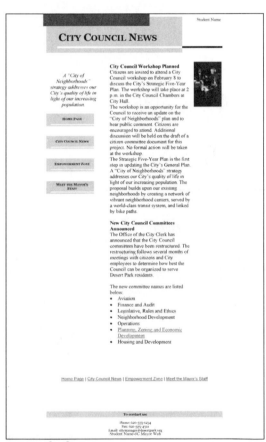

Figure 6.56B

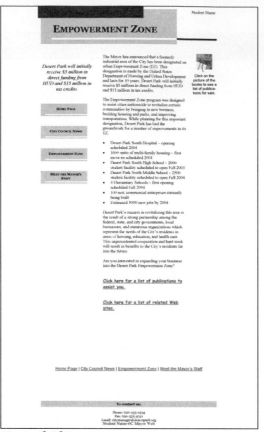

Figure 6.56C

Figure 6.56D

Figure 6.56E

Figure 6.56F

1. Take a moment to look at the structure of the Web site that you will be creating, as shown in Figure 6.57. Then, start Publisher, display the New Publication task pane and the Publication Gallery. Under By Publication Type click Web Sites.

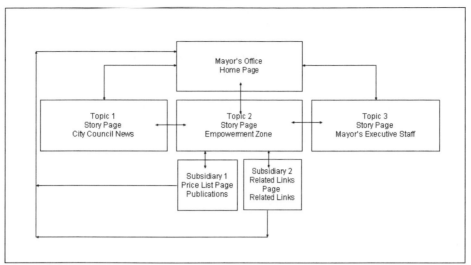

Figure 6.57

2. Click the Bars Web Site. Display the Edit menu, and then click Personal Information. Compare your screen to Figure 6.58, make any necessary changes, and then click Update. If you need the City of Desert Park logo for any of the Web pages, insert 6C_DesertParkLogo from your student files.

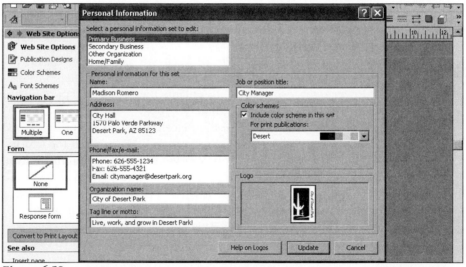

Figure 6.58

3. Display the View menu, and then click Header and Footer. The format of this Web design places headers and footers in the center of the page. For the header to display, you must change it so that the name appears at the extreme right side. In the Header frame, press Tab⇄ two times to move to the right edge of the page, and then type only your name. Use the Nudge feature as necessary to position your name just below and to the left of the blue guides. Insert a footer in the center position by typing `Firstname Lastname-6C Mayor Web`. Use the Nudge feature as necessary so that the footer aligns just above the blue layout guide. Close the Header and Footer toolbar.

4. On the menu bar, click File, and then click Save As. To save the publication as a Web page, move to the bottom of the Save As dialog box, locate the Save as type box, and then click the Save as type arrow. Scroll the displayed list as necessary, and then click Web Page. Use the Save in arrow at the top to navigate to the location in which you are storing your files, and then at the bottom, in the File name box, delete the existing text and type Firstname Lastname-6C Mayor Web

5. In the Web Site Options task pane, under Navigation bar, be sure that Multiple is selected. Under Form, be sure that None is selected.

6. At the bottom of the task pane, click Insert page, accept the default Story page, and leave the check box checked so that the page displays on the navigation bar. Click OK. This page will become the City Council News page. Click Insert page again, accept the default Story page, and leave the check box checked. Click OK. This will become the Empowerment Zone page. Your Web should now have three pages.

7. On the menu bar, click Insert, and then click Page. Click the Available page types arrow, and then click Price list. At the bottom of the page, click to remove the check mark from the check box so that this page does not appear on the navigation bar—it will be accessible only from the Empowerment Zone page. Click OK.

8. Using either the task pane or the Insert menu, display the Insert Page dialog box, and from the list of page types, click Related links. At the bottom, remove the check mark so that the page does not display on the navigation bar. It will be accessible only from the Empowerment Zone page. Click OK.

9. Insert a Story page. Leave the check mark in the check box so that the page displays on the navigation bar. Click OK. This will be the final page, which will contain information about the Mayor's executive staff. Your Web now has six pages. On the Standard toolbar, click Save to save your changes.

10. Navigate to page 1. Close the task pane, zoom to 75%, and position the top of page 1 in the center of your screen. Check that the navigation bar displays four blocks—the Home Page and three Story Pages.

11. Replace Home Page Title with Office of the Mayor. Select the picture of the coffee cup, right-click, and then use the Change Picture command to insert 6C_CityHallPIC. Use the lower right resize handle to enlarge the picture to approximately 1 inch tall. Visually center the picture above the large text box.

12. In the large text box, replace the placeholder text with 6C_MayorHomeText. When the message regarding text flow displays, click No to place the text in overflow. Then, drag the bottom boundary of the text box down to 10 inches on the vertical ruler. Select all of the text you just inserted, left align the text and remove hyphenation.

13. In the fourth paragraph of the text you just inserted, select the words "City Council." On the Standard toolbar, click the Insert Hyperlink button. In the Insert Hyperlink dialog box, on the Link to bar, click Place in This Document. Under Select a place in this document, click Page 2, Story Page. Use the Change Title button to change the title of this page to City Council News. Click OK twice to close the dialog boxes.

14. In the last paragraph of the text you just inserted, select the words "Empowerment Zone." On the Standard toolbar, click the Insert Hyperlink button. Insert a hyperlink in this document on Page 3, Story Page. Use the Change Title button to change the title of this page to Empowerment Zone. Click OK twice to close the dialog boxes. Click Save to save your changes.

15. Navigate to page 2. Change "Story Page Title" to City Council News and then click in the gray scratch area to view the change to the navigation bar. In the large text box, replace the placeholder text with 6C_CouncilText. Left align the text and remove hyphenation.

16. In the third paragraph of the City Council text, select the sentence "A City of Neighborhoods strategy addresses our City's quality of life in light of our increasing population." On the Standard toolbar, click Copy. Then, click to select the placeholder text in the pull quote frame located in the upper left corner of the page, and click Paste.

17. At the bottom of the large text box, in the bulleted list, select the text of the next to last item, "Planning, Zoning, and Economic Development," and use the Insert Hyperlink dialog box to link it to the Empowerment Zone page. At the upper right, ungroup the picture from its caption and then click in the gray scratch area. Click the border of the caption text box to display a pattern of dots, and press ⒟ⓔⓛ. Click to select the picture. Right-click and use the Change Picture command to insert 6C_CouncilPIC. Resize and position the picture to fit in the approximate location as the deleted picture and caption. Click Save to save your changes.

18. Navigate to page 3. Change the page title to Empowerment Zone. In the large text box, replace the placeholder text with 6C_EmpZoneText. Left align the text and remove hyphenation. In the first paragraph, select the last sentence that begins "Desert Park will initially" and then click Copy. Paste the copied text into the pull quote frame in the upper left corner. Point to the small Paste Options button that displays, click the arrow, and then click Keep Text Only. This will keep the text, but retain the italic formatting of the pull quote frame.

19. In the upper right corner, ungroup the caption box from the picture. Click in the gray scratch area, and then click to select the picture only. Right-click and use the Change Picture command to insert 6C_BookPIC. Replace the caption text with Click on the picture of the books to see a list of publications for sale. Then, select the caption text you just typed, change the font size to 9 and center the text.

20. On the Objects toolbar, click the Hot Spot button. On the displayed Insert Hyperlink dialog box, make sure the Link to bar indicates Place in This Document. Then, link the Hot Spot to Page 4, Price List. Click OK, and then position the AutoShape over the book picture. Resize the shape so that it is the approximate size of the picture.

21. To ensure that visitors have ample opportunity to get to the Price List page, go to the bottom of the large text box and select the text "Click here for a list of publications to assist you." Insert a hyperlink to Page 4, Price List. Then, select the text "Click here for a list of related Web sites." Insert a hyperlink to Page 5, Directory of Related Links. Click Save to save your changes.

22. Navigate to page 4. Replace the title "Price List" with Call 626-555-1234 to Order. Change the font size of the text you just typed to 20. Open Word, and then open the document 6C_PriceList. Click anywhere in the table. On the Word menu bar, click Table, point to Select, and then click Table. On Word's Standard toolbar, click Copy. Close the document and close Word. In your publication's Price List table, zoom to 66%, and then drag to select the first eight rows. With the first eight rows selected, move to the Standard toolbar and click Paste. Select the empty table rows, and on the menu bar click Table, click Delete, and then click Table. This will delete the smaller four-row table. Click Save to save your changes.

23. Navigate to page 5. In the text box beginning "Hyperlinks are," replace the placeholder text with For more information on Empowerment Zones, urban revitalization, and small business, please visit the following sites: Select the text you just typed, change the font size to 18 and remove hyphenation. Right-click on the first coffee cup picture and use the Change Picture command to insert 6C_LinksPIC. Use the lower left resize handle of the inserted picture to enlarge it slightly—to approximately the size of the coffee cup picture it replaced. Replace the next three coffee cup pictures in the same manner. Then, delete the remaining two coffee cups and their accompanying text boxes.

24. Open Word, and then open the document 6C_RelatedLinks. Select the two lines of text representing the first link, and then on Word's Standard toolbar, click Copy. Use the task bar to switch back to Publisher. In the first Web site text box, click and then use ⒞ⓣⓡⓛ + Ⓐ to

select all the text. On Publisher's Standard toolbar, click Paste. Repeat this Copy and Paste technique for the remaining three link sites. Close the Word document and close Word. Click Save to save your changes.

25. Navigate to page 6. Change the title to Meet the Mayor's Staff. Delete the pull quote frame, delete the picture and its caption frame, and then move the upper boundary of the large text box down to 3.25 inches on the vertical ruler. On the Objects toolbar, click the Picture Frame button and draw a frame beginning at 2 inches on the horizontal ruler and 1.5 inches on the vertical ruler. Drag down and to the right to 3.5 inches on the horizontal ruler and 3 inches on the vertical ruler. Insert 6C_StaffPIC. With the picture selected, display the Format Picture dialog box and click the Size tab. Place a check mark in the check boxes for Lock aspect ratio and Relative to original picture size. Then use the spin box up arrow to change the Height to 1.595 inches. Click OK. Visually center the picture above the large text box.

26. In the large text box, replace the placeholder text with 6C_StaffText. Click Save to save your changes.

27. Navigate to page 1. Display the File menu, and click Web Page Preview. Preview your Web site pages, and check the hyperlinks. When you are finished, click File, and then click Close. On the menu bar, click File, and then click Page Setup. Click the Printer & Paper tab. Change the paper size to Letter. Click OK. On the Standard toolbar, click the Print button. Twelve sheets will print. Publication 6C Mayor Web is complete!

Publication 6D

Police Web

In the following Skill Assessment, you will convert an existing brochure to a Web site. Your completed publication will look like the one shown in Figure 6.59. You will save your publication as *Firstname Lastname-6D Police Web.*

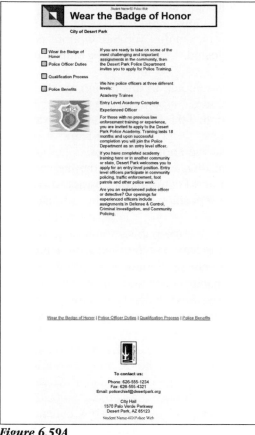

Figure 6.59A

Figure 6.59B

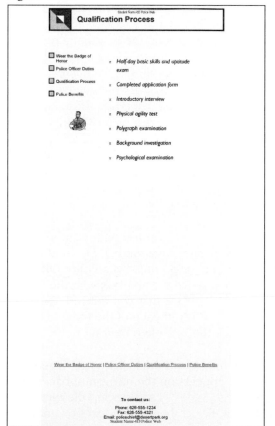

Figure 6.59C

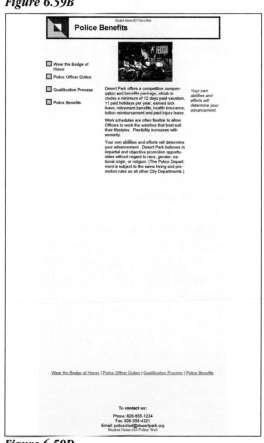

Figure 6.59D

1. Start Publisher. From your student files, open the publication 6D_PoliceWeb.

2. On the menu bar, click Format, and then click Brochure Options. At the bottom of the Brochure Options task pane, click Convert to Web Layout. On the Web Site Options task pane, be sure that under Navigation bar, Multiple is selected. Under Form, be sure that None is selected. Close the task pane.

3. On the menu bar, click View, and then click Header and Footer. In this design, the Header and Footer are positioned in the center. In the Header frame, type Firstname Lastname-6D Police Web. Select the text you just typed and change the font to Arial Narrow and the font size to 8. Then use the Nudge feature as necessary to position your name about one-quarter inch below the blue layout guide. Switch to the Footer. If necessary, zoom to a smaller view to resize and position the Footer frame. Insert your name and the file name. Close the Header and Footer toolbar. View the Header and Footer on the displayed page, and if necessary, open the Header and Footer again to reposition them so they are clearly visible.

4. On the menu bar, click File, and then click Save As. To save the publication as a Web page, move to the bottom of the Save As dialog box, locate the Save as type box, and then click the Save as type arrow. Scroll the displayed list as necessary, and then click Web Page.

5. At the top of the dialog box, use the Save in arrow to navigate to the location in which you are storing your files for this lesson. Then, at the bottom of the dialog box in the File name box, delete the existing text, type Firstname Lastname-6D Police Web and click the Save button.

6. Zoom to 75% and position the top of page 1 in the center of your screen. Delete the picture of the child at the computer. Select the text box with the bulleted items, and move it into the gray scratch area for later use. Move the picture of the badge directly under the vertical navigation bar. Click in each of the three text boxes that comprise the vertical navigation bar and click the Left Align button on the Standard toolbar. Delete the text box containing "Live, work, and grow in Desert Park." At the bottom of the page, delete the text box with the text beginning "Features."

7. Change the Home Page Title to Wear the Badge of Honor. On the Objects toolbar, click the Text Box button. Draw a text box beginning at 2 inches on the horizontal ruler and 1.5 inches on the vertical ruler, and drag down and to the right to 4.5 inches on the horizontal ruler and 7.5 inches on the vertical ruler. Insert the text file 6D_RecruitText, left align the text if necessary, and remove hyphenation. Click Save to save your changes.

8. Navigate to page 2. Select the title text and replace it with Police Officer Duties. Select the text you just typed and change the font size to 24. Move the picture of the policewoman directly below the vertical navigation bar. Click to select the large text box, and delete all of its text. Then, extend its upper boundary to 1.5 inches on the vertical ruler. Insert the text file 6D_DutiesText. In the second paragraph, select the first sentence, which begins "As a Police Officer." Copy this text and then Paste it into the pull quote. Click in each of the three text boxes that comprise the vertical navigation bar and click the Left Align button on the Standard toolbar. Click Save.

9. Navigate to page 3. Select the title text and replace it with Qualification Process. Move the picture of the policeman directly under the vertical navigation bar. Delete the yellow pull quote frame, delete the small text box with text beginning "As a Police Officer," and delete the large text box. From the gray scratch area, move the text box with the bulleted items into the approximate location of the large text box that you deleted. Expand its lower boundary as necessary to accommodate its text. Click in each of the three text boxes that comprise the vertical navigation bar and click the Left Align button on the Standard toolbar. Click Save.

10. Make sure you are on page 3. On the menu bar, click Insert, and then click Page. Insert a Story page and leave the check box checked so that it appears on the navigation bar. This becomes page 4. On page 4, change the title to Police Benefits. Ungroup the picture from its caption, and then click in the gray scratch area. Select the caption text box and

delete it. Select the picture, and use the Change Picture command to insert 6D_CyclePIC. Move the inserted picture up directly beneath the box surrounding the title, and then use the lower right resize handle to enlarge it to meet the top edge of the text box. Visually center it above the text box.

11. Select the placeholder text in the large text box and insert 6D_BenefitsText. In the third paragraph, select and Copy the first sentence and then Paste it into the pull quote. Click in each of the four text boxes that comprise the vertical navigation bar and click the Left Align button on the Standard toolbar. Navigate to page 1. Now that an additional page has been added to the Web, move the badge picture down so that it is not blocking the new link on the navigation bar. Make the same adjustment on pages 2 and 3. On each of the four pages, change the alignment of the final navigation button to Left Align. Navigate back to page 1, and click Save.

12. Display the Format menu, and then click Background. In the Background task pane, under Apply a background, click the third block—30% tint of Accent 2. Then under More colors, in the second row, point to the first block (14% tint of Accent 2) and click its arrow. Click Apply to All Pages. Click Save.

13. Preview your Web. Test the navigation bar to make sure that it links to the appropriate pages. When you are finished, click File, and then click Close. On the File menu, click Page Setup, and then click the Printer & Paper tab. Change the paper size to Letter, click OK, and then click the Print button on the Standard toolbar. Eight pages will print. Publication 6D is complete!

Publication 6E

Water Web

In the following Performance Assessment, you will create a Web site for Desert Park's Department of Water Resources. The site will have a Home Page and three topic pages. Your completed publication will look like the one shown in Figure 6.60. You will save your publication as *Firstname Lastname-6E Water Web*.

Figure 6.60A

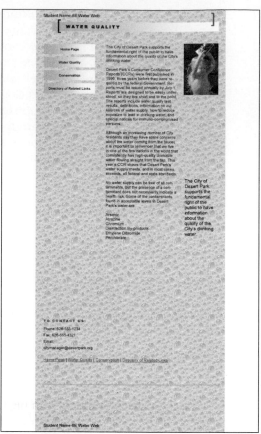

Figure 6.60B

Figure 6.60C

Figure 6.60D

1. Start Publisher. Display the New Publication task pane and the Publication Gallery. Under By Publication Type, click Web Sites. Click the Axis Web Site. Insert both a header and footer with your name and the file name. Adjust the frames as necessary so that your name displays on each page. Use the Personal Information Set for the City Manager, as shown in Publication 6C Figure 6.58, making any necessary changes. Save the file *as a Web page* in your storage location with your name and the filename.

2. In the Web Site Options task pane, under Navigation bar select Multiple, and under Form select None. Insert a Story page as page 2, and leave the check mark so that it displays on the navigation bar. Insert another Story page as page 3 and have it display on the navigation bar. Insert a Related links page as page 4 and have it display on the navigation bar. Your Web now has four pages. Close the task pane and click Save to save your changes.

3. Navigate to page 1. Change the Home Page title to Water Resources. In the main text box, replace the placeholder text with 6E_HomeText. Remove hyphenation. Select the picture and use the Change Picture command to insert 6E_DrinkPIC. Drag the lower right resize handle of the picture down and to the right to enlarge the picture to the same width as the text box above it. In the last line of text, select the word "Conservation" and link it to Page 3. In the same line, select the words "Water Quality" and create a link to Page 2. Click Save to save your changes.

4. Navigate to page 2. Replace the title with Water Quality. In the main text box, insert 6E_WaterQuality. Select the first paragraph of the text and paste it into the pull quote. Ungroup the caption and picture. Delete the caption text box, and change the picture to 6E_ChildPIC. Click Save.

5. Navigate to page 3. Replace the title with Conservation. In the main text box, replace the placeholder text with 6E_ConserveText. Ungroup the caption and picture. Delete the caption text box, and change the picture to 6E_GorgePIC. Delete the pull quote frame. Click Save.

6. Navigate to page 4. In the text box beginning "Hyperlinks," delete the placeholder text and type Because water supply and quality are so important, we encourage City residents to learn more by reviewing the information available at these sites:

7. Remove hyphenation from the text you just typed, and change the font size to 14. Open Word, and then open 6F_LinksText. Use the Copy and Paste method that you used in Publication 6C to copy each link into one of the text boxes. Delete any unused boxes. Click Save.

8. Navigate to page 1. Display the Format menu, and then click Background. Under More colors, scroll to row 9 and click the Water droplets background. Apply it to all pages. Display the Format menu again, and click Color Schemes. Apply the Marine color scheme. Close the task pane and click Save. Preview the Web site. Then, change the paper size to Letter and print. Publication 6E Water Web is complete!

Publication 6F

Course Web

In the following Performance Assessment, you will convert an existing brochure to a Web site. Your completed publication will look like the one shown in Figure 6.61. You will save your publication as *Firstname Lastname-6F Course Web*.

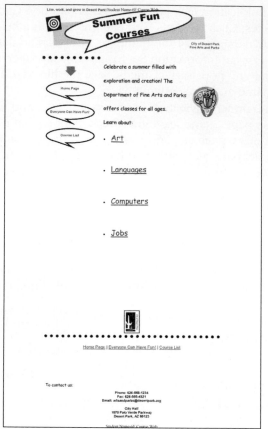

Figure 6.61A

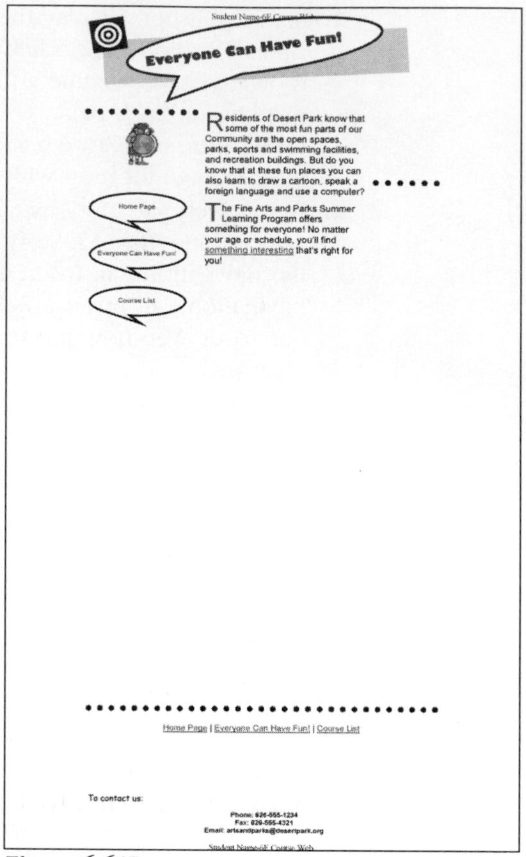

Figure 6.61B

Figure 6.61C

1. Start Publisher. From your student files, open publication 6F_Course. Display the Format menu, click Brochure Options, and then click the Convert to Web Layout command on the task pane. Be sure that under Navigation bar, Multiple is selected, and that under Form, None is selected. Close the task pane. Insert a header and footer by typing `Firstname Lastname-6F Course Web`. Resize and position the header and footer frames as necessary. Save the publication as a Web page in your storage location.

2. On page 1, change Home Page Title to `Summer Fun Courses`. Select the text in the main text box, left align the text, change the font to Comic Sans MS, and the font size to 12. Delete the text box at the bottom beginning "Features." Drag the bottom boundary of the main text box down to 8 inches on the vertical ruler. Select the four lines of bulleted text. On the menu bar click Format, and then click Line Spacing. Change the spacing between lines to 3 and change the font size of the bulleted items to 18. Select the picture and change it to 6F_Art. Create a link for each of the four bulleted items to page 3. Click Save.

3. Navigate to page 2. Change the title to `Everyone Can Have Fun!` Delete the pull quote frame. In the last sentence of text, select the phrase "something interesting" and link it to page 3. Change the picture to 6F_World.

4. Navigate to page 3. Select the first six rows, which is the first table. Left align all the text and change the font to Comic Sans MS. Apply the same formatting to the four rows in the second table. Change the title of the page to `Course List`. Draw a picture frame just under the navigation bar that is about the width of the navigation bar and about 1 inch tall. Insert the picture 6F_Computer. Visually center the picture under the navigation bar. Save your changes.

5. Navigate to page 1. Display the Background task pane. Under Apply a background, click the fourth block. Then, under More colors, to the right of the X block, click 30% tint of Accent 3. Apply this background to all pages. Close the task pane. Preview your Web, save any changes, and then change the paper size to Letter and print. Close the file. Publication 6E Course Web is complete!

On the Internet

Microsoft Publisher is a good Web development tool for small Web sites composed of a few pages. For larger Web sites, or Web sites with more that 10 pages, investigate Microsoft FrontPage. You can take an interactive computer tour of FrontPage by visiting **www.microsoft.com/frontpage**.

Glossary

Adjustment handle   A small yellow diamond, attached to an AutoShape, with which you can change the most prominent feature; for example, the width of an arm on a star.

Align Left   The positioning of text at the left boundary of the text box, leaving the right margin uneven.

Align Right   The positioning of text at the right boundary of the text box, leaving the left margin uneven.

Alignment   The placement of a paragraph relative to the left and right boundaries of the text frame or column in which it is contained.

Articles   The informative stories contained in a newsletter.

Aspect ratio   The proportional relationship of a picture's width and height.

AutoCorrect   A feature that corrects common typing, spelling, and grammatical errors as you type.

Autoflow   A process to distribute text that is too large to fit into the selected frames, and in which additional frames are automatically located by Publisher.

AutoShapes   A collection of ready-made shapes that includes basic shapes—such as rectangles and circles—plus a variety of lines and connectors, block arrows, flowchart symbols, stars, and banners.

Berners-Lee, Tim   The scientist who created hypertext markup language, known as HTML.

Bitmaps   Graphic files composed of a pattern of thousands of dots (called pixels).

Blue dotted layout guides   Nonprinting guides that indicate where frames should be aligned so they do not run into each other and which create a safety zone for the margins.

Booklet   A publication that describes products, services, or other information in detail.

Brightness   A term used to describe how well paper reflects light.

Brochure   A small pamphlet that describes an event, product, program, or service.

Browser   Software used to view information coded in hypertext markup language.

Bulk mail   A program of the United States Postal Service that provides lower postage rates for mail that is presorted by Zip code.

Bulk mailing   When a copy of the same publication is sent to a large number of addresses— also referred to as mass mailing.

Business forms   Printed documents, such as invoices, purchase orders, and expense reports, used by organizations to document various business transactions.

Business stationery   Letterhead, envelopes, and business cards personalized with an organization's name, address, and logo.

Callouts   Interesting quotations taken from the text of the story to draw the reader into the story, usually in a larger font size than the story and in bold or italic. Also called pull quotes.

Caption   Text that briefly describes a photo or graphic.

Catalog   A printed list of items arranged systematically.

Cell   The intersection of a column and a row in a table.

Cell diagonal   A feature that draws a diagonal line through a cell in a table.

Center   Alignment of text so that it is positioned an equal distance from the left and right boundary of the text box.

Clip art   Predefined graphic images that are included with the Microsoft Office software and can be purchased from other software vendors.

Column   An arrangement of short lines of text, such as a newspaper, because it is easier to read than long lines of text. Also, a vertical array of cells in a table.

Composite RGB   Colors that are intended to display on a monitor.

Continued notice   A message at the bottom of a story column indicating on what page an article is continued or from what page an article was continued.

Convert to Web Layout   An option available in Microsoft Publisher that enables you to convert either a newsletter or a brochure to a Web publication.

Copyfitting   The process of sizing text to fit in a text box.

Crop marks   Lines that print when your publication is smaller or larger than a piece of paper.

Cropping handles   Handles surrounding an image with which you can hide portions of the image.

Cropping pointer   The mouse pointer when it is in the shape of the cropping tool.

Crosshair pointer   The mouse pointer when it is in the shape of a small plus sign and used to form frames.

Data source   An electronic file where you store the names, addresses, and other contact information about individuals who will receive a copy of a publication.

Dateline   Lines of text that indicate the date and/or the volume or issue number of the newsletter. The volume or issue number informs the reader how long the newsletter has been published.

Design Checker   A Publisher feature that checks your publication for errors such as an empty frame, text left in the overflow area, broken hyperlinks, or an object that is partially covered by another object.

Design Gallery Live   Microsoft's Web site that provides free downloadable media files.

Design set   A group of preformatted publications that share the same graphic design elements and font formatting.

Desktop publishing program   A program that allows you to mix text and graphics on a page to create publications of professional quality.

Dingbats   A small typographical symbol or ornament used to embellish a printed page, often used at the start and end of chapters in a book.

Docked   The position of a toolbar when it is aligned with other toolbars or with the edge of the window.

Document size   The area of a sheet of paper that contains the text and graphics and is determined by the margin settings.

Drop cap   An effect that enlarges the selected character, usually the first character of an article or newsletter, and lowers the character into the paragraph or suspends the character in the left margin.

Editing   The process of making changes to text or objects in a publication.

Embedded graphics   Graphics that are stored as part of a publication's file.

Entry blank   A printed form to be filled out.

Field   The elements, such as name, address, and zip code, that comprise a record.

Field code   A placeholder for changeable data.

Fill color   The inside color of an object or text box.

Fill effects   Textures, patterns, color fades, and pictures that can be applied to the inside of a frame.

Finish   A term used to describe the smoothness of paper.

Flyer   A one-page message with minimal text and graphics that is convenient for last-minute communications, such as an upcoming event.

Font   A set of characters with the same design and shape.

Font descenders   The lower parts of letters, such as p and g, that extend slightly below the line of text.

Font styles   Bold, italic, and underline enhancements to text.

Footers   Text, page numbers, graphics, and formatting that print at the bottom of every page, or on specific pages.

Form   A structured document with spaces reserved for entering information.

Form controls   The individual boxes and buttons with which a Web site visitor enters information.

Formatting   The process of determining the overall appearance of the text within the publication, and the overall appearance of the publication itself.

Forms   A document in your Web site that enables interaction between you and the visitor to the Web site.

Frames   Boxes into which you place text or images, and which can be moved, resized, and formatted.

Gradient fill   A color combination in which one color fades into another.

Grain   A term used to describe the direction in which the majority of the fibers run in paper.

Graphics   Anything on the page that is not text.

Grayed out   Shading applied to a command or option indicating that it is unavailable for use.

Grouping   The process of selecting two or more objects and combining them into one object for the purpose of moving, copying, or formatting.

Grow to Fit Text   A Publisher feature that expands a cell to accommodate your typing.

Gutters   The term used to refer to the area defined by the blue dotted guidelines that create a safety zone for the margins.

Handles   Small black circles or squares on the edges of a frame, text box, or other object used to change the size of the object, and indicate that the object is selected.

Headers   Text, page numbers, graphics, and formatting that print at the top of every page, or on specific pages.

Headline   The title of an article written in a way that informs the reader of the article's content.

Help   A system that provides information about Publisher features and step-by-step instructions for performing tasks.

Home Page   The first page of a Web site.

Horizontal navigation bar   An area on a Web site, arranged horizontally, indicating the names of the pages that are linked directly to the page and with which the visitor can access with just a click.

Horizontal Rules   A Publisher feature that formats a horizontal line under text or between paragraphs, and which, unlike the Underline style, does not cut through font descenders.

Hot spot   An area of an object that is a hyperlink.

Hyperlink   Text or graphics that you click, the result of which is that your computer is directed to display a different Web page.

Hypertext Markup Language (HTML)   A programming language that communicates color and graphics in a format that most computers can understand with the help of a browser.

Hyphenation   A process for breaking words between syllables at the end of a line of printed text for the purpose of making the right margin look more even.

Hyphenation zone   The amount of space at the end of a line within which automatic hyphenation will be activated.

Import   The process of bringing into your publication text from another electronic file.

Insert mode   The default setting for entering text in Publisher in which, as you type, existing text moves to the right to make space for the new text.

Internet   The worldwide network of computers that connects other, smaller, networks of computers.

jpeg   A file format created specifically for photographs.

Justify   The alignment of text that adds additional space between words so that both the left and right margins are even.

Keyboard shortcut   A combination of keys that can be held down in combination to start a command.

Landscape   A page orientation in which the paper is wider than it is high.

Layer   The process of overlapping frames.

Layout   The size, number, and placement of graphics on a page.

Layout guides   Nonprinting dotted lines that assist you in positioning objects precisely on the page.

Legal size paper   Paper that is 8.5 inches wide and 14 inches tall.

Letter size paper   Paper that is 8.5 inches wide and 11 inches tall.

Letterhead   Paper printed with the name, address, and contact information of an organization or individual.

Line spacing   The amount of space between lines of text in a paragraph.

Linked graphics   Graphics that are part of a publication, but are stored as separate electronic files.

Logo   A letter, symbol, or sign used as an identifying element for an organization.

Mail merge   The process of combining a data source with a publication to print a group of individually customized publications.

Mailing panel   Space provided on the back of the newsletter for the recipient's name and address (or a preprinted label containing the recipient's name and address), and includes the organization's name, address, logo, and phone number.

Mass mailing   When a copy of the same publication is sent to a large number of addresses—also referred to as bulk mailing.

Master Page   A special page that acts as a background for your publication. Items placed on the Master Page will display on any or all pages in the publication.

Master set   A design name that includes a complete set of preformatted publications sharing the same graphic design elements and font formatting.

Masthead   The top of the first page that contains the title of the newsletter, often in a different font than the rest of the newsletter.

Media files   Electronic files consisting of pictures, movies, or sound recordings.

Menus   Lists of commands within a category.

Navigate   To move within a publication.

Navigation bar   An area on a Web page containing a set of hyperlinks to other pages in the Web site.

Navigation structure   The order in which the pages of a Web site will be arranged.

Newsletter   A periodical used to distribute news and information to a special group.

Nudge   A command used to move an object in small increments.

Object   Any element that can be selected, such as a graphic frame or text frame.

Office Assistant   An animated character that provides general and specific help in response to your questions.

Opacity   A term used to describe the degree of transparency of an image.

Overflow   An area where extra text is held until you decide how you want to distribute the text.

Pack and Go Wizard   A process that creates linked graphics and embeds fonts in your publication so your printing service has access to the graphics and typefaces you want to use in your publication.

Panels   Distinct surfaces on which frames are arranged.

Personal Information Set   Commonly used business information such as the name, address, phone numbers, and logo of an organization.

Pink dotted layout guides   Nonprinting guides that indicate the actual margin boundaries of the page.

Pixels   An abbreviated term for picture element, which are the dots that comprise an image.

Placeholder text   Default text in a placeholder that you replace with your own text.

Points   The unit of measurement for fonts. One point equals 1/72 of an inch.

Points of Interest   A list of key points from the various articles, intended to entice readers to read the entire article.

Postcards   Cards, with proper stamps or postage, on which a message is written for mailing without an envelope.

Printer's marks   A collection of marks that direct a printing press operator at a commercial print shop as to the size, alignment, and color of a publication.

Process colors (CMYK)   A Publisher option that converts colors to their CMYK (cyan, magenta, yellow, and black) equivalents—a formula for color formation that is understood by professional printing organizations.

Program   A printed outline describing the events, people, and features of a play, dinner, agenda, performance, or public event.

Pt.   The standard abbreviation for point—the unit of measurement for fonts.

Pull quotes   Interesting quotations taken from the text of the story to draw the reader into the story—

usually in a larger font size than the story and in bold or italic.

Purchase order   A business form generated when an organization makes a request to buy goods or services from a vendor and to be billed for the amount.

Pushed   The highlighted and bordered appearance of a button on a toolbar to indicate that it is active.

Quick Publication   One of Publisher's pre-formatted design templates consisting of one page and three frames—one each for a picture, a heading, and a message—plus some color and graphic design elements.

Raster objects   Another name for vector objects.

Record   Each individual's information stored in a data source.

Rotation handle   A small green handle displayed on a selected image with which the image can be rotated in various directions.

Rows   A horizontal array of cells in a table.

Ruler guide   A green dotted line that acts as a visual ruler for the purpose of aligning objects when no pink or blue layout guide is available.

Sans serif fonts   Fonts with no lines on the ends of characters, and which are more suitable for headings and titles.

Scratch area   The gray area of the screen outside of the publication window.

ScreenTip   A small yellow box that displays the name of a button on a toolbar or some other part of a Windows screen when you pause the mouse pointer over it.

Selecting   Highlighting text or clicking on objects for the purpose of editing, formatting, copying, or moving.

Serif fonts   Fonts that have lines or extensions on the end of the characters, and are good choices for body text because they are easy to read.

Sheet size   The size of the paper on which you print your publication.

Side fold card   A sheet arrangement which, when folded, results in four pages in the style of a greeting card.

Sizing handles   Small black circles or squares on the edges of a frame, text box, or other object used to change the size of the object, and indicate that the object is selected.

Smart object   A preformatted design element that has a wizard associated with it.

Snap to   The ability of an object to automatically line up with guides or other objects in a quick and easy manner.

Story   A chain of connected text boxes.

Style   A group of formatting instructions that are stored by Publisher with a specific name, and with which you can quickly retrieve and apply to text in a publication.

Submenu   A secondary menu that displays when pointing to the right-pointing arrow next to an item on a menu.

Subsidiary pages   The subset of a topic page in a Web site.

Table AutoFormat   A Publisher command that can quickly and easily apply a predefined format to a table.

Table of Contents   The titles of the articles in the newsletter.

Tables   An arrangement of information in columns and rows.

Tabloid paper   Paper that is 11 inches wide and 17 inches high, frequently used for printing newsletters.

Tabloid size paper   Paper that is 11 inches wide and 17 inches tall.

Task pane   A window within a Microsoft Office application that provides commonly used commands, and whose location and small size allow you to use these commands while still working on your files.

Templates   A model publication upon which you can build your own new publication.

Tent fold card   A sheet arrangement that, when folded, results in two pages in the style of a tent card—commonly used at a meeting table to display the names of people in large letters.

Text boxes   Containers into which you can type or insert text; also referred to as text frames.

Text frames   Containers into which you can type or insert text; also referred to as text boxes.

Text juxtaposition   The relationship of a graphic to its surrounding text.

Top fold card   A sheet arrangement that, when folded, results in four pages in the style of a personal note card.

Topic pages   Pages in a Web site to which the Home Page directly links.

Trapping   A process used on professional printing presses to compensate for errors on the printing press that result from paper being moved on the press.

Tri-fold brochure   A brochure folded into thirds.

Trim size   The actual size of a publication after the paper is cut.

Two-Page Spread   The display of two facing pages side by side on the screen.

URL   The abbreviation for Uniform Resource Locator, which is the electronic address of a Web site.

Vector objects   Graphic images whose files contain a mathematical description about how to form the lines, shape, and fill of the graphic.

Vertical navigation bar   An area on a Web site, arranged vertically, indicating the names of the pages to which a visitor can link directly from the page.

Web pages   Documents that contain the text and graphics of a Web site.

Web site   One or more pages stored on a computer on the World Wide Web.

Web Sites Wizard   A tool that takes you step by step through the process of creating a Web site in Publisher.

White space   Blank, unused space on a publication's printed page.

Wizard   A tool that takes you step by step through a process, such as building a publication based upon a pre-designed template.

Word count   A feature in Microsoft Word that counts the number of words in a document; useful when inserting Word files into Publisher story chains because you can get an idea of how well the text is going fit.

Word wrap   The action that takes place when the insertion point reaches the right margin and automatically moves down and to the left margin of the next line.

WordArt   An application within Microsoft Office XP that transforms text into a stylized graphic object.

World Wide Web   The multimedia branch of the Internet.

Wrapping   The ability to have text appear to flow around graphic images, even though each is held in different frames.

Wrapping styles   Visual arrangements by which text can flow around, or position itself relative to, a graphic object.

Zoom   The action of making the screen view of the page larger or smaller.

Index